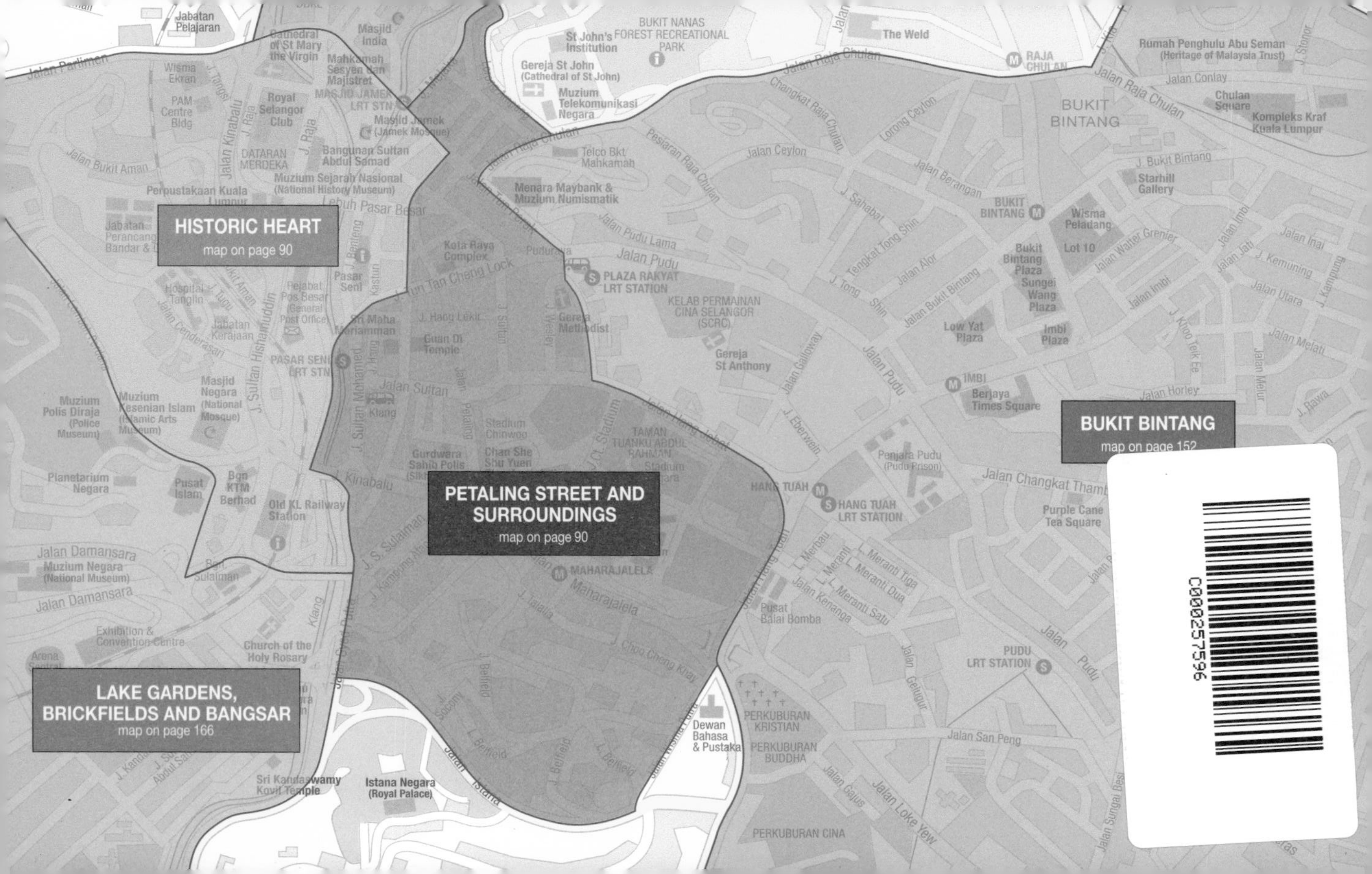

HISTORIC HEART
map on page 90
PETALING STREET AND SURROUNDINGS
map on page 90
BUKIT BINTANG
map on page 152
LAKE GARDENS, BRICKFIELDS AND BANGSAR
map on page 166
BUKIT NANAS FOREST RECREATIONAL PARK
St John's Institution
Gereja St John (Cathedral of St John)
Muzium Telekomunikasi Negara
The Weld
Rumah Penghulu Abu Seman (Heritage of Malaysia Trust)
Chulan Square
Kompleks Kraf Kuala Lumpur
BUKIT BINTANG
Starhill Gallery
Wisma Peladang
Lot 10
Bukit Bintang Plaza
Sungei Wang Plaza
Imbi Plaza
Low Yat Plaza
Berjaya Times Square
Cathedral of St Mary the Virgin
Masjid India
Mahkamah Sesyen dan Majistret
Royal Selangor Club
Masjid Jamek (Jamek Mosque)
DATARAN MERDEKA
Bangunan Sultan Abdul Samad
Muzium Sejarah Nasional (National History Museum)
Perpustakaan Kuala Lumpur
Wisma Ekran
PAM Centre Bldg
Jabatan Pelajaran
Hospital Tanglin
Jabatan Kerajaan
Pejabat Pos Besar (General Post Office)
Sri Maha Mariamman
Guan Di Temple
Kota Raya Complex
Gereja Methodist
Menara Maybank & Muzium Numismatik
Telco Bkt Mahkamah
PLAZA RAKYAT LRT STATION
KELAB PERMAINAN CINA SELANGOR (SCRC)
Gereja St Anthony
Stadium Chinwoo
Chan She Shu Yuen
Gurdwara Sahib Polis
TAMAN TUANKU ABDUL RAHMAN
MAHARAJALELA
HANG TUAH LRT STATION
Penjara Pudu (Pudu Prison)
PUDU LRT STATION
Purple Cane Tea Square
Pusat Balai Bomba
Dewan Bahasa & Pustaka
PERKUBURAN KRISTIAN
PERKUBURAN BUDDHA
PERKUBURAN CINA
Istana Negara (Royal Palace)
Sri Kandaswamy Kovil Temple
Church of the Holy Rosary
Old KL Railway Station
Bgn KTM Berhad
Pusat Islam
Masjid Negara (National Mosque)
Muzium Kesenian Islam (Islamic Arts Museum)
Muzium Polis Diraja (Police Museum)
Planetarium Negara
Muzium Negara (National Museum)
Exhibition & Convention Centre
PASAR SENI LRT STN
MASJID JAMEK LRT STN
Pasar Seni
Jalan Parlimen
Jalan Raja Chulan
Jalan Pudu
Jalan Pudu Lama
Jalan Ceylon
Jalan Sultan
Jalan Tun Tan Cheng Lock
J. Sultan Hishamuddin
Jalan Kinabalu
Jalan Damansara
Jalan Bukit Bintang
Jalan Changkat Thambi Dollah
Jalan Hang Tuah
Jalan Hang Jebat
Jalan San Peng
Jalan Loke Yew
Jalan Istana
Jalan Maharajalela
Jalan Sungai Besi
Leboh Pasar Besar
Jalan Imbi
Jalan Alor
J. Sahabat
Jalan Galloway
J. Eberwein
Jalan Kenanga
Jalan Gelugur
Jalan Gajus
Jalan Bukit Aman
Jalan Cenderasari
Jalan Conlay
Jalan Walter Grenier
Jalan Beranggan
Lorong Ceylon
Changkat Raja Chulan
Pesiaran Raja Chulan
Tengkat Tong Shin
J. Tong Shin
Jalan Horley
Jalan Melur
Jalan Melati
Jalan Utara
J. Khoo Teik Ee
Jalan Inai
J. Kemuning
Jalan Jati
J. Rawa
J. Kampung
J. Stonor
J. Bukit Bintang
Jalan Petaling
J. Hang Lekir
J. Sultan
J. Wesley
J. Sultan Mohamed
J. S. Sulaiman
Choo Cheng Khay
J. Belfield
L. Belfield
J. Jalalia
L. Meranti Tiga
L. Meranti Dua
L. Meranti Satu
L. Merbau
Jalan Raja
J. Tangsi
J. Raja
Klang
Jalan Kastun
J. Benteng

INSIGHT GUIDES

KUALA LUMPUR

APA PUBLICATIONS
Part of the Langenscheidt Publishing Group

How to Use This Book

This book is carefully structured both to convey an understanding of the city and its culture and to guide readers through its attractions and activities:

◆ The Best Of section at the front of the book helps you to prioritise. The first spread contains all the Top Sights, while the Editor's Choice details unique experiences, the best buys or other recommendations.

◆ To understand Kuala Lumpur, you need to know something of its past. The city's history and culture are described in authoritative essays written by specialists in their fields who have lived in and documented the city for many years.

◆ The Places section details all the attractions worth seeing. The main places of interest are coordinated by number with the maps.

◆ Each chapter includes lists of recommended shops, restaurants, bars and cafés.

◆ Photographs throughout the book are chosen not only to illustrate geography and buildings, but also to convey the moods of the city and the life of its people.

◆ The Travel Tips section includes all the practical information you will need, divided into five key sections: transport, accommodation, activities (including nightlife, events, tours and sports), an A–Z of practical tips and a handy phrasebook. Information may be located quickly by using the index on the back cover flap of the book.

◆ A detailed street atlas is included at the back of the book, with all restaurants, bars, cafés and hotels plotted for your convenience.

Places and Sights

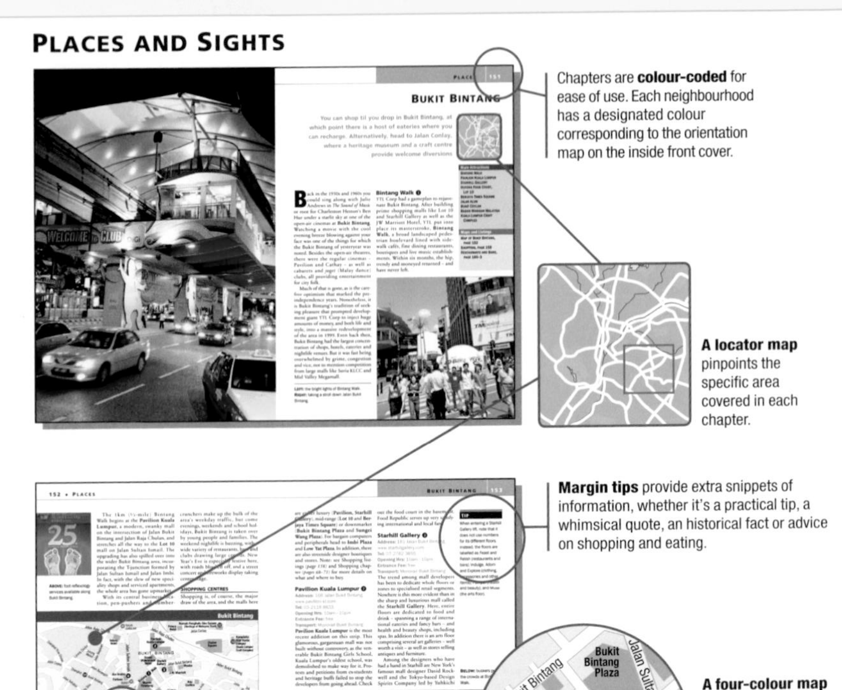

Chapters are **colour-coded** for ease of use. Each neighbourhood has a designated colour corresponding to the orientation map on the inside front cover.

A locator map pinpoints the specific area covered in each chapter.

Margin tips provide extra snippets of information, whether it's a practical tip, a whimsical quote, an historical fact or advice on shopping and eating.

A four-colour map shows the area covered in the chapter, with the main sights and attractions coordinated by number with the text.

Photo Features

Photo features offer visual coverage of various aspects of the city, from fashion and clothing to auspicious signs and symbols in Malaysian culture.

Shopping and Restaurant Listings

Shopping listings provide details of the best shops in each area. **Restaurant listings** give the establishment's contact details, opening times and price category, followed by a useful review. Bars and cafés are also covered here. The coloured dot and grid reference refers to the atlas section at the back of the book.

an array of curries as well as vegetables.
Tanjung Bungah
117 Jalan SS2/6. Tel: 03-7877 4531. Open: Fri–Wed 10am–3pm, 5–10pm. **$$**
Penang Nyonya food with an infusion of Thai flavours. Dishes include *jiu hu char* (dried cuttlefish

Travel Tips

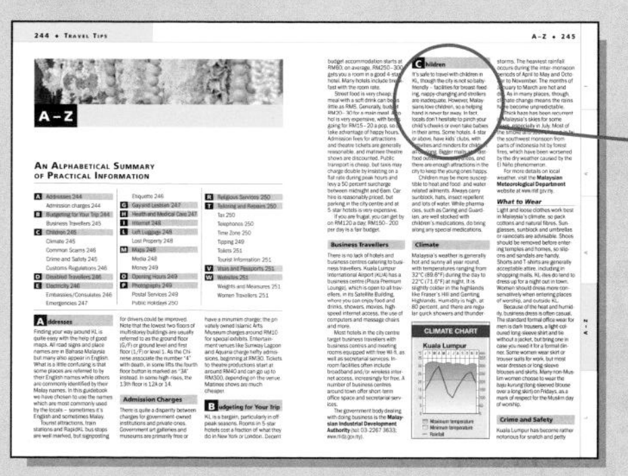

Children
It's safe to travel with children in KL, though the city is not so baby-friendly – facilities for breast-feeding, nappy-changing and strollers are inadequate. However, Malaysians love children, so a helping hand is never far away. In fact, locals don't hesitate to pinch your child's cheeks or even take babies in their arms. Some hotels, 4-star or above, have kids' clubs, with activities and minders for children all day long. Bigger malls and fa...

Travel Tips provide all the practical knowledge you'll need before and during your trip: how to get there, getting around, where to stay and what to do. The A–Z section is a handy summary of practical information, arranged alphabetically.

Contents

Introduction

History

Features

Insights

MINI FEATURES

PHOTO FEATURES

Places

LEFT: KL's Twin Towers dominate the skyline.

Travel Tips

Maps

The Best of Kuala Lumpur: Top Sights

At a glance, the attractions in and around Kuala Lumpur that you can't afford to miss, from iconic architecture to religious sites, and antiques to food stalls

△ The **Batu Caves** are an important site for Hindu pilgrims, especially devotees of Lord Murugan. The rear walls are a popular hang-out for rock-climbing fanatics. *See page 182.*

▷ No visit to KL is complete without enjoying the gastronomic experience that is **Jalan Alor**. It's best to visit after dark, when the hawkers are out in full force, and order dishes from more than one stall as is expected. *See page 156.*

◁ The **KL Tower Observation Deck** offers an eye-popping view of the city. If you're a speed junkie, check out the Flying Fox zip wire or the F1 simulator as well. *See page 138.*

△ **Jamek Mosque** is situated at the confluence of the Klang and Gombak rivers, which gave birth to Kuala Lumpur. This domed, colonnaded mosque still stands dignified after 100 years. *See page 89.*

◁ You can't miss the majestic, Mughal-inspired **Sultan Abdul Samad Building.** The clock tower, KL's very own Big Ben, overlooks the historic Dataran Merdeka, site of cricket matches and all sorts of play.
See page 94.

▷ If you only have time for one museum, it should be the **Islamic Arts Museum.** Dedicated to the history and pursuit of Islamic arts around the world, this is a treat and a treasure.
See page 168.

△ **Aquaria KLCC** is the country's only oceanarium, with more than 5000 marine creatures, including sharks, eels and colourful coral. You can also feed the sharks if you're game. *See page 134.*

△ You'll definitely find something to buy at the **Central Market**; not all of it is local, but you'll have fun deciding.
See page 92.

▷ The **Petronas Twin Towers** are still the most breathtaking sight in KL. Stand on the junction of Jalan Ampang and Jalan Yap Kwan Sang to take in the full majesty of this Islamic-inspired building. *See page 129.*

The Best of Kuala Lumpur: Editor's Choice

Setting priorities, saving money, unique attractions... here are our recommendations, plus a few insider tips

Best for Families

These attractions are popular with children, though not all will suit every age group.

- **Aquaria KLCC**. Giant aquariums filled with all sorts of marine wonders. *See page 134.*
- **Cosmo's World**. This exciting indoor theme park is just the thing for rainy days. *See page 155*.
- **Craft Village**. Kids can paint their own batik or try their hand at woodcraft. *See pages 159.*
- **Genting Theme Park**. Enjoy over 50 exciting rides, and both "smell" and "feel" while you watch a 4D Motion Master movie. *See page 198.*
- **KLCC Park**. Children can cool off in the wading pool during the day and watch the fountains dance at night. *See page 134.*
- **Kuala Gandah Elephant Conservation Centre**. A chance to ride, feed and observe Asian elephants at play. *See page 198.*
- **Petrosains**. Learning about science and the oil and gas industry has never before been this fun. *See page 132*.
- **School of Hard Knocks**. Even little ones can hammer out their own pewter products at this smithing workshop. *See page 243.*
- **Sunway Lagoon**. Water fun galore with an artificial beach and pool, plus all sorts of water rides. *See page 214*.

Best Festivals and Events

- **Chinese New Year**. Red for luck dominates everything from decorations to clothes during this 15-day celebration. Petaling Street becomes especially busy. *See page 49*.
- **Colours of Malaysia (Citrawarna)**. A colourful parade with traditional dance and music kicks off this month-long cultural and gourmet fest. *See page 50*.
- **Hari Raya Puasa**. The month preceding the fasting month of Ramadan is just as fascinating as the festival itself. *See page 51.*
- **Petronas Malaysian F1 Grand Prix**. Held annually in April, this action-packed event draws top drivers from the world over. *See page 50.*
- **Thaipusam**. This fascinating celebration sees Hindus skewering their bodies and carrying large metal structures called *kavadi*. *See pages 49 and 186–7*.

Left: Sunway Lagoon Water Theme Park in Klang Valley provides fun for the young-at-heart. **Above:** Citawarna, or Colours of Malaysia, celebrates Malaysia's cultural diversity.

Only in Kuala Lumpur

- **The Annexe Gallery** is KL's alternative, no-holds-barred art space, filled with works that will stimulate and inspire. *See pages 63 and 92.*
- **Conservatory of Rare Plants and Orchids**. Beautiful begonias, unusual palms and rare orchids are among the 1,500 plants found here. *See page 214.*
- **Giant Flagpole**. A neck-craning 95-metre-tall (310ft) flagpole is among the large monuments that have come to represent this city. *See page 96.*
- **Hokkien *Mee***. This all-time KL hawker favourite is a flash-fried dish of noodles in a sticky dark sauce with slices of pork and seafood. Try it out at **Hong Ngek Restaurant**.
- **Kampung Kuantan Fireflies**. Male fireflies flashing synchronously to an invisible beat makes for a remarkable sight. *See page 207.*
- **Museum of Asian Art**. Excellent display of Malaysian and Southeast Asian ceramics, textiles and woodcarvings, including the world's largest *kendi* (water jug) collection. *See page 212.*

Best Architecture

- **Dayabumi Complex**. This modern building is a graceful representation of Islamic symbolism with its lovely fretwork and arches. *See page 101.*
- **National Museum**. One of the city's first post-independence buildings, it incorporates traditional Malay architectural elements and motifs to fine effect. *See page 169.*
- **PAM Centre Building**. This well-preserved colonial bungalow combines European neoclassical architecture with Chinese craftsmanship. *See page 99.*
- **Petronas Twin Towers**. Still among the world's tallest buildings, this glass-and-steel engineering feat is a wonder to behold. *See page 129*.
- **Rumah Penghulu Abu Seman**. A reconstructed early 20th-century Malay timber house that was once a village headman's home. *See page 157.*
- **Sultan Abdul Samad Building**. This Mughal-inspired colonial edifice with arched colonnades and minarets is one of the city's most photographed sights. *See pages 94–95.*
- **Wisma Ekran**. Strong vertical and horizontal lines and abstract motifs distinguish this Art Deco masterpiece. *See page 99.*

Above: traditional Malay architecture.

Best Rainforest Encounters

- **Chiling Waterfall**. Trek through riverine and lowland dipterocarp vegetation and six river crossings to this spectacular 20-metre (660ft) waterfall. *See page 192.*
- **Fraser's Hill**. See tree ferns, oaks, laurels and other species that characterise the montane forest here. Fraser's is also a birder's paradise. *See pages 192–7.*
- **Canopy Walkway**. Catch a rare top-down perspective of the rainforest canopy, and the life it supports, at the Forest Research Institute of Malaysia. *See page 179.*
- **Kuala Selangor Nature Park**. Walkways thread through mudflats and around lakes in a highly specialised mangrove ecosystem with unique fauna and flora; of note is its large heron colony. *See pages 201–7.*
- **Rimba Ilmu**. Dubbed the "rainforest for beginners", this botanical garden has excellent information on the millennia-old Malaysian rainforest; the guided tour is recommended. *See page 213.*

Below: the Canopy Walkway at FRIM is not recommended for those who suffer from vertigo.

Best Shopping Experiences

- **Central Market**. Find Malaysian and southeast Asian handicrafts, souvenirs and gifts here, from kitschy fridge magnets to handcrafted Kelantanese silverware. *See page 92.*
- **Jalan Masjid India**. The city's Indian Muslim quarter has shops selling colourful saris, sarongs, brassware, gold jewellery and all things ethnic. *See page 121.*
- **Kuala Lumpur Craft Complex**. A one-stop centre for Malaysian arts and crafts, it also has a museum and artists' workshops where you can see products being created. *See page 159.*
- **Low Yat Plaza**. Nothing but computers, peripherals, software and electronic gadgets are sold here. A true haven for techies. *See page 158.*
- **Petaling Street Bazaar**. Almost everything on sale here is fake, whether a movie DVD, handbag or electronic gadget; only the food is authentic. *See page 108.*
- **Pavilion.** This gargantuan mall has everything from luxury goods to electronics and furniture, plus a fantastic food court. *See page 153.*
- **Ramadan Bazaar**. Timing is imperative as it only happens during the annual Ramadan fasting month. Expect a staggering range of Malay delicacies, Islamic paraphernalia and household products. *See page 147.*
- **Sungei Wang Plaza**. This is the mall that locals head to for bargains galore and a wide range of products and services. *See page 158.*
- **Suria KLCC**. Slick and well designed mall – with many good eateries – that you can spend an entire day at. *See pages 132 and 138.*

Best Bars and Clubs

- **Alexis Bistro Ampang**. Good food, great ambience and even better music make a combination that is hard to beat. *See page 172.*
- **Bar Italia**. Classic yet contemporary, this three-storey building also has a rooftop lounge and the best *gelato* in town. *See page 143.*
- **Envie Clublounge**. Chic joint with rooftop lounge, popular with DJs and young patrons, who enjoy their themed nights. *See page 237.*
- **Frangipani**. Friday nights at Frangi are legendary now, especially if you are gay and/or love to shake your booty. *See page 161.*
- **No Black Tie**. This performance space for top local musicians, who play everything from jazz to classical, also dishes up Japanese-inspired food. *See page 238.*
- **The Laundry Bar**. The slight trek from the city is well worth the effort, as this bar hosts rising musos and regulars. *See page 238.*
- **Zouk Club**. Mambo-Jambo nights on Wednesdays attract a retro-loving crowd but every night is just as hot and happening at this trendy dome-shaped club with four outlets. *See page 136.*

Above: the Sungei Wang Plaza, the place for bargains. **Right:** mixing cocktails at legendary gay club Frangipani.

Best Places of Worship

- **Batu Caves**. An important pilgrimage site for Hindus, the limestone cave temple here hosts the world's largest statue of the Murugan deity. *See pages 182–3.*
- **Cathedral of St Mary the Virgin**. One of the earliest Anglican cathedrals in this region,

it still impresses with its Gothic architecture and stained-glass windows. *See page 97.*
- **Chan She Shu Yuen Clan Association**. This lovely Chinese clan association building, with ornate altars and ancestral tablets, has fine curved gables and intricate ceramic friezes. *See page 110.*
- **Jamek Mosque**. Built in the Mughal style, this domed and colonnaded mosque sits at the historic river confluence where KL was founded. *See pages 89–91.*
- **Masjid Sultan Salahuddin Abdul Aziz**. Also known as the Blue Mosque, its large blue-and-white dome is anchored by four equally impressive minarets. *See page 215.*
- **Sin Sze Si Ya Temple**. This Taoist temple honours Yap Ah Loy and two other Chinese leaders of early Malaya. *See pages 116–17.*
- **Wat Chetawan**. This elaborate Thai-style Buddhist temple with multi-tiered roofs and intricate carvings is in the suburbs of PJ. *See pages 211–12.*

Above: ride the whitewater at Sungai Selangor.
Left: temple offerings.

Adrenalin-Rushing Activities

- **Adventure caving**. Climb, slide and crawl through four caverns inside the Dark Caves. *See page 183.*
- **Cameroon Climb**. This double-tube water ride at Sunway Lagoon drops riders from as high as 15 metres (49ft), then shoots them up again to a height of 8 metres (26ft). *See page 214.*
- **Flying Coaster**. Experience almost zero gravity on this hang-gliding roller-coaster at Genting Theme Park as it swoops, twists and drops. *See page 198.*
- **F1 Simulator.** Ever wanted to be inside a racing car? If so, try the simulated Formula 1 experience at KL Tower. Earplugs not included. *See page 139.*
- **Whitewater sports**. Shoot up to Class 4 rapids – including steep and technical sections – in a raft or kayak on Sungai Selangor, near Kuala Kubu Bharu. *See pages 190 and 241.*

Money-Saving Tips

Pay cash Payment by credit card at the smaller shops will incur a 3 percent surcharge. Also, shop early: according to local superstition, the first customer deserves a good deal for bringing luck and starting the "flow" of cash. Alternatively, shop near closing time, when salespeople tend to give in to fierce bargaining.

Free food Sample festive goodies during "open house" celebrations at community halls and politicians' residences during major festivals, like Hari Raya Puasa or Chinese New Year. You can also freely imbibe alcohol and finger food during exhibition openings at art galleries. Announcements for these appear in the newspapers.

Matinee concerts Matinee tickets for Petronas Philharmonic Hall classical concerts can go as cheap as RM10 a pop. Also, check other theatre listings for previews or work-in-progress presentations of local productions, which are usually free.

Open-air classes At dawn, join groups of *t'ai chi* and line dancing practitioners at Lake Gardens or Titiwangsa Lake Gardens. There is usually an instructor in front, and anyone can just join in.

Taxis Note that there is a 50 percent surcharge for taxis taken between midnight and 6am. Get to bed early!

Cheap sports For the cost of a cup of tea, get a seat at a 24-hour *mamak* outlet (Indian coffee shop) and enjoy live coverage of global sporting events, such as English Premier League soccer matches and Formula 1 races, on giant TV screens. Food orders are optional.

護國庇民天
勅封忠義關
都天至富財帛

A MULTI-LAYERED CITY

Although Kuala Lumpur is outwardly cosmopolitan, its rhythms are profoundly Asian and multi-ethnic: Malay, Chinese, Indian and Western influences are everywhere, from architecture to fast-food menus

The incessant engine drone of a million vehicles and the click-clacking of countless computer keyboards, the melodic *azan* – the Muslim call to prayers – and the three-tone chimes announcing the arrival of commuter trains. This buzz is about aspiration. By 2020, Kuala Lumpur, known to everyone as KL, intends to reach "world-class city" status. Most of the work was done in the 1990s during Malaysia's Asian Tiger economic heyday, when former strongman Prime Minister Mahathir Mohamad's penchant for almost manic mega-project building transformed the capital.

Since then, KL has struggled with world financial crises and competition from India and China. Yet it continues to build on being a cosmopolitan commercial centre driven by capitalism and globalisation, although the slightly more liberal climate post-Mahathir has seen the creative use of urban spaces for artistic and political expression. Tourists expecting to experience Malaysian culture in some quaint, simplistic form will be sorely disappointed. More likely, they will find multinational companies, global consumer labels, international cuisines and a heaving nightlife scene.

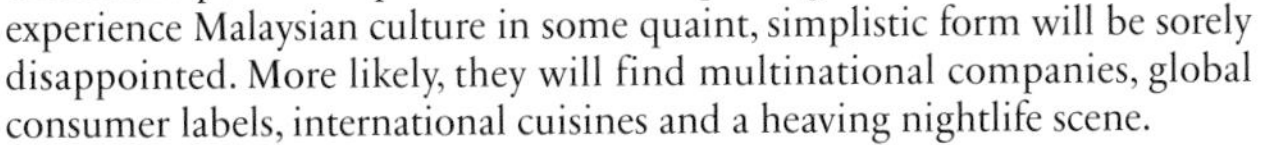

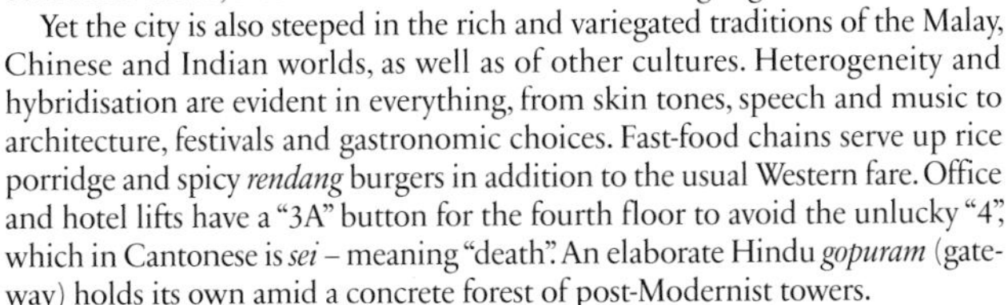

Yet the city is also steeped in the rich and variegated traditions of the Malay, Chinese and Indian worlds, as well as of other cultures. Heterogeneity and hybridisation are evident in everything, from skin tones, speech and music to architecture, festivals and gastronomic choices. Fast-food chains serve up rice porridge and spicy *rendang* burgers in addition to the usual Western fare. Office and hotel lifts have a "3A" button for the fourth floor to avoid the unlucky "4", which in Cantonese is *sei* – meaning "death". An elaborate Hindu *gopuram* (gateway) holds its own amid a concrete forest of post-Modernist towers.

Big-city living may have led more KL-ites to assume the urbanite's steely mantle, but smiles, a probing curiosity and genuine friendliness are still palpable during encounters with locals, whether conducted in Malay or in sing-song Malaysian English. The city's hues, rhythms and vibrancy are the result of an organic growth fertilised by time, ideas and even mishaps – scratch below the surface and you will uncover its multi-layered personas. ❑

PRECEDING PAGES: Malaysia's 50th Independence Day celebrations; shopping for saris on Jalan Tuanku Abdul Rahman. **LEFT:** Guan Di Temple. **ABOVE:** Bazaar Baru Chow Kit.

2.00
1kg
SUZUKI

PEOPLE

Living in a city that embodies the aspirations of the nation, the people of Kuala Lumpur are recipients of the first, best and latest of everything, from fashion to technology, but many of these city slickers are still in touch with their humbler *kampung* (village) roots

One thing has not changed since the 19th century, when settlers first dug their heels in to deal with malaria, civil war and hardship – Kuala Lumpur is where wealth is made, and the people of Malaysia know it. The Federal Territory's area of 244 sq km (94 sq miles) is home to a population of 1.6 million. During the day, the total swells to over 2.5 million, with workers streaming in from the surrounding Klang Valley.

The wealth carrot

Kuala Lumpur has a per capita gross domestic product (GDP) of over RM49,000 – almost double the national average. Likewise, the employment-to-population ratio is almost twice that of other metropolitan areas, with over 80 percent of the total in the service sector. A large migrant labour force also plays an indispensable role in driving the economy. Because of its obvious affluence, the capital attracts the best and the brightest in the country. National literacy levels are close to 100 percent, and the percentage of KL-ites with tertiary education (35 percent) is one-and-a-half times that of the national average. Internationally, Kuala Lumpur is a very important city that links major economic regions into the world economy, according to the UK-based Globalization and World Cities Study Group and Network to measure "world city-ness". In 2008, Kuala Lumpur was ranked an "alpha city", equal to Brussels and Chicago, and higher than Zurich and Los Angeles.

KL-ites go to war when they get behind the wheel of a car or onto a motorcycle. Traffic rules are broken, road rage is rampant and parking is a real work of art.

LEFT: a Chinese hawker frying up chestnuts at the Petaling Street bazaar. **RIGHT:** *tudung*-clad young Malay students.

Hometown links

KL-ites generally do not exhibit a characteristic regional identity. Furthermore, the city's economic boom and irresistible pull have resulted in a generation of migrants who settled here only in the early 1960s. Many are from the rural areas, and their ties to their hometowns and vil-

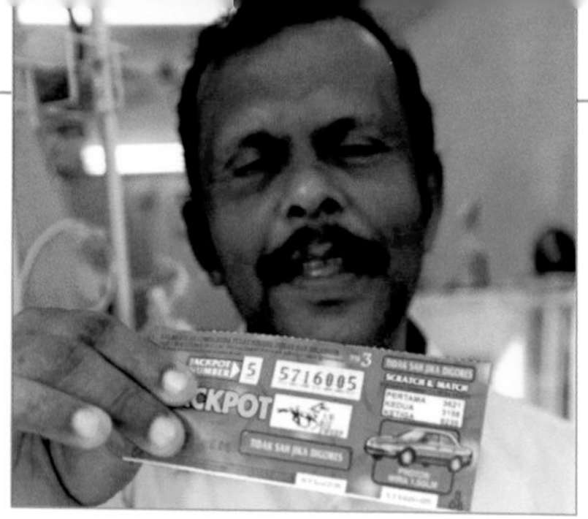

lages remain strong. This is manifested in the periodic exodus from the city – called *balik kampung*, literally "going home to the village" – during the major festive periods of Hari Raya Aidilfitri, Chinese New Year and Deepavali. This is when the notorious Kuala Lumpur traffic chokes up every outbound transport artery.

Of course, as city-dwellers, KL-ites tend to manifest many of the traits of an urbanised population. Though relatively less sophisticated and hard-edged than their more affluent and industrialised neighbours in Hong Kong and Singapore, KL-ites do have a more international outlook compared to residents in the rest of the country. They tend to be more well-travelled and are more influenced by global trends. Indeed, it is feared that a globalised, middle-class, iPod-toting younger generation that holidays in Sydney, shops in Hong Kong and wants a Harvard education is becoming increasingly disjointed from the rest of the country, particularly the rural areas and their attendant issues.

Like many newly moneyed communities, KL-ites enjoy the modern infrastructure of their city but lack the maintenance mentality and high service standards that should naturally follow; they mimic the latest trends but need to work harder on their social graces and civic consciousness. On the other hand, a hard-nosed, big-city imperviousness is blissfully absent. The good life has come easily, and so the approach to life is laid-back – even sluggish – rather than edgy and competitive. KL-ites are warm, friendly and curious to the point of being *kaypoh* (nosy, in local parlance).

Traits from their small town and rural backgrounds are also endearingly retained. Spirit mediums, Malay faith healers (*bomoh*) and fortune tellers are frequently consulted. Playing the lottery (the "4D" – four digits, or *empat ekor*) is an obsession. In fact, traffic jams worsen when there is a road accident because of a combination of the *kaypoh* factor and passersby who hurriedly scribble down what might just be the lucky number to that RM1 million jackpot!

Ethnic *rojak*

Kuala Lumpur as an entity may be relatively new, but it is part of a Malaysia whose human diversity is centuries old. Among KL-ites,

Mobile Madness

Given that every KL-ite owns at least one mobile phone, you could be forgiven for thinking they are as indispensable as air to these city dwellers. Many mobile phone owners do not even have fixed line telephones. Mobile phone trends change rapidly and the use of the Short Message Service (SMS), particularly among the tech-generation youth, is almost rabid. Bizarrely, the Syariah Court allows Muslim men to divorce their wives via SMS, something that women are, not surprisingly, fighting. Mobile phone etiquette is generally nonexistent, so don't be surprised to hear a ringtone in a cinema or see a little rectangular screen light up in a concert hall.

Above: KL-ite obsessions – mobile phones and lottery tickets. **Right:** birthday celebrations. **Far Right:** motorbikes are many families main form of transport.

SONS OF THE SOIL

The Malay (Melayu) people arrived in the archipelago 3,000–5,000 years ago from southern China and Taiwan. Over time, they interacted and intermarried with the Arabs, Indians, Thais and Chinese. The resulting culture and language therefore show strong Javanese, Sumatran, Siamese and, especially, Indian influences. The Malays were largely Hindu before they converted to Islam in the 15th century, and were shifting cultivators and coastal rice planters before the British introduced individual land ownership for the purpose of tax collection.

The word "Malay" is thought to have been either the name of a kingdom or a river in Sumatra, or a Javanese or Mandailing word for "run", since the peninsula's first Malay sultan had fled from war and poverty in Sumatra. Malaysia's Federal Constitution defines a Malay as one who practises Islam and Malay culture, who speaks the Malay language and whose ancestors are Malays.

The language belongs to the Austronesian family and is related to the indigenous tongue called Jakun, but vocabulary is borrowed from Arabic, Chinese, Dutch, English, Portuguese, Sanskrit and Tamil languages.

Today, the Malays – along with the Orang Asli, Indian Muslims, Thais and Portuguese Malaysians – are officially categorised as *bumiputra*, literally "sons of the soil".

affluence and the pursuit of material gain tend to level out differences, but state-led categorising along ethnic lines – a tool courtesy of the British colonialists – is occasionally wielded for political purposes, and is most obvious in institutional life. It certainly does no justice to the colourful, multi-wefted complexity of a population that has shared the same land and experienced hundreds of years of heterogeneity and hybridisation. While core ethnic values are largely preserved – particularly in religion and marriage – borrowings and adaptations are rampant and creative, from food and dress to social mores and customs, language and attitudes.

Decried by some, celebrated by others, but unavoidable when cultural boundaries are so porous, the results are what Malaysians call *rojak*, after a popular local salad of mixed vegetables and fruit doused in a pungent sauce.

The Malays

The indigenous Orang Asli community predates the arrival of the present-day Malays, but urbanisation has pushed this traditionally forest-dwelling group to the fringes of the city. The ethnic Malays are now the dominant *bumiputra* *(see above)*. Kuala Lumpur's first Malay settlers were Sumatran, Bugis, Rawa and Mandailing traders and miners. Their *kampung* (villages) were located north of the river confluence. By 1900, however, the number of Malays in Kuala

Lumpur had decreased, and the British had to set aside Kampung Baru (literally, "new village") as a Malay Agricultural Settlement, to encourage them to eventually partake in government administration. In the wake of the capital's economic progress, the trend has reversed, and today, Malays and other *bumiputra* make up about 40 percent of Kuala Lumpur's population. Most work in the government, community, social and service sectors.

The Chinese

Chinese migrants began to pour into Malaya in great numbers in the 19th century. Around

> *Many middle-class couples have left their children in their hometowns, in the care of family members and live-in maids, usually Indonesian or Filipino.*

Kuala Lumpur, many ended up working in the mines, and a predominantly Hakka and Cantonese community soon sprang up east of the river confluence. Under the third Kapitan Cina, Yap Ah Loy, they built the respectable brick town that the British took over in 1880. Eventually, the Chinese came to dominate business and commerce. Today, they make up about 40 percent of the city's population, and most of them are engaged in the wholesale and retail trade, and food and hospitality industries.

The Indians

About 10 percent of KL-ites are Indians. The majority are Tamils, and a sprinkling are Malayalis, Punjabis and Telugus. The largest numbers arrived as labourers during the rubber boom of the 1880s, although the British era also saw a steady immigration of administrative clerks and moneylenders. Indians today have a strong presence in the wholesale and retail trade, but are equally active in the community, social and personal-services sectors.

Migrant communities

Today, almost 9 percent of Kuala Lumpur's population – or a whopping 82,000 people – make up the migrant labour force. It is no surprise, then, to encounter a Bangladeshi or Burmese waiter, a cleaner who is Indonesian, a hotel manager who is German, or a security guard who is a Nepali Gurkha. Together, these non-Malaysians actually outnumber some of the city's smaller communities, such as Sikhs, Eurasians and Sri Lankans.

Playing the race card

The state paints two diametrically opposed pictures of multiculturalism. One is encapsulated by Tourism Malaysia's tagline, "Malaysia, Truly Asia", which projects the image of perfect utopian harmony. Yet, when the balance of power is threatened, the state issues dire warnings and paints a scenario of a society on the brink of tribal bloodshed, invoking the spectre of the May 13 Incident in 1969. In fact, for 50 years after independence, political representation has been along ethnic lines, serving to keep the ethnic groups divided.

Street-level perceptions and realities are greyer. According to influential pollster Merdeka Centre, about 40 percent of respondents had previously ranked ethnicity before nationality, considering themselves, for example, Chinese or Malay first and Malaysian second. But a more recent poll of young people found that 77 percent indicated faith in multiethnic party representation. Opinion polls have also shown that while some Malaysians felt the country's biggest problem was the lack of national unity, twice as many polled were more worried about the economy. ❑

It's English *lah*!

The English language as spoken in KL by a people who interact across multiple languages has sprouted – and continues to sprout – richly colourful varieties

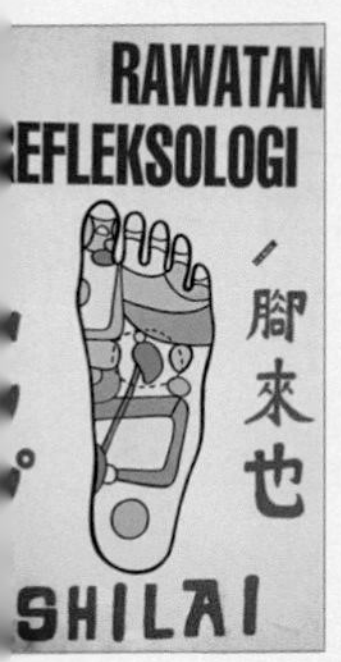

Listening to Malaysians speak English can be by turns bewildering and amusing, particularly in Kuala Lumpur, where the language is widely used. Referred to collectively by the outside world as "Manglish", the varieties of English spoken in Malaysia are as fluid and complex as its multicultural peoples.

English gained a foothold in the region under 19th-century British rule, and was the language used to teach in schools until the late 1960s, when Malay became the main medium of instruction and English was taught as a second language. Yet the common tongue has always been Malay (Bahasa Malaysia), the national language, while English is often still linked to elevated social status and education, and, increasingly, is used in business. In Kuala Lumpur, it is an emerging lingua franca, serving to level out ethnic differences.

English has evolved into an array of colourful vernaculars, which have an undeserved reputation for being ungrammatical, even pidgin. In reality, they have systematic and coherent grammar and vocabulary, understood and used by all speakers. The syntax often involves the restructuring and simplification of sentences, and the omission of certain words. For instance, "Came from where?" translates as "Where did you just come from?"

There are also borrowings from local languages. "They already *makan*" ("They have already eaten") uses the Malay word for food or eating. In "Don't so *kiasu* lah", the Hokkien Chinese word *kiasu* means "afraid to lose out", but also carries a load of cultural connotations for which there is no exact English equivalent. *Lah* is probably the best-known feature of Malaysian English, a sentence particle that, depending on how it is intoned, is used to cajole or tease, or to signify impatience or firmness.

When it comes to pronunciation, the door is thrown wide open. Although British English is the normative standard, elements of American speech are steadily creeping in – due to media influence – particularly in Kuala Lumpur. Depending

on the speaker and situation, one might hear Received Pronunciation, East Coast American or staccato unintelligibility – sometimes in the same conversation.

What is certain is that Malaysians love their English and have fun with it – and not just in conversation. Malaysian English is occasionally used and celebrated in the local English-language media, literature and theatre. ❑

LEFT: soccer fans. **RIGHT: ABOVE:** advertisement for a reflexologist. **RIGHT:** T-shirt illustrating Malaysian English usage, on sale at the Central Market.

DECISIVE DATES

EARLY HISTORY

800–200 BC
Miners from what is today Vietnam mine tin in Klang, but do not settle in the area permanently.

c.300 BC
The Bronze and Iron Age ancestors of today's Malay people settle on the peninsula.

c.200 BC
Trading with China and India begins.

AD 700–1400
The Malay Peninsula comes under the control of the Indianised kingdom of Srivijaya.

c.1400
The port and sultanate of Melaka, the first great maritime power on the peninsula, is founded. Islam, first brought by traders and missionaries, becomes the state religion in 1446.

1511
Melaka falls to the Portuguese. The deposed ruler establishes the Sultanate of Johor, which nominally controls what is present-day Selangor.

1641
The Dutch capture Melaka with the help of the Johor Sultanate.

1700s
Bugis migrants from Sulawesi displace the Minangkabau settlers and establish the present the Sultanate of Selangor.

1824
Melaka is ceded to the British under the Anglo-Dutch Treaty; forms the Straits Settlements with Penang and Singapore.

THE BIRTH OF KUALA LUMPUR

1857
Raja Abdullah, chieftain from Klang, sends Chinese labourers up the Klang River to search for tin. The prospectors alight at the confluence of Sungai Gombak and Sungai Klang, and continue on foot to Ampang, where tin is found. Shacks are built near the confluence. Kuala Lumpur is founded. Large numbers of Chinese labourers start working in the mines.

1859
Hiu Siew becomes KL's first Kapitan Cina ("Chinese captain"), the leader of the Chinese community.

1864
Sin Sze Si Ya Temple, the oldest Chinese temple in KL, is built by Yap Ah Loy.

1867
Selangor Civil War breaks out as rival Malay princes in Klang fight for control of the tin trade.

1868
Yap Ah Loy becomes KL's third and most influential Kapitan Cina.

1873
Selangor Civil War ends. Yap Ah Loy rebuilds the town and revives the mining industry.

BRITISH MALAYA

1874
Pangkor Treaty establishes the British Residential system. The Selangor Resident is installed in 1876.

1878–79
The price of tin doubles.

1880
British Resident Bloomfield Douglas shifts Selangor's capital from Klang to KL.

1881
A massive fire and. later, flood destroy KL's buildings. Yap Ah Loy rebuilds the town twice.

1882
British Resident Frank Swettenham reorganises KL's layout and stipulates that its buildings be built with bricks and mortar, resulting in KL shophouse architecture.

1896
Selangor, Perak, Negeri Sembilan and Pahang are brought together as the

LEFT TOP: the Dutch attack Melaka in 1606. **LEFT:** Yap Ah Loy, Kapitan Cina, 1868–85. **ABOVE:** workers in a tin mine at the turn of the twentieth century. **RIGHT:** Japanese troops launch amphibious assault at Kota Bharu, 1941.

Federated Malay States, with KL as the capital and Frank Swettenham its first Resident. Mughal-style administrative buildings begin to be constructed.

1897
Kampung Bharu established to entice more Malays to settle in KL.

1910
Rubber, introduced in the 1880s, becomes lucrative with the advent of the auto industry and rich Malayans switch from their horse-drawn gharries to the motorcar. Large numbers of Indians are brought in as indentured labour to work on rubber estates.

1926
A great flood hits Kuala Lumpur, causing extensive damage.

1937–38
As the world economy recovers from the Great Depression, KL experiences a building boom.

TIME OF UNREST

1942
Japanese troops reach KL on 11 January 1942. They occupy Malaya till their surrender in August 1945.

1945
The British reoccupy Malaya.

1946
The British propose the

formation of a British crown colony, the Malayan Union, but the scheme is opposed. This leads to the formation of the United Malays National Organisation (UMNO), whose demands result in the inauguration of the Federation of Malaya in 1948.

1948–60
A guerrilla insurgency by the Malayan Communist Party results in a state-declared "Emergency".

1955
Ethnic-based Alliance Party sweeps first local elections.

1957
At midnight on 30 August the Union Jack is lowered and the Malayan flag raised. Malaya's first prime minister, Tunku Abdul Rahman, declares *merdeka* (independence). KL is the new nation's capital. Thereafter nationalistic and modernist architecture shape the city.

1963
On 31 August, the Federation of Malaysia is formed, incorporating Malaya, Singapore, British North Borneo (Sabah) and Sarawak. This leads Indonesia to adopt a policy of *konfrontasi* (confrontation) against Malaysia until 1966.

1965
Singapore separates from the Federation to become a republic, resulting in Malaysia's present national boundaries.

1969
Politically motivated race riots break out in Kampung Bharu and Chow Kit on 13th May. Parliament is suspended and the country is run by a National Operations Council until 1971.

1970
The New Economic Policy, aiming to adjust colonial-era economic imbalances, is unveiled, and includes affirmative rights for Malays, at the time the most economically disadvantaged.

1972
KL is accorded city status.

1973
Alliance Party, with members from Sabah and Sarawak, renamed Barisan Nasional (National Front), and retains stronghold on Malaysia.

1974
KL is declared a Federal Territory. Steady migration from rural areas to KL begins, lasting till the 1980s.

Mahathir Era

1981
Mahathir Mohamad becomes the country's

fourth and longest-serving prime minister.

1988–1997
Malaysia experiences double-digit GDP growth; sees massive industrialisation and mega-projects such as the national car project, Proton, launch of first satellite and building of new administrative capital, Putrajaya.

1996
The iconic Petronas Twin Towers are opened – the tallest buildings in the world till 2003. Malaysia's Silicon Valley, the Multimedia Supercorridor, is launched.

1997
Asian financial crisis causes currency and stock markets to collapse. KL's building boom ends abruptly and many projects are abandoned.

1998
The arrest of Mahathir's successor, popular Deputy Prime Minister Anwar Ibrahim, on charges of sodomy and corruption, provokes a political crisis and the Reformasi movement for political change. The Kuala Lumpur International Airport opens.

1999
Federal government's offices move to Putrajaya. KL remains the legislative capital, as well as financial and commercial centre. Economic rebound begins.

LEFT TOP: show of patriotism on National Day. **LEFT:** Mahathir Mohamad was prime minister for 22 years. **RIGHT TOP:** analysing at the stock market. **RIGHT:** the infamous Anwar Ibrahim.

2003
Mahathir retires. Abdullah Ahmad Badawi takes over as the fifth prime minister.

POLITICAL TSUNAMI

2007
Large street demonstrations show public dissatisfaction with Barisan's administration and policies.

2008
Historic elections on 8 March see the Anwar-led Pakatan Rakyat win four states, denting Barisan's parliamentary majority for the first time since independence. Development blueprint for KL, the KL City Plan 2020, launched.

2009
Badawi pressured to step down. Najib Abdul Razak takes over as prime minister, shadowed by controversy.

2010
Economic restructuring announced to help Malaysia recover from global downturns. Anwar on trial again for sodomy.

南興旅店
Green Spot
南興旅

FROM TIN TO TWIN TOWERS

Kuala Lumpur was a remote mining town that grew to become the capital of Malaysia. For a long time it played second fiddle to other Southeast Asian capitals; it was only in the "can-do" era of the 1990s that the city came of age

Viewed from the bridge of the six-lane Lebuh Pasar Besar, it is difficult to believe that about 150 years ago, there was nothing but swamps and shrubs where glass and steel skyscrapers today sprout. The bridge itself was, in 1880, just a pair of tree trunks placed across the river. But it was here, at the confluence of two rivers, Sungai Gombak and Sungai Klang, that the city of Kuala Lumpur had its humble beginnings.

A town is born

The muddy Sungai Klang (Klang River) is no longer a transport artery today, but in the 19th century and long before that, it served as the main route inland from its estuary 35km (20 miles) west, now the location of Port Klang.

Historians typically trace the founding of Kuala Lumpur to 1857, when Raja Abdullah, a Malay chieftain from Klang in today's state of Selangor, and Raja Jumaat, his brother, from Lukut, sent 87 Chinese coolies (labourers) upriver in search of veins of tin. The prospectors were forced to disembark at the confluence of the two rivers as it was too shallow to accommodate their fully laden flotilla. From here, they followed jungle paths to a place now called Ampang, where tin was found. When this pioneering group were killed by mosquito-borne malaria, they were replaced by another gang of 150. When most of them died, yet another group of labourers was sent up till there were enough to work the mines economically. In this way, thousands of Chinese labourers were brought in, and they soon dominated population numbers.

LEFT: High Street (Jalan Tun HS Lee) and Foch Avenue (Jalan Tun Tan Cheng Lock), c.1960. **RIGHT:** most early Chinese migrants worked as labourers.

The Sungai Klang soon became a busy "highway", with boats packed with miners moving upriver and boatloads of tin being sent down. Since tin was the primary commodity traded along the river, it is plausible that the river got its name from an archaic Malay word for tin, *kalang*.

It is possible that mining activities took place as early as 800–200 BC in parts of Selangor and perhaps along Sungai Klang – three bronze Dong Son bells and a drum tympanum were

unearthed near Klang – but it appears that no permanent settlement sprang up. In contrast, the 1860s saw rows of houses on stilts, with roofs made of *attap* and walls of wooden planks or bamboo lattices, some right by the river. Shops selling provisions, foodstuffs and drinks were set up by enterprising businessmen. To entertain the rough and tough miners, booze stalls, brothels and gambling halls were also opened. In this rickety manner, the city of Kuala Lumpur was born.

Civil unrest

Being something of a frontier town, the settlement was a wild place. The Chinese miners organised themselves into secret societies that constantly fought one another. The Selangor aristocracy did not interfere, being content to just collect export duties from the mined ore. They left control of the Chinese immigrants largely in the hands of a community leader called the 'Kapitan Cina' (literally, "Chinese Captain").

Yap Ah Loy, the third and most illustrious Kapitan Cina, headed the Chinese community from 1868 till his death on 15 April 1885. He was reported to have been a ruthless peacekeeper: during the Selangor Civil War of 1867–73, he paid 50 silver dollars for every enemy head delivered to his home, and, as it was reported, business was brisk.

With the rise of the canning industry at the end of the 19th century, demand for tin shot up, and the rush to mine the metal precipitated widespread unrest. Malay chiefs with rich tin deposits in their domains became powerful magnates whom the sultan could no longer control. A conflict over administrative authority and taxation between Raja Abdullah, the administrator of Klang, and a rival chief, Raja Mahdi, resulted in the Selangor Civil War.

Initially, the war focused on gaining control of the forts sited at the river estuaries where the Malay royalty were based. Fearing the war, the miners shipped their ore through whatever river route was open to them. As duties from tin slowly dwindled in the ports, the warring parties moved into Kuala Lumpur.

Raja Abdullah was supported by Tengku Kudin, the Viceroy of Selangor, who in turn had the support of Yap Ah Loy. When their enemies overran Kuala Lumpur in 1872, razing it to the ground, Tengku Kudin enlisted the help of a Malay army from Pahang to regain the town in 1873. Yap Ah Loy is credited with rebuilding Kuala Lumpur after the war and ensuring that it did not disappear back into the marsh.

Meanwhile, the outbreak of unrest provided the British with the opportunity to assert their presence in the tin-mining states of Selangor, Perak and Negeri Sembilan.

The British Residential system

British presence in the Malay Peninsula had begun earlier, in 1785 in Penang, followed by Singapore and Melaka. By 1826, the three were administered as part of the Straits Settlements, and, with their strategic location and free port status, they came to dominate trade in the region.

The British initially pursued a policy of non-intervention in the affairs of the Malay states. But with the rising demand for tin and with civil unrest threatening investments in the mines, the Straits Settlements merchants

Left: a tin mining site near Kuala Lumpur, c.1906.
Right: Selangor royalty, c.1874.

pressured the British administrators to intervene. The signing of the Pangkor Treaty in 1874 settled a dispute over the throne of Perak, but imposed on the new sultan a British "Resident", whose advice had to "be asked and acted upon on all questions other than those touching Malay religion and custom". A similar agreement was made soon after in Selangor.

Thus, ultimate control rested with the British Resident. Captain Bloomfield Douglas, who became the Resident of Selangor in 1876, introduced a policing and legal system based on British principles, and the town soon began to take shape.

Ethnic settlements

Many of Kuala Lumpur's early roads were once named after the origins of the people living there, or the destinations they led to.

In the 1850s, there were only two cart tracks – Java Street (now called Jalan Tun Perak) and Market Street (now Lebuh Pasar Besar). Java

THE GOLDEN CHERSONESE AND SELANGOR BEFORE 1857

From the beginning, the Malay Peninsula's position on the shipping routes linking East and West influenced its economy through maritime trade, attracting cultural and religious influences, and exposing it to colonial subjugation.

The peninsula was known to early geographers as the "Golden Chersonese", a rich source for aromatic woods and spices, as well as birds' nests, prized by the Chinese. Port-kingdoms along the coast waxed and waned depending on the strength of their dominance over trade routes.

By the 7th century, the peninsula had become part of the Indianised empire of Srivijaya, centred on Sumatra, but by the end of the 15th century, it had come under the rule of the Muslim sultanate of Melaka, the first great maritime power based on the peninsula itself.

When Melaka fell to the Portuguese in the 16th century, what is present-day Selangor came under the nominal rule of the Sultanate of Johor. With the arrival of the Dutch and the British in the 17th and 18th centuries, pitched struggles for control of the Melaka port continued, but Selangor would remain relatively unaffected until later, when tin became a new source of wealth and contention.

In the 18th century, Bugis migrants from Sulawesi displaced the original Minangkabau settlers and established the present Sultanate of Selangor.

Yap Ah Loy – Man of Steel

This intrepid leader fought against human and natural calamities to prevent the settlement from sinking back into swampland, winning respect from both locals and colonials

The story of Kuala Lumpur is not complete without the mention of Yap Ah Loy, a Hakka immigrant who arrived in Malaya when he was only 17. Though he was the third Kapitan Cina (Chinese

Captain) of the city, he is often considered the founder of Kuala Lumpur, much to the chagrin of Malay nationalists, who would prefer that the founder of their capital were Malay.

Yap's rise to fame was legendary: he rebuilt Kuala Lumpur at least thrice, ruled it like his own little kingdom before the British Resident turned up in 1880, was the richest man around, and was a great fighter and a gang leader (or *daaigo* – Cantonese for 'big brother').

The first time Yap rebuilt Kuala Lumpur was after the Selangor Civil War, when he returned to find the town in ruins, with the mines flooded, equipment damaged and houses burnt. With borrowed money, he rebuilt the town and revived the mines, almost going bankrupt when the world price of tin collapsed. A sudden doubling in the tin price in 1878–79 saved him.

A fire at the beginning of 1881 razed the entire town except Yap's house, and the wooden shacks had to be erected again. Unfortunately, a great flood at the end of that year swept away the homes. Yap stoically went about rebuilding the town again.

His personality is documented in a Chinese account: "He was not very big or tall but when he spoke his voice was sonorous. His temper was like fire and he had the strength of an elephant."

Frank Swettenham thought highly of him, and commented in his book, *Malay Sketches* (1895), that Yap was a "remarkable man... whose instincts were distinctly warlike and his authority with his countrymen supreme".

Yap was, indeed, mayor, police chief, developer, judge, tax collector, opium den operator, casino owner and brothel keeper. He maintained order, ran a hospital, operated the market and gambling booths, and had a prison. He owned between one-third and almost two-thirds of the city (the most reliable statistics have him owning 64 out of the 200 houses in 1880).

Yap died in 1885 at the age of 48, and his successors did not achieve his level of eminence. The position of Kapitan Cina was eventually replaced by the government's Protectorate of Chinese.

Today, nothing much remains of Yap's wealth – one of his three sons gambled away almost all of the family's fortune. Yap is honoured by a road named after him, but it's the shortest in town, measuring a mere 80 metres (260ft). ❑

Left: Yap Ah Loy, Kapitan Cina 1868–85.

Street was populated by people from Sumatra, while Market Street was, well, where the market was located. Other roads in early Kuala Lumpur were Ampang Street and Petaling Street, which led to the mines in Ampang and Petaling. Market Square had two side roads named Macao Street and Hokkien Street, whose residents were, unsurprisingly, from Macau and Fujian Province in China.

The Malays and Indonesians lived mostly north of the confluence in the vicinity of Java Street and Malay Street. The Chinese settled east of Sungai Klang along Petaling Street, High Street, Sultan Street, Klyne Street and Pudu Street, which was at the fringe of the jungle back then and is still called *Bun Saan Ba* ("half-jungle" in Cantonese) by the Chinese today. In 1875, the town's population was estimated at 1,000 Chinese and 500–700 Malays. Today, a few of these streets still retain their old names.

The British settled mostly west of the river, building their bungalows on leafy, green lawns in the classier part of town. It was here that the Residency, home of the British Resident, was assembled.

Building the city

In 1880, the state capital of Selangor was moved to Kuala Lumpur, and in 1882, Frank Swettenham took over as the Resident. It was in the era of his stewardship, which lasted till May 1889, that wooden shanties were pulled down and brick buildings were introduced, roads were widened and some of Kuala Lumpur's grand colonial structures were erected.

From the 1850s till 1881 at the earliest, most locals lived in wooden or bamboo structures. There was no planning, houses were built too near each other, sanitation was poor and some areas were described as "pestilential". In October 1882, Swettenham reported, "The present state of the town is not only a disgrace to the Government, but I should think it is dangerous to health."

In January 1881, a massive fire razed almost all of Kuala Lumpur, and when the town was rebuilt, some houses and shops were constructed using bricks and tiles. But on 21 December that year, a great storm flooded the city, and many buildings were again damaged.

Tin from mines in Kuala Lumpur continued to be shipped downriver to Klang or ferried on a cart track to Damansara, about 26km (16 miles) away, where there was a jetty and boats that went to and from Klang. But by 1901, tin was being transported by train to Port Swettenham (now called Port Klang), the new transshipment centre for tin.

Meanwhile, in 1896, Selangor, Perak, Negeri Sembilan and Pahang were brought together as the Federated Malay States (FMS), with the aim of facilitating administration and promoting quicker economic development. Kuala Lumpur

ABOVE: Frank Swettenham. **RIGHT:** floodwaters (December 1881) at Java Street (Jalan Tun Perak).

was chosen as its capital, and Swettenham was appointed the first Resident-General. The seat of the colonial government, the Bangunan (Malay for "building") Sultan Abdul Samad *(see page 94)*, was opened in April 1897. Around the grand block, other buildings in complementary style were later erected, prompting a British architect who visited Kuala Lumpur to comment on "the total fantasy of the nearly theatrical setting". The city rapidly grew to become a centre of administration, business and trade.

Prewar prosperity

Kuala Lumpur entered the 20th century amid much optimism. A newspaper reported on 25 November 1903 that "Java Street is not much to look at, in fact it has been called the slum of slums of our local paradise, yet it is a street of no little activity, for in it are congregated a large number of native shops which, to judge from the crowds continually around them, should be doing a roaring trade."

By this time, the peninsula was producing more than half the world's supply of tin. Towards the end of the 19th century, *Hevea brasiliensis*, or the rubber tree, was introduced to Malaya. Planters were initially unreceptive to the Brazilian crop, but when the price of coffee collapsed and the birth of the automobile industry triggered a demand for rubber tyres, it was quickly embraced, and migrant Indian labourers were brought in to work on the rubber estates. Fortunes were made in the rubber boom that followed, and the industry remained a mainstay of the Malaysian economy up to the 1970s.

Profits from the rubber boom also heralded the age of the motorcar in Kuala Lumpur. Richer residents abandoned bullock carts, horse-drawn gharries and rickshaws for this classy new conveyance.

After the Great Depression (1929–34), Kuala Lumpur experienced a building boom in 1937. Developers invested about $2 million in property projects, including the five-storey Oversea-Chinese Banking Corporation building at the junction of Rodger Street and Market Street; the three-storey offices of the tin company Anglo-Oriental (Malaya) Ltd behind the Selangor Club; the Pavilion and Odeon cinemas; the Central Market; and the offices of the top rubber company, Harrisons, Barker & Co Ltd, on Ampang Road. While the Pavilion cinema has since been demolished, the other buildings are still standing.

The Japanese occupation

The era of Britain's "benevolent imperialism" in Malaya came to an end when Japanese Imperial Army troops invaded on 8 December 1941. Initially, when the Japanese reached Kuala Lumpur on 11 January, they were more intent on passing through to reach and overpower the British garrison in Singapore. Nevertheless, residents of Kuala Lumpur remember well the beheading of Chinese men, whose heads were then placed on poles at strategic points around the town – a fear tactic to cow the inhabitants into submission.

Eventually, due to poor strategies (guns were pointed in the wrong direction), weak airpower and other factors, the British suffered a humiliating defeat in Malaya, ushering in a harrowing 44-month period of the Japanese Occupation. Despite persuasive propaganda about an "Asia for Asiatics", the Japanese ruled with an iron fist in order to control a resentful population suffering from spiralling inflation and shortages of food and other essential goods.

In 1904, the Memorandum on the Future Policy of Municipal Schemes stated: "It is too late ... to hope that Kuala Lumpur can ever become a city of great grandeur."

Tens of thousands of Chinese were rounded up and executed, and other ethnic groups were not spared either. Europeans suffered appalling conditions in detention camps, and Indians and Malays were forced to work on the notorious "Death Railway" in Thailand.

The birth of a nation

The British returned soon after the war ended, but the sun had started to set on the British Empire. Virtually bankrupt, the British adopted a policy to return its colonies to self-rule. Meanwhile, in the Malay peninsula, the Japanese occupation had also prompted the formation of a largely local Chinese-based Communist anti-Japanese movement, which turned into an anti-colonialist movement. The Japanese had also fostered limited Malay nationalism as part of their plans for the region.

The British had intended to merge the various polities of the Malay Peninsula into a Malayan Union under the sovereignty of the British Crown, but this idea was strongly opposed by Malay nationalists. In 1946, some 41 Malay associations formed the United Malays National Organisation (UMNO), which today remains Malaysia's dominant political party. Their demands resulted in the formation of the Federation of Malaya in 1948. The Communists, shut out of public life, embarked the same year on guerrilla warfare as the path to independence, resulting in the British declaring a state of emergency which was to last 13 years.

Against this background of war and insurgency, the colonials strengthened government and imposed draconian laws, legacies that lasted till the present. British rule had also been based on economic expediency. The colonialists practised ethnic identification with economic sectors on a divide-and-rule basis. However, when it came to independence talks, they switched tacks,

Left: Sultan Abdul Samad Building, *c.*1906. **Above Left:** Malaysian soldiers, 1941. **Above:** British troops' failed attempt to stop the Japanese at Singapore. **Right:** Japanese surrender ceremony on 22 Feb 1946.

emphasising instead a multiracial "Malayan" identity to enforce loyalty to the state. This became a condition for independence.

As a multiracial Malaya struggled with identity, position and welfare in the context of a nation-state, what resulted politically was not a "fusion" but accommodation of the different ethnic groups in a social compact. A cooperative partnership was formed by UMNO with two other ethnic-based political parties, the Malaysian Chinese Association and the Malaysian Indian Congress. The Alliance won the first Malayan election in 1955. Two years later, Malaya became an independent state, with Kuala Lumpur as its capital.

Stadium Merdeka was ready in time to allow tens of thousands of proud, excited and anxious Malayans to witness the first prime minister, Tunku Abdul Rahman, shout "Merdeka" on 31 August 1957. The period of nation-building that followed resulted in the completion of other large-scale public projects, such as the Parliament House, the National Museum, the National Monument, the National Mosque and the Subang airport.

In 1963, the Federation of Malaysia was formed, incorporating Malaya, Singapore, British North Borneo (Sabah) and Sarawak. For various reasons Singapore was expelled in 1965, resulting in the present national boundaries of Malaysia. The Alliance expanded to include political parties in the peninsula as well as Sabah and Sarawak – all of them ethnic-based – and became the Barisan Nasional (BN, the National Front). BN have led the country since independence, and all Malaysian prime ministers have come from its majority party, UMNO.

Affirmative action

However, colonial-era inequalities among Malaysians were not addressed fully at the country's independence. The rights of Malays, the identity of non-Malays, wealth distribution, language and education soon became key issues of contention. In 1969, emotionally charged elections shockingly eroded the traditional majority support for BN in favour of two majority-Chinese opposition parties. Immediately afterward, politically engineered bloody clashes occurred between Malays and Chinese on 13 May.

The clashes were centred on the Kampung Baru and Chow Kit areas, where Chinese shops and houses were razed and fighting broke out between gangs of Malays and Chinese. An emergency was declared, and the police and army were mobilised to try and control the situation.

The violence was contained in less than a week, fewer than 200 lives were lost and the events were largely confined to Kuala Lumpur. However, the May 13 Incident, as it has come to be known, had a lasting impact on the whole country. Parliament remained suspended for two years and the country was governed by a 10-man civilian military council. In 1970, the New Economic Policy was introduced to address ethnic and economic inequality and to eradicate poverty by growing the economic pie. In 1970, 75 percent of Malaysians living below the poverty line were Malay and so affirmative action for the *bumiputra* (which include Malays) became part of institutional life.

Today, the policy is mired in controversy – the criticisms are numerous, but the chief one is that it has resulted in lulling the Malays into complacency and engendered a stratum of society that has become dependent on state hand-outs. However, among Malays themselves there was growing dissatisfaction with the abuses of the policy by the political elite and their business associates – a group sometimes referred to scathingly as "Umnoputra" – to enrich themselves.

ABOVE LEFT: Tunku Abdul Rahman (at podium), Malaya's first PM, declaring Independence on 31 Aug 1957. **LEFT:** social divide: children in refugee centre, Stadium Merdeka. **RIGHT TOP:** damage caused in May 13 Incident.

The era of mega projects

Kuala Lumpur was declared a Federal Territory in 1974. In the same decade, the government launched an ambitious programme to transform Malaysia from its agro-mining foundation to a mixed economy with a strong manufacturing sector.

Riding on industrialisation, particularly the lucrative electronics and computer industries, and on commodities such as palm oil (which had replaced rubber) and petroleum, Malaysia became a major trading nation and economic growth was a given. Malaysians from rural areas, and especially Malays, flocked to cities. Kuala Lumpur, in particular, flourished. To ease housing issues, vast housing estates were built outside the city, including the satellite town of Petaling Jaya (PJ). Incomes and the standards of living improved, and the Malay middle class grew.

Growth jumped even more and Malaysia's ambitions became truly international during the 22-year leadership of Mahathir Mohamad (1981–2003). However, Mahathir is also decried by critics for authoritarian steps such as muzzling the judiciary, royalty and media, and for breeding cronyism and corruption through

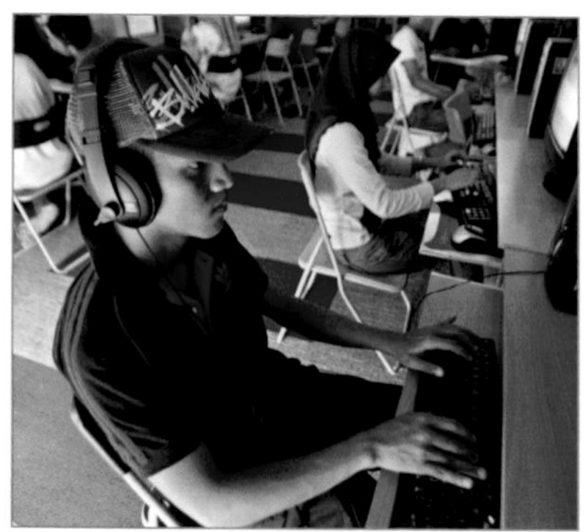

corporate nationalism. Still, he raised Malaysia's global profile, became a spokesman for the Third World against the West, and forged links with the South and Muslim countries.

It was in the last decade of Mahathir's tenure, when GDP averaged 10 percent per annum, that billion-ringgit mega-projects were implemented, including a new federal capital, Putrajaya, a car industry and the launching of a satellite. Migrant labour poured into the country in even greater numbers, Kuala Lumpur's skyline was dramatically transformed and the economic spillover into Selangor saw the rapid development of the Klang Valley. The conurbation today covers 4,000 sq km (1,500 sq miles), and spreads southwest to Klang and south to the Kuala Lumpur International Airport. Vision 2020, a nationalist and developmentalist blueprint, was launched, aiming to propel Malaysia to developed-nation status by 2020.

The mega-projects of the 1990s included the Kuala Lumpur City Centre and the Petronas Twin Towers; the Multimedia Super Corridor; a new administrative capital, Putrajaya; and the international airport.

Then in 1997, the Asian financial crisis wreaked havoc in the region. Overnight, many projects in Kuala Lumpur were abandoned and capital controls imposed. Meanwhile, the popular deputy prime minister, Anwar Ibrahim, was sacked and jailed on charges of sodomy and corruption, provoking the *Reformasi* movement and historic demonstrations on the streets of the capital, pushing for political change.

In 1999, the executive and judicial branches of Malaysia's government moved to Putrajaya, leaving Kuala Lumpur as the seat of Parliament and the financial and commercial centre. After reining in the economy and the social unrest, Mahathir passed the baton in 2003 to the consensus-seeking Abdullah Ahmad Badawi. The change in leadership led to both BN's biggest general election win a year later, as Malaysians looked forward to more open governance, and its biggest loss four years after that, when that did not materialise.

Political tsunami

The shock 2008 "political tsunami" resulted from many dissatisfactions since *Reformasi*: the abuse of affirmative-action policies, corruption, the lack of judicial independence, the Islamisation of the government machinery and totalitarian laws. The winners were the multi-ethnic Pakatan Rakyat, a new opposition coalition put together by Anwar. The Pakatan comprised Anwar's new Parti Keadilan Rakyat (People's Justice Party) along with two longtime "foes",

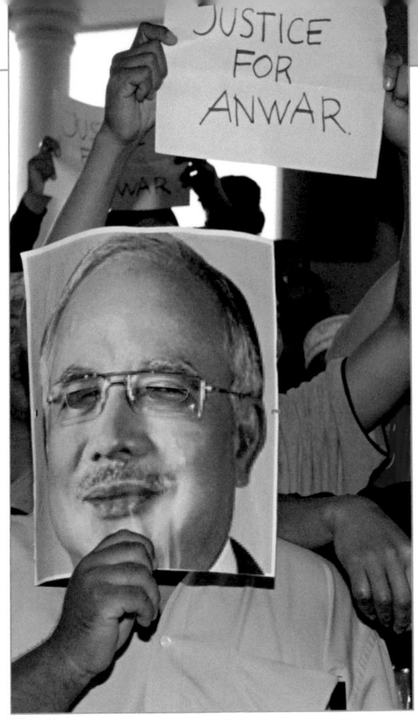

the largely Chinese-based Democratic Action Party (DAP) and the Pan-Malaysian Islamic Party (PAS). They won an unprecedented four states while Kuala Lumpur voted in a historic number of opposition Members of Parliament. 2010 saw their leader brought to trial once again after he was accused of sodomizing an aide.

In 2009, Najib Razak took over as prime minister under a cloud of controversy, and BN have been struggling since to regain lost ground. BN's tactics include stepping up racialised politicking and abuses of power. Nonetheless, they are also addressing Malaysians' key concern – the economy, which is exposed to global financial trends and competition from China and India. Strategies include economic liberalisation and further emphasis on the services and high technology industries, a move led by a Kuala Lumpur aiming to be a "world-class city" by 2020.

FAR LEFT: Petronas Towers. **LEFT TOP:** around 16 million Malaysians regularly use the internet. **ABOVE LEFT:** supporters of opposition leader Anwar Ibrahim outside the courthouse in Kuala Lumpur in February 2010. **ABOVE RIGHT:** a Pakatan Rakyat supporter waves a campaign poster outside a polling station in 2010.

Meanwhile, Pakatan Rakyat are consolidating power-sharing among their component parties and building efficient and transparent governance in the states they lead. They are aiming to win federal government in the next general elections. KL-ites, like many Malaysians, have never been so politicised. Just over 50 years after independence, change is in the air, with the possibilities now of representative democracy, the beginning of the end of race-based politics, and a more liberal and inclusive society. ❑

DIGITAL EXPRESSIONS

Launched in 1996, the ambitious Multimedia Super Corridor aimed to transform Malaysia into a "knowledge society". Today, 16 million Malaysians are internet users; about 70 per cent use social media. The proliferation of political online newspapers and blogs circumvents stifling media laws, while singer-songwriters and independent film-makers reach international audiences through platforms like YouTube. Meanwhile, community mobilisation and grassroots activism have never been more effective. However, even as connected Malaysians are more globalised and engaged, the digital divide threatens to widen the socio-economic divide.

RELIGION

In a city where temples and churches stand alongside mosques, and where Muslims and non-Muslims celebrate festivals together, the designation of Islam as the country's official religion comes not without its share of debate and compromise

Malaysia is a country with a Muslim majority, with 60.4 percent of its people practising Islam. Of the remaining, 19.2 percent are Buddhist, 9.1 percent are Christian, 6.3 percent Hindu, 2.6 percent subscribe to Chinese folk beliefs, while the remaining 2.4 percent practise other faiths.

The religious composition of the capital, however, has come to mirror the national statistics only in the last three decades. Owing its origins to the activities of Chinese tin prospectors and British colonialists as much as to the patronage of the Selangor royal family, Kuala Lumpur only saw its Malay Muslim population increase after it was proclaimed a Federal Territory in 1974. This increase was due to several migratory waves of people, mostly from rural areas, looking for jobs and a better life in the thick of the aggressive industrialisation policies of the late 1970s and most of the 1980s.

> *Article 3(1) states: "Islam is the religion of the Federation; but other religions may be practised in peace and harmony …." Article 11(1) states: "Every person has the right to profess and practise his religion."*

A diversity of faiths

A walk through the neighbourhood of Brickfields puts the city's de facto religious plurality into perspective. Along a single road, one will come across Syrian Orthodox, Lutheran, Catholic and Methodist churches, along with a Buddhist wat, several Hindu temples and a Muslim madrasah, all within minutes of each other. At the end of the street is a small Chinese folk temple, and scattered around the neighbourhood are several Chinese ancestral shrines.

LEFT: a man at prayer in Masjid India. **ABOVE:** religious icons on sale in Jalan Ampang.

In fact, this mix of religious persuasions is not peculiar to Brickfields. The same concentration of houses of worship can be found in the older parts of the Klang Valley, in residential areas that have grown organically in spite of the government obsession with imposing

racial and religious quotas in most aspects of public life.

Yet, beneath this rose-tinted image of peaceful coexistence, religious divisions can sometimes be rigorously upheld. Non-Muslims are occasionally barred from entering some of the mosques in Kuala Lumpur. A French Muslim visitor was once reportedly prevented from performing his midday prayers at Masjid Jamek, as the caretakers did not believe he was Muslim – he was white and did not go by a Muslim name.

Syariah Criminal Offences Act

Syariah laws are binding upon Malaysian Muslims. They designate criminal offences that are not listed in the secular Penal Code. For example, the consumption of alcohol or the non-observance of fasting during the month of Ramadan are designated as crimes for Muslims even though they are not crimes under the Penal Code. These crimes are prosecuted in the Syariah Court. A common criticism of these laws is that they turn the personal obligations of a Muslim to his or her religion into crimes against the State. Proponents of these laws, however, assert that they are essential to keeping the moral fabric of an Islamic Malaysia intact.

Islam and the state

The Constitution of Malaysia designates Islam as the official religion of the Federation *(see text box on page 43)*, but precisely what this means is still hotly debated. The central question is whether the Constitution guarantees freedom of religion, and whether Malaysia is really a secular or an Islamic state.

Constitutional enshrinement of Islam has meant the heavy involvement of the state in determining the kind of Islam practised by its citizens. As a consequence, a distinct set of laws has been created to govern Muslims and a state-sanctioned hierarchy of Islamic authority makes pronouncements on how Malaysians must live their lives *(see box below)*.

A sinister example of this is the outlawing of Shi'ism in the country. Malaysia's Muslims follow the Sunni branch of Islam and the Shafi'i school of jurisprudence. In the not-so-distant past, Malaysia has witnessed more than one state crackdown on professed Shi'ites, many of whom were detained without trial under the Internal Security Act. In fact, a council of *muftis* (state-appointed legal experts on Islam) even released a *fatwa* (a "legal opinion", which in Malaysia carries the force of law), declaring Shi'ism to be a threat to national security and to Malaysian Muslims.

A moderate Muslim nation?

This example of how Islam is regulated by the state is incongruent with the widespread perception of Malaysia as a moderate Muslim nation with a stable government and enviable prosperity in the post-colonial era. Indeed, American think-tanks such as the New America Foundation hold up Malaysia as a model that "shows what moderate Islam can look like".

Internally, this image has been cultivated by the governing political party, the United Malays National Organisation (UMNO), for political leverage in multi-religious Malaysia. UMNO uses secular, nationalist rhetoric in contrast to the opposition Pan-Malaysian Islamic Party (PAS), whose founding principle is the ideal of an Islamist state.

Both UMNO and PAS are vying for the majority ethnic Malay Muslim vote, and this rivalry has catapulted the country into divisiveness.

Painted by UMNO as an "Islamic fundamentalist party," PAS has led the largely Muslim state

of Kelantan since independence. It imposes strict regulations on Muslims in terms of alcohol, dressing and entertainment, but respects the rights of non-Muslims.

Meanwhile, under UMNO leadership, the nation has seen the rise of authoritarian politics and moral policing to secure political power. Since the Islamisation of the government machinery under former prime minister Mahathir Mohamad, the state's role has been extended to policing values, beliefs and private lives.

This has ranged from banning rock performers from the West to entering homes to apprehend Muslim adulterers. Non-Muslims have been told they have no right to comment on matters Islamic. In the last decade, the Islamic bureaucracy has worsened, with the criminalising of differences of opinion in Islam and the mishandling of the rights of non-Muslims in high-profile cases of divorce and conversion.

Even trivial matters come under the spotlight. For years, it's been a popular practice for Malaysians to celebrate the major festivals of different faiths together. Sometimes, festival dates coincide, and the affectionally dubbed "Kongsi Raya" and "Deepa Raya" are jointly celebrated. This has been declared by state-appointed religious authorities as un-Islamic.

Alarmed Muslims and non-Muslims voiced their dissatisfaction over these and other issues through the ballot box in 2008. And so PAS now has the opportunity within the Anwar Ibrahim-led Pakatan Rakyat opposition coalition to work with non-Muslim political parties and to serve mixed constituencies in terms of ethnicity and religion.

> *"Kongsi Raya" is when Hari Raya Aidilfitri coincides with Chinese New Year ("kongsi" is the Chinese festive greeting). "Deepa Raya" is when Hari Raya coincides with Deepavali.*

Meanwhile, even as some segments of society have intensified efforts to assert the supremacy of a particular brand of Islam, others – including Muslims and Malaysians of other faiths – are constantly trying to adjust to the ever-changing religious landscape. ❑

FAR LEFT: Hindu priests at the Sri Maha Mariamman Temple. **ABOVE LEFT:** traditional jewellery at a market in Kampung Baru, Malaysia's oldest district. **ABOVE RIGHT:** men prepare themselves for Friday prayers at Masjid Jamek.

Of Signs and Symbols

Symbols, numbers and colours of various kinds have special significance in Malaysia – a significance that often transcends religious and ethnic differences

Symbols, iconography and numerology are evident in everyday life in Kuala Lumpur.

Drawn from the people's various religions, cultures and traditions, these developed independently or through synthesis, from within or imported. A number have roots in the past, others are contemporary. Some are subscribed to by all Malaysians; some are observed by specific groups; yet others are dismissed as superstition or censured by the establishment.

But many belong to the common domain and are a common language that articulates community, a shared shorthand for complex, layered and fluid histories, values and knowledge. In multicultural Malaysia, this collective acknowledgement consolidates collective identity.

From colours to numbers and food to fables, symbols and icons shape the world of Kuala Lumpur. For example, celebration is coloured: Chinese New Year by red, the colour of luck, and the Muslim celebration of Hari Raya Aidilfitri by green, the colour of Islam. Houses, streets and clothing are adorned accordingly. Multicultural neighbours not only put up with it, some wear the appropriate colour when visiting each other for "open house."

Present-day injections of meaning into these symbols, usually by the establishment, sometimes bear round peg-square hole results. Those that never get accepted are quietly forgotten. More disturbing, though, are attempts to racialise the relevance of these symbols and icons or worse, abuse them for political mileage. In trying times, Malaysians articulate and work hard to stand by that commonality forged by the unifying bonds of signs and symbols.

Above: red is an auspicious colour associated traditionally with Chinese culture. It is dominant during Chinese festivals and weddings, and is an absolute taboo at funerals.

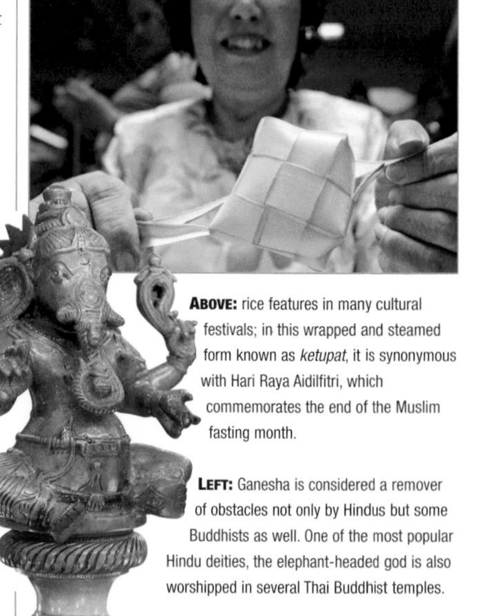

Above: rice features in many cultural festivals; in this wrapped and steamed form known as *ketupat*, it is synonymous with Hari Raya Aidilfitri, which commemorates the end of the Muslim fasting month.

Left: Ganesha is considered a remover of obstacles not only by Hindus but some Buddhists as well. One of the most popular Hindu deities, the elephant-headed god is also worshipped in several Thai Buddhist temples.

NATURAL ICONS

Nature is an important wellspring of symbols and icons. Indigenous peoples believe spirits live in all living things, from plants to rivers and mountains. Among these would be the fig tree, a large tree family in Malaysian forests. But the Ficus features in many religions and is revered across faiths. So it is that in over-built Kuala Lumpur, even if all other signs of nature have been concreted over, the fig is left well alone, especially towering and old specimens. That it is meaningful to Malaysians of many faiths is evident in the offerings left around it, ranging from a *nasi lemak* breakfast to miniature icons of Hindu gods and Taoist joss sticks.

Of nature's bounties, the domesticated paddy is uniform in its ritualistic importance across ethnic groups. Wedding couples are traditionally blessed with rice; Indian and Malay couples also feed each other rice as part of the ceremony, and an Indian bride must tip over a vessel of rice at the entrance of the couple's new home to invite prosperity in. Tamils celebrate Ponggal by boiling a rice concoction over first thing in the morning to signify an abundance of luck and blessings.

ABOVE: with the number eight signifying prosperity, 08.08.08 saw 238 Chinese Malaysians partake in a mass wedding to ensure a head start in conjugal success.

BELOW: the keris is a double-edged dagger that symbolises Malay royalty and has recently become a marker of Malay supremacy, a racial- and tension-provoking redefinition by certain political parties.

EVENTS AND FESTIVALS

Kuala Lumpur's multicultural society celebrates in spectacular fashion all year long. Anywhere and at any time, there are lots of opportunities for the visitor to join in the festivities, whether religious and cultural, or contemporary and hip

Kuala Lumpur has a year-round calendar of traditional festivals and contemporary events. The lead-up to festivals sees different parts of the city and all shopping malls decked in the respective cultural decorations, and offering festive goodies and clothing for sale. Most Malaysians celebrate with "open house", inviting both family and friends home for meals and refreshments. Government-run "open houses" are also held in public venues, and everyone is welcome. The timing of major festivals, such as Hari Raya Aidilfitri and Chinese New Year, is variable as they adhere to the lunar calendar. Check the local dailies or **Tourism Malaysia** (tel: 03-2615 8188; www.tourism.gov.my) for details.

January/February

Federal Territory Day (1 February): Kuala Lumpur observes this public holiday with fireworks, cultural shows, sports activities and other events around the city.

National Craft Day: A month-long festival at the National Craft Complex on Jalan Conlay, this showcases handicrafts from all over the country, together with craft-making demonstrations, performances and participatory activities.

Thaipusam: On the eve, Hindu worshippers gather at the Sri Maha Mariamman Temple near Petaling Street. At dawn, a procession with a chariot carrying the deity Lord Murugan's statue makes its way to Batu Caves outside the city, the priests giving blessings at Hindu temples en route. At Batu Caves, devotees carry altars and pots of milk to the hilltop temple *(see pages 46–7)*.

Chinese New Year: Traditionally celebrated over 15 days, the run-up to the new year centres around Petaling Street, with decorations and treats galore from mandarin oranges to barbecued pork. On the eve, families gather for reunion meals, while the rest of the festival sees lion dances herald new beginnings, and youngsters receive "red packets" – cash gifts from their elders for good luck.

March/April

Le Tour de Langkawi: Regarded as the best annual cycling road race in Asia, this action-packed event attracts top international teams.

LEFT: dancers at Citrawarna (Colours of Malaysia) parade.
ABOVE: children carry lanterns for the Mooncake Festival.

It starts from the northern island of Langkawi and ends in Kuala Lumpur at Dataran Merdeka (Independence Square).

Formula 1 Petronas Malaysian Grand Prix: Enjoy top-speed Formula 1 action at the Sepang International Circuit near the Kuala Lumpur International Airport. The Kuala Lumpur Grand Prix City Festival in the city takes place at the same time, with road races, street parties, concerts, vintage car parades and shopping sales.

> *New year starts in mid-April for several communities, including Tamils, Punjabis and Malayalis – and Thais, who celebrate with the wet Songkran water festival in Thai Buddhist temples.*

Vaisakhi: The most important religious festival for Sikhs commemorates the day the Khalsa, or order of baptised Sikhs, was formed. It is celebrated with prayers, traditional performances and games and food in gurdwaras.

KL Tower International Forest Towerthon Challenge: The world's top tower runners race for 1km (½ mile) up a forest trail, then the 2,058 steps of KL Tower in a challenge of speed and stamina. The forest trail goes through Kuala Lumpur's last remaining virgin forest.

May/June

Wesak Day: Commemoration of Buddha's birth, enlightenment and death. Devotees offer prayers and give alms to monks at Buddhist temples. Decorative float and candle processions begin and end at several major Buddhist temples.

Colours of Malaysia (Citrawarna Malaysia): A colourful festival that showcases Malaysia's cultural diversity with exhibitions on Malaysian culture and handicrafts, a food festival, an extravagant parade of dancers and musicians, and other highlights.

July/August

Malaysia Mega Sale Carnival: The best time to shop, as stores and malls nationwide offer discounts and special deals for nearly two months.

National Day (31 August): Malaysia celebrates its independence day with pomp and pageantry. Join the countdown and free open-air concert on the eve at Dataran Merdeka. The grand National Day parade, if hosted in Kuala Lumpur, is usually along Jalan Raja in front of Dataran Merdeka.

September

Festival of the Hungry Ghosts: Chinese believe that during the seventh month of the lunar calendar, the gates of hell open and lost souls in purgatory roam the earth. Believers offer food, joss sticks and burn "hell money" on

pavements, while Chinese operas and concerts are staged to appease the spirits.

Mooncake Festival: This commemorates the overthrow of China's Mongol dynasty through messages to galvanise revolt hidden in mooncakes. Today, mooncakes come filled with chocolate and fruit besides the traditional lotus seed or bean paste. Children light lanterns and Taoists pray to the moon goddess.

October/November

KL Tower International Jump Malaysia: Daring BASE (Buildings, Antennas, Spans and Earth) jumpers leap off the 300-metre (980ft) KL Tower. Attracting the global BASE fraternity, it ends a BASE-jump circuit around towns in Malaysia.

Malaysia-International Fashion Week: Fashionistas will appreciate this showcase for established and up-and-coming fashion designers from Malaysia and the region. Both a trade and a public event, its offerings are noteworthy, particularly in Islamic fashion.

Malaysia International Gourmet Festival: A month-long fine-dining event with special menus, food and beverage promotions, door gifts, cooking lessons and even special hotel packages.

Deepavali: Hindus celebrate the triumph of good over evil in the seventh month of the Hindu calendar. They perform cleansing rituals and thanksgiving at home and in temples, and oil lamps are lit to receive blessings from Lakshmi, the goddess of wealth.

December

Christmas: Christians celebrate with carolling, nativity plays and midnight masses on Christmas Eve. At home, they partake in gift-giving and family gatherings over meals, which could range from roast turkey to curry, while decorations include imitation fir trees and fake snow.

New Year's Eve: Countdowns are celebrated in different parts of the city with free concerts, fireworks and much merry-making. Restaurants offer special menus, while clubbers party till dawn.

Variable dates

Hari Raya Puasa: Muslims celebrate this festival, also known as Hari Raya Aidilfitri, by visiting ancestral graves and offering prayers, seeking forgiveness from their elders, and much feasting. The festival follows the month of fasting and prayers known as Ramadan. Ramadan is exciting for its food bazaars, found throughout the city.

Hari Raya Haji: This Muslim festival marking the *haj*, or religious pilgrimage to Mecca, is more solemn than Hari Raya Aidilfitri. Donated cows and sheep are slaughtered and their meat is distributed to the poor and needy at mosques. ❑

FAR LEFT: a Wesak Day float procession in Brickfields. **LEFT:** a daredevil BASE jumper. **RIGHT:** watching street entertainers on Bintang Walk.

THE MALAY WEDDING

Visitors who venture into the suburbs may just chance upon the festive din and colour of a Malay wedding in progress. On the wedding day, the groom presents a dowry of cash, jewellery and other gifts for all to see. A troupe singing hymns to the beat of hand drums then leads the nuptial couple in a procession to the wedding venue. The wedding is a regal affair, where the bride and groom are treated like king and queen for the day. The most significant event is the *bersanding* ceremony, during which the couple sit on a bridal dais as relatives and guests sprinkle perfumed water, flower petals and rice on their palms to signify good wishes.

SILA BERATUR
TERIMA KASIH

CUISINE

The sophistication of the city's palate has spawned cosy cafés, trendy bistros and fine-dining restaurants offering European and Asian cuisines. But the unassuming stars of the eating-out scene are still the hawker stalls and coffee shops serving humble local specialities

Eating is an experience to be savoured when in Kuala Lumpur. The locals take to it with great gusto – and increasingly, panache – often plotting the next meal even as they polish off a feast of Chinese fried noodles, Indian breads with curry, or fragrant Malay coconut rice with a chilli *sambal*.

The centuries-long mixing of cultures is manifest in the availability of both so-called "authentic" preparations as well as fusion fare. These can range from using an ingredient not normally used in China or the Malay world in a traditional dish, to quirky East–West experiments. An example of adaptability and inventiveness is the widespread use of the humble noodle. Originally Chinese, different ethnic groups have come up with their own, unique preparations.

Meanwhile, economic migrants to Kuala Lumpur from all over the country have also brought their regional cooking styles with them, and so the variety can be staggering but never boring. Chinese and Indian vegetarian food is quite widespread, while eateries that cater to Muslims are *halal*, and therefore do not serve pork.

Chinese food

With its fastidious concern about the balance of flavours and textures, Chinese cuisine ranges from the delicate to the zesty, and from the smooth and silky to the springy and the crispy. A typical meal of fluffy steamed rice accompanied by a soup, some stir-fried vegetables, a meat or fish dish, and beancurd cooked in a clay pot, would incorporate diverse flavours and contrasting "mouth feels".

LEFT: rice features heavily in Malaysian cuisine.
RIGHT: roasted chicken among the dim sum choices.

Malaysia's Chinese hail from the southern provinces of China, and today, each dialect group has contributed its characteristic œuvre to the multitudinous Chinese food options.

From the Cantonese come such perennial favourites as *chaa siu* (barbecued pork) and roast duck, as well as a refined banquet cuisine renowned for the delicacy of its flavours and the rarity – or strangeness, depending on one's perspective – of its prized ingredients. Dim sum

CHINESE STREET EATS

Petaling Street, Jalan Imbi and Jalan Alor in the old city centre are where you can find good Chinese food. Have a bowl of the city's best *yeung dau fu* (a Hakka dish of fishpaste-stuffed vegetables) at Petaling Street, then go for *wan tan* (dumpling) noodles, beefball noodles, prawn noodles or Hainanese chicken rice in various stalls down the road. Jalan Imbi is known for *bak kut teh* (herbal pork bone soup), fishhead noodles, *saang ha min* (noodles with big prawns), fried beef *kway teow* (flat rice noodles) and porkball noodles. Walk down Jalan Alor and decide whether it's claypot seafood noodles, fishhead noodles or roast-duck rice you fancy.

straddles both worlds, with at least 30 varieties of steamed, fried or baked morsels, from dumplings of shrimp or pork to radish cakes, custard tarts and more.

A characteristically Kuala Lumpur dish, and representative of the hawker style of cooking, is Hokkien *mee*, a dish of thick yellow wheat noodles fried in dark soy sauce with pork, prawns and squid. Another contribution of the Hokkiens is *bak kut teh*, a fragrant herbal soup of pork ribs served with Chinese crullers.

The Teochews are perhaps most famous for their plain rice gruel eaten with a panoply of salty, preserved foods, but they are also known for richer fare like the sensuously smoky braised goose and the sweet and creamy yam custard.

From the Hakkas comes the ubiquitous *yeung dau fu*, a delightful assortment of beancurd and vegetables stuffed with fish paste. This has become a staple of Malays too.

Many Hainanese worked in the plantations as cooks for the British, serving up curry "tiffin" and accruing a reputation for their good cooking and high service standards. From them come Chinese-influenced "Western" dishes such as chicken chop with Worcestershire sauce and pork chop with tomato ketchup, as well as thoroughly local favourites like Hainanese chicken rice.

These days, contemporary trends have also influenced and refined the way Chinese food is presented in restaurants. The decor is elegant, the food healthier, and experiments, such as baked prawns with foie gras and Chinese-style rack of lamb, are beginning to appear on discerning menus.

Malay food

Malay cuisine is less well known around the world, but is an adventure that is worth experiencing. A cornucopia of chillis, herbs, roots and spices such as lemongrass, galangal, ginger, turmeric and lime leaf imparts a heady bouquet to the dishes. Some find, though, that the robust flavours and sometimes rich, oily textures do not make for gourmet-style subtlety.

The Malays have a tradition of eating at home, so Malay restaurants are not as common a sight in Kuala Lumpur as might be expected. But hawker stalls are plentiful. *Nasi lemak*, traditionally a breakfast favourite for all Malaysians, consists of rice cooked in coconut milk and

served with an array of condiments like fried anchovies, peanuts, slices of cucumber, egg, and the all-important *sambal tumis*, a sweet and spicy chilli paste.

Another popular treat is satay (sometimes spelled "sate"): kebabs of marinated chicken, beef or mutton, skewered and tenderly grilled over charcoal, then served with a thick sweet and spicy peanut sauce and accompanied by *ketupat* (pressed rice cakes).

The mainstay of Malay cuisine, however, is the meal of plain white rice accompanied by several meat and vegetable dishes. The Malays traditionally use the fingers of the right hand to eat (the left hand is considered unclean), so you may not automatically be given cutlery; on request eating establishments will usually provide you with a fork and spoon.

Standard dishes include *sotong* (squid) cooked in *sambal*; *rendang*, a dry beef curry simmered

Rice is a staple meal for Malaysians. At communal meals, typically each diner has an individual portion of rice, while the side dishes are shared.

with shallots, coconut milk, cumin, lemongrass and other herbs; *ayam masak merah*, a piquant chicken dish cooked with tomatoes and chillis; and *asam pedas*, a bracingly astringent broth boiled with fish, tamarind, chillis and *daun kesum*, a fragrant Vietnamese mint leaf. Common vegetable dishes include *sambal goreng*, long beans fried with chilli paste, beancurd and *tempeh*; and *kangkung* (water spinach) stir-fried with *belacan* (shrimp paste). For a fresher taste, try *ulam*, an assortment of raw vegetables, leaves and herbs eaten with rice. This dish can be eaten with *budu*, a fermented fish sauce from the eastern states.

Malay food has its share of regional innovations and peculiarities, so one might encounter such dishes as beef simmered in the spicy *rendang tok* style, with slices of young coconut in it, a Perak speciality; or *ayam percik* from Kelantan, spicy chicken with coconut sauce skewered and roasted over a charcoal flame. Food from the eastern states tends to be sweeter and richer,

FAR LEFT: eating out in Bintang Walk. **ABOVE LEFT:** Malay street food made to order. **TOP:** food stalls at Bangsar Night Market. **ABOVE:** typical Thai dish found at the famous Ginger Restaurant. **RIGHT:** fresh produce at Bangsar Night Market.

while food from Johor in the south has more pronounced Arab influences.

Indian food

The majority of Malaysia's Indians came from the southern part of the subcontinent. They brought with them griddled breads like *roti canai* and *thosai*, furiously spicy curries eaten with rice, and a tradition of using the hand to eat food heaped on banana leaves. Nothing quite beats the experience of having hot rice piled onto a leaf, with at least three different types of vegetables accompanying it, a choice of curries in small plates placed beside, and an order of fried or spiced (masala) chicken, mutton or seafood, as well as *rasam*, a spicy soup said to be good for curing colds. Vegetarian and vegan options are easily available. Remember to fold the leaf towards you after your meal as a sign of your satisfaction with the meal.

In the earlier years, Indian Muslim hawkers would carry a pot of rice (*nasi*) and a pot of curry in two baskets balanced on a *kandar*, or pole, to serve the labourers at Penang's port. This is how *nasi kandar* came about, and it can now be found on just about every street corner and in 24-hour food outlets in Kuala Lumpur. There is a wide choice of dishes to go with the rice – from fish-head curry and tiger prawns masala to crabs, mutton, chicken and fish.

NYONYA FOOD: THE ORIGINAL FUSION CUISINE

The cooking of the Peranakans, also known as the Straits Chinese, is similar to Malay food but has decidedly Chinese twists. The community is said to have its roots in the 15th century, when a princess from China, Hang Li Po, married Sultan Mansur Shah of Melaka. The members of her royal retinue settled down in Melaka, married local women, and over the years, their descendants assimilated many local Malay customs, thus fashioning a unique fusion culture of their own.

The terms *nyonya* and *baba* refer to the Peranakan womenfolk and menfolk respectively, and their style of cooking is often referred to as Nyonya food. Jealously guarded recipes are handed down from mother to daughter, complex spice pastes are painstakingly pounded by hand, and Nyonya *kuih*, or sweet confections, for which they are well known, are time-consuming to prepare. This exacting attention to detail is no doubt the product of an era when a *nyonya*'s cooking skills were highly valued and improved her chances of getting married.

Peranakan dishes such as *lemak nanas* (pineapple curry) or *kari kapitan* (chicken curry) are more Malay in character, while dishes like *itik tim*, a clear soup of duck and salted mustard cabbage, or *pongteh*, a salty-sweet gravy redolent of soy bean paste, are more Chinese.

A popular hawker choice is *mee goreng*, a spicy thick yellow noodle dish, stir-fried with tofu, vegetables and sometimes meat. Evening tea choices include potato-filled curry puffs, *vadai* (lentil doughnuts) and samosas with ground meat. *Rojak*, also known as *pasembor*, is another delicious spicy snack, comprising dough fritters, potatoes and other vegetables, mixed with a peanut sauce. This is washed down with the popular *teh tarik* (frothy hot tea).

North Indian or Mughal cuisine became popular in Kuala Lumpur in the 1980s. The easily recognisable mainstays of tandoori chicken and naan are now available even in casual, open-air eateries, while the finer dishes of the maharajahs are replicated and served to an appreciative audience – for a price – in the ambience of grand old colonial houses or sumptuously appointed restaurants.

Flavours from around the world

The dining scene has assumed a more international and sophisticated flavour in recent years.

FAR LEFT: spicy Indian food served on banana leaves.
LEFT TOP: elegant Café Café in downtown Kuala Lumpur.
ABOVE: trendy Shook! restaurant in Starhill Gallery.

Said to have an aphrodisiac effect is spicy nasi kandar, *which makes the body feel hot. Sometimes a drowsy feeling follows, perhaps because of the poppy seeds in the curry.*

French, Italian, German, Austrian, Swiss, Spanish, Mexican and Middle Eastern restaurants are everywhere, as are Japanese, Korean, Thai and Vietnamese ones. Five-star hotels will have a continental restaurant and shopping malls usually offer a variety of cuisines, whether in the city centre or expatriate areas such as Bangsar and Mont Kiara.

As Kuala Lumpur is now popular with Middle Eastern tourists, many restaurants that cater to them, cheek by jowl in the Golden Triangle area, observe later hours, even serving dinner at 10pm or thereabouts. But in any case, in a city whose favourite pastime is sitting down to eat, rest assured there are eateries open at any hour of the day or night. ❑

• *Restaurant recommendations are listed at the end of each chapter in the Places section.*

THE ARTS SCENE

Malaysian arts and culture are a reflection of the rich historical influence of the Malay Archipelago, centuries of interaction with traders from the Middle East, India and China, and the hand of European colonialism. KL's artistic and cultural life is a distillation of this heady mix

While Kuala Lumpur is not the heartland of the country's traditional arts and culture, it offers an active and unique scene that comprises varied forms and genres. These range from traditional Chinese opera to avant-garde theatre, from Islamic calligraphy and Chinese scroll paintings to internationally acclaimed visual art, and from sitar recitals to underground gigs by black metal groups.

Historical snapshot

Indigenous art and cultural practices were ritualistic in nature, following the dictates of belief systems, seasonal changes and agrarian cycles. With the arrival of Hinduism came Indian dance drama, puppet theatre and the use of plots and characters from the literary epics *Mahabharata* and *Ramayana*, which have endured until today. Islam, which made its way to the shores of Melaka in the 14th century, introduced the cultures of the Middle East and South Asia. Folk tales from Persia, Mesopotamia and Egypt became part of the local literature and theatre repertoire, while musical styles and instruments from the Middle East enriched the already complex musicology of the region.

One of KL's greatest strengths is that its array of modern inter-cultural works allow visitors to encounter ancient arts and culture in new and startling ways.

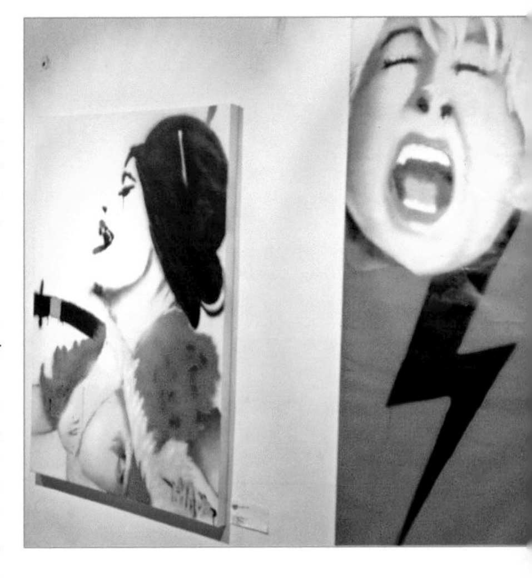

LEFT: traditional *gamelan* musicians. ABOVE: artworks at the Annexe Gallery in Kuala Lumpur's Central Market.

Western values and ideas were an inevitable part of the colonial era, which dates back to the 16th century. Contact with the Portuguese and the Dutch left an impression which can be discerned, for example, in the use of the accordion and the violin in traditional music forms such as the *ronggeng*, *asli* and *joget*.

Contemporary influences

Modern Western forms in the performing arts, visual arts and literature emerged under British rule in the first half of the 20th century.

The KLPAC

The Kuala Lumpur Performing Arts Centre (KLPAC) is the centrepiece in a gentrification project of the formerly working-class neighbourhood of Sentul. Located five minutes from the CBD, KLPAC *(see also page 104)* is a gem of an arts centre which uses part of an abandoned 1930s railway godown as its architectural backbone. Set in the grounds of a landscaped park, the space includes two theatres, a café and a water feature. Aside from the chance to catch some good local and foreign performances, it's a great place to have a picnic and enjoy the park or catch a quick meal at the adjoining Japanese garden restaurant. For more details, see www.klpac.com.

The British not only imported their cultural practices into the colonies but also instituted an anglicised education system that raised a middle-class elite who were eager to embrace European ways. Local artists subsequently created works with a bias towards Western arts and culture – which were seen as more sophisticated and "civilised". Thankfully, Malaysian artists have reacquainted themselves with indigenous art forms over the years, and in the process, developed works that exploit both Asian and Western forms to produce critically acclaimed projects.

During the economic boom of the 1990s, the government invested substantially in the arts infrastructure. Important venues are the National Theatre (*see page 148*), the National Art Gallery (*see page 148*) and the National Library (*see page 149*), all on Jalan Tun Razak. Privately owned venues include the Kuala Lumpur Performing Arts Centre (KLPAC; *see left*) and the Petronas Philharmonic Hall (*see page 133*). Smaller, experimental spaces abound, such as the Central Market's Annexe Gallery. The following is a guide to Kuala Lumpur's arts scene.

Theatre

Bangsawan, sometimes referred to as Malay opera, traces its genealogy to *wayang Parsi* (Persian theatre), brought by traders to Penang in the late 1800s. By its heyday in the 1930s, *bangsawan* had taken on a uniquely Malaysian character by combining didactic tales taken from Malay myths, Chinese legends, Arab tales and Shakespearian tragedies, interspersed with bawdy vaudeville and the latest hit songs performed by cabaret girls. Primarily an urban

theatre, *bangsawan* was unencumbered by the ritualistic or ceremonial imperatives that formed the basis of pre-existing forms such as *mak yong* (an ancient Malay dance drama originating from Kelantan) and *wayang kulit* (shadow puppet theatre). By the 1940s, however, *bangsawan* had fallen into decline. Today, *bangsawan* productions are staged at Istana Budaya and the Panggung Bandaraya by semi-professional groups, and by students of the National Arts, Culture and Heritage Academy (ASWARA; 464 Jalam Tun Ismail; www.aswara.edu.my; tel: 03-2697 1777).

Chinese opera, which found its way into Malaya via Chinese immigrants in the late 19th century has, unfortunately, lost much of its popular appeal in contemporary Kuala Lumpur, and is now primarily staged to coincide with religious festivals. To attract the younger generation and compete with other forms of popular entertainment, karaoke, pop songs and other contemporary modifications have been included. It is worth tracking down a performance, however, as the operas, which are staged in the open, are communal affairs where the audience can provide as much interest as the actors on stage.

Wayang kulit troupes from Malaysia's east coast states sometimes travel to perform in the capital. It is also possible to catch these performances at the National Theatre or ASWARA. The Malaysia Tourism Centre stages occasional performances as well.

Kuala Lumpur is the centre of the contemporary drama scene in Malaysia, and there is a plethora of productions, from avant-garde plays to West End comedies and politically astute dramas. The quality can vary, but the drama scene can provide an insight into issues the country faces and makes for an enjoyable experience of the city's social and cultural life.

Among the companies that stage credible English-language works are the Five Arts Centre, which is known for its cutting-edge dance, drama, music and visual art; Instant Café Theatre, which serves up biting political satire in its hugely popular productions; and The Actors Studio, which stages slick mainstream fare. The main performance venues include Istana Budaya, The Actors Studio @Lot 10, The Annexe Gallery, MAP and the Kuala Lumpur Performing Arts Centre *(see text box on page 60)*.

Dance

Traditional Malay dance performances are held several times a day at the Malaysia Tourism Centre, and in the evenings at places such as the Sri Melayu Restaurant (1 Jalan Conlay; tel: 03-2145 1833). These cater to tourists, so for more sophisticated offerings, check the performance schedule of ASWARA. The academy has an active dance faculty and stages public performances regularly, including traditional and contemporary dance offerings.

LEFT: Bangsawan (Malay opera). **ABOVE:** performer in a solo Indian classical dance. **RIGHT:** Malay dancers.

Tari-drama, or dance drama, are large-scale spectacles with elaborate song-and-dance sequences starring legends. Performances staged by the Petronas Performing Arts Group at the Dewan Philharmonic Petronas feature an excellent Asli (traditional Malay) orchestra performing on traditional instruments such as the *rebab* (a bowed string instrument), *serunai* (a double-reed oboe) and *gamelan* metallophones.

There is also a very active classical Indian dance movement in Kuala Lumpur, with regular performances presented by groups like Sutra House *(see text box below)* as well as the Temple of Fine Arts. The quality is uniformly good.

Malaysian dancers and choreographers have the advantage of drawing on the traditions of some of the most developed dance cultures in the world and, as a result, the contemporary dance scene here is one that is particularly rich. The scene is largely informal but groups to look out for include the Kwantung and Kwangsi dance groups, Batu Dance Theatre, Dua Space and Nyoba Kan, led by extraordinary Buto master Lee Swee Keong.

Sutra House

Sutra House is an art gallery, dance studio, performance venue, library and home to one of Malaysia's leading choreographers, Ramli Ibrahim. Situated next to the beautiful Titiwangsa Lake, it hosts Sutra, primarily a dance company with an active performance programme, mainly of classical Indian dance. These performances are staged here on a hexagonal stage in an amphitheatre set in a lush tropical garden. The small but good art and culture library is open to the public, while the art gallery holds a series of eight exhibitions a year, featuring both international and local artists. For details, visit www.sutradancetheatre.com.

Music

Nothing encapsulates Kuala Lumpur's aspirations of becoming a world-class city better than the Petronas Philharmonic Hall, or Dewan Philharmonic Petronas (DFP). Housed in the Petronas Twin Towers and funded by Petronas, the national petroleum company, DFP is one of the most technically sophisti-

Above: Ramli Ibrahim (second from left) performing at a classical Indian dance recital. **Above Right:** contemporary art gallery.

cated concert halls in the world, and is home to the Malaysian Philharmonic Orchestra (MPO) – which unfortunately is largely made up of non-Malaysian musicians. While it could be argued that resources could have been better spent on, say, a *gamelan* orchestra, to represent the country's cultural heritage, the MPO is nonetheless an excellent orchestra, often performing with internationally acclaimed soloists and conductors.

Dama Orchestra is an ensemble of virtuoso musicians who perform largely on traditional Chinese instruments. Their repertoire is wide, and they specialise in popular Chinese music from the first half of the 20th century, usually featuring the sublime vocalist Tan Soo Suan.

There are several Malaysian Indian cultural organisations that organise traditional music recitals, of which the Temple of Fine Arts is the best known and the most consistent. Of groups that feature a fusion of the old and new, Hands Percussions offers adrenaline-pumping performances using traditional Chinese drums. The critically acclaimed Rhythm in Bronze is the only *gamelan* orchestra that performs contemporary music.

Visual arts

Malaysia's traditional visual arts and crafts, such as *songket* (brocade) weaving, traditional ceramics, silver and brass work, woodcarving, batik painting and basketry can be found in places like Central Market *(see page 92)* and the Kuala Lumpur Craft Complex *(see page 159)*. If you're looking for quality, visit the Pucuk Rebung Museum Gallery *(see page 132)*, which is part antique shop, part museum.

The National Art Gallery and the Petronas Gallery *(see page 133)* both hold regular exhibitions of works by local and international artists. The Islamic Arts Museum *(see page 168)* houses a fine collection from the Muslim world, including the Middle East, China, South Asia, Southeast Asia and Eastern Europe.

Like any big city, Kuala Lumpur has an active contemporary visual-arts scene. Works range from lush landscapes in oils to video installations and performance art. There are several good places to catch art by Malaysian artists who are making waves in art biennials around the world. Commercial galleries abound, a testimony to the healthy art market. Among the leading galleries are Valentine Willie Fine Art, Wei-Ling Gallery, NN Gallery, Taksu, Tangsi and Art Case Galleries.

Artists' collectives like Rumah Frinjan, Matahati and Rumah Air Panas are working studio spaces as well as exhibition venues that run active programmes like artists' talks and alternative festivals. Experimental and alternative works are the forte of The Annexe Gallery *(see box below)*. ❑

• *See Travel Tips (pages 235–6) for listings of performing arts venues and art galleries.*

THE ANNEXE AND THE MAP

"Integrated" arts spaces that blur the lines between arts disciplines were pioneered by Central Market's Annexe Gallery. Its mid-town location, mix of spaces and eclectic programming have boosted the production of creative works while broadening the public appeal of all art forms. These range from *wayang kulit* to student work and the regular "Art for Grabs" art and craft bazaar. A higher-end setting, launched in 2009, is MAP at Solaris Dutamas in Mont Kiara. Designed by the same architects as the Annexe, MAP integrates the arts into an entire shopping centre, with indoor and outdoor installation and performance spaces, art tenancies and three festivals a year.

BSN

AFTER DARK

An evening out in Kuala Lumpur always starts with food, and often ends with food too. In between, the diversions are plenty – underground music gigs, fervent partying in trendy clubs, or simply relaxing at a roadside coffeeshop

As darkness descends on Kuala Lumpur, many KL-ites unwind and partake of their three favourite after-sundown activities – eating out, partying and taking it easy. They come out to play – for they know that once Kuala Lumpur's frenetic daytime persona is shed, the city is gentler and cosier, its temperature slightly cooler, its grime obscured and its contours delightfully lit and softer.

Eating out

On weekdays, dinner is usually the only meal a KL-ite family has together, a sit-down and substantial affair usually partaken at home. But for nuclear families and the many couples and singles living in the city, dining out after work or college has become a norm, not only because of the remarkable variety and quality of the food, but also because of its affordability and convenience.

On weekends, eating places, especially child-friendly outlets and new ones recently featured in the media, can be particularly crowded. KL-ites will also travel great distances to sample the best – even if it means driving to another town. Often, ambience and cleanliness do not really matter – it is the taste of the food that counts.

Supper is the KL-ite's favourite bookend to an evening, with many thronging the hawker stalls and 24-hour *mamak* eateries (Indian Muslim coffeeshops or stalls). These casual eateries are some of the best places for glimpses of local colour. Spent from an evening of drinking and dancing, customers settle on plastic stools, just after midnight or even much later, and tuck into supper staples like Indian *roti canai* (flat bread with curry), fried Chinese-style noodles or a glass of *teh tarik* (literally, "pulled tea", a frothy tea concoction). Occasional buskers or illegal DVD pedlars are part of the scene.

LEFT: Zouk dance club in the shadow of the Petronas Twin Towers. **RIGHT:** roadside hawker stall at Jalan Alor.

Partying

Kuala Lumpur's clubbing scene is so hot even worldly Singaporeans come up regularly to party here. Kuala Lumpur has some of the best clubs in the region, with a large selection of sophisticated spaces, talented international and local DJs, and live acts playing everything from house and hip-hop to Latin and retro.

The chi chi of local society – starlets, yuppies, expatriates and social butterflies – hit the clubs late on Friday and Saturday nights and don't emerge until the wee hours. Clubbers tend to dress up, and some of the classier places have a no T-shirt, shorts or sandals rule.

Some clubs are housed in hotels but most are clustered in entertainment areas such as Bukit Bintang and Changkat Bukit Bintang in the city, and the suburban enclaves of Bangsar and Sri Hartamas. The city nightspots tend to be big and glamorous; established "institutions" include Modesto's, The Beach Club, Asian Heritage Row and Zouk. The suburban spots are more intimate, smaller places.

Clubs are usually frequented by an even mix of ethnic groups, although there is a sprinkling with patronage that largely follows ethnic lines. Canto-pop outlets are invariably favoured by the Chinese, who are also the main patrons of karaoke outlets; pubs and clubs playing Bollywood hits are almost exclusively Indian; while a mainly Malay and Indonesian clientele enjoys places with Indonesian-style *dangdut* music. Malay clubbers tend to frequent places with rock, R&B and hip-hop playlists.

While weekends offer great action, Kuala Lumpur shifts into party overdrive on special occasions, like New Year's Eve and National Day (31 August), or when an event, such as Formula 1, hits town. Then the streets are closed off to traffic, concerts featuring local pop groups are held, and fireworks light up the sky. Popular venues for these events are the Kuala Lumpur City Centre (KLCC) and Bukit Bintang.

Illegal Bike Races

A Saturday night congregation of motorcycles at Dataran Merdeka on Jalan Raja is usually a sign of an illegal street race in the early hours of the next morning. Despite police crackdowns, racers on souped-up two-wheelers called *kapchai* ride dangerously on highways and the city's streets, beating traffic lights and weaving in and out among vehicles. The racing is almost exclusive to lower-income speed-loving Malay men under 30. They are often referred to as *mat rempit* (from "ramp it") and their girls – and there are always girls – are called *minah rempit.* The races are often linked to crime, but many participate for the glory and as a show of anti-authoritarianism.

Gay Kuala Lumpur

Nightlife choices for the gay community in Kuala Lumpur are burgeoning, though they are not advertised blatantly as such because of secular and religious laws as well as low-key harassment by the police and religious authorities. Nonetheless, the society is generally open and the city is dotted with gay-friendly eateries, spas and saunas, and bars and clubs such as Frangipani and Market Place. Straight clubs also regularly hold gay and/or lesbian nights.

Police raids at these places are occasional. The downside to the strict policing is that these establishments have become afraid to stock contraceptives and health information supplied by organisations like the PT Foundation, an AIDS/HIV outreach organisation.

Underground music

The underground music scene is an established, independent urban music scene that traces its roots back to the early 1980s. It largely comprises rock musicians writing and playing a wide range of sub-genres including punk, hardcore, experimental and post-grunge. English is the preferred language choice, although a small group of songwriters are expressing themselves in Tamil and in Mandarin or Cantonese too.

These individuals and bands perform in underground clubs and community halls, many crossing over into the mainstream. For underground music gigs and dates, check out ricecooker (www.ricecooker.kerbau.com).

LEFT: Luna bar, one of the city's trendier nightspots.
ABOVE: dancing at the popular Boreno Baruk Club.

Hanging out

Other than eating and partying, KL-ites really know how to *lepak*. *Lepak* is a lyrical Malay term that describes a state of mind that appreciates relaxing and taking it easy; in short, an epicurean appreciation for idling. *Lepak* is a lovely *kampung* (village) and small-town inheritance that Kuala Lumpur urbanites put to good practice in the evenings, particularly on weekends. After a good dinner, the KL family enjoys strolling at open spaces like Dataran Merdeka or the KLCC Park, while friends and couples *lepak* for hours at the city's alfresco *mamak* stalls.

Football has an obsessive following in the city, and *mamak* outlets and pubs cash in by having giant TV screens and LCDs that show live matches. Meanwhile, café culture is big and while the younger set has not abandoned the *teh tarik* stall, they do enjoy the cushier and trendier air-conditioned atmosphere of a Starbucks outlet, where they can also surf the internet.

> *Movies are sometimes released in KL before the US or Europe to curb video piracy. The Suria KLCC, Pavilion Kuala Lumpur and the Mid Valley Megamall have excellent cinemas.*

A perennial favourite among all KL-ites, though, is to browse the itinerant *pasar malam* (night market), which brims with local life and where everything from local sweets to pirated DVDs can be purchased – a great place just to be Malaysian. ❑

• *Recommendations for pubs, bars and nightclubs can be found at the end of Places chapters and in the Travel Tips (see pages 237–9).*

SHOPPING

At first glance it may seem Kuala Lumpur's retail scene is all about designer boutiques and high-gloss mega-malls. But beneath the glitz there are also crafts and cultural finds, street markets and ethnic neighbourhoods that will appeal even to those who usually detest shopping

People in Kuala Lumpur take their shopping very, very seriously, indulging in bargains offered by retail environments that range from hectic street markets to luxurious malls. Shopping centres can even be considered the great equalisers of Malaysian society – their mix of convenience and comfort allows people from all walks of life to *lepak*, or hang out, on weekends.

KL-ites celebrate consumerism by immersing themselves for hours in retail complexes, especially during sale seasons. Of note is the annual Mega Sale Carnival, held every year from July to August, when most shops throughout Malaysia offer discounts of up to 70 percent. This is when shopping becomes a competitive sport requiring speed and endurance. Smaller sales periods also occur in March/April and December *(see pages 50–1)*.

It is no understatement to say that on the opening days of sale seasons, the city comes to a virtual halt with traffic jams. Thankfully, there has been an effort to integrate public transportation with the construction of shopping centres in recent years. Accessibility to malls via carefully planned train or monorail links has helped enhance the popularity of big retail spaces like Suria KLCC, Berjaya Times Square, Pavilion, Mid Valley Megamall and The Gardens.

The Klang Valley has about 3 million square metres (32.3 million sq ft) of retail space, with more in the pipeline. Given the furious competition, the shopping can only get better.

Branding the city

Apart from brand-name boutiques, shopping in Kuala Lumpur can be reasonably inexpensive even outside of sales periods. As a typically modern Asian city, Kuala Lumpur has always been attracted to high-end fashion labels. There are enough international designers to satisfy any fashionista with up-to-date collections from labels such as Hermès, Prada and Armani. Boutiques are located in upscale versions of shopping malls such The Gardens at Mid Valley

City and Sungei Wang in Bukit Bintang, while premium malls like Suria KLCC and Pavilion have the very best labels.

Shopping malls

Pavilion Kuala Lumpur (*see page 153*) is the city's top retail space, right in the shopping district of Bukit Bintang. This impressive mall boasts top designer labels, swanky restaurants and lots of eye candy for those who really have money to spend.

The Starhill Gallery (*see page 153*), also in Bukit Bintang, is a particularly interesting experiment in the branding of space within Kuala Lumpur. Designer David Rockwell has created a sophisticated retail space, where boutiques cluster around a garden atrium and escalators look like tree trunks between floors. Above the designer shops, an upper floor is dedicated to art, with small galleries and art exhibitions. The lowest level is entirely devoted to eateries that offer varied Asian cuisines. These are designed with such eclectic and chic decor ideas that they provide a feast for the eyes as well.

Apart from Starhill, many shopping centres also have identities that help distinguish one mall from the next. Mega-developments such as 1 Utama, Mid Valley Megamall and The Gardens hold entire worlds, complete with cinemas, restaurants and hypermarkets. Suburban centres like IOI Mall in Puchong attract residents mainly from surrounding housing estates, but other malls like Bangsar Village and Bangsar Village II attract a more status-conscious crowd to its eclectic mix of boutiques. Department stores, such as Isetan from Japan and the home-grown Parkson Grand, are found in most major malls and always feature huge cosmetic and perfume departments.

Suria KLCC occupies the premier shopping address at the base of the Petronas Twin Towers, with international boutiques and restaurants to match. Apart from the floors of designer labels, Pucuk Rebung on the fourth floor is worth a visit for its collection of heritage items. Ombak, on the same floor, is a furnishings shop, with sleek contemporary tableware and rustic home accessories. Kinokunya on the fourth floor remains a favourite among Kuala Lumpur book-lovers for its wide range of titles and a breathtaking view over KLCC Park.

LEFT: bargain-price wallets at a roadside stall.
ABOVE: sari shop along Jalan Masjid India.

More consumer heavens

The Bukit Bintang area, especially Bintang Walk, remains the undisputed retail hub of the city, with more than seven shopping centres in one area. Berjaya Times Square is the newest and biggest of them all, with over 1,000 shops and an indoor theme park – the mall feels almost too big

MALAYSIAN BRANDS

You can find all the international designer labels in Kuala Lumpur, but the truly great buys are Malaysian-designed fashion brands. The Vincci chain does trendy, affordable women's shoes and accessories, while Padini and Seed carry seasonal knock-offs and reasonably priced clothing basics. British India is more upmarket, with ethnic home furnishings and well-designed clothes using natural fabrics. Zang Toi Collection in Sungei Wang Plaza carries the lower-priced diffusion lines while Salabianca and Eclipse have more glamorous fashion. Aseana in KLCC showcases the desirable chic, short, sequinned dresses from KL socialite and businesswoman Farah Khan.

Government policy on pirated goods has never really made an impact, despite increasing prosecution and surprise raids. Bear in mind, however, that low prices often reflect poor imitations.

to take in and is best explored in stages. Sungei Wang Plaza is one of the city's oldest shopping malls but it is always packed with crowds, thanks to a mix of funky streetwear boutiques and good eateries. The narrow corridors can feel maze-like and the thumping club music from each unit is disorienting, but this is a genuine Kuala Lumpur experience with good, affordable buys.

A number of shopping malls in Bukit Bintang are also devoted completely to everything that beeps, records or has a processor. Imbi Plaza was the first complex to specialise in computers well before they became a part of everyday life, but eventually lost ground to its neighbours, Sungei Wang Plaza and Low Yat Plaza. The latter is now the biggest IT retail hub in Kuala Lumpur, with over five floors of shops selling competitively priced personal computers, PDAs and mobile phones.

Diverse heritage

Move away from the big brands and electronic gadgets in contemporary malls and you will discover the cultural side of Kuala Lumpur's shopping landscape. The Art Deco Central Market in the historic area was once a produce market, but has been renovated as a major retail hub for Malaysian arts and crafts. Visitors can easily pick up souvenirs that are proudly made in Malaysia, from silverware to ikat to shadow puppets. If some of the goods seem like tourist tat, the restaurants and fortune tellers upstairs might be of more value and interest. Another popular shopping attraction is the Kuala Lumpur Craft Complex (Kompleks Kraf Kuala Lumpur) in Bukit Bintang *(see page 159)*. Locally produced handicrafts such as baskets, batik clothing and woodcarvings are available here, although prices are on the high side. The artists' workshops provide a good insight into Malaysia's craft heritage.

Along the tree-lined Jalan Masjid India, multicoloured saris, *salwar kameez* (a long tunic worn over loose trousers) and jewellery spill out from shops. The largest complex here is the Madras Store, which sells fabrics, brassware and oil lamps, while other smaller shops along the same stretch sell a combination of saris, accessories and jewellery. A nearby market at the end of the street provides a bit of theatrical relief, as peddlers of home-brewed medicines testify to the effectiveness of their products in curing everything from bad breath to impotence. Parallel to Jalan Masjid India, Jalan Tuanku Abdul Rahman also has stores selling lovely fabrics and collectables.

For gifts that are uniquely Malaysian, the Royal Selangor pewter showroom in Setapak Jaya, north of KLCC, has an extensive range of finely crafted pewterwork from tableware to children's gifts.

LEFT: batik artist at Kuala Lumpur Craft Complex. **ABOVE:** high-end jewellers, Bvlgari. **RIGHT:** jewellery and trinkets at Petaling Street Bazaar.

Further away from the city centre, the Alamanda Putrajaya in Putrajaya has the same retail chains as any other shopping centre but, notably, there are also several boutiques selling traditional Malaysian clothing such as the Nyonya *kebaya* (*see page 73*).

Street markets

The shopping experience that best encapsulates Kuala Lumpur's vibrancy is not found in its air-conditioned shopping malls, but in the *pasar malam*, or night markets. Different from the traditional "wet" markets selling fresh produce in the early morning, these usually comprise rows of stalls along a commercial street. Most residential areas, including Ampang and Kampung Baru, have regular night markets once a week. Good markets to visit include the Bangsar night market on Sundays, which starts at 6pm. Shoppers walk in the cool of the evening with the hum of electric generators all around, and makeshift stands display fresh fruit, flowers and plastic trinkets. The nightly Chow Kit market has RM5 'bundles', or jeans, shirts, jackets sold in piles. Lorong Tuanku Abdul Rahman near Masjid India is closed to traffic on Saturday evenings, and has stalls selling handicrafts and Malay delicacies spilling out on to the road, while Jalan Berhala in Brickfields has a Thursday market that starts before sunset.

The city's most famous street market, at Petaling Street, lost a bit of its allure when the roof canopy was added. Nevertheless, its stalls are still packed with tourists and locals browsing copies of branded accessories, pirated DVDs and ethnic jewellery. There's authenticity to be found in the goldsmiths, coffee shops, haberdashers, medicine shops and dried herbs; otherwise, most goods here are counterfeit and probably won't hold up well to close scrutiny. Vendors are always ready to bargain. The atmosphere is vibrant and bustling, which adds to the urgency of price negotiations. When the buyer pretends to walk off in a show of disinterest, a counter offer is made at once and both parties complete the transaction, each happily thinking they've got the better deal. Now isn't this what shopping is all about? ❑

• *For more recommended shops and markets, see the Shopping listings in the Places section chapters.*

FLEA MARKET SHOPPING

It has taken a while, but flea markets are now beginning to catch on in the Klang Valley. The first and most popular weekend bazaar is Amcorp Mall Antiques Flea Market, which has an assortment of old records, books, antiques and toys. Higher-end flea markets are found in Mont Kiara and Bangsar, where stalls purvey fashion, jewellery and homemade biscuits. If you want fashion that is trendy and a bit different, check out websites like www.tonguechic.com and www.bijoubazaar.blogspot.com, which are forums for young entrepreneurs who regularly tout their funky wares at mobile flea markets. They also do the rounds of the nightclubs.

Fashion and Clothing

Cosmopolitan KL-ites blend traditional elements with modern flair for a unique everyday fashion style

The fashion styles on Kuala Lumpur's streets are varied and colourful. You are likely to find traditional dress worn alongside designer labels and street fashion. The Indian sari, Malay *baju kurung* and Chinese *cheong sam* are not confined to religious events and festive occasions but are worn every day to work. What's more, these are worn by different ethnic groups. The *tudung*, a headscarf or veil covering the hair while leaving the face exposed, is a standard element of office wear and uniforms for many Muslim women. However, it's not unusual to pair distressed blue jeans and designer heels with a *tudung* – many Muslim women wear it with panache.

Malaysian designers, from Bernard Chandran to Melinda Looi, are also embracing heritage in their contemporary collections. While traditional clothing remains a key part of Malaysians' cultural identity, designer brands are equally important for the growing middle class. Stroll through any shopping centre in Kuala Lumpur and you will see how well dressed and creative the city's urbanites are. It is not unusual to find an embroidered Nyonya *kebaya* (*see opposite*) blouse worn over trousers, or an Indian kurta with punk attire – either way, Malaysians are using their cultural influences to create their own unique styles.

Above and Below: the Malaysian equivalent to Gap, the Padini brand, is well loved for its everyday style. Cheaper and unlabelled but fashionable alternatives abound in street stalls.

ABOVE: it's not all grey suits in the CBD: office workers also wear traditional dress, such as the *baju kurung* and sari, as everyday attire.

ABOVE AND BELOW: the trendy, new or just unusual are available in shopping centres which are always packed to the brim with KL's young and fashion-conscious set. Tailors and seamstresses can skilfully produce any desired design.

NYONYA KEBAYA

The delicate Nyonya *kebaya* best represents the fusion of cultures in Malaysia. From the Arabic word *kaba* for "clothing", the blouse has evolved since the 16th century with European and Chinese influences. Unlike the long and looser Malay version, the Nyonya *kebaya* is hip-length, form-fitting and often made with semi-transparent materials such as voile, silk and muslin. Exquisitely embroidered front panels, usually with floral themes in vivid colours, are its characteristic feature. Fine needlework is one way to distinguish a well-made Nonya *kebaya*, and status is also associated with the *kerosang*, linked gold brooches used to fasten the blouse. The Nyonya *kebaya*, more likely worn on formal or festive occasions, had once faded away with modernisation but antique pieces have now become collectors' items. Modern versions can be found from Malaysian fashion designers. Interest was renewed largely through the efforts of Endon Mahmood, the late wife of former Prime Minister Abdullah Ahmad Badawi. Her book, *The Nyonya Kebaya: A Century of Straits Chinese Costume*, is an excellent resource on both the outfit and the women who wore it so well.

BELOW: embracing one's culture through traditional clothing: a modern-day bride wears a Peranakan (Straits Chinese) wedding dress with ornate embroidery and gold accessories.

ARCHITECTURE

From traditional village to glass-and-steel megapolis, Kuala Lumpur's built heritage offers fascinating variations on a theme as it tries to merge a vernacular aesthetic with Islamic symbolism and a capital-driven economy

While stone monuments of lost civilisations may be found elsewhere in the region, evidence of the past is less obvious in Malaysia. References before 1400 are fragmentary at best. All we know of Kuala Lumpur's murky past is that it began as a humble tin trading outpost at the confluence of the Klang and Gombak rivers. The temporary settlement from which the city grew would have followed the traditional *kampung* (village) tradition closely. Early photographs show the Kuala Lumpur of 1884 as groups of thatched *attap* (palm) houses set in compounds and surrounded by jungle.

Vernacular traditions

The basic design of the Malay house has evolved over centuries to meet local climatic and social conditions. Vernacular styles were distinguished by their roof forms, which indicate a regional influence with their decorative elements on the gables and open verandahs. With a floor raised on stilts, the house was kept free from rising damp and floods, and safe from forest creatures, while large windows provided views and natural airflow. Chinese miners adapted the *kampung* house, transforming it to a ground level structure, sans stilts, with a covered verandah and thatched roof.

These early structures, however, were purely utilitarian and had little expression of regional decoration styles. Flexible construction methods using locally available materials of hardwood or bamboo allowed extensions to the building whenever necessary, enabling the town to grow on the east bank of the river.

LEFT: Putrajaya Corp's overarching steel mesh gateway.
ABOVE: wooden house in Jalan Raja Muda Musa.

Building a national identity

Traditional *kampung* houses have almost completely disappeared from the Klang Valley, except in Kampung Baru *(see page 144)*. Thankfully, in parts of the city today, elegant roof forms that follow a vernacular tradition are cast in concrete and used to crown highrise structures.

Exploration of a national architectural identity after independence in 1957 began with public buildings such as the Parliament House

Tropical Architecture

Even before the age of global environmental awareness, traditional Malaysian houses were already designed to adapt to the local climate. Design features included elements like terraced landscaping and sunshade louvres to enhance natural light and ventilation. Contemporary Malaysian architects have won awards for their innovative adaptations of traditional solutions for energy conservation in modern buildings. One such leading architect is Ken Yeang, whose bioclimatic skyscrapers, such as the Menara Mesiniaga in Subang and the Central Plaza on Jalan Sultan Ismail, are global showcases for ecologically sustainable high-rises.

(Banhunan Parliamen; see *page 167*) and the National Museum (Muzium Negara; see *page 169*). Such landmarks developed a functionalist design, drawing inspiration from traditional residential architecture in order to construct recognisably Malaysian symbols. The National Museum, completed in 1963, uses a literal adaptation of Melakan and Bugis elements in its double-pitched gable roofs, with ornamentation on the underside columns that clearly departs from the Modernist integrity.

Traditional elements are also included in the *kampung* roof forms of the podium blocks of two high-rise buildings, the CIMB Bank building on Jalan Tun Perak, and the Putra World Trade Centre *(page 126)*. Paying little heed to either scale or proportion, vernacular components are used in these buildings as expressions of nationalism. The city's humble beginnings meant that a new identity had to be established by using overt visual symbolism in the absence of context.

Colonial adaptations

While a singular Malaysian national identity has yet to be found among the people of the nation's capital city, establishing a built style has always been an important prerogative for Kuala Lumpur's builders and designers.

The British administration left a legacy that represents the colonial invention of Kuala Lumpur generated from 19th-century Positivism. The British Resident Frank Swettenham's administration, for instance, showed its Orientalist flair when dissent occurred in 1897 over an official style for the city's first civic building, the Sultan Abdul Samad Building *(page 94)*. The colonial government architect at the time had a taste for a classical style modelled on Greek temples. In fact, the design eventually chosen for the Old Town Hall *(page 94)* was neo-Saracenic, a hydrid style developed in India that combines some features of Islamic architecture with Gothic elements. The building

is constructed of red brick, with three large Mughal-inspired domes covered in copper, and surrounded on all sides by wide and shady verandahs. It was certainly something quite new in Malaya and would be later reproduced in buildings such as the Federated Malay States Survey Office *(page 94)* and the fabulously ornate Old KL Railway Station *(page 102)*.

Symbols in the capital

To mark Merdeka (independence), significant public buildings were commissioned to be built in the centre of the city, beginning with Stadium Merdeka *(page 112)*. Set on high ground and completed in 1957, the open arena was built in the Modernist style, which was seen as befitting the country's newly independent status. The architecture of statehood also found expression in buildings like the National Theatre (Istana Budaya; *page 148*) and the Perpustakaan Negara, or National Library *(page 149)*, both found along Jalan Tun Razak. These buildings were designed to portray the country's heritage, economic strength and technological prowess.

As the country's economy expanded, new building typologies, notably hotels, condominiums and shopping centres, emerged. Urban space became a scarce commodity in booming Kuala Lumpur during the 1980s and 1990s, and new buildings pushed upwards in order to maximise land values. But the economic rationale for skyscrapers is far outweighed by the drive towards immortality: the soaring edifices, if one cares to delve deeper, are really displays of technical virtuosity and economic virility.

LEFT: Mughal-inspired Bangunan KTM Berhad. **ABOVE:** inside Asy-Syakiri Mosque. **RIGHT:** Petronas Twin Towers with mosque in foreground.

Within the CBD, known as the Golden Triangle, almost every available plot of land is a testament to the corporate dominance of landscape. The next surge in vertical building is now taking place around the Kuala Lumpur City Centre (KLCC): upmarket residential buildings that reflect the world-class character of the area are being constructed. One such development is the Troika apartments. Designed by eminent British architect Norman Foster, it is one of the most expensive condominiums in Malaysia.

> *The landscape is changing, and, apart from the very rich, Kuala Lumpur's residents now contend with mass residential housing that resemble uniform rows of Victorian models.*

Rising above the dense city skyline, the Petronas Twin Towers, the work of US-based Argentine Cesar Pelli, are considered the epitome of this new metropolis. The completion of the towers can be interpreted as an apogee in Kuala Lumpur's contribution to nation building. In a sense, they represent a merger between ultimate capitalist power and the religious symbolism of an assumed vernacular aesthetic. But authenticity has always been a very hazy notion in Kuala Lumpur – in the Twin Towers' case, the overlaid Islamic-influenced geometrics and floor plans form a tenuous link at best to local conditions.

Ambition and imagination

The aspirations expressed by Kuala Lumpur's architecture have always included both the real and the imagined. The Egyptian-themed Sunway Pyramid shopping mall *(page 214)*, on the outskirts of Kuala Lumpur, is a piece of kitsch that seems to have come straight out of Disneyland or Las Vegas, with little relation to its surrounding urban sprawl.

Putrajaya *(pages 216–7)* and Cyberjaya in the Klang Valley are two new purpose-built cities that were part of former Prime Minister Mahathir Mohamad's legacy of mega-projects. Cyberjaya was created as the IT centre of the Multimedia Super Corridor – to that end it mostly resembles a massive high-tech park filled with office buildings designed as space-age structures. Few clues to their identities are given beyond the gleaming glass and steel cladding, except for signage and logos that have global recognition.

Former plantation land was transformed on a massive scale equal to that in Canberra, Australia, into a new urban hub for Putrajaya's federal administrative centres. Faced with the blank canvas of a site, contemporary architects made every effort to build monumental forms. The prevailing use of Islamic elements on major buildings, from the Perdana Putra (Prime Minister's Office Complex) to Putrajaya Mosque, is but a continuation of a trend that began with the British Raj. But where the Raj style originated as a response to the Muslim demographics of early Malaya, the architecture of Putrajaya is an artificial attempt to unify a diverse country through a built agenda.

Growing with the times

Through floods, civil war, colonial rule, independence and economic boom, Kuala Lumpur's built environment has never stopped growing, and its streets have not stopped radiating out to the rest of Malaysia. Yet amid change, the

ABOVE: Putrajaya Mosque anchors one end of Putrajaya Lake. **RIGHT:** shophouse buildings at Medan Pasar.

THE EVOLUTION OF THE SHOPHOUSE

Along with infrastructure, municipal sanitation was one of the colonial administration's first concerns for Kuala Lumpur. After a fire destroyed the town in the 1880s, the commercial quarter on the east bank was redeveloped street by street. Flimsy shacks were replaced with masonry shophouses modelled after the Melakan town house, set in rows with uniform facades and a continuous 1.5-metre (5ft) wide ground floor passages, with roof tiles for fire protection and sanitation alleys at the rear. The continuous verandah provided a shaded walkway while allowing its occupants a view of the street. The traditional two-storey shophouse was usually up to 30 metres (100ft) deep. As the shophouse typology developed with more storeys and eclectic decorative styles, increasing exposure to European culture led to a variety of ornamentation, from Baroque to neoclassical and Art Deco, up until World War II.

Today, historic shophouses in the old city centre conceal their history either behind neon signs and renovations or beneath the veneer of decay. But along the Asian Heritage Row off Jalan Sultan Ismail, and in Changkat Bukit Bintang near Bukit Bintang, prewar buildings have been transformed into trendy bars and restaurants, while intrepid migrants have infused new life into the shophouses near Petaling Street.

past can still be found in the layout of the city's old centre, where Jalan Ampang and Petaling Street retain the same alignment as the paths along which tin was first extracted. Remove the congestion of traffic and buildings near Lebuh Pasar Besar, and Medan Pasar Lama *(page 91)* will reveal itself to be remarkably similar to the old market area of Yap Ah Loy's time.

Time and air conditioning may have initiated the decline of the shophouse and changed the face of Kuala Lumpur, but it's the motorcar that has been instrumental in the city's growth. The expanding middle class, commuting to the city for work, has led to the proliferation of triple-deck flyovers and endless housing estates beyond Kuala Lumpur's boundaries. The city's development today closely approximates that of any other developing metropolis.

As agricultural land and *kampung* areas on the city's fringe continue to be consumed by new suburbs, illegal squatter settlements are also disappearing. Migrants attracted by the promise of the city built their houses in communities, much like the first village at Kuala Lumpur's river confluence. Since the nationwide initiative to achieve developed status began, squatter areas have been demolished in favour of high-rise projects. It seems that at any given time, a part of Kuala Lumpur is under some sort of construction. Both the planned and the projected will continue to overlap, with their fleeting histories left behind. ❑

HOTEL ISTANA

ORAN
estaurant
ரெஸ்டாரண்ட்
குடி மெஸ்
782217 FAX: 03-20726479
EDAI EMAS PRASAD
பிரசாதி நகைக் கடை
ow Flat Rate

KEDAI TEKSTIL
LETCHIMY NARAYANA STORE
KEDAI KAIN
LETCHIMY
NARAYANA
STORE
எங்கள் நிறுவனம்
JLN LEBUH AMPANG 50100 K.L.
KEDAI MENJUAL
PERALATAN SEMBAHYANG
VETRIVEL
AGENCY
LOTUS
FIVE STAR AV
PUSAT
MUZIK
LOTUS
FIVE
STAR
(M) SDN BHD
AV
P. RISHA ENTERPRISE
National

PLACES

A detailed guide to Kuala Lumpur and its surroundings, with principal sites numbered and clearly cross-referenced to the maps

The capital of Malaysia, Kuala Lumpur is a thriving, fast metropolis, a hub for commerce and cosmopolitan souls and a congregation of all that is truly Asia. This veritable city, a gateway to the rest of Malaysia, is a hotchpotch of old and new, traffic snarls and smiles, great sights and even greater food. While the streets are far from pedestrian-friendly, the slowly improving system of public transport by bus and train makes the city easy to navigate with a map.

The old city centre, around the confluence of the rivers Klang and Gombak, is chock-a-block with historical attractions. Head southwest, and minaret-and-spire colonial architecture dominates the skyline; to the south is the red-lantern-adorned Chinatown of Petaling Street, while the north hosts the Malay enclave, Kampung Baru, and the Indian Muslim district around Masjid India. The latter adjoins the garment district of Jalan Tuanku Abdul Rahman.

To the northeast is the Kuala Lumpur City Centre (KLCC), anchored by the stunning Petronas Twin Towers. Although they are no longer the world's tallest buildings, these edifices still impress with their stature and iridescent facade. The KLCC sits in the Golden Triangle, the financial and commercial district marked by contemporary swathes of steel and glass. To its south is the swanky district of Bukit Bintang, which has Bintang Walk, a window-shopping extravaganza of high and low fashion, and offers pedestrians access to the pulse of the city.

A patch of pristine rainforest occupies prime land in the city. The Bukit Nanas Forest Recreational Park offers lovely walks, and the spindly KL Tower offers eye-popping 360-degree views. In the manicured Lake Gardens, west of the old city centre, more leisurely alternatives await.

To the south is Brickfields, an old Indian neighbourhood, which has the city's largest concentration of multiracial places of worship.

If you get lost in this city's maze, don't hesitate to ask locals for directions. Many speak English and will be curious, so be friendly back – engaging them is a great way to get to know the city. ❑

PRECEDING PAGES: the distinctive city skyline; a cluttered street in Jalan Ampang. **LEFT:** trendy Village Bar at the basement level of Starhill Gallery. **ABOVE LEFT:** the chic Frangipani club. **ABOVE RIGHT:** fabric shops along Jalan Tuanku Abdul Rahman.

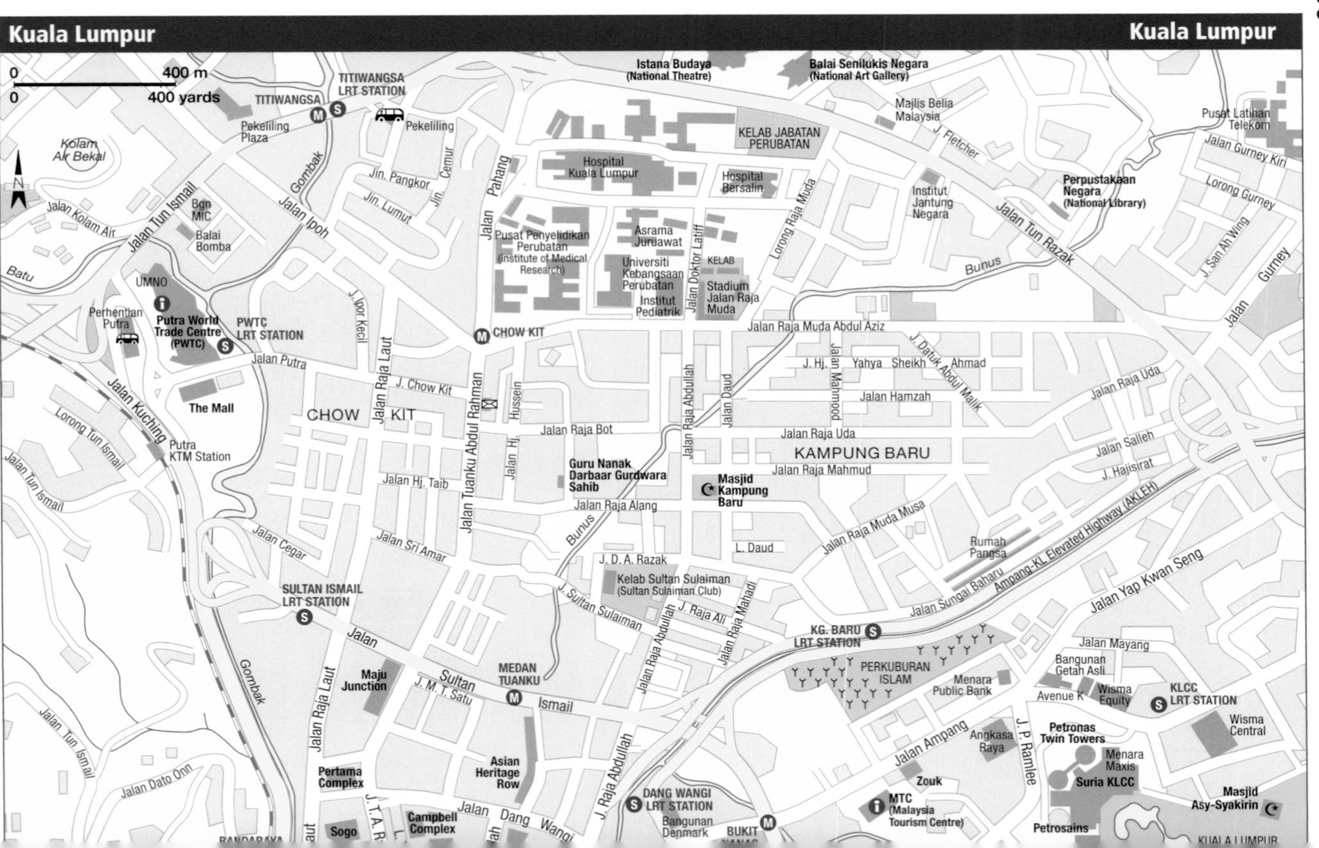
Kuala Lumpur
Kuala Lumpur
0 400 m
0 400 yards
N
TITIWANGSA
TITIWANGSA LRT STATION
Pekeliling Plaza
Pekeliling
Kolam Air Bekal
Jalan Kolam Air
Jalan Tun Ismail
Bgn MIC
Balai Bomba
Gombak
Jalan Ipoh
Jln. Pangkor
Jln. Cemur
Jln. Lumut
Batu
UMNO
Perhentian Putra
Putra World Trade Centre (PWTC)
PWTC LRT STATION
Jalan Putra
J. Ipor Kecil
Jalan Raja Laut
J. Chow Kit
CHOW KIT
The Mall
Jalan Kuching
Putra KTM Station
Lorong Tun Ismail
Jalan Tun Ismail
Jalan Cegar
Jalan Hj. Taib
Jalan Sri Amar
SULTAN ISMAIL LRT STATION
Jalan Sultan Ismail
Gombak
Jalan Raja Laut
Maju Junction
J. M. T. Satu
MEDAN TUANKU
Jalan Tun Ismail
Jalan Dato Onn
Pertama Complex
Sogo
J. T. A. R.
Campbell Complex
Asian Heritage Row
Jalan Dang Wangi
Jalan Pahang
Pusat Penyelidikan Perubatan (Institute of Medical Research)
CHOW KIT
Jalan Tuanku Abdul Rahman
Hussein
Jalan Hj.
Istana Budaya (National Theatre)
Hospital Kuala Lumpur
KELAB JABATAN PERUBATAN
Hospital Bersalin
Asrama Juruawat
Universiti Kebangsaan Perubatan
Institut Pediatrik
Jalan Doktor Latiff
KELAB
Stadium Jalan Raja Muda
Lorong Raja Muda
Balai Senilukis Negara (National Art Gallery)
Majlis Belia Malaysia
J. Fletcher
Institut Jantung Negara
Bunus
Jalan Tun Razak
Perpustakaan Negara (National Library)
Pusat Latihan Telekom
Jalan Gurney Kiri
Lorong Gurney
J. San Ah Wing
Jalan Gurney
Jalan Raja Muda Abdul Aziz
J. Hj. Yahya Sheikh Ahmad
J. Datuk Abdul Malik
Jalan Mahmood
Jalan Hamzah
Jalan Raja Abdullah
Jalan Daud
Jalan Raja Bot
Jalan Raja Uda
KAMPUNG BARU
Jalan Raja Mahmud
Guru Nanak Darbaar Gurdwara Sahib
Masjid Kampung Baru
Jalan Raja Alang
Bunus
L. Daud
J. D. A. Razak
Kelab Sultan Sulaiman (Sultan Sulaiman Club)
J. Sultan Sulaiman
Jalan Raja Abdullah
J. Raja Ali
Jalan Raja Mahadi
Jalan Raja Uda
Jalan Salleh
J. Hajisirat
Jalan Raja Muda Musa
Rumah Pangsa
Jalan Sungai Baharu
Ampang-KL Elevated Highway (AKLEH)
Jalan Yap Kwan Seng
KG. BARU LRT STATION
PERKUBURAN ISLAM
Menara Public Bank
Jalan Mayang
Bangunan Getah Asli
Avenue K
Wisma Equity
KLCC LRT STATION
Wisma Central
Jalan Ampang
Angkasa Raya
J. P. Ramlee
Petronas Twin Towers
Menara Maxis
Suria KLCC
Zouk
MTC (Malaysia Tourism Centre)
Petrosains
Masjid Asy-Syakirin
J. Raja Abdullah
DANG WANGI LRT STATION
Bangunan Denmark
BUKIT

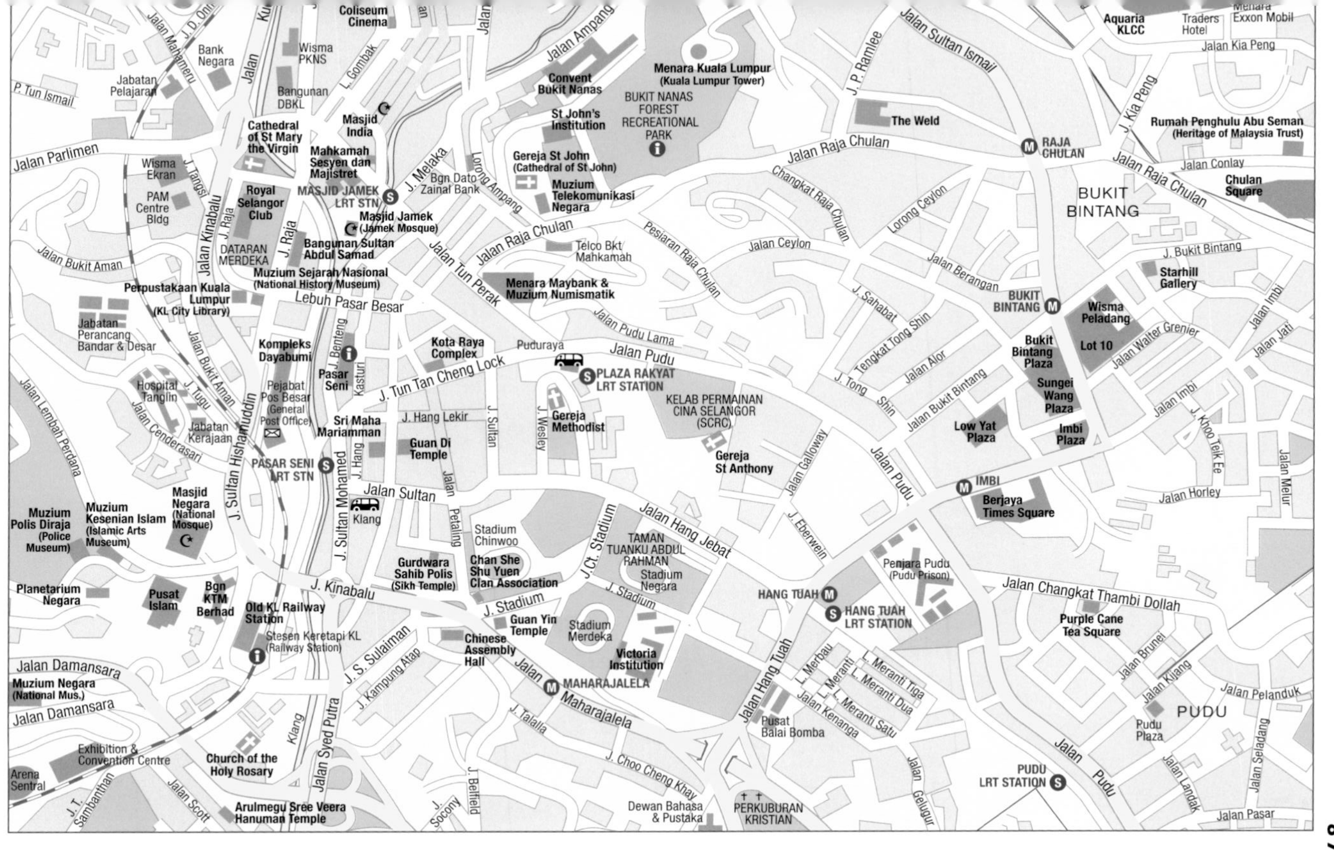

Coliseum Cinema
Jalan Mahameru
Bank Negara
Wisma PKNS
L. Gombak
Jalan Ampang
Menara Kuala Lumpur (Kuala Lumpur Tower)
Convent Bukit Nanas
BUKIT NANAS FOREST RECREATIONAL PARK
St John's Institution
J. P. Ramlee
Jalan Sultan Ismail
Aquaria KLCC
Traders Hotel
Exxon Mobil
Jalan Kia Peng
J. Kia Peng
Rumah Penghulu Abu Seman (Heritage of Malaysia Trust)
The Weld
Jabatan Pelajaran
P. Tun Ismail
Bangunan DBKL
Masjid India
Cathedral of St Mary the Virgin
Mahkamah Sesyen dan Majistret
Jalan Parlimen
Wisma Ekran
J. Tangsi
PAM Centre Bldg
J. Melaka
Bgn Dato Zainal Bank
Lorong Ampang
Gereja St John (Cathedral of St John)
Muzium Telekomunikasi Negara
Jalan Raja Chulan
RAJA CHULAN
Jalan Conlay
Chulan Square
BUKIT BINTANG
Royal Selangor Club
MASJID JAMEK LRT STN
Masjid Jamek (Jamek Mosque)
J. Raja
Jalan Kinabalu
DATARAN MERDEKA
Bangunan Sultan Abdul Samad
Changkat Raja Chulan
Lorong Ceylon
Jalan Ceylon
Pesiaran Raja Chulan
Telco Bkt Mahkamah
J. Bukit Bintang
Starhill Gallery
Jalan Bukit Aman
Muzium Sejarah Nasional (National History Museum)
Jalan Tun Perak
Menara Maybank & Muzium Numismatik
Jalan Berangan
BUKIT BINTANG
Wisma Peladang
Perpustakaan Kuala Lumpur (KL City Library)
Lebuh Pasar Besar
Jalan Pudu Lama
J. Sahabat
Tengkat Tong Shin
Jalan Imbi
Jalan Jati
Jabatan Perancang Bandar & Desar
Kompleks Dayabumi
J. Benteng
Kota Raya Complex
Puduraya
Jalan Pudu
Jalan Alor
Bukit Bintang Plaza
Lot 10
Jalan Walter Grenier
Hospital Tanglin
J. Tugu
Pasar Seni
Kasturi
J. Tun Tan Cheng Lock
PLAZA RAKYAT LRT STATION
KELAB PERMAINAN CINA SELANGOR (SCRC)
J. Tong Shin
Jalan Bukit Bintang
Sungei Wang Plaza
J. Khoo Teik Ee
Jalan Lembah Perdana
Jalan Cenderasari
Jabatan Kerajaan
Pejabat Pos Besar (General Post Office)
Sri Maha Mariamman
J. Hang Lekir
J. Sultan
J. Wesley
Gereja Methodist
Low Yat Plaza
Imbi Plaza
Jalan Melur
J. Sultan Hishamuddin
PASAR SENI LRT STN
J. Hang
Guan Di Temple
Jalan Galloway
Gereja St Anthony
Jalan Pudu
IMBI
Jalan Horley
Jalan Sultan
Muzium Polis Diraja (Police Museum)
Muzium Kesenian Islam (Islamic Arts Museum)
Masjid Negara (National Mosque)
J. Sultan Mohamed
Klang
Jalan Petaling
Stadium Chinwoo
J.Ct. Stadium
Jalan Hang Jebat
J. Eberwein
Berjaya Times Square
TAMAN TUANKU ABDUL RAHMAN
Stadium Negara
Gurdwara Sahib Polis (Sikh Temple)
Chan She Shu Yuen Clan Association
Penjara Pudu (Pudu Prison)
Planetarium Negara
Pusat Islam
Bgn KTM Berhad
J. Kinabalu
J. Stadium
Jalan Changkat Thambi Dollah
Old KL Railway Station
Guan Yin Temple
Stadium Merdeka
HANG TUAH
HANG TUAH LRT STATION
Purple Cane Tea Square
Stesen Keretapi KL (Railway Station)
Chinese Assembly Hall
Victoria Institution
J. S. Sulaiman
Jalan Damansara
J. Kampung Atap
Jalan Hang Tuah
L. Merbau
L. Meranti
L. Meranti Tiga
L. Meranti Dua
Jalan Brunei
Jalan Kijang
Muzium Negara (National Mus.)
Jalan Maharajalela
MAHARAJALELA
Jalan Kenanga
L. Meranti Satu
Jalan Pelanduk
Jalan Damansara
J. Talalla
Pusat Balai Bomba
PUDU
Pudu Plaza
Exhibition & Convention Centre
Church of the Holy Rosary
Klang
Jalan Syed Putra
J. Choo Cheng Khay
Jalan Gelugur
Jalan Seladang
Arena Sentral
J. T. Sambanthan
Jalan Scott
Arulmegu Sree Veera Hanuman Temple
J. Belfield
J. Socony
Dewan Bahasa & Pustaka
PERKUBURAN KRISTIAN
PUDU LRT STATION
Jalan Landak
Jalan Pasar

Maybank

HISTORIC HEART

The cradle of modern-day Kuala Lumpur, this district was once the core of the colonial administration and the centre of its recreational life. Today, its architectural heritage, by turns monumental and humble, bears witness to its glorious past

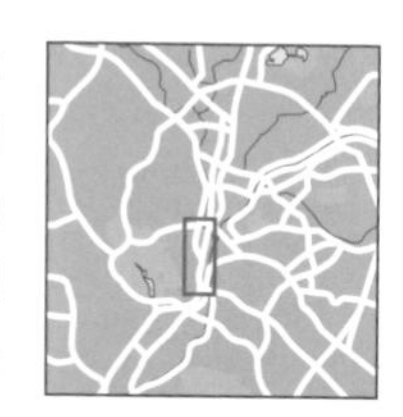

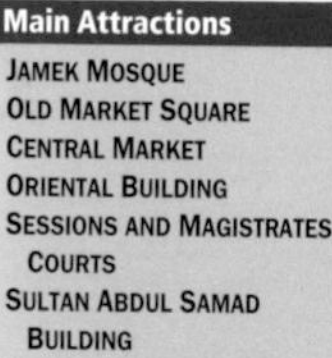

Main Attractions

Maps and Listings

Malaysia's unrelenting pursuit of economic progress – especially under the guiding hand of former firebrand Prime Minister Mahathir Mohamad – has seen modernity encroach upon literally every corner of the capital, and its historical heart has not been spared. As a result of the furious construction that assailed Kuala Lumpur in the 1980s and 1990s, many charming late 19th- and early 20th-century structures have either been demolished or are now hemmed in by light rail tracks and loomed over by skyscrapers. Yet the area remains an essential part of any tour of the city, for in this historical nucleus one might still stumble across nostalgic reminders of the Kuala Lumpur of old.

Jamek Mosque ❶

Address: Jalan Tun Perak
Tel: 03-2274 6063
Opening Hrs: Sat–Thur 8.30am–12.30pm, 2.30–4pm, Fri 8.30–11am, 2.30–4pm
Entrance Fee: free
Transport: LRT Masjid Jamek

It all began at the confluence of the Klang and Gombak rivers, where Chinese labourers prospecting for tin in the late 19th century alighted from their boats – as the waters were too shallow to accommodate their full-laden vessels – before continuing on foot to Ampang, where tin was eventually found. Today, the triangular piece of land where the two rivers meet and where the tin miners settled is the location of the **Jamek Mosque** (Masjid Jamek). This is Kuala Lumpur's first brick mosque, built in 1909 and designed by Arthur Benison Hubback, who was appointed by the colonial government. Hubback was

LEFT: the Jamek Mosque.
RIGHT: the historic Klang and Gombak river confluence.

Historic Heart and Petaling Street

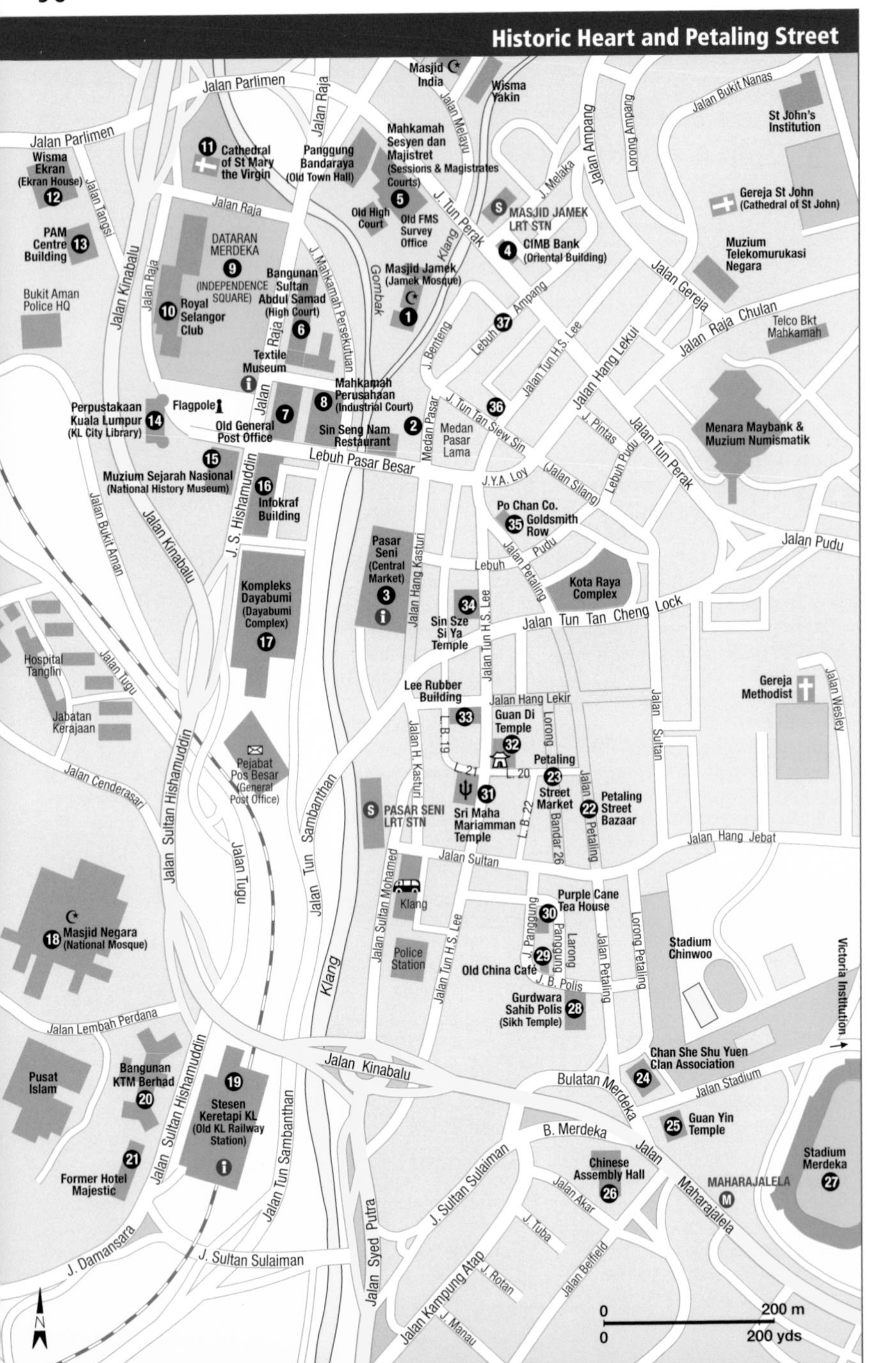

also the architect responsible for the Old KL Railway Station *(see page 102)*. The mosque has two striped minarets, from which the call to prayer is made five times daily, and three domes above the prayer hall; it was the first mosque in the Federal Territory to sport an onion-shaped dome.

A wall surrounds the compound, preserving the mosque as a peaceful place of prayer and saving the historic confluence from being overwhelmed by the surrounding buildings. Looking into the colonnaded forecourt of the mosque, you are likely to see a worshipper or two in quiet contemplation. With a backdrop of coconut trees, the soothing symmetry of the arches frames a cool oasis that seems almost unreal in the surrounding press of humankind, noise and urban grit.

Until the National Mosque *(see page 101)* was built, Jamek Mosque was the main place of worship for the city's Muslims. Visitors must be properly attired, meaning no bare arms and legs, in order to be allowed into its compound.

Old Market Square ❷

Close to the river confluence, bordered by Market Street (now Lebuh Pasar Besar) and Hokkien Street (now Medan Pasar), is the **Old Market Square** or Medan Pasar Lama. There is no signage as the original demarcations of the square have disappeared due to urban renewal. Look out instead for the rather grimy **clock tower** to the right of the bus-stop. Notable for its signature Art Deco sunburst motif at the base, it was built to commemorate the coronation of England's King George VI in 1937. Not long after Art Deco swept across the Western world in the early 20th century, it began to be adopted for buildings in the booming colonial outpost of Kuala Lumpur. The Art Deco style is also visible in two nearby buildings, Central Market and Oriental Building *(see pages 92–3)*.

ABOVE: Old Market Square is framed by ornate old shophouses; Sin Seng Nam restaurant is at one end. **BELOW:** the clock tower in the Old Market Square.

Medan Pasar was the business and social centre for the local mining setlements in the early days. Besides a bustling market, there were gambling booths, opium dens and brothels, all made of wood and *attap* thatching, and presided over by the Chinese community leader, or Kapitan Cina, Yap Ah Loy *(see page 32)*. Most of it was destroyed, however, by a massive fire in 1881, so this was where the first brick houses in Kuala Lumpur were erected. These new buildings, funded by Yap, were built more spread apart, both as a fire prevention measure and as a way to improve sanitary standards. However, they were eventually demolished to make way for the ubiquitous double-storey shophouses seen here and in several locations around the city.

A legacy of earlier times, shophouses were built in a design seen in many parts of Southeast Asia where immigrants from southern China settled. These buildings extend 30–60 metres (100–200ft) to the back, with

ABOVE: the Art Deco entrance to Central Market. **BELOW:** bargain hunting in Central Market.

EAT

On the corner of Old Market Square is a notable Dutch-gabled restaurant where British colonial planters in the old days used to spend their evenings. Previously called The Vatican, it is now the Sin Seng Nam restaurant (see *page 103*), famous for its good breakfasts as well as its rude waiters. With the Malaysian Bar Council just opposite and the courts nearby, it attracts mostly legal professionals.

the ground level used to conduct business (typically, a "shop"), while the upstairs was where the proprietor's family lived (the "house"). New lots of three-storey shophouses were built around the market square in 1906–7, incorporating Western decorative details like fluted pilasters and ornate window frames and fanlights.

Central Market ❸

Address: Jalan Hang Kasturi, www.centralmarket.com.my
Tel: 03-2274 9966
Opening Hrs: daily 10am–10pm
Entrance Fee: free
Transport: LRT Pasar Seni

After Yap Ah Loy died, the original market on Medan Pasar was moved south to the place now occupied by **Central Market,** or Pasar Seni, on Jalan Hang Kasturi. In 1936, this fresh-produce market was relocated to this high-ceilinged Art Deco edifice. It continued to serve the community for decades before it made history as the city's first heritage building to be rescued from demolition and converted on such a large scale for a different use – in this case, as a mall.

Since it opened in 1986, the Central Market has remained one of the city's most popular tourist stops, hawking culture in the form of food, performances and exhibitions, as well as a gamut of souvenirs, from portraits done on the spot and tacky "I Love Kuala Lumpur" T-shirts to delicate batik silk scarfs, antiques and pricey pewterware. Along the side of Central Market, Jalan Hang Kasturi is a pedestrian mall on which other prewar buildings have been turned into souvenir shops too. **The Annexe Gallery** located behind the Central Market, which dubs itself "the art and soul of KL" (www.annexegallery.com; tel: 03-2070 1137; Mon–Thur 11am–8pm, Fri and Sat 11am–9.30pm) is KL's most alternative art space. Be sure to catch something here, as you might be surprised at the quality and diversity of the work from some of KL's most inspired artists.

Oriental Building ❹

North of the river confluence is another clutch of interesting old

buildings constructed in the early 20th century. The most interesting of these is the striking Art Deco-inspired **Oriental Building**, located on the corner of Jalan Tun Perak and Jalan Melaka, close to the Masjid Jamek LRT station. If from a distance the building vaguely resembles the facade of an antiquated radio, it's because the structure originally housed the offices of the old Radio Malaya. Today, the building is occupied by the CIMB Bank.

Colonial district

Lugging heavy briefcases and files, lawyers in their mandatory black and white attire can often be seen scurrying along Jalan Raja, where courthouses now occupy what was once the colonial administrative quarter. The architectural harmony of the colonial cluster is a testament to the thought and planning that went into the shaping of the cityscape between 1894 and 1917. The domes, minarets and large arches of the Islamic Mughal style were used not just for mosques, but also feature in many administrative buildings.

The goals were multifarious: the buildings had to befit a colonial capital, inspire confidence in investors, reflect the Islamic mores of the land, and take into account the tropicalclimate. Therefore, based on their earlier experience in another colony, the British adopted – and adapted – the Mughal style of North India.

Sessions and Magistrates Courts ❺

The first cluster of colonial buildings is found at the corner of Jalan Tun Perak and Jalan Raja. Not immediately obvious to most passers-by is the fact that three adjoining structures make up this complex, which houses the offices of the **Sessions and Magistrates Courts** (Mahkamah Sesyen dan Majistret), a function that befits the grandeur and solemnity of these buildings.

The first building, occupying part of Jalan Tun Perak and stretching

ABOVE LEFT: local artists will paint your portrait at Central Market. **ABOVE:** the Sessions and Magistrates Courts. **BELOW:** the Old Town Hall.

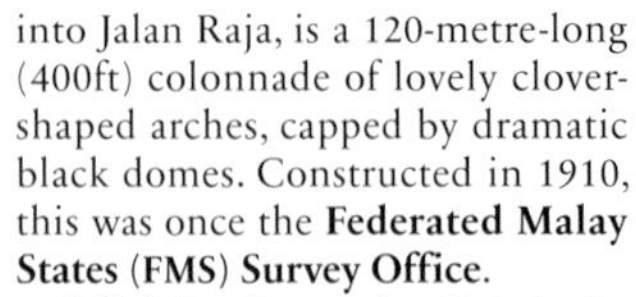

TIP

Detailed histories of many of the buildings in the historic heart can be found on the website of the Badan Warisan Malaysia (Heritage of Malaysia Trust). Look up www.badanwarisan.org.my/cultural_tourism/kl_heritage_trails.

into Jalan Raja, is a 120-metre-long (400ft) colonnade of lovely clover-shaped arches, capped by dramatic black domes. Constructed in 1910, this was once the **Federated Malay States (FMS) Survey Office**.

Adjoining it on Jalan Raja is the city's **Old Town Hall** (stand back and scrutinise the architecture in order to see where the first building ends and the second one begins), dating back to 1904. The British Sanitary Board offices installed here were the first real attempt to administer the city's public services. Part of the old building is now the **City Hall Theatre** (Panggung Bandaraya), best known for having been gutted by fire and whose long-drawn-out restoration took a full 11 years to complete. These new renovations – the massive *wau* or traditional kite splayed on the ceiling, and overused hibiscus motifs – are somewhat garish and tacky and have unfortunately deterred local theatre groups from using this once beautiful and revered theatre.

The last building in this cluster is the **Old High Court** (*c.*1915), located just behind the Town Hall. The offices of the present High Court have moved to the Old General Post Office building *(see page 95)* across the river. The Old High Court building, with its four towers topped by quaint "pepper pot" turrets, was ravaged by fire but was, thankfully, rebuilt in 1992, restoring it to its former glory.

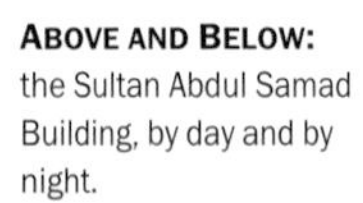

ABOVE AND BELOW: the Sultan Abdul Samad Building, by day and by night.

Sultan Abdul Samad Building ❻

Just across the river on Jalan Raja and facing the expanse of greenery known as the Dataran Merdeka, or Independence Square *(see page 95)*, is the first Mughal-style structure built in Kuala Lumpur, the **Sultan Abdul Samad Building** (Bangunan Sultan Abdul Samad). This is by far the most imposing building on Jalan Raja and arguably the centrepiece of the historic district. Named after the Sultan of Selangor at the time, it took three years to construct – and officially opened in April 1897 as the Supreme Court. A factory was actually set up to supply the millions of bricks required to construct it. The main architect of the building was Arthur Charles Norman, although colonial records indicate that others like C.E. Spooner and R.A.J. Bidwell had a hand in its execution as well. Both symmetrical and rhythmically patterned, and anchored in the middle by a square clock tower flanked by two circular towers, the building was like nothing Kuala Lumpur had ever seen.

Today, the building houses the Finance Division of the Ministry of Information, Communication and Culture and the **Textile Museum** (tel 03-2691 7136; daily 9.30am–6pm; charge), which serves as a repository of stunning textiles from various traditions and influences from around the country. There are fine examples of batik and *songket* from the east coast states of Kelantan and Terengganu as well as the ceremonial *pua kumbu* weavings from the Ibans of Sarawak.

In the days before the Petronas Twin Towers, this grand structure was the pre-eminent and endlessly photographed icon of the city. It is still popular with photographers, and is particularly pretty at night when it is all lit up.

Old General Post Office ❼

A covered arched walkway connects Sultan Abdul Samad Building with the **Old General Post Office**, with its distinctive leaf-shaped pediments, rows of pointed arches and pinnacles jutting out at the top. Easily mistaken for part of the Sultan Abdul Samad Building, it was taken over by the High Court when the latter expanded and needed more space. The General Post Office in turn was relocated in 1981 to the Dayabumi Complex *(see page 101)*.

Industrial Court ❽

Just behind the Old General Post Office are two buildings that house the **Mahkamah Perusahaan** (Industrial Court). The first is the rather nondescript **Straits Trading Building**, but it is the second and more elaborate pastel pink and white coloured building that is of greater interest. This used to be a department store – Kuala Lumpur's first, in fact. Established in the early 1890s by Loke Chow Kit, a businessman and municipal councillor, **Chow Kit & Co.**, as the department store was called, catered to the British colonials of the day and offered everything from food and booze to clothing and horse-riding gear. A succession of government offices took over the building until it was renovated and turned into the Industrial Court. The building was constructed in neo-Renaissance style, with its windows and pediments showing Dutch and other European influences, its alternating square and arched windows setting a strong rhythm.

Dataran Merdeka ❾

The Bangunan Sultan Abdul Samad and its surrounding lofty buildings along Jalan Raja form an impressive abutment to the historically pivotal **Dataran Merdeka** (Independence Square). Originally called **Padang** (Malay for "field"), this parade ground was renamed in post-colonial times to commemorate Malaysia's independence from colonial rule. For it was here, just before midnight on 30 August 1957, that Britain's Union Jack was lowered and the flag of the newly independent Malaya flown for the first time – on

ABOVE: the pink and white Industrial Court, once a department store. **BELOW:** the green expanse of Independence Square.

ABOVE: celebrations on Dataran Merdeka.
BELOW: the ornate Victorian fountain, towards the southern end of Dataran Merdeka.

31 August. Since then, every year on this anniversary, the hoisting of the Malaysian flag has been replicated, witnessed by a spirited crowd of citizens who riotously count down to midnight along with the Bangunan Sultan Abdul Samad clock.

The annual National Day parade was for years held along Jalan Raja and on Dataran Merdeka. The parade has since moved to the new administrative capital at Putrajaya *(see pages 216–18)*. Nonetheless, June sees the square host a colourful cultural parade that kicks off the tourism event Colours of Malaysia (Citrawarna Malaysia), a month-long promotion of cultural events and food hosted by hotels, restaurants and tourist venues all over the country.

Dataran Merdeka and Jalan Raja remain very much a place for the people. Every Saturday evening, the road is closed to traffic, and teenagers, lovers and families hang out here or stroll along the road, enjoying the night breeze and the bright lights. Men in white flannels are occasionally seen on the green bowling at wickets, but cricket, unlike rugby, never really caught on with the general populace in post-colonial Malaya.

Fountain and a flagpole

Towards the southern end of Dataran Merdeka is a strikingly ornate **Victorian fountain**. Some sources say it was commissioned and brought from England to be placed at Market Square, but was moved here because the former site was too congested.

The monumental buildings seen around Dataran Merdeka include one more structure, a veritable high point of the area – the tallest **flagpole** in Malaysia and one of the tallest in the world. It anchors the southern end of the field at a neck-craning height of 95 metres (310ft); the Guinness World Record holder in Aqaba, Jordan, is 37 metres (121ft) taller. The original flagpole that stood here was of much humbler stature and is long gone, but the flag of Malaya that was raised for the first time on 31 August 1957 is on display in the National History Museum *(see pages 101–102)*; this is just behind the giant flagpole and somewhat overlooked because of the grandeur of the structures around.

Royal Selangor Club ⑩

One side of Dataran Merdeka is flanked by the imposing **Royal Selangor Club**, distinguished by its rather pretentious mock-Tudor architecture. A members-only social club now frequented mostly by lawyers, it still houses the famous **Long Bar** where colonial administrators and planters once gathered for their evening *pahit* (gin and tonic) and *stengah* (whiskey soda). This was the nexus of late 19th-century social life *(see page 98)* for the British in Kuala Lumpur.

While its original purpose was to serve the colonials, the Selangor Club also became the first multiracial club in its later years, although local membership was mainly confined to Malay royalty or community leaders. There is speculation that not all the Europeans were happy with this – one theory is that its moniker, "The Spotted Dog", alluded to the "spots" that were the darker-skinned Malays and Indians against the fairness of the Europeans. However, some sources ascribe this reference to a pair of Dalmations that the wife of the police chief at the time used to bring to the club, and the club today is fondly known simply as "The Dog".

In another throwback to colonial times, there is still a gender bias: women are not allowed into the Long Bar, nor are they allowed to vote at club elections or hold positions on the Board. Not surprisingly this archaic law is a sore point with women's rights groups in the city.

Cricket on the Padang

One of the legacies left by the British is cricket. It was played on the Padang after the arrival of Ernest Birch, who was the British Resident, in 1892. This quintessentially British sport had been played in KL as early as 1884, but it was Birch who popularised it. At a time when British administrators selected recruits based on how well they played the game, Birch's excellence as a cricketer got him the billet to KL, where he quickly worked on filling in the swampy parts of the Padang, down near the Chartered Bank, and getting it ready for cricket. The game was later picked up by locals, especially the Indians, who kept the colonial tradition alive long after the wane of Pax Britannica.

ABOVE: entrance to the mock-Tudor Royal Selangor Club. **BELOW:** a stained glass panel at the Cathedral of St Mary the Virgin.

St Mary's Cathedral ⑪

Address: Jalan Raja, www.stmaryscathedral.org.my
Tel: 03-2692 8672
Opening Hrs: daily 7am–3pm
Entrance Fee: free
Transport: LRT Masjid Jamek

Just to the right of the Royal Selangor

Colonial Pursuits

The British Colonial era remains one of the most fascinating periods of Malaysian history but has been remarkably neglected by local historians

Before the Royal Selangor Club *(see page 97)* was built, there were few recreational places for the colonials. Where the "natives" lived, there were gambling halls and brothels, but only the bravest of colonial souls would have visited the "pestilential" part of town for entertainment.

The British Resident Frank Swettenham requested $2,500 from the Colonial Office in London, which existed to supervise the British colonies, including Malaya, for "the erection and furnishing of a Reading Room facing the Parade Ground", which would have a billiard table and serve as a "pavilion for cricket and lawn tennis". After the Selangor Club opened in October 1884, the colonial officers had a clubhouse where they could wind down by playing billiards and drinking when the sun went down.

In 1890, a breakaway group of Selangor Club members set up an elitist whites-only club near Lake Gardens *(see page 165)*. Called the Lake Club, it had a strict dress code, and it was only in 1958 that non-whites were allowed to be members. Feeling slighted, the working-class Europeans who were denied entry started their own club in 1896 and called it the Selangor Recreation Club. With a clubhouse located across the road from the Royal Selangor Club, it offered more of the same vices.

In 1920, the Coliseum theatre was built to stage Malay opera and English plays. Behind it was a bakery which was renovated into a hotel called Coliseum Café and Hotel *(see page 124)*, and it quickly became yet another popular watering hole. In fact, there was an informal arrangement among the out-of-town planters and miners to stay at the Coliseum and meet at the Royal Selangor Club for socialising and drinking on the first Saturday of every month. A favourite beverage was the *stengah* (derived from the Malay word *setengah*, meaning "half"), a mix of whiskey and water.

While the menfolk spent much of their energy lifting mugs of beer from the bartop or playing cricket, soccer or rugby on the Padang on weekends, the women would sit around on the verandah to exchange gossip about the latest love affairs, occasional scandals, the "delinquencies of the 'boy'", that is , the antics of their houseboys, and the prices of things.

Outside of the social clubs, a day at the paddocks was another highlight for the ladies, and the races were also another opportunity to be seen in the latest fashions. As historian G.M. Gullick describes it, "There was something in the nature of a dress parade after the last race." ❑

ABOVE: the Lake Club. **LEFT:** the Padang (framed by Sultan Abdul Samad Building) was the cricket ground for the British.

Club is the first brick church in the Federated Malay States and one of the oldest Anglican churches in the region, the **Cathedral of St Mary the Virgin**. The church was consecrated in 1887 and proclaimed a cathedral only a century later. In the colonial days, St Mary's served as the main place of worship for the British and, often, as a venue to meet and exchange news as well.

Built in the early English Gothic style, the current structure was rebuilt in 1922 following a fire, and now stands on a spot once occupied by stables. The church has some interesting features, including wall plaques honouring lives sacrificed in service to Malaya. Among the most prominent figures honoured is the former British Resident Sir Henry Gurney, whose funeral was held here and in whose memory the pipe organ panelling is dedicated. Stained-glass windows also honour the colonial planters and recognise tropical crops, such as rubber and oil palm, that were the agricultural mainstays of the Malaysian economy.

Today, services are conducted in English, Malay and, interestingly, Iban – to cater to the indigenous people originally from Sarawak who moved to Kuala Lumpur to work in the police and armed forces.

Ekran House ⓬

Beside St Mary's Cathedral is a roundabout with traffic lights – the only point where pedestrians can attempt to cross the extremely busy Jalan Kinabalu to reach the corner of Jalan Tangsi and Jalan Parlimen. Here you will find **Ekran House** (Wisma Ekran), a fine example of elaborate and eclectic Art Deco style, whose monochromatic grey facade throws its strong geometric forms into greater relief. The entrance at the curved corner of the building is flanked by two prominent pylons topped by flagpoles. Erected in 1937 as the Anglo-Oriental Building, it used to be occupied by Malaysian construction and property conglomerate Ekran, but now, sadly, it is empty and abandoned.

PAM Centre Building ⓭

Address: 4 & 6 Jalan Tangsi
Tel: 03-2693 4182
Opening Hrs: Mon–Fri 9am–5.30pm, Sat 9am–1pm
Entrance Fee: free
Transport: LRT Masjid Jamek

Further down the street from Ekran House, at Nos 4 and 6 Jalan Tangsi, is another colonial-era gem. Dating back to 1907 is the **PAM Centre Building**, home of the Malaysia Institute of Architects (Persatuan Arkitek Malaysia). The building is another legacy of magnate Loke Chow Kit, who had it constructed after a tour of Europe. Called Loke Hall, it was designed by the same architect, A.K. Mosdeen, who designed the Chow Kit & Co. building *(see page 95)*. The neoclassical structure features high-quality Chinese artisanal craftsmanship and many interesting architectural details, such as elegant

ABOVE: Ekran House is a fine example of stylish Art Deco architecture.
BELOW: PAM Centre Building, another colonial era gem.

ABOVE: the distinctive Infokraf Building is used as an extension of the High Court. **RIGHT:** detail of a bronze etching at the National History Museum.

Regency-style balconies. Originally used as a town house and offices, the building was converted into a hotel in 1908.

In 1973, the Loke family sold the building. Slated for demolition, it was saved by vehement protests led by PAM, which later restored the building. There are no tours, but visitors are allowed to roam the halls. The building is also home to a contemporary art space, **Galeri Tangsi**, which showcases Malaysian and Asian art (tel: 03-2691 0805/13; Mon–Fri 10.30am–6.30pm, Sat 10am–2pm, Sun by appointment only; free).

Kuala Lumpur City Library ⓮

Address: Dataran Merdeka
Tel: 03-2692 6204
Opening Hrs: Mon 2–6.45pm, Tue–Sat 9.30am–6.45pm, Sun 11am–5pm
Entrance Fee: free
Transport: LRT Masjid Jamek

At the southern end of Dataran Merdeka is the **Kuala Lumpur City Library**, known as Perpustakaan Kuala Lumpur. The library has a good digitised collection of materials about the city – including photographs, video and newspapers. The building is of more recent pedigree, but the architects have taken pains to make it blend into the area's architectural landscape.

The empty building next to it was the former home of the library, and bears the sign **Pustaka Peringatan Kuala Lumpur**. It was originally built to house the government printing office, and is, architecturally, the odd one out in the area. Though it was built in the same period as the other Mughal-style buildings around the city, it sports a neo-Rennaisance design and was built without the breezy verandahs so necessary in Malaysia's climate.

National History Museum ⓯

Address: Dataran Merdeka
Tel: 03-2694 4590
Opening Hrs: daily 9am–6pm
Entrance Fee: free
Transport: LRT Masjid Jamek

Next door to the library is the **National History Museum** (Muzium Sejarah Nasional), with exhibits from the independence period right back to the country's prehistory,

SHOPPING

Ethnic Arts

Art House Gallery
Lot 3.04 & 3.05, Level 1, The Annexe, Central Market, 10 Jalan Hang Kasturi. Tel: 01-2388 6868. p261, E2
This museum-cum-shop sells gorgeous things made by tribal societies around Asia. Prices range from tens of ringgit to tens of thousands.

Music

The Ricecooker Shop
Sub-Basement 18, Bangunan Cahaya Suria, Jalan Tun Tan Siew Sin. www.thericecookershop.com Tel: 01-7315 0734 (Mat Norr). p261, F2
This DIY music shop is run by the iconic Joe Kidd, godfather of Malaysian punk, and his friends. Sells one-of-a-kind T-shirts, underground music, fanzines and much more.

Toys

Wau Tradisi
Lot M 51, Level 1, Central Market, Jalan Hang Kasturi. www.centralmarket.com.my Tel: 03-2274 1906. p261, E2
The best place to find the traditional kite, or *wau*, and traditional spinning tops (*gasing*).

including a 520-million-year-old metamorphic sandstone and a *Homo sapiens* skull that is more than 40,000 years old.

The building originally housed the Chartered Bank of India, Australia and China; it was the dominant bank on the peninsula before World War II and held the government accounts till the country's independence. Built in 1909 and designed by A.C. Norman, the architecture echoes the Mughal style, especially in its roof and in the arches on the ground floor.

Infokraf Building ⓰

At the traffic junction near the History Museum, Jalan Raja changes into Jalan Sultan Hishamuddin. Across this road is yet another prominent example of the Mughal-inspired style. Referred to as the **Infokraf Building** because it served as a centre for Malaysian arts and crafts before it closed down, this is another monument attributed to colonial architect A.B. Hubback. The building, dating back to 1896, housed the FMS Railway headquarters during colonial times. Distinguished by its alternating red and white stripes of brick and plaster, the building is used today as an extension of the Sessions and Magistrates Courts.

Dayabumi Complex ⓱

South along Jalan Sultan Hishamuddin is the **Dayabumi Complex** (Kompleks Dayabumi), the city's first steel-frame skyscraper. Completed in 1984, the 35-storey structure, with its Islamic-influenced fretwork and arches, blends with the Mughal elements of the colonial buildings around it. The tower saw the start of a trend in buildings that adopted a local Islamic identity. Housing offices, a shopping centre and the General Post Office, the building is impressive at night when floodlit.

ABOVE: the dramatic roof design of the National Mosque.

National Mosque ⓲

Address: Jalan Sultan Hishamuddin
Tel: 03-2693 7905
Opening Hrs: Mon–Thur 10am–noon, 2–4pm, Sat, Sun and holidays 9am–noon, 2–6.30pm
Entrance Fee: free
Transport: LRT Pasar Seni

South of the Dayabumi Complex, a pedestrian tunnel leads underneath Jalan Sultan Hishamuddin to the **National Mosque** (Masjid Negara). Completed in 1965, this is the first local mosque to depart from the Mughal style. It also marks what is arguably a watershed in Malaysia's experiment with contemporary architecture. Its circular and dramatically ridged blue roof symbolises an open royal umbrella, while its pointed, spindly minaret resembles a closed umbrella. The lower floor is for public use, administration and religious instruction, while the upper floor, which sits on stout columns, is for prayer. The main prayer hall can accommodate 15,000 worshippers.

Built from funds raised by the city's various ethnic groups, the Modernist National Mosque was erected to honour Malaysia's first Prime Minister, Tunku Abdul Rahman, but he insisted that it be called the National Mosque.

Old KL Railway Station

South of the National Mosque, the familiar Mughal-style architecture greets the eye again. The last two buildings to be constructed in this style are the Old KL Railway Station and, across Jalan Sultan Hishamuddin, connected by an underpass, the Bangunan KTM Berhad. With a flurry of minarets, colonnades and arches, the two complement each other and together form a lovely gateway into the city centre.

The **Old KL Railway Station** (Stesen Keretapi KL) ⓳ is as photogenic today as it was when completed in 1911. Designed by the colonial architect A.B. Hubback, the station was built to cater to increased human traffic when trains started chugging between Kuala Lumpur and Port Swettenham (now Port Klang) in 1886. One of the construction specifications at the time was that the roof be able to support 1 metre (3ft) of snow, a curious feature for a building in the tropics. The building also houses the Station Hotel.

Today, the station is a shadow of its former glory and the hotel is now a backpackers' lodge. The main rail terminus was moved to the modern **KL Sentral** in 2001; only the luxurious Eastern and Oriental Express trains still stop here en route to and from Singapore or Bangkok. Suggestions that the building be turned into a railway museum have so far come to nought.

KTM Berhad Headquarters

Luckily, the same fate has not befallen the **KTM Berhad Building** (Bangunan KTM Berhad) ⓴ across the road. Comprising a pastiche of various architectural motifs, from Mughal minarets to large Gothic windows and ancient Greek columns, the building has withstood several disasters – its north wing, in particular, survived a World War II bombing and a 1969 fire. Today, the interior has been refurbished and air-conditioned, and is used as the offices of ktm Berhad (Malaysian Railways).

BELOW: Mughal-style elements of the Old KL Railway Station Building.

Hotel Majestic ㉑

Like the Station Hotel, another former colonial hotel whose glory days are long gone sits forlornly further down the road. **Hotel Majestic**, built in 1932, was the largest in town and heralded as the equivalent of Singapore's Raffles Hotel. However, over the years, it acquired a reputation for attracting everyone from spies and Japanese soldiers, to ghosts and guerrilla artists who have used it for site-specific work. It briefly served as the National Art Gallery from 1984 to 1992, after which it was acquired by developers. It is currently being restored, and conservationists hope that it will be revived as a heritage hotel. From the outside, the neo-Renaissance building, designed by a Dutch architect, is still impressive, with its symmetrical structure and giant arches. ❑

Best Restaurants

Indian

Restoran Ahamedia
18 Medan Pasar. Tel: 03-2031 3982. Open: daily 6.30am–10.30pm. **$**
1 p261, E2
Overlooking the Klang River with the historical Jamek Mosque behind, this restaurant serves an excellent fish-head (mackerel or red snapper) curry, thick with coconut milk and vegetables. Naans, best eaten with lentil curry, are always served fresh from the tandoor oven. Try also its other Indian breads like *roti canai* (flaky bread), *chapati* (flat bread) and *thosai* (a paper-thin pancake). The moist and fragrant *nasi briyani* (rice cooked with spices and ghee) is delicious with chicken curry.

Restoran Yusoof Dan Zakhir
44 and 46 Jalan Hang Kasturi. Tel: 03-2026 8685. Open: daily 24 hours. **$**
2 p261, E2
A clean and brightly lit setting, abuzz with locals who come for the good variety of Indian *roti* (breads) – from *roti pisang* (with banana) and *roti planta* (with margarine), to *roti telur* (with egg), *murtabak* (with spicy mutton) and naan with tandoori chicken. Service is quick and attentive – your *roti*, served on a banana leaf, lands on your table seconds after you order it.

Price per person for a three-course meal without drinks:
$ = under RM30
$$ = RM30–60
$$$ = RM60–90
$$$$ = over RM90

International

Restoran Seri Asia
20 Medan Pasar. Mobile tel: 017-615 5626. Open: Mon–Sat 8am–9pm. **$**
3 p261, E2
This café, with plenty of old-world charm, has a varied menu of Chinese, Malay, Indonesian and Western dishes. Excellent *mee goreng* (fried noodles), fish in black pepper sauce, and a mouth-watering *nasi lemak* (coconut rice). Come afternoon teatime, delicious local snacks like deep-fried bananas and Peranakan cakes make their appearance. The icy treats, such as *cendol pulut* (green pea jelly strips with glutinous rice), are simply heaven-sent after a day of sightseeing.

Secret Recipe
3 Medan Pasar. Tel: 03-2070 5323. Open: Mon–Sat 10am–9pm. **$**
4 p261, E2
A cool, comfortable spot with a good selection of cakes, pastries and café nosh, such as New York cheesecake, Cornish pasties, *tom yam* spaghetti and braised lamb shank. The set lunches offer good value for money: choose fish and chips, spaghetti or roast duck with turmeric sauce, to go with an iced lemon tea and a brownie for dessert. Serves a really good white coffee too.

Malay

Ginger Restaurant
Lot M12, Central Market, Jalan Hang Kasturi. Tel: 03-2273 7371. Open: daily 11am–10pm. **$$**
5 p261, E2
Opulently decorated Ginger serves a Malaysian and Thai selection. You can't go wrong with its mango salad, seafood *tom yam* (hot and sour soup) and green curry. Other fine complements are garlic prawns, grilled beef salad, stir-fried chicken with basil and *asam* fish (fish in a spicy tamarind soup).

Oh Malaya
Lot 2.07, Central Market Annexe, Jalan Hang Kasturi. Tel: 03-2072 7700. Open: daily 11am–10pm. **$$**
6 p261, E2
This place harks back to the old days of Malaya, replete with memorabilia from the 1950s and 60s. It's a nice pit-stop for a cheap, cold beer after shopping and if you're hungry, the *nasi lemak* is a excellent choice. It's also a good spot for people-watching and is popular with the patrons who frequent the Annexe Gallery upstairs.

Sin Seng Nam Restaurant
2 Medan Pasar. Open: Mon–Fri 7am–4.30pm. **$**
7 p261, E2
Never mind the surly, elderly waitstaff and old decor. This Hainanese coffee shop is a worthy stop for fabulous Hainanese chicken rice and chicken chops. Other must-tries include fish curry, *mee rebus* (noodles in a spicy gravy) and Indian *rojak* (salad). It's excellent for breakfast too; try the comforting local-style breakfast of toast with *kaya* (coconut jam), soft-boiled eggs and coffee.

Peranakan

Precious Old China Restaurant and Bar
Lot 2, Mezzanine Level, Central Market, Jalan Hang Kasturi. Tel: 03-2273 7372. Open: daily L & D. **$$**
8 p261, E3
Eclectically decorated with Vietnamese deities, Victorian furniture and antique Chinese wall panels, this restaurant's real draws are its delicious Peranakan favourites: "top hats" (pastry cups) filled with shredded yam bean, fish-head curry with salted fish, *kapitan* chicken (Peranakan-style chicken curry) and beef *rendang* (dry beef curry).

Preserving Malaysia's Built Heritage

Conservationists have saved many of Kuala Lumpur's historic buildings by reinventing them for contemporary purposes

Kuala Lumpur may have lost many of its buildings to urban renewal, but a growing awareness of Malaysia's architectural heritage has led to continual efforts to save historic properties from the wrecking ball. Key to this campaign is the Badan Warisan Malaysia (the Heritage of Malaysia Trust; *see page 157*), which promotes the conservation of buildings significant to the country's heritage. As of 2010, fewer than 20 buildings in the capital are protected by the National Heritage Act 2005.

The real reward for retaining properties with historical significance has so far been financial. One successful example of conservation is the Central Market (*see page 92*). The Art Deco-style former fresh produce market was rescued from demolition and turned into a shopping complex, now popular with tourists. Prewar shophouses, especially around the Changkat Bukit Bintang and Asian Heritage Row areas, have been converted to trendy bars and restaurants. For now at least, gentrification is the only means of saving such historic gems.

Above: the Carcosa Seri Negara in Lake Gardens was built as British Resident Frank Swettenham's official home. Now reinvented as a luxury hotel, it still bears a distinct colonial style.

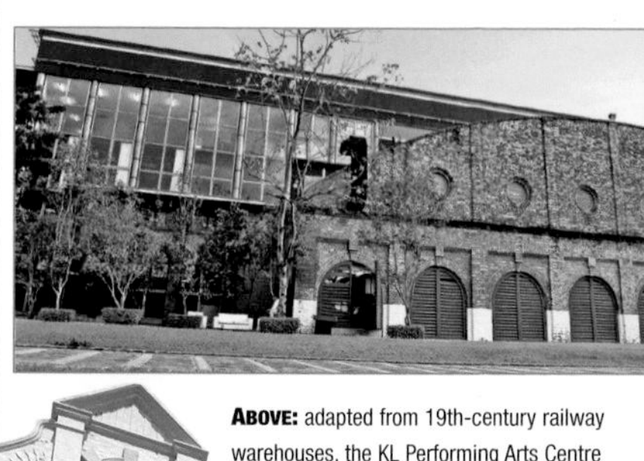

Above: adapted from 19th-century railway warehouses, the KL Performing Arts Centre retains the volume of industrial space with a contemporary aesthetic.

Above: an Art Deco gem, Central Market was the first heritage building to be conserved and converted for a different use.

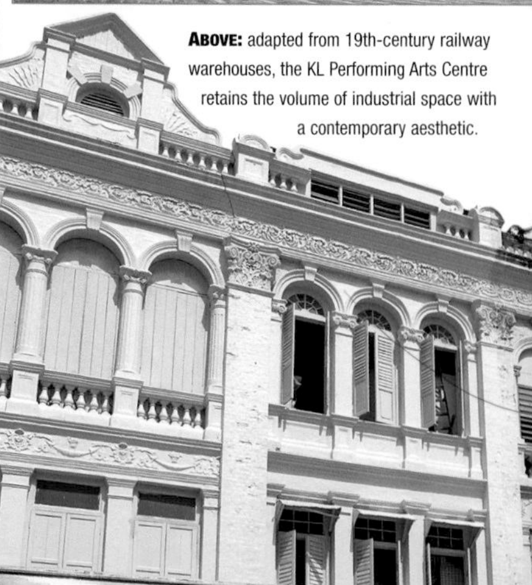

BELOW: in the foothills of Ampang, a colonial bungalow surrounded by lush greenery has been transformed into the chic Tamarind Springs restaurant.

BELOW: many pre-war shophouses are now settings for trendy bars and restaurants, but on Medan Pasar they are still a part of everyday life and business.

MODERNIST CONSERVATION

Following independence in 1957, buildings were designed in the Modernist style to reflect a progressive society. The National Mosque, for instance, completed in 1965, is an icon of Modernist architecture. Its unique folded concrete roof was renovated with blue aluminium panels and it has been kept as a working mosque. Unfortunately, many other post-independence Modernist buildings face demolition threats. Some significant structures have already been lost to development, for example the old Subang International Airport, which was completed in 1965. When the new KL International Airport in Sepang opened in 1998, Subang's Terminal 1 was torn down. Stadium Merdeka, completed in 1957 to mark independence, was also threatened with demolition. Its significant historical value finally prevailed, and it was completely renovated to its original shape, even winning a Unesco award for conservation in 2008.

BELOW: the Rumah Penghulu Abu Seman, a traditional Kedah house, has been rebuilt on Badan Warisan's premises, with the original timber and roof tiles from the same period.

BISKUT FUNG WONG SDN. BHD.
鳳凰餅家有限公司
KEDAI MAKANAN SALAI
16

PETALING STREET AND SURROUNDINGS

Chinatown, centred around Petaling Street, may be a colourful shopping magnet for tourists, but this bustling area with its numerous shops, eateries, temples and clanhouses is where locals have gathered since the city first took shape

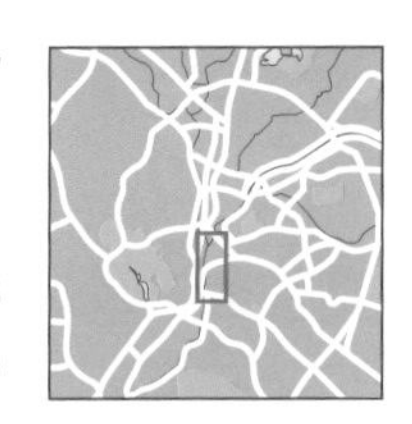

Main Attractions

PETALING STREET BAZAAR
CHAN SHE SHU YUEN CLAN ASSOCIATION
GURDWARA SAHIB POLIS
JALAN BALAI SHOPHOUSES
SRI MAHA MARIAMMAN TEMPLE
GUAN DI TEMPLE
SIN SZE SI YA TEMPLE

Maps and Listings

MAP OF PETALING STREET, PAGE 90
RESTAURANTS, PAGE 119

From classic Rolexes and sleek Ray-Bans to fancy Gucci leather belts and Manchester United T-shirts, the bootleg goods peddled on **Petaling Street** (Jalan Petaling) have made it the undisputed House of Fake. Such blatant disregard for copyright and trademarks is casually defended as a means for the small-timer to *wan sek* (a Cantonese phrase that means, literally, to earn money to eat).

This need to eke out a living was what drove tens of thousands of desperate Chinese migrants from the grinding poverty and overpopulation of mainland China in the 19th century to foreign lands such as Malaysia. Armed with a single-minded focus to accumulate as much wealth as possible to send home to their families, the migrants slogged hard and assiduously scrimped and saved.

Today, few of Malaysia's Chinese residents, barring recent arrivals from China, have ties with their kinsfolk in China. With Malaysia being the land of plenty it is today, the penurious lifestyle of old has been left behind. Nevertheless, *wan sek*, with its connotations of need and basic survival, is still very much a cornerstone of not just Chinese, but also Malaysian, society. In fact, it has found acceptance across all ethnic groups in its Malay version of the phrase, *cari makan*.

KL's Chinatown

In 2003, Petaling Street was given a facelift to "improve" it, by giving it a purportedly more distinct Chinese character. This took the form of building stock gateways, as found in cities around the world, at either end of the Petaling Street Bazaar. Residents were opposed to the

LEFT AND RIGHT: Petaling Street is popular day and night, among both locals and tourists.

gates, feeling they gave KL's Chinatown a generic, "Western" feel, and were inappropriate for a city where the Chinese had been the majority ethnic group from the 19th century to the 1970s and lived spread out. While there is still a strong Chinese presence in Petaling Street, there are unmistakable infusions of other ethnic influences. The renovation has, in fact, stripped the area of some of its chaotic colour. Many bazaar stalls are now boringly identical, while the all-weather modern roofing obscures what used to define the area during the Chinese New Year period – strings of pretty red lanterns framed by the night sky.

Petaling Street Bazaar ㉒

The most visible sight in this area is **Petaling Street Bazaar**, a thriving den of cut-rate commerce. The bazaar runs along Jalan Petaling between Jalan Tun Tan Cheng Lock and Jalan Sultan, and also spills over into the eastern section of Jalan Hang Lekir, all the way to the Jalan Sultan junction. From 10am onwards, the shops and stalls lining the pavements start coming to life. By 4.30pm, Jalan Petaling is closed to traffic and the street is taken over by makeshift stalls, with the action on the street and in the shops behind ending only at around 10pm.

The stalls sell a wide variety of counterfeit goods, including entire product lines and the latest designs fresh off the factory floor. The fake watches are particularly popular, and look and feel very much like the real thing. Some also do inexpensive on-the-spot repairs of watches and mobile phones. For local flavour, look out for souvenirs like postcards and T-shirts emblazoned with Kuala Lumpur landmarks and fun "Manglish" (Malaysian English) text. Keep an eye out also for off-beat items like Russian binoculars and Nepalese jewellery. In addition, there are stalls offering piles of local fruit, Chinese biscuits and titbits such as barbecued pork, roast duck and chicken floss. Behind the stalls that line the pavement are shops selling yet more clothes, shoes, food and other items.

The browsing and shopping experience here can be fun, but the press

BELOW: A chicken to the slaughter at a Petaling Street Market stall.

The Art of Bargaining

Other than in department stores and boutiques, goods are always priced with the expectation that they will be knocked down by the customer. Shop around so you know what the price range is. Start by knocking 50 percent off the price, then increase the amount you are prepared to pay as the salesperson reduces the price, until hopefully you meet somewhere in the middle. Throw in a few local terms like "*Mahal sangat*!" (too expensive!) or "*Boleh kurang*?" (can you reduce the price?). If you are not prepared to pay the "final price" offered, walk away. If your price is within the stallholder's profit range, they will call you back. If not, you know you have gone too low.

of bodies and being called out to constantly may start to grate. Prices, also, are sometimes horribly inflated, so bargain hard – many of the operators speak English well enough to haggle with. Shop around, too, as the same products are usually available in more than one stall.

At night, the atmosphere intensifies as the lights come on and the number of stalls and people double. Some restaurants along Jalan Hang Lekir are filled almost entirely by tourists dining alfresco and gawking at passers-by (who stare right back). Other eateries have their fair share of local regulars too – a testament to how good the food is along this street. For despite its kitschy patina and tourist appeal, Petaling Street and its vicinity are, at heart, still the home ground of locals. Here, along one of the city's first streets, the Chinese have for over three generations gone about their daily lives: this is where they built their homes, haggled over fish and other produce at the markets, breakfasted on dim sum, sought advice from the traditional healers, used remedies from the medicine shops and prayed for health, wealth and wisdom at the temples.

Petaling Street Market ㉓

The **Petaling Street Market** (daily 7am–3pm), formerly known as the Madras Lane Market, is over a century old, and is one of the city's oldest traditional "wet" produce markets. Sprawled behind the buildings bounded by Lorong Bandar 20, Jalan Tun H.S. Lee, Jalan Hang Lekir and Jalan Petaling, it comes alive from dawn, when women carrying baskets, sometimes with Indonesian maids in tow, navigate the slippery cement floors to buy the freshest of vegetables, fruit, poultry, pork, seafood and various herbs and condiments. The market's main entrance is on Jalan Hang Lekir next to Hotel Malaya, where a gateway reads "Penjaja Gallery Jalan Hang Lekir". This market captures the essence of early-morning Chinatown and is worth a jaunt if you're up early. If you're adventurous, you'll be tempted to

TIP

An excellent thirst quencher on Petaling Street is brownish *air mata kuching*, which mean's cat's eye water in Malay, but is really juice made from dried longan, an Asian fruit. The drink is available at the stall at the junction of Petaling Street and Jalan Hang Lekir.

ABOVE LEFT: chilled soft drinks keep the temperature down. **BELOW:** bright bouquets in the market.

ABOVE: the multi-armed Goddess of Mercy statue at the Guan Yin Temple. **ABOVE RIGHT AND BELOW:** entrance to the Chan She Shu Yuen Clan Association and decorative exterior building motifs.

try some of the local breakfasts.

The shophouses around the market also sell groceries and other household goods. While bigger and more ornate shophouses were built north of Jalan Tun Tan Cheng Lock, simpler buildings were constructed here, albeit in the same mould – double-storey Chinese-style shophouses fronted by a narrow pavement called the "five-foot way".

Chan She Shu Yuen Clan Association ㉔

Address: 172 Jalan Petaling
Tel: 03-2078 1461
Opening Hrs: daily 8am–5pm
Transport: Monorail Maharajalela, LRT Pasar Seni

At the southern end of Petaling Street, towards the left, is the **Chan She Shu Yuen Clan Association.** Although the building was built in 1906, the association has been serving the needs of early Chinese migrants bearing the surname Chan (as well as Chen and Tan, which are spelling variations of the same name) since 1896. While Chinese clan association buildings are generally quite decorative, few possess the ornate pottery roofs and friezes that this one has. The colours have faded over time, but the terracotta figures depicting mythological tales, popular dramas and historical episodes are still a marvel. The ceramic artform is called *shek wan*, after the area in Guangdong Province, famous throughout China for its pottery during the Ming and Qing dynasties.

Another distinctive feature of the building is its unusual curved gables. This undulating shape typifies the type of symbolism used in Chinese architecture to reflect a belief in humankind's affinity with nature.

Guan Yin Temple ㉕

Address: Jalan Maharajalela
Tel: 03-2070 8650
Opening Hrs: daily 8am–5pm

Transport: Monorail Maharajalela, LRT Pasar Seni

From the Chan She Shu Yuen building, turn the corner on Jalan Maharajalela and go up a flight of stairs guarded by a pair of lion statues to reach a temple that has fewer embellishments but is equally charming. The century-old **Guan Yin Temple**, with its widely curving roof, honours Sakyamuni Buddha as its principal deity. Next to the statue of the sitting Sakyamuni Buddha is an icon of Guan Yin, the Goddess of Mercy, in her thousand-armed and thousand-eyed form. This represents Guan Yin as the omniscient and omnipresent saviour, simultaneously looking in all directions, sensing the afflictions of humanity and extending her many arms to alleviate them.

Unlike the many other Cantonese temples and clan houses in the city, this is a Hokkien temple, and is cared for by the Selangor Hokkien Association. It was apparently built in the 1890s as a place of worship for visitors to the adjoining cemetery (now occupied by Stadium Merdeka). The current structure, however, is the result of an almost complete rebuilding after a fire ravaged it in 1989, its second fire in 30 years. Miraculously, none of the primary icons were affected on either occasion.

Chinese Assembly Hall ㉖

In the colonial era, Chinese immigrants newly arrived in Kuala Lumpur were divided by surname, locality, dialect or trade. Feeling displaced and lonely, many immigrants naturally formed clan associations with people of their own ilk so that their needs could be represented. In 1921, a nationwide Associated Chinese Chambers of Commerce of British Malaya was founded. It looked after not only the economic well-being of the Chinese but also their political and educational welfare. Today known as the Associated Chinese Chambers of Commerce and Industry of Malaysia, it was based for a time across the road at the **Chinese Assembly Hall** on Jalan Maharajalela, just opposite the Chan She Shu Yuen Clan Association. In 1988, the organisation helped Malaysia renew ties with China that had been

BELOW LEFT: the venerated Victoria Institution.
ABOVE: step back in time at the Old China Café.

The Victoria Institution

Behind Stadium Merdeka is a distinguished school known as the **Victoria Institution**, or "VI" for short (closed to outsiders) but ask the guard for permission to enter; gates are open Mon–Fri 6.30am–2pm, and up to 7pm when sports events are held). Formerly one of the city's premier schools, it was established in 1893 using funds for the commemoration of Queen Victoria's Golden Jubilee, together with donations by the Sultan of Selangor and three local tycoons. The current building dates from 1929 and its classic Western architecture still impresses. Its domed, octagonal tower with four clocks is the only school clock tower in Malaysia. Symmetrical blocks of classrooms emanate from the tower in an "E" shape – to symbolise Education for the Elite – while a pavilion sits in front of the main entrance overlooking the sports field.

Many of the first group of local students won scholarships to England and returned to the school as teachers, training two further generations of teachers or becoming school heads elsewhere in Malaysia. The list of VI's "old boys" reads like a Who's Who of Malaysia, in all arenas from education and politics to theatre and law.

strained since 1948 by the communist insurgency in Malaysia. Today, the Chinese Assembly Hall is used mainly for talks and seminars.

Purple Cane Tea Art Cultural Centre

Address: Chinese Assembly Hall, 1 Jalan Maharajalela, www.purplecane.com.my
Tel: 03-2272 3090
Opening Hrs: 10am–10pm
Entrance Fee: free
Transport: Monorail Maharajalela

One corner of the Chinese Assembly Hall is occupied by the **Purple Cane Tea Restaurant**, which serves Chinese food whose main ingredient is Chinese tea. This unique company also promotes Chinese culture through the art of brewing and drinking tea, and there is a shop here that sells all manner of teas and tea-drinking paraphernalia. Both are part of the Purple Cane chain, which has outlets throughout the city *(see pages 113 and 156)*.

Stadium Merdeka ㉗

Walk out of the side entrance on the right of Guan Yin Temple and up a flight of steps to Maharajalela monorail station, which leads to a car park that adjoins **Stadium Merdeka**. The stadium is where Malaysia's independence was proclaimed in 1957 – in fact, it was specially built for the event. The image of the country's first prime minister, Tunku Abdul Rahman, punching the air and shouting "*merdeka*" (freedom) seven times, echoed by those present, is one that is familiar to every Malaysian. Afterwards, it served as the city's main stadium until the Bukit Jalil Stadium was built in 1998.

Gurdwara Sahib Polis ㉘

Return to Petaling Street and turn left into Jalan Balai Polis. At No 6 is **Gurdwara Sahib Polis** (daily 9am–5pm; free), one of two police *gurdwara* (Sikh temples) in the city. In many parts of Malaysia, *gurdwara* are found in the compounds of old police barracks because Sikhs made up a large part of the early police force. In fact, it was to fill the police force that Sikhs from Punjab in India were first brought by the British to

ABOVE: serving tea at the Purple Cane Tea Restaurant. **BELOW:** chefs prepare garlic, an essential cooking ingredient.

the Malay Peninsula in the 1870s. In the 1880s and 1890s, the Sikh contingent played an invaluable role in quelling civil unrest in Kuala Lumpur.

As with all Sikh temples, it houses the *Guru Granth Sahib*, the Sikh holy book, and is identified outside by a triangular pennant with the Sikh emblem. The temple is a modest structure and continues to be managed by policemen and their families today.

Old China Café 29

Address: 11 Jalan Balai Polis, www.oldchina.com.my
Tel: 03-2072 5915
Opening Hrs: 11am–10.30pm
Entrance Fee: free
Transport: LRT Pasar Seni

Jalan Balai Polis has a row of lovely refurbished shophouses. Besides bookshops and teahouses, there is a restaurant and antique shop at No 11 called **Old China Café**, which used to be a Chinese laundry association. Its charming 1930s ambience has been well preserved, including elements like the *pintu pagar* (swing doors) and pulley-drawn lights. The eatery serves Peranakan food, a fusion of Malay and Chinese cooking styles unique to Malaysia's Straits Chinese community.

Purple Cane Tea House 30

Address: 6 Jalan Panggung, www.purplecane.com.my
Tel: 03-2072 1349
Opening Hrs: 11am–8pm
Entrance Fee: free
Transport: LRT Pasar Seni

Take the opportunity to visit some of the lovely speciality Chinese tea shops in the Jalan Balai Polis, Jalan Sultan and Jalan Panggung area. These are graceful establishments that sell a range of Chinese teas, and porcelain and clay teapots as well as associated paraphernalia. Shop assistants are usually quite happy to show tourists the range of products and let visitors sample a few different teas. They will demonstrate time-honoured Chinese methods of brewing tea that most modern city-bred KL-ites know little about, much less practise. Though somewhat less ritualistic than the more well-known Japanese

In 1975 Stadium Merdeka hosted the 27-round Muhammad Ali–Joe Bugner boxing match, the fight that preceded the famous final match between Ali and Joe Frazier in Manila.

BELOW LEFT: flower garlands on sale.
BELOW: the nostalgic interior of Old China Café.

ABOVE: a Hindu priest at the Sri Maha Mariamman Temple. **ABOVE RIGHT:** the elaborate, 5-tiered gateway tower into the temple.

tea ceremony, the Chinese methods of brewing bring out the full and intense flavours of the tea. For those who cannot be bothered, convenient teabags are also sold.

One of the early pioneers is the **Purple Cane Tea House**, north of Jalan Balai Polis. Its products are a little more expensive than in other places, but it has a good reputation. Purple Cane has branches throughout the city, holds tea appreciation courses, runs a restaurant, and was the first to start up the "tea art house" concept, which promotes the culture of reading and tea drinking.

At the end of Jalan Panggung, head left into Jalan Sultan, then right along **Jalan Tun H.S. Lee**, taking the time to appreciate some fine examples of the city's remaining prewar structures, especially the shophouses. The road's original name was High Street, simply because it was built on higher ground and did not suffer the floods that often denuded the colonial core.

Sri Maha Mariamman Temple ㉛

Address: Jalan Tun H.S. Lee
Tel: 03-2078 3467
Opening Hrs: daily 6am–1am
Entrance Fee: free
Transport: LRT Pasar Seni

Look out on the left-hand side for an unmissable testament to the religious plurality of the city, the **Sri Maha Mariamman Temple,** one of the most important Hindu temples in the country. It is immediately distinguishable by its enormous *gopuram* (gateway tower). Rising to a height of 23 metres (75ft), its tiers are arrayed with statues of Hindu deities carved by artisans from South India. This elaborate entryway, the threshold between the material and the spiritual worlds, is said to represent the "feet" of the temple. The "head" of the temple is the inner sanctum, the *garbagraham*, where the main deity, the Divine Mother goddess Mariamman, is enshrined and worshipped. Also worshipped here are

TIP

Statues of the main deities in all Hindu temples, including the Sri Maha Mariamman, are bathed and prayed to at dawn and dusk each day: these are the best times to visit.

the elephant-headed god Ganesh and the god Subramaniam (better known to South Indians as Murugan).

Established in 1873 by an influential member of the Indian community, the temple occupies an important place in the city's Hindu religious life, as it is from here that the annual Thaipusam festival pilgrimage to the Batu Caves begins *(see pages 182–3 and 186–7)*. Both the statue of Murugan and the massive silver chariot on which it sits for the pilgrimage to Batu Caves are kept in this temple.

Guan Di Temple ㉜

Address: Jalan Tun H.S. Lee
Opening Hrs: daily 7am–5pm
Entrance Fee: free
Transport: LRT Pasar Seni

Further up Jalan Tun H.S. Lee on the right is **Guan Di Temple**, one of the city's oldest Cantonese temples and one of its finest, with many traditional architectural features. Large and slow-burning spiralling coils of incense hang above the entrance courtyard, sending prayers to the heavens. Go through the enormous entrance doors and on the central altar you will see the icon of the main deity after which the temple is named: Guan Di, the God of War and Literature, a red-faced and bearded sword-wielding folk deity worshipped for advice, guidance and protection. To his right is the image of the Goddess of Mercy, Guan Yin, and to his left is the Tiger God. This is one of the few temples in the city where the Tiger God is worshipped.

The temple is often referred to as the Kwong Siew Temple as it was originally a clanhouse of the Kwong Siew Association, established in 1888 by migrants from the Guangdong (Canton) Province of China – where many of Kuala Lumpur's original, Cantonese-speaking Chinese families come from. The association's name is derived from the groups it serves: people originating from the Kwong and Siew prefectures. Typical of clan associations, the Kwong Siew Association originally catered to the economic, social and religious

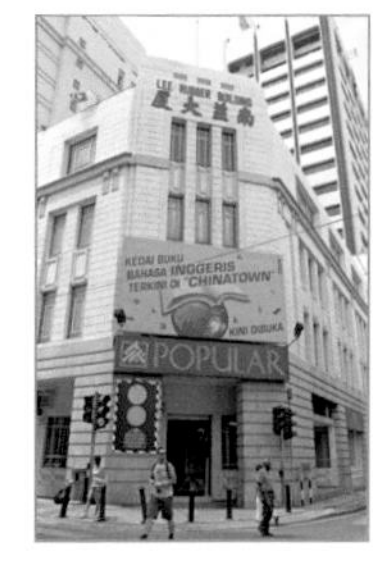

ABOVE: the Guan Di icon – God of War and Literature – at Guan Di Temple. **BELOW LEFT:** gifts galore at Peter Hoe. **BELOW:** the Art Deco Lee Rubber Building.

needs of its members. Now located in a modern building opposite the temple, its role is largely organising ancestor and deity worship.

Lee Rubber Building 33

On the corner of Jalan Tun H.S. Lee and Jalan Hang Lekir is a geometric Art Deco structure from the 1930s, the **Lee Rubber Building**. Its narrow entrance facade facing the street corner is particularly striking, with vertical bands emphasising the building's height. It is named after one of the country's most successful rubber companies, which today is worth over US$266 million and whose famous trust fund is one of the most generous, particularly in contributions to education. The company was set up in the southern state of Johor by Chinese businessman Lee Kong Chian, who was also instrumental in creating what has become Singapore's third largest bank, the Oversea-Chinese Banking Corporation (OCBC). Lee eventually became famous throughout Southeast Asia as the "Rubber and Pineapple King".

The first two floors of the building are taken up by a branch of **Popular** bookshop (daily 10.30am–8.30pm), but the real draw here, located on the third level, is **Peter Hoe** (tel: 03-2026 9788; daily 10am–7pm), one of the best souvenir shops in town. The artist-designer produces an eclectic range of pan-cultural clothes, home furnishings, jewellery and gifts, arrayed in a beautiful setting. He has a smaller shop selling more touristy items at No 2 Jalan Tun H.S. Lee (tel: 03-2026 0711; daily 10am–7pm), opposite the Central Market.

Sin Sze Si Ya Temple 34

Address: Jalan Tun Tan Cheng Lock
Tel: 03-2072 9593
Opening Hrs: daily 7am–5pm
Entrance Fee: free
Transport: LRT Pasar Seni

Continue on Jalan Tun H.S. Lee past the intersection with Jalan Tun Tan Cheng Lock. Almost completely hidden behind a group of pre-war shophouses is the **Sin Sze Si Ya Temple**, which can be accessed through a narrow, ornate gateway adorned with a red sign painted

ABOVE: petitions asking for favours from the deities at the Sin Sze Si Ya Temple. **BELOW:** Chinese devotee at the Sin Sze Si Ya Temple.

with an image of a pair of dragons. This temple was built by Yap Ah Loy in 1864 to honour the deities Sin Sze Si Ya and Si Sze Ya. The former was associated with a Kapitan under whom Yap had once served, and the latter was one of Yap's loyal lieutenants. Both died in battle before Yap did, and in keeping with the Chinese practice of ancestor worship, they were accordingly deified.

Three years before Yap's death, the original *attap* (thatch-roofed) building was replaced by a brick edifice, but care was taken to ensure that the new worship hall had the same diagonal orientation as the original, with its entrance facing a corner. This position was specifically selected in accordance with feng shui principles.

Built in the traditional symmetrical layout, the temple comprises a main hall and two side halls. The main altar in the main hall is where the statues of Sin Sze Si Ya and Si Sze Ya are placed. After Yap Ah Loy passed away in 1885, members of the Yap clan held a ceremony to formally enshrine their illustrious ancestor in the temple for worship. An altar to Yap Ah Loy is on the left of the main altar, and holds a photograph of him. A bust of him sits nearby. Buddha images and other deities are worshipped in the other halls, including Guan Yin, or the Goddess of Mercy, one of the deities most widely worshipped by the Chinese.

Today, this is regarded as one of the most important Taoist temples in the city. It is administered by a trust with representatives from the city's 12 different Chinese clans.

Goldsmith row 35

Continue north on Jalan Tun H.S. Lee past Lebuh Pudu. On the right, where it intersects with Jalan Yap Ah Loy, is a row of goldsmith shops. No one is sure why the goldsmiths congregated here, but this is still a popular location for buyers of the precious metal. One of the oldest shops here is **Po Chan Co.** at No 110 (tel: 03-2078 2763; Mon–Sat 10.30am–4pm, closed public holidays). Established in 1912, it is now run by the second generation. The owners take pride in their product knowledge, honesty and customer service, and several employees have been with the company for over two decades. All of Po Chan's products are locally made, and it can also custom-make jewellery. Gold is much sought after by Malaysians of all races, both as jewellery and as a means of investment.

ABOVE: images and deities fill the Sin Sze Si Ya Temple. **BELOW LEFT:** worshippers at Sin Sze Si Ya Temple. **BELOW RIGHT:** a Burmese restaurant and internet café at Jalan Tun Tan Siew Sin.

Migrant territory 36

Jalan Tun H.S. Lee soon meets **Jalan Tun Tan Siew Sin** (formerly called Jalan Silang) on the right, a hangout for more recent arrivals to Malaysia who, although transient, play an invaluable role in building the local economy. Here, signboards in Urdu, Burmese and Nepali advertise shops, restaurants and even hairstylists, all of which accommodate some of the city's roughly 100,000-strong migrant labour force. Malaysia sources its foreign labour from over 10 countries in Asia, and those who work in Kuala Lumpur often gather in this area to catch up with friends for dinner or a drink and for news of home.

At places like Kham Myint, Burmese customers browse *The Myanmar Times* and shop for *longyi* (sarongs) and *thanaka* sunscreen paste. At Theid Di Win restaurant, they slurp up Burma's national dish, *mohinga*, a fish noodle dish. Meanwhile, at the Himalaya Restaurant, Nepalis dine on mutton *bhat* – Nepali-style meat curry with rice – and at Bhijaya Export, they purchase toothpaste and other toiletries as well as groceries. On public holidays, the pavements are also crowded with Bangladeshis, Indonesians and other nationalities.

ABOVE: roadside fortune tellers at Lebuh Ampang. **BELOW:** colonial shophouses at Lebuh Ampang.

Lebuh Ampang 37

Back on Jalan Tun H.S. Lee, turning left into Jalan Tun Perak leads to **Lebuh Ampang**. This is one of the former strongholds of the Nattukottai Chettiar people, a diasporic community from South India whose members were the fathers of modern banking in Malaysia. It was here that they set up their traditional moneylending establishments, called *kittinghi*. The Chettiars played a key role in funding the local economy in the recent past, especially between the two World Wars. Known for their business acumen, the Chettiars lent money to locals who could not obtain credit from the British to buy land and expand their businesses. Chettiar moneylenders operated on trust and a strict code of honour, requiring no collateral but charging interest rates of 12 to 15 percent per annum. As foreigners, they took large risks; they were also part of a tight trading network that covered countries like Burma, Sri Lanka, Vietnam and Singapore. So synonymous were they with moneylending that the word "chettiar" has seeped into common usage to mean "moneylender".

However, modern banking and illegal loan sharks have forced the 1,000 or so Chettiar families in Malaysia to turn to other professions. Today, along Lebuh Ampang, the ground floors of the ornate shophouses that once were *kittinghi* have been taken over by restaurants and shops with an Indian flavour. But keep an eye out for the facades with concertina metal gates flanked by simple barred windows and, perhaps, a remnant signboard that states "Licensed Money Lender". A peep through the gates will reveal concrete floors and bare walls: the "banks" from which men in crisp white shirts and *dhoti* (traditional white sarongs) once ran an economy. ❑

BEST RESTAURANTS

Chinese

Chinatown Seng Kee
50 Jalan Sultan. Tel: 03-2072 5950. Open: daily 11am–4.30pm. **$** 9 p261, E3
Around for some 30 years now, Seng Kee is famous for its *lo shee fun* – short, fat rice noodles – served in a claypot with a minced pork sauce, topped with a raw egg to be stirred in. The *saang ha meen*, noodles with tiger prawns in an eggy sauce, and the *siu yoke*, roast pork noodles, are also irresistible.

Hong Ngek Restaurant
50 Jalan Tun H.S. Lee. Tel: 03-2078 7852. Open: Mon–Fri 10.30am–7pm, Sat 10.30am–5pm. **$** 10 p261, F2
Tuck into sweet-sour pork ribs, *yin-yang* pomfret in two styles (steamed and deep-fried), and healthful double-boiled winter melon soup. The Hokkien noodles are also a must – thick yellow noodles in a sticky dark sauce with pork crackling, seafood and vegetables.

Koon Kee
Jalan Hang Lekir. Open: daily 10am–9.30pm. **$** 11 p261, E3
A hole-in-the-wall place serving the best *wan tan* (meat dumpling) noodles in town for some 50 years. Its other egg noodle varieties,*chaa siu* (barbecued pork) and chicken in oyster sauce, are also excellent. Try its *sui kau* (meat and prawn dumplings) soup too.

Nam Heong Restaurant
56 Jalan Sultan. Tel: 03-2078 5879. Open: daily 10am–3pm. **$** 12 p261, E3/4
Well known for Hainanese chicken rice. Be early for lunch. If the succulent chickens have sold out – usually by 1pm – the *chaa siu* (barbecued pork) rice and *siu yok* (roast pork) rice are good bets too.

The Oriental Bowl
5 & 7 Lebuh Pudu. Tel: 03-2032 5577. Open: Mon–Sat 11am–6.30pm. **$$** 13 p261, F2
Stop here for a nutritious bowl of double-boiled soup. Soups like "Dancing Buddha" – with wild American ginseng, dried scallops and sea cucumber – have the sweet, mellow goodness of pork bones and chicken simmered for hours in superior stock.

Soong Kee Beef Noodles
3 Jalan Tun Tan Siew Sin. Tel: 03-2078 1484. Open: Mon–Sat 11am–midnight; closed public holidays. **$** 14 p261, E2
The best beef balls in the city since 1945. You can enjoy these perfectly chewy morsels in soup, accompanied by springy egg noodles tossed in a soy-based sauce with minced beef and garlic, and a home-made hot and sour garlic-chilli dip.

Indian

Lotus Family Restaurant
79 Lebuh Ampang. Tel: 03-2026 1689. Open: daily 6.30am–11pm. **$** 15 p261, E2
Southern Indian cuisine. A wide variety of sides – chicken curry, *sambal* (chilli) prawns and more, to go with your *briyani* rice, *pappadam* (spicy lentil wafers) and *rasam* (spicy tomato and pepper soup). Savoury snacks – samosas, curry puffs, onion *pakora* (fritters) and dhal patties – are served for tea.

International

Peter Hoe Beyond
Level 2, Lee Rubber Building, 145 Jalan Tun H.S. Lee. Tel: 03-2026 9788. Open: daily 10am–7pm. **$** 16 p261, E3
After shopping at Peter Hoe's homeware store, head for his café. Order the tuna-capsicum quiche or chicken burger on homemade bread. The eclectic menu also features a tofu and orange salad and oven-roasted pumpkin soup. The fairy-coloured cupcakes are irresistible too.

Malay

Old Town Kopitiam
23 Jalan Hang Lekir. Tel: 03-2031 4321. Open: daily 9am–10pm. **$** 17 p261, E3
A coffee-shop chain with decor harking back to a bygone era. The fragrant coffee is perfect with *kaya* (coconut jam) toast, soft-boiled eggs and *pulut kaya* (glutinous rice pudding with coconut jam). For a bigger meal, opt for the curry noodles or Ipoh-style *kway teow* (flat rice noodles with shredded chicken).

Vegetarian

Cintamani
37 and 39 Jalan Hang Lekir. Tel: 03-2072 1491. Open: daily 7am–10pm. **$** 18 p261, F3
Nestled in a prewar building now restored as the budget Cintamani Travellers' Lodge. On the menu are eggplant-mushroom lasagna, *roti canai* (Indian flaky bread), *nasi lemak* (coconut rice) and even Hungarian goulash. Lunch buffet from Monday to Friday.

Yin Futt Kuok
52 Jalan Hang Lekir. Tel: 03-2070 7468. Open: daily 10am–9pm. **$** 19 p261, F3
Popular vegetarian restaurant. Dishes like *asam* "fish" in a spicy tamarind soup, "prawns" on hot plate, and sweet and sour "pork" are prepared with gluten and bean curd sheets.

Price per person for a three-course meal without drinks:
$ = under RM30
$$ = RM30–60
$$$ = RM60–90
$$$$ = over RM90

PENJUAL BARANG
ENTERPRISE
BHD.

JALAN MASJID INDIA AND JALAN TUANKU ABDUL RAHMAN

Kuala Lumpur's Indian Muslim quarter has lots of shops selling saris and intricate gold jewellery. Along the parallel Jalan TAR are fabric stores galore and shopping centres old and new. Further north is Chow Kit, a little sleazy but famous for its night bazaar

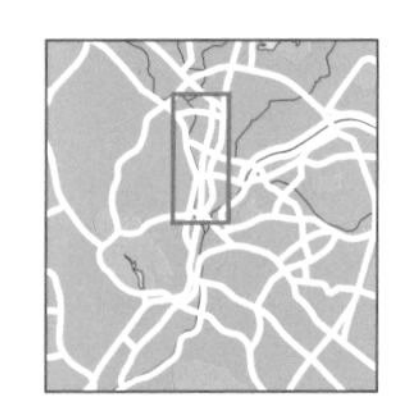

Main Attractions

JALAN MASJID INDIA
MASJID INDIA
GOLD AND JEWELLERY SHOPS
SEMUA HOUSE AND PLAZA CITY ONE
JALAN TAR
COLISEUM CAFÉ AND HOTEL
KAMDAR AND EURO MODA
CHOTIRMALL AND P. LAL

Maps and Listings

MAP OF JALAN MASJID INDIA AND JALAN TAR, PAGE 122
SHOPPING, PAGE 124
RESTAURANTS, PAGE 127

During the glory days of the Malaccan empire in the 15th and 16th centuries, Indian textiles were a principal trading commodity, and, together with spices, were the currency that fuelled the world's greatest global trading empire. The textiles were brought by the shipload to the Malay isles by Indian traders, usually from Gujarat in northwest India. The Indian weavers also adapted their designs and styles to reflect local tastes and traditions. Today, these Indian influences are finely woven into the wholesale quarter of Jalan Tuanku Abdul Rahman and Jalan Masjid India. Many Indian trading businesses here are several generations old.

Anytime a nice outfit is required, grannies, mothers, sisters, daughters and aunts – with their men reluctantly in tow – head to Jalan Tuanku Abdul Rahman and Jalan Masjid India. In these enclaves, fabrics of every hue (and price) are to be found, whether wholesale or retail, knitted, woven or felted, natural or synthetic, local or imported, in the form of bales or ready-made clothing.

JALAN MASJID INDIA

Centred on the pedestrianised **Jalan Masjid India** and the roads leading off it is a chaotic, crowded and noisy yet colourful district known for its very visible Indian Muslim flavour and speciality shops. This is one of the best places to buy batik, whether locally made or Indonesian. One such shop is **Goodluck Trading Company** (No 5 and 7 Jalan Melayu; tel: 03-2691 6006; Mon–Sat 9am–6.30pm), a wholesaler set up in 1895 by Chennai Indians. The shop is also noted for its *kain pelikat chop gadja*, for which it is the sole agent in the country. These are sarongs of hand-loomed

LEFT: trader in religious paraphernalia on Jalan Masjid India. **RIGHT:** barber shop.

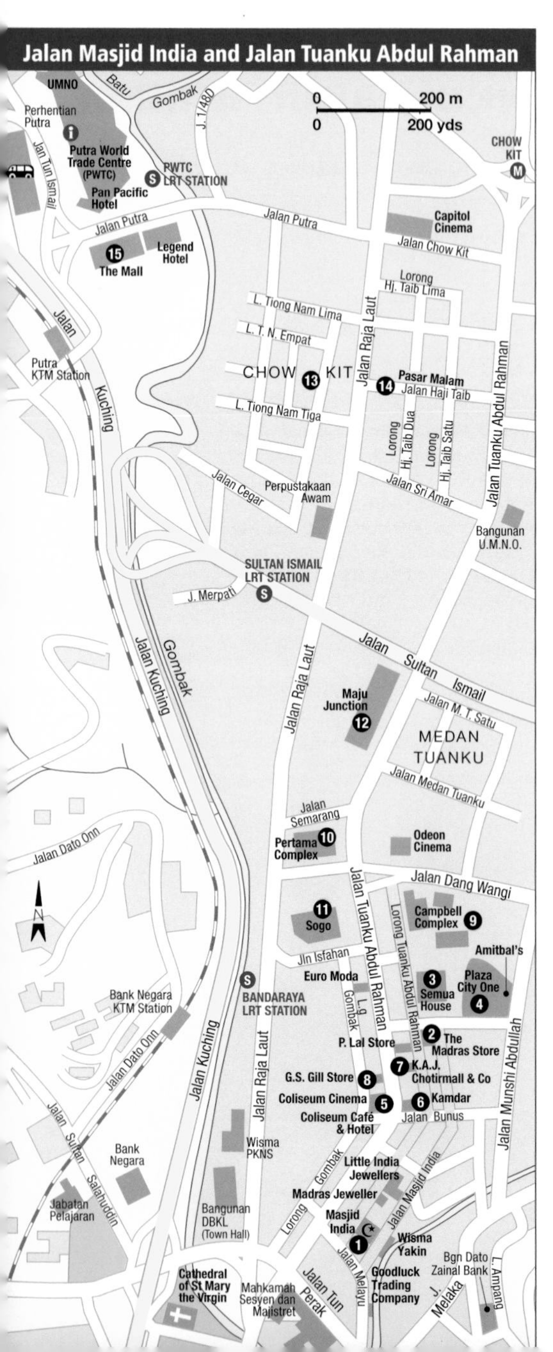

Jalan Masjid India and Jalan Tuanku Abdul Rahman

checked fabric – imported from the textile-producing area of Pulicat near Chennai in India – that are frequently donned by Malaysian men of all races.

Masjid India ❶

The name of this area and its main street derives from a late 19th-century Indian Muslim mosque known as **Masjid India** (no entry to non-Muslims) located near the Jalan Melayu intersection. Now covered in giant slabs of dull-brown tile, it has lost some of its original Moorish grandeur. The first floor is still the prayer hall for men and the second for women – in line with some mosque designs. Built and maintained by donations from the city's Indian Muslim community, the mosque conducts services in Arabic and Tamil.

In front of the mosque, beneath a covered and paved walkway, is a **bazaar** of stalls selling Malay and Islamic knick-knacks. A recent makeover of this stretch has overlaid its original Indian persona with a more Malay character. Here are pyramids of *songkok* (Malay headwear for men), bunches of colourful headscarfs for women, Malay outfits of every design and pattern, Islamic religious books, as well as *jamu*, traditional herbal concoctions for health and beauty. More of such products are sold at **Wisma Yakin** (daily 9am–9.30pm), located on the other side of the bazaar.

Gold and jewellery shops

Walk further along Jalan Masjid India, and look out for jewellery shops which offer a broad range of ethnic and contemporary designs in gold. Shops like **Little India Jewellers** (No 48; tel: 03-2693 3443; daily 10am–8pm) and **Madras Jeweller** (Nos 54 and 96; tel: 03-2691 5715; daily 9.30am–8pm) source their jewellery both locally and from India and Dubai. Establishments like the **Madras Store** ❷ (No 100; tel: 03-2693 0072; Mon–Sat 10am–8pm, Sun 10.30am–8pm) are one-stop shops for Indian brassware and household items, incense and other religious paraphernalia.

Semua House ❸

Address: 3 Lorong Bunus 6
Tel: 03-2691 2829
Opening Hrs: daily 10am–10.30pm
Entrance Fee: free
Transport: LRT Bandaraya

At the north end of Jalan Masjid India, a peeling orange facade denotes **Semua House**, meaning "house of everything", a multistorey air-conditioned mall on Lorong Bunus 6. This is where Malays get everything they need for a wedding, from fabrics and tailoring services to gift baskets, artificial flowers, ribbons and lace. Shops stock outfits from all over the world – including trendy Bollywood outfits – for the elaborate costume changes that are part of the ceremony. At the entrance to the mall is **Kafe Bangles Restaurant** (tel: 03-2691 3088), one of the oldest North Indian eateries in town, reinvented as a trendy sidewalk café.

Next to Semua House is **Plaza City One** ❹ (daily 9am–10pm), a veritable Little India in a high-rise. Bollywood music blares from competing shops, where yards of saris, like multicoloured waves, are creatively hung and draped from the ceiling and walls. Long skirts called *lehnga* are hung by the dozens on racks, as are *salwar kameez*, two-piece ensembles of blouse and trousers. For men, there is a staggering choice of *kurtas* (Indian shirts) in crisp cotton or fine silk. Glass and metal bangles are piled high, and Indian costume jewellery is laid out in glass displays. **Amitbals** (tel: 03-2691 7009; Mon–Sat 10.30am–7pm, Sun 11.30am–5.30pm; *see box, page 124*) at No 1-03 Plaza City One in particular stands out with its ornate Indian clothing and accessories for weddings and formal wear.

JALAN TUANKU ABDUL RAHMAN

Compared to the narrow, congested lanes of Jalan Masjid India, the parallel **Jalan Tuanku Abdul Rahman** seems like a civilised highway, in part because it was turned into a one-way street to ease congestion. Jalan TAR, as it is commonly called, is a long road that stretches all the way north

ABOVE: intricate Indian jewellery on display along Jalan Masjid India. **BELOW:** there are many sari shops in this colourful district.

TIP

A traditional colonial non-alcoholic drink found throughout the former British Empire is the "gunner", consisting of equal parts ginger ale and ginger beer, with a dash of Angostura bitters. It is a refreshing thirst-quencher. Be sure to order one at the Coliseum Café.

through the seedy Chow Kit neighbourhood before becoming Jalan Pahang. Originally called Batu Road, it was renamed to honour the first king, or *Yang di-Pertuan Agung*, of the Federation of Malaysia in 1963.

Over the years, as the number of shops along Jalan TAR increased, it became the city's main shopping precinct, thus earning the moniker "Golden Mile". This area was dominated by tradesmen from the Indian subcontinent in the early 20th century. Remarkably, some businesses have stayed within the same family for several generations, and have thrived despite stiff competition from the city's glitzy new mega-malls.

Today, while the more derelict prewar buildings flanking the road have been replaced, there are still several surviving double-storey shophouses with interesting features such as neoclassical columns, bay windows and decorative gables.

Coliseum Café and Hotel ❺

Address: 98–100 Jalan TAR
Tel: 03-2692 6270
Opening Hrs: daily 10am–10pm
Entrance Fee: free
Transport: LRT Bandaraya

Many of the traders along Jalan TAR have probably spent a good amount of time at another venerable institution – the bar at the **Coliseum Café and Hotel** (*see page 230*). In colonial times the hangout of Somerset Maugham types nursing their drinks, the bar today attracts mainly lawyers, barflies and tourists. Both the bar and its adjoining restaurant are soaked in 1920s nostalgia, thanks to old furniture and memorabilia. Upstairs, there are 10 slightly musty rooms where the colonial out-of-towners, not quite worthy of the grand Majestic or Heritage hotels of the time, once bunked.

While the waiting staff in the restaurant seem to be mostly young Turks, there are still a few grizzled

SHOPPING

The earliest shopping strip in the city is still bustling with traders that have been here since the beginning. Masjid India and Jalan TAR sell everything from gold to saris. Both locations are good places to shop for batik.

Antiques

Melaka Junk Store
397 Jalan TAR. Tel: 012-329 9081/03-4041 1148. p256, B2
Owned by the Kutty family, who used to rule the antique trade in Melaka, this is arguably the most reputable dealer in town. Restored colonial furniture, lamps and curios.

Clothing

Amitbals
Lot No 1-03, Level 1, Plaza City One, 6 Lorong Bunus, off Jalan Masjid India. Tel: 03-2691 7009. p256, B4
This is India at your doorstep: saris, *kurtas*, *salwar kameez*, sandals, jewellery, bedspreads and more. Amitbals stocks the latest textiles and fashions from the boutiques of Delhi and Mumbai.

Malls

Maju Junction
1001 Jalan Sultan Ismail. www.majujunction.com Tel: 03-2772 8536. p256, B3
This ultra-sleek steel-and-glass mall has over 70 shops, including the warehouse-styled WH by British India, international brands and food outlets. Concierge services are also available.

The Mall
Jalan Putra. www.themallkl.com Tel: 03-4042 7122. p256, A2
Opposite the Putra World Trade Centre, this is one of the oldest shopping centres in town, and has undergone renovations several times. Anchored by the classy Parkson department store and Cold Storage, it is popular with families.

Pertama Complex
Jalan TAR (corner of Jalan Dang Wangi). Tel: 03-2672 7457. p256, A/B3
Built in the 1970s, this shopping centre remains *the* place to head for cheap leather products, from shoes to belts and handbags. Jeans are also a good buy here, as is tailoring, especially for Malay clothes.

Sogo
190 Jalan TAR. www.klsogo.com.my Tel: 03-2698 2111. p256, A/B4
Located opposite the Pertama Complex, this eight-storey Japanese chain caters to the Japanese market with services like orchid delivery to Japan, and a good supermarket and food court. Its periodic sales offer genuine value for money.

throwbacks to an earlier age when Hainanese cooks dominated the local hotel and service industry. If you order the café's famous sizzling steak, the waitstaff will tuck a giant napkin into your shirt, wheel out the hot plate on a trolley, and serve you with precise, if expressionless, flair.

Next door is **Coliseum Cinema**, a neoclassical structure built in 1920 to showcase "the highest type of films", as a 1921 daily put it, to a targeted patronage of Europeans. Today, Malay, Indonesian and Bollywood films are shown here.

Kamdar and Euro Moda

A number of speciality fabric stores line both sides of Jalan TAR, attracting even store-owners from Singapore, who come all the way to purchase their goods in bulk here. During festival periods, the place brims with locals and Asian tourists.

Most visible of these stores is **Kamdar** ❻ (www.kamdar.com.my; tel: 03-2692 5571; Mon–Sat 9.15am–6.30pm), located just opposite the Coliseum Café and Hotel. This textile and furnishings emporium has four outlets along the street, the largest at No 113. Established in the town of Ipoh in 1950 by three brothers from India, it is now a public-listed company with a presence all over the country. The family – now into the third generation – still has a hand in the business. Besides home furnishings and fabrics, Kamdar also carries ready-to-wear clothing, particularly in Malay and Indian styles.

Further down the road on the left, No 126/128 is taken up by the poshest fabric house in town – where you are most likely to spot high-society *Mak Datin* (wealthy older Malay women), starlets and politicians' wives. Called **Euro Moda** (tel: 03-2694 0805; Mon–Fri 10.30am–8.30pm, Sat 10.30am–9pm, Sun 11am–9pm), it offers a wide range of medium- to high-end fabrics, attentive personalised service, as well as design and tailoring consultation. Creatively lit displays show off fabrics and garments from India and South Korea, as well as Italian, French and English designer textiles. Prices can reach RM10,000 per metre/yd.

Chotirmall and P. Lal Store

Past Kamdar, at No 131 is **K.A.J. Chotirmall & Co.** ❼, one of the oldest Indian regional trading firms (www.chotirmall.com; tel: 03-2692 8228; Mon–Sat 10.30am–7pm, Sun 11.30am–5.30pm). Set up in 1875, it now has its headquarters in Hong Kong and stores in seven countries. The initials in the company name are those of the three brothers who established the firm. They belong to the commercially minded Sindhi ethnic group, who were among the first traders to venture out of India in the 19th century. Today, the Kuala Lumpur branch specialises in tailoring, menswear, lawyers' gowns and winter clothing.

Adjacent, at No 135, is one of Kuala Lumpur's oldest businesses, the venerable **P. Lal Store** (www.plal.com; tel: 03-2692 7062; Mon–Sat 10am–7pm). The company was set up in 1929 by Prabhulal G. Doshi from India, but it

ABOVE AND BELOW: speciality fabric and garment stores are found along both sides of Jalan Tuanka Abdul Rahman.

Chow Kit is named after a rags-to-riches millionaire from Penang, who, in the early 20th century, had a hand in everything from transport and real estate to tin and rubber.

was his son's business acumen that was behind its growth. Now in the hands of the third generation, it continues to be successful, selling mainly men's leather shoes, tobacco pipes and winter clothing sourced from Europe. These days, it even takes orders online, aiming "to become a leading cyber-retailer of the very wares that we sell so well in our brick and mortar retail store". But the physical store retains some specialised services that few contemporary shoe shops offer, such as its shoe-stretching service.

G.S. Gill ❽

Across from Chotirmall at No 106 is **G.S. Gill ❽** (www.gsgill.net.my; tel: 03-2698 3477; Mon–Fri 9.30am–7pm, Sat 10am–7pm), a store synonymous with sports goods. It started off in 1946 as an importer of bicycles (along with jam and cigarettes). Today, the Sikh-owned company is a manufacturer, licensee, wholesaler and exporter of a range of sporting goods, including its own house brand of racquets, soccer balls and a range of best-selling golf equipment (McGill), which is exported to Holland, Germany and Australia. Even today you might see the owner himself keeping an eye on things behind the counter.

BELOW: an ad hoc game of street chess along Jalan Chow Kit.

Newer shopping malls

North of Jalan Isfahan, the old-world family-owned shops give way to a slew of shopping centres dating from the 1970s onwards, with architectural styles that attest to the period they were built. These include places like **Campbell Complex ❾** (Kuala Lumpur's first shopping centre), **Wilayah Complex** and **Pertama Complex ❿** (1970s–80s), the large Japanese chain **Sogo ⓫** (1990s) and the more recent (and very slick) **Maju Junction ⓬**.

CHOW KIT ⓭

The northernmost stretch of Jalan Tuanku Abdul Rahman runs from Jalan Dang Wangi all the way up to Jalan Ipoh, through an area known as **Chow Kit**, bordered on the west by the Gombak River and on the east by Kampung Baru. In the daytime, Chow Kit is a popular place to buy household items and fresh produce, but is also teeming with transsexual sex workers. The area is sleazy, so beware of pickpockets.

Nonetheless, if you are undaunted (or curious), there is a small handful of attractions worth seeing here. South of Jalan Chow Kit is the bustling ***pasar malam*** (daily 4–11pm) at **Jalan Haji Taib ⓮**, a Malay version of the night bazaar on Petaling Street. Bargain items here include RM5 'bundles' that incorporate jeans, jackets, and second-hand denims from the US; pirated DVDs; cheap electronic devices; and all manner of kitsch.

At the northern end of Jalan TAR, a left turn onto Jalan Chow Kit, which becomes Jalan Putra, leads to the headquarters of UMNO and the **Putra World Trade Centre** (PWTC), a popular venue for exhibitions and trade shows. Just opposite is **The Mall ⓯**, a modern shopping centre with a large food court on level 4 *(see page 124)*. ❑

BEST RESTAURANTS

Chinese

Maju Palace
Suite 5.6–5.11, Level 5, Maju Junction Mall, Corner of Jalan Sultan Ismail and Jalan Tuanku Abdul Rahman. Tel: 03-2691 8822. Open: daily L & D. **$$**
⓴ p256, B3
Modern Cantonese cuisine in five-star surroundings. Dim sum lunch is served daily; don't miss the prawn dumplings, mango rolls and egg tarts. À la carte offerings include baked New Zealand lamb fillet, steamed crabs with glutinous rice, and braised shark's fin soup in a claypot.

European

O'Briens
Ground Level, Menara OCBC, 18 Jalan Tun Perak. Tel: 03-2698 2281. Open: Mon–Sat 7am–8pm. **$**
Off map
Satisfying sandwiches are made fresh before your eyes at this Irish café. The choices are eclectic and plentiful – how about a chicken and turkey bacon triple-decker or the toasted Crambo Club Tootsie with turkey ham, bacon and cheese, topped with mustard and mayonnaise? Great gourmet coffee and fresh juices.

Price per person for a three-course meal without drinks:
$ = under RM30
$$ = RM30–60
$$$ = RM60–90
$$$$ = over RM90

Indian

ABC Foods Corner
1009 Selangor Mansion, Jalan Masjid India. Tel: 03-2693 3314. Open: daily 11am–11.30pm. **$**
㉑ p256, B4
The varied menu here does not disappoint, especially if you're seeking spicy, oily and pungent Chettinad cuisine from southern India. The *dum briyani* (rice with spiced mutton or chicken) is excellent, and the crab masala wonderfully redolent of spices and fiery chilli. There's also a flavoursome mutton soup with chunky meat, tomatoes and spices.

Mohd Yasseen Nasi Kandar Penang
351–353 Jalan Tuanku Abdul Rahman. Tel: 03-2694 8927. Open: daily 24 hours. **$** ㉒ p256, B3
The *nasi kandar* (Penang-style rice and curries) is among the best in KL and popular with Penang-ites who swear by the succulent beef drenched in a thick, brown, spicy sauce. Choose an assortment of side dishes to go with the rice; if you don't mind spicy, the curried crab should not be missed. Don't be put off by the grubby counter – food here moves fast, so a splattered counter is a good sign. And yes, eat with your hands.

Saravana Bhavan
1007 Selangor Mansion, Jalan Masjid India. www.saravanabhavan.com. Tel: 03-2287 1228. Open: daily 8am–10.30pm. **$**
㉓ p256, B4
Outstanding Indian vegetarian food is served in this pretty restaurant with Indian lamps and oil paintings. Have a banana-leaf meal – rice served on a banana leaf with an assortment of sides, from pumpkin mash and chilli *paneer* (fried cottage cheese with chillies and onions) to cauliflower Manchuria and mushroom *roghan josh* (mushrooms cooked in yoghurt and spices).

International

Coliseum Café
98–100 Jalan Tuanku Abdul Rahman. Tel: 03-2692 6270. Open: Mon–Sat 10am–10pm, Sun 9am–10pm. **$** ㉔ p256, B4
You're here for the nostalgia as much as the food. Dating back to 1921, the café conjures up the old British colonial days with its decor – high ceilings, swinging doors and a wooden bar counter. Shake up your appetite with a cocktail first – try a gunner *(see page 124)* or a gin sling – then have a sizzling ribeye, baked crabmeat or an English pot pie from the wood-fired oven. Chinese and Malay dishes offered too.

Malay

Capital Café
213 Jalan Tuanku Abdul Rahman. Tel: 03-2698 2884. Open: daily 6am–8.30pm. **$** ㉕ p256, B4
A Chinese coffeeshop from the 1950s, complete with marble-top tables and wooden chairs. Choose from a variety of noodles, from Cantonese fried *kway teow* (flat rice noodles) to *mee Hailam* (Hainanese-style yellow noodles fried in a soy sauce gravy). The *nasi padang* (Indonesian-style rice with an assortment of sides) stall does brisk business, while delicious satay is available after 6pm.

Yut Kee
35 Jalan Dang Wangi. Tel: 03-2698 8108. Open: Tue–Sun 7am–6pm. **$**
㉖ p256, B3
A Hainanese coffeeshop dating from the 1920s, well known for *roti babi*, a sandwich filled with minced pork and crabmeat, dipped in egg and then deep-fried, served with Worcestershire sauce. Equally good are the *asam* (tamarind) prawns, *belacan* (shrimp paste) fried rice and beef tripe stew. Grab a Swiss roll with *kaya* (coconut jam) or a slice of marble cake from the wood-fired oven on your way out.

KLCC AND JALAN AMPANG

Close to the world's tallest pair of buildings are several attractions: chic Suria KLCC mall, a family-friendly park, assorted galleries, a concert hall and an aquarium. All these are set within the commercial district known as the "Golden Triangle", which is also famous for its nightlife

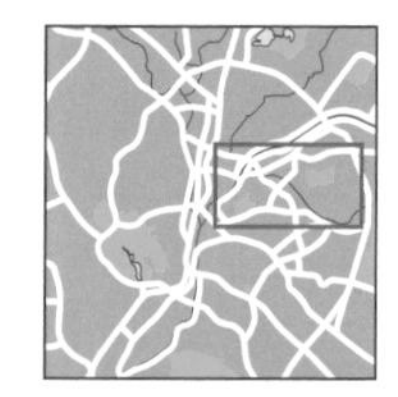

Main Attractions

Maps and Listings

MAP OF KLCC AND JALAN AMPANG, PAGE 130
SHOPPING, PAGE 138
RESTAURANTS AND BARS, PAGES 141–3

The statuesque Petronas Twin Towers anchor the **Kuala Lumpur City Centre (KLCC)**, a 40-hectare (100-acre) area that the Mahathir administration decided should be the eminent centre of a country hurtling towards developed-nation status. Slowly but surely rising up around the towers are more than 20 developments, including skyscrapers, luxury hotels and condominiums – the area will look quite different in a decade. Already occupying prime postions in KLCC are luxury hotels like the Mandarin Oriental, Trader's Hotel and The Ascott serviced apartments. In addition, there are several fine hotels on the periphery of KLCC, such as the Crowne Plaza Mutiara, the Shangri-La and the boutique Hotel Maya.

PETRONAS TWIN TOWERS ❶

Address: Kuala Lumpur City Centre, www.petronastwintowers.com.my
Tel: Tower 1 03-2331 4444, Tower 2 03-2331 8240, skybridge 03-2331 8080
Opening Hrs: daily 10am–10pm
Entrance Fee: free
Transport: LRT KLCC

It was said that they had to keep pouring concrete into its foundation for days, that the towers were slanted, that the government ran out of money half-way through the project – the rumours were rife. Unsurprisingly, during the three years (1994–6) that it took to build the 452-metre-tall (1,480ft) **Petronas Twin Towers** the stories and hype that surrounded it ballooned in proportion.

The towers did make the Guinness Book of Records for the world's tallest building, and they held the record

LEFT: looking up at the magnificent Petronas Twin Towers.
RIGHT: children having fun at the KLCC Park's wading pool.

KLCC, Jalan Ampang and Kampung Baru

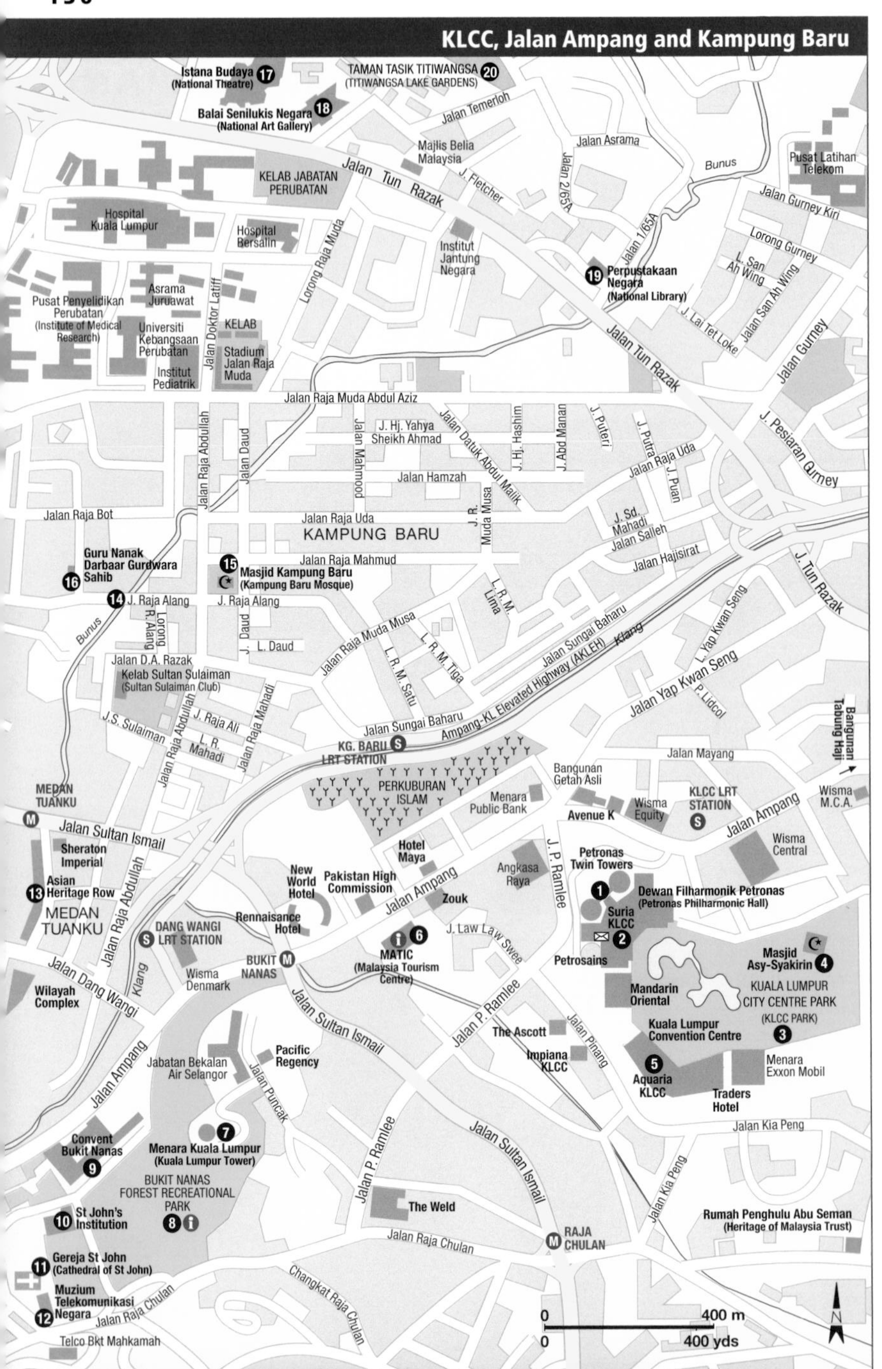

from April 1996 to October 2003, until the Taipei 101 tower topped it by 56 metres (190ft). However, the towers are probably still the world's tallest *pair* of buildings, as proud Malaysians are apt to point out to visitors. In any case, it achieved its goal of putting Malaysia firmly on the global radar as a modern city deserving of the world's attention – which one hopes was worth the US$1.2 billion price tag.

Going up close to the glass-and-steel structures, you basically see just a lot of glass and steel. It is only when you stand further away that you can appreciate the physical beauty of this monument as well as the architectural and engineering feat that it is. Good views can be had from the adjoining KLCC Park *(see page 134)*, although shutterbugs also like to photograph the towers from the fountain-lined pavement by the Tower 2 exit.

Named after and owned by the national petroleum corporation, Petronas, the towers are a concerted effort to reflect a Malaysian identity. The cross-sectional form of the buildings is patterned after a traditional Islamic geometric motif, consisting of two interlocking squares inset with small circles, forming an eight-pointed star. Eight is a lucky number for the Chinese (it is homophonous with the word for prosperity in Chinese), and it's no coincidence that 88 floors make up the tower.

Visitors are not allowed to go up to the top of the towers unless they know someone who works there – Tower 1 is occupied by Petronas, Tower 2 by various multinational companies. Since 9/11, security has been beefed up, particularly with the US Embassy situated close by on Jalan Tun Razak.

However, tourists can go halfway up the towers to the double-deck viewing platform called the **skybridge** (tel: 03-2331 8080/7619; Tue–Sun 8.30am–5.30pm, groups of 20 allowed entry every 15 minutes; free). Located at levels 41 and 42, at 170 metres (560ft) above street level, the view from the bridge is not as spectacular as one might imagine. Still, those wanting to satisfy an "I was there" urge should start lining up from 8am onwards at the information

TIP

Come back after dark – nighttime presents a whole different view of the Towers. Likewise, the National Day and New Year's Eve fireworks here are quite spectacular.

BELOW: dancing fountains at KLCC Park.

The Petronas Twin Towers were designed by New York-based Cesar Pelli and Associates while the KLCC Park was the work of Brazilian landscape artist Roberto Burle Marx. Here's some trivia for fans of statistics: the glass on the Twin Towers covers 77,000 square metres (92,100 sq yds) – about 11 football fields. There are 37,000 tonnes of steel beams, trusses and reinforcement and 65,000 sq metres (78,000 sq yds) of stainless steel cladding.

BELOW: display at Pucuk Rebung. **RIGHT:** Suria KLCC mall.

desk of the Tower 2 foyer. Only 1,300 tickets are issued a day and they run out fast. The towers do sway slightly with the wind and other factors, as all very tall buildings imperceptibly do.

SURIA KLCC MALL ❷

At the base of the towers is the six-storey mall, **Suria KLCC**. This is a slick and well-designed shopping centre with large department stores (Isetan, Parkson and Marks & Spencer), over 270 speciality and designer shops and a 10-hall cineplex. On level 4 is a slew of restaurants with cuisines from all over the world, while level 3 has an expansive food court. Walkways are generously proportioned and expansive skylights give it a sense of space. You could easily spend an entire day at this mall and not come out for fresh air. There are shops here for every kind of budget and if you're in the mood to splash out on something nice, this is the definitely the place to stretch your plastic. Japanese bookshop **Kinokuniya** (daily 10am–9.30pm) on level 4 is one of KL's top bookshops *(see page 138)*.

Petrosains

Address: Level 4, Suria KLCC, www.petrosains.com.my
Tel: 03-2331 8181
Opening Hrs: Tue–Sun 9.30am–5.30pm
Entrance Fee: charge
Transport: LRT KLCC

Children will want to spend hours at **Petrosains**, a terrific interactive museum about science and the oil and gas industry. A modest entrance on level 4 belies the 7,000 square metres (75,000 sq ft) of space inside. Your visit begins and ends with a ride in an oil-drop-shaped vehicle, and there is a special area for two- to eight-year-olds called Galeria, which introduces them to science through play. For souvenirs with a difference, head to the photo area in the gift shop where blue screen and digital photography technologies produce amusing results.

Pucuk Rebung Museum Gallery

Address: 302A, Suria KLCC
Tel: 03-2382 0769
Opening Hrs: daily 10am–10pm
Entrance Fee: free

Transport: LRT KLCC

The **Pucuk Rebung Museum Gallery** is on level 3 of Suria KLCC. Owned by Malaysian antiques enthusiast Henry Bong, this is both a gallery and shop space, with excellent displays of beautiful Malaysian antiques, arts and crafts, fabrics and objets d'art. The goods are pricey but the quality is unsurpassed. Even if you don't buy anything, a browse through this place is recommended for its museum-like documented displays of artefacts.

Petronas Gallery

Address: 341–343, Suria KLCC, www.galeripetronas.com
Tel: 03-2051 7770
Opening Hrs: Tue–Sun 10am–8pm
Entrance Fee: free
Transport: LRT KLCC

Another worthy stop in Suria KLCC is the spare but elegant **Galeri Petronas**. Both contemporary and traditional works are exhibited here; check its website for details of what's on. Look out also for art demonstrations, forums, classes and lectures, performances and other art-related activities held periodically in its multimedia and lecture rooms.

Petronas Philharmonic Hall

Address: Ground Fl, Petronas Tower 2, www.dfp.com.my
Tel: 03-2051 7007 (box office)
Opening Hrs: Mon–Sat 10am–6pm
Entrance Fee: charge
Transport: LRT KLCC

Giving a huge boost to Kuala Lumpur's classical music scene is the **Petronas Philharmonic Hall** or Dewan Filharmonik Petronas, a spectacular performance venue in the style of a 19th-century European concert hall. It hosts a varied concert season each year, featuring both international and local performers and compositions, including world music and jazz genres.

It is also home to the Malaysian Philharmonic Orchestra (MPO), which currently comprises mainly international musicians but has the

ABOVE: the interactive science museum Petrosains is a sure-fire hit with children
BELOW: a bird's-eye view of the expansive KLCC Park.

intention of encouraging home-grown talent. It has an educational and outreach programme in addition to a Malaysian Philharmonic Youth Orchestra. Though piano and violin lessons are increasingly *de rigueur* for middle- and upper-income Kuala Lumpur children, few pursue a career in music and virtually none who have been successful as musicians abroad return to their homeland because of lack of opportunity. Things are now changing, with the city's orchestra slowly making a name for itself on the world stage.

KLCC PARK ❸

Most of the eateries in the shopping mall command a view of the "dancing" fountains behind the mall. The fountains are programmed to perform 150 movements, and they are pretty when lit at night. The steps fronting the fountains are often crowded, particularly on weekends.

The restaurants on the higher floors also provide views of the artfully laid-out **KLCC Park**, a sprawling 20-hectare (50-acre) area of landscaped greenery, with walking and jogging trails, and a playground and wading pool (Tue–Sun 10am–7.30pm; free) for children. The greenery consists mainly of indigenous species, including local fruit trees.

On the northeast corner of the grounds is **Masjid Asy-Syakirin** ❹ (tel: 03-2380 1293; daily 9am–5pm, except Muslim prayer times; free), a mosque with a modern, metallic dome and walls that sport intricate Islamic patterns and calligraphy handmade by Uzbek craftsmen. The dome allows sunlight to enter the mosque in the day and the interior lighting to shine out at night.

Aquaria KLCC ❺

Address: Kuala Lumpur City Centre, www.klaquaria.com
Tel: 03-2333 1888
Opening Hrs: daily 11am–8pm, last admission at 7pm
Entrance Fee: charge
Transport: LRT KLCC

On the southwest corner of the park is the **Kuala Lumpur Convention Centre**, a high-tech space for trade shows, conventions and theatre productions (www.klccconventioncentre.com;

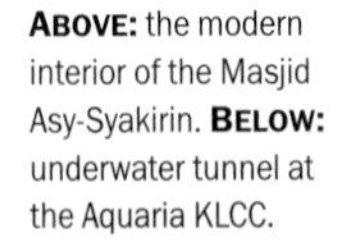

ABOVE: the modern interior of the Masjid Asy-Syakirin. **BELOW:** underwater tunnel at the Aquaria KLCC.

ABOVE LEFT: a photo opportunity at KLCC Park. **ABOVE:** the Malaysia Tourism Centre occupies an old French-style building.

tel: 03-2333 2888; daily 9am–5pm). Connected to Suria KLCC by a tunnel, its concourse level is occupied by the **Aquaria KLCC**. This is a family-oriented, interactive "edu-tainment" rainforest display and aquarium stocked with more than 5,000 fish and other marine life within the confines of a 5,500sq metre (60,000 sq ft) tank. The Living Oceans tunnel, with a moving walkway and assorted fish (including sand tiger sharks, moray eels and giant groupers) swimming around you, is a highlight. Feeding sessions for the various creatures, including sharks and piranhas, start at 11am and go on till 3pm. For an extra fee, visitors can also dive with the sharks – under supervision, of course.

Animal-rights supporters may find certain exhibits rather upsetting. While the marine life seem to have enough space to swim unencumbered, the snakes, tree frogs and other small creatures in the Jewels of the Jungle section are displayed in painfully small glass display boxes.

GOLDEN TRIANGLE

Jalan Ampang, which runs along the front of KLCC, was one of the city's first roads. Today, it is the main artery through what is called the **Golden Triangle**, the city's main commercial and financial district. The three points of the triangle are roughly at the Klang–Gombak river confluence in the west; the junction of Jalan Yap Kwan Seng and Jalan Tun Razak in the northeast; and the junction of Jalan Imbi and Jalan Pudu in the southeast. Contemporary high-rises dominate in the Golden Triangle, many of which incorporate elements from the local culture and environment, particularly Islamic symbolism. An elegant example of this is the **Bangunan Tabung Haji** on Jalan Tun Razak. Designed by Hijjas Kasturi, one of Malaysia's top architects, it is built on five curved pillars representing Islam's five pillars of faith. Most of the high-rises in the Golden Triangle house large corporations, banks and government-linked companies – the latter are a Mahathir-era way of using the private sector to drive the Malaysian economy.

Jalan Ampang mansions

In the late 19th and early 20th centuries, Jalan Ampang was but a trail cut through forest and swampland,

'Ampang' *or* 'empangan' *– from where Jalan Ampang gets its name – is Malay for "dam", a reference to the fact that a lot of water was needed in the Chinese method of open-cast tin mining.*

TIP

If house and hip-hop is not your music style and you're more of a 1980s child, head to the Zouk club on Wednesday for its Mambo Jambo night. Hits by retro stars like Rick Astley, Crowded House and Bananarama get the crowds onto the dance floor.

leading about 5km (3 miles) to the tin mines upstream. Once the city started to grow, rich Chinese miners and businessmen built their ostentatious mansions – some of which have survived to the present day – along this road. Fashioned after the bungalows of British India, these sprawling mansions were built with the hard-earned cash of these *towkay* (rich Chinese businessmen) owners who arrived penniless from China but had slogged and saved their way to riches.

The architecture usually combined a mixture of Chinese features, such as moongates, enclosed courtyards and spacious verandahs at the back of the house, with European elements like Roman pillars, multi-tiered roofs, balconies and fancy Art Deco finishes. Inside, the sumptuous furnishings were often a mishmash of the Oriental and Occidental too.

Malaysia Tourism Centre (MATIC) ❻

Address: 109 Jalan Ampang, www.matic.gov.my
Tel: 03-9235 4848/4800
Opening Hrs: Tourist Information Centre, daily 8am–10pm
Entrance Fee: free
Transport: Monorail Bukit Nanas

Thankfully, a palatial historical house further along Jalan Ampang at No 109, close to the Jalan Sultan Ismail junction, was restored by the government and put to good use. Built in 1935 as the residence of a wealthy miner and planter, Eu Tong Sen, the house served briefly as a war office for the British Army until World War II broke out. The Japanese Army used it as their headquarters until the end of the war in 1945, after which it was taken over by the Federation of Malaya. Since 1989, the building has served as the **Malaysia Tourism Centre** (**MATIC**).

Besides a tourist information desk, the MATIC also has a tourist police counter, a tour agency, the office of the interstate Transnasional Coach company, a craft centre and the **Saloma Theatre Restaurant** (www.saloma.com.my; tel: 03-2161 0122), named after the 1950s singer and screen siren Saloma. The auditorium in the back is where the country's

BELOW: the Beach Club Café is one of the city's most popular nightlife hubs.

first parliament sat in 1959, and is where several *agung* (kings) were installed. It served as the first space for the national art gallery, and is now a theatre where performances are sometimes held. In the MATIC's **Mini Auditorium**, cultural performances are held four times weekly (Tue, Thur, Sat and Sun 2–2.30pm; admission charge).

Across the road from the MATIC at No 132 and behind high walls is another elegant colonial mansion. Housing the offices of the **Pakistan High Commission**, the bungalow sports an octagonal corner tower like the MATIC, in addition to a dome and casement windows on all its three floors.

Entertainment hub

Several other old bungalows on Jalan Ampang east of Jalan Tun Razak are used as diplomatic missions as well as housing for their staff. A few have been converted into restaurants, like **Ma Maison** and **Bangles** *(see page 141)*, offering a charming dining experience in an old-world interior or alfresco on verandahs and patios.

Alexis Bistro Ampang, further down, in Great Eastern mall, is one of KL's top live jazz venues.

Meanwhile, new buildings, many of which reflect post-modern sensibilities, are taking over Jalan Ampang, including the four-venue dance club complex **Zouk** with its futuristic pod-shaped domes at No 113, and the zen-like slick boutique **Hotel Maya** just opposite it.

Together with Zouk, the establishments west of the KLCC in the zig-zagging streets of **Jalan Sultan Ismail, Jalan P. Ramlee** and **Jalan Pinang** make up the main entertainment hub in the city centre. Here, hotels, restaurants, clubs and pubs dominate, including haunts like **7atenine,** the **Beach Club Café** and **Quattro** *(see nightlife listings on pages 237–8)*. Loud, pulsating music and heaving bodies are the main scene here, making it difficult to believe that you are in the capital of a largely Islamic country. KL-ites like to party hard, and though the clubs here are technically supposed to close at 3am, many stay open till the chill dawn.

ABOVE LEFT: a photo opportunity at KLCC Park. **ABOVE:** the Malaysia Tourism Centre occupies an old French-style building.

Heritage at Risk

Jalan Ampang is known for its historic mansions, but unfortunately these grand old ladies are perpetually at the mercy of different priorities and weak conservation laws that are supposed to guard heritage sites (*see page 104*). A prime example is the demolition of Bok House in late 2006. It was one of Jalan Ampang's most impressive neoclassical-style buildings, designed by Singapore-based colonial architectural firm Swan & McLaren in 1929 and erected by a city pioneer called Chua Cheng Bok to woo his lady love. It is just one of several beautiful houses in downtown Kuala Lumpur that has met the wrecker's ball in the last decade or so.

TIP

Instead of taking a taxi to the KL Tower, take the free shuttle bus at the base of the tower just off Jalan P.Ramlee. These operate at 15-minute intervals. Note: your admission ticket to the KL Tower also gives you free guided tours of the surrounding Bukit Nanas Forest Recreational Park. Tours start at 10.30am, 12.30pm, 2.30pm and 4.30pm daily, and begin from the park entrance just outside the ticket office of the KL Tower.

BUKIT NANAS

KL Tower 7

Address: 2 Jalan Punchak, off Jalan P. Ramlee, www.menarakl.com.my
Tel: 03-2020 5444
Opening Hrs: daily 9am–10pm
Entrance Fee: charge
Transport: Monorail Raja Chulan or Bukit Nanas

West of the KLCC is where the "other tower" stands – Menara Kuala Lumpur, popularly known as the Kuala Lumpur Tower or **KL Tower.** This pink telecommunications tower rises out of the lush greenery of Bukit Nanas. People comparing the KL Tower with the Petronas Towers on the same horizon are usually puzzled because the former looks taller. This is because the KL Tower is perched atop a hill, its pinnacle reaching 515 metres (1,690ft) above sea level. But the tower's actual height is 421 metres (1,380ft), which still makes it the second-tallest building in town.

Visitors are only allowed to go up to 276 metres (900ft). An ear-popping super-fast lift delivers you to the observation deck here, where a self-guided audio tour and telescopes provide a good, if vertigo-inducing, overview of the city – including the Petronas Towers, weather permitting. The view at dusk, when the cityscape is enveloped by darkness, is especially spectacular. The building also houses a theatrette, souvenir shops and a revolving restaurant.

The tower's design is influenced by Islamic motifs. Of note are the dome-shaped arches of the lobby entrance, which are decorated with glass to resemble diamonds. The tower's pinnacle is sometimes lit with combinations of hues, maybe to add to its playful character: the tower was inspired by the Malay spinning

SHOPPING

The area's shiny malls are filled with some good specialist shops as well as designer names.

Antiques

Acacia Tree
Lot 1.67, Level 1, Wisma Cosway, Jalan Raja Chulan. www.acacia-tree.biz Tel: 03-2142 8880. p260, A1
Owner Sandra Chia scours Southeast Asia for authentic textiles and jewellery. The gold pieces from the Hindu Majapahit era are stunning.

Books

Kinokuniya
406–408, Level 4, Suria KLCC. www.kinokuniya.com Tel: 03-2164 8133. p257, D3
There is a dearth of good bookshops in KL, but this is probably the best. The sections on art, Asian history, culture and religion are extensive, and there are plenty of foreign-language titles. The best place for Japanese manga.

Crafts

Tenmoku Pottery
Concourse, Suria KLCC. www.tenmokupottery.com.my Tel: 03-2382 0135. p257, D3
Noted for its fossil-like appearance, Tenmoku pottery is a home-grown product line comprising tea sets, vases and decorative items. Also available at Central Market and at major department stores.

Malls

Avenue K
156 Jalan Ampang. Tel: 03-2168 7888. p257, D3
Located opposite the Petronas Twin Towers, this spacious French-designed trapezoidal mall exudes luxury with arty video installations and fashion retrospectives alongside boutiques selling international brands. It beautifully complements the smart K residences alongside it.

Suria KLCC
Petronas Twin Towers, Jalan Ampang. www.suriaklcc.com Tel: 03-2382 2828. p257, D3
This spacious and classy shopping venue has large department stores – including Isetan, Parkson and Marks & Spencer – a Cold Storage supermarket, and more than 270 speciality shops and food outlets. For ethnic goods, check out the Pucuk Rebung Museum Gallery, and Ombak shops.

Shoes

Shuz
102–103A, Level 1, Suria KLCC. Tel: 03-2166 3309. p257, D3
Manolo Blahnik, Christian Louboutin, Rene Caovilla, Sergio Rossi: all the names shoe fans know and love are here.

top or *gasing*. The *gasing* itself has lost its popularity among the new generation of kids weaned on high-tech toys, but the tower does host a battery of recreational options and thrills that will likely appeal to older children.

Bukit Nanas Forest Recreational Park ❽

Address: Jalan Punchak, off Jalan P. Ramlee
Opening Hrs: daily 7am–6pm
Entrance Fee: free
Transport: Monorail Bukit Nanas

Moving from the modern, concrete and fast-paced to the ancient, natural and calming, one comes upon the beautiful rainforest that surrounds the KL Tower. Gazetted as protected land in 1906, the 10-hectare (25-acre) **Bukit Nanas Forest Recreational Park** is the city's oldest forest reserve, and is amazingly lush considering its dense urban location. The park is an excellent introduction to a typical Malaysian lowland tropical rainforest: key plant species are labelled in both Latin and local terms, insects, birds and amphibians abound, and even silver leaf monkeys call this forest home.

Three short and well-marked educational trails, a small nursery of traditional herbal and medicinal plants and an **information centre** are located at the Jalan Raja Chulan end of Jalan Bukit Nanas. Other facilities in the park include a picnic area, children's playground and jogging trails. Be sure to apply insect repellent before you enter the forest.

Colonial-era schools

At the foothills of Bukit Nanas are two of the city's top schools. Many of the schools built by the British colonial government from the 1850s to the early 20th century sported a readily identifiable classical style imported from the West. A good number were modelled after the Penang Free School on Penang island, the first of such schools to be built.

Convent Bukit Nanas ❾, on the northern end of Jalan Bukit Nanas, was the city's first convent, and was established by three French nuns. Built in the English Gothic style, the main building has a typical strong vertical emphasis and pointed arches. Its brother school down the same road,

When the KL Tower was built in the 1980s, enormous effort went into minimising damage to the forest around it. For example, right next to the tower is a gigantic, 100-year-old native jelutong tree, which was protected with a special retaining wall at a cost of RM430,000.

Extreme Sports

Adrenalin junkies will appreciate the extreme sports that revolve around the **KL Tower** on Bukit Nanas. The mildest is the **Flying Fox**, essentially a zip wire where visitors are strapped into a safety harness and launched down a 100-metre-long (330ft) rope across the treetops. If you have ever dreamt of being inside an F1 car, head for the **F1 Simulator** – guaranteed to make your hair stand on end. In addition two annual events are held here: the **KL International Towerthon Challenge** (basically a run up the stairs of the tower) and the **KL International Tower Jump**, a BASE jumping event held since 1999, which involves a heart-stopping parachute-aided freefall.

BELOW: a BASE jumper freefalls during the KL International Tower Jump.

St John's Institution ⓾, has a more elaborate design, with a red-brick facade resembling a Greco-Spanish structure. The school was set up by the head of the Catholic mission in Kuala Lumpur, who had been distressed that Catholic boys had no choice but to attend a Protestant school, the Victoria Institution *(see page 103)*. The two schools remain fierce rivals today.

Cathedral of St John ⓫

Address: Jalan Bukit Nanas
Tel: 03-2078 1876
Opening Hrs: daily 6am–6.30pm
Entrance Fee: free
Transport: LRT Masjid Jamek

Next to the boys' school on Jalan Bukit Nanas is the **Cathedral of St John**. This Roman Catholic cathedral – the only one in downtown Kuala Lumpur – was built in 1883. It is in the shape of a crucifix, and has lovely stained glass windows illustrating Biblical stories. Sunday mass at 10.30am sees a large number of Filipinos here (the Tahanang Filipino Ministry holds a mass there in Tagalog every second Sunday). The church also hosts a Migrant Services Secretariat that caters to the pastoral care of migrant workers, and a Community Services Centre which operates a daily soup kitchen for the needy.

ABOVE: a Silver Leaf monkey at the Bukit Nanas Forest Recreational Park. **BELOW:** Mass is conducted in Tagalog for the city's Filipino community at the Cathedral of St John.

National Telecomunications Museum ⓬

Address: Jalan Gereja
Tel: 03-2031 9966
Opening Hrs: Tue–Sun 9am–5pm
Entrance fee: free
Transport: LRT Masjid Jamek

Close to the Lorong Ampang and Jalan Raja Chulan junction is a graceful Greek-inspired neoclassical structure fronted by eight imposing columns – the National Telecommunications Museum or **Muzium Telekomunikasi Negara**. Once known as the Central Battery Manual Telephone Exchange, it now houses a museum that traces the history of telecommunications in Malaysia back to the 1870s. There is a re-creation of a telegraph office from colonial times as well as exhibits of modern telecoms equipment.

ASIAN HERITAGE ROW

The very name smacks of kitsch and artifice, but it doesn't seem to bother the well-heeled and trendy who are attracted by the bright lights of the **Asian Heritage Row** (www.asianheritagerow.com) ⓭. Located on Jalan Doraisamy, off Jalan Sultan Ismail and next to the Sheraton Imperial Hotel, this row of refurbished colonial-era shophouses has earned accolades from both the local and foreign press, including *Time Asia*, who called it the city's "swankiest night neighbourhood". It is home to ultra-hip dance clubs and pubs like **Vanity Mansion, The Loft** and **Bar SaVanh**, and trendy eateries like **CoChine** and **Mezza Notte** *(see pages 142–3)*, which dish up fusion and gourmet fare from the world over. Most punters on this strip are hip, young trendsetters out on club crawls, especially on Friday and Saturday nights, when the streets are heaving. ❑

BEST RESTAURANTS AND BARS

Restaurants

Chinese

Chef Choi
159 Jalan Ampang. www.chefchoi.com Tel: 03-2163 5866. Open: daily L & D. **$$$** Off map
Chef Choi excels in Cantonese cuisine with modern twists. The foie gras in a caramelised superior stock is sublime, but it's the "Buddha Jumps Over the Wall" soup, rich with morsels of abalone, dried scallops and blackened chicken, that truly steals the thunder. Other popular favourites include prawns in wine and saffron sauce, and fragrant duck wrapped in pancakes.

Hakka Restaurant
6 Jalan Kia Peng. Tel: 03-2143 1908. Open: daily L & D. **$$** 27 p257, D4
With a heritage of over 40 years and solid Hakka culinary traditions, this family-run restaurant is the best place for authentic Hakka Chinese food. Try the Hakka noodles with minced pork sauce, *mui choy kau yuk* (braised pork belly layered with preserved vegetables) or the unique stewed fish head with fermented red rice.

Soo Kee Restaurant
373–1, 4th Mile, Jalan Ampang. Tel: 03-4257 0767. Open: Tue–Sun L & D. **$** Off map
Good old-fashioned Chinese food in a basic, but air-conditioned, restaurant. Roast meats (barbecued pork, roast duck) aside, there are wonderful cooked dishes such as *kon cheen ha lok* (dry-fried prawns in soy sauce and chilli), steamed marbled goby and vegetable stir-fries. The *chaa siu* (sweet barbecued pork) here is legendary.

French

Lafite
Shangri-La Hotel, 11 Jalan Sultan Ismail. Tel: 03-2074 3900. Open: Mon–Fri L & D. **$$$$** 28 p257, C4
Modern French cuisine is the order of the day at this well-established chic restaurant. The chefs turn out exquisite dishes such as morel essence consommé with glazed chicken wings, artisanal pasta with artichokes, and grilled sea bream fillet with a lovely *beurre blanc* sauce. The Buffet Tree is popular with the ladies who lunch.

Ma Maison
32 Persiaran Ampang. Tel: 03-4256 5410. Open: Wed–Mon L & D. **$** (set lunch), **$$$** (à la carte). Off map
French chef-owner Bertrand Langlet serves classic French cuisine in this restaurant, which is furnished like a cosy house. Excellent set lunch: appetiser buffet with salads, pâté and breads, with mains like *emince* of beef, fisherman's terrine and salmon pasta. For dinner, there's the *escalope de foie gras Miss Chan*, named after a regular diner who loved it, and the grilled duck breast with green pepper sauce.

Indian

Bangles Restaurant
270 Jalan Ampang. Tel: 03-4252 4100. Open: daily L & D. **$$** Off map
Objets d'art and some 30,000 glass bangles hanging from the ceiling adorn this restaurant in a grand old mansion. The cuisine is northern Indian: *dum briyani* (rice cooked with spiced meat), shish kebab, fish *tikka masala* and butter chicken Mughlai. Alfresco seating in the garden with a barbecue. This is one of the oldest northern Indian restaurants in KL, dating from the early 1970s. It is still run by the Jethwani family, whose business also imports the Indian artefacts you will see strategically placed around the restaurant.

Nasi Kandar Pelita
149 Jalan Ampang. Tel: 03-2162 5532. www.pelita.com.my Open:

Price per person for a three-course meal without drinks:
$ = under RM30
$$ = RM30–60
$$$ = RM60–90
$$$$ = over RM90

RIGHT: taking a break at Chinoz on the Park.

daily 24 hours. **$**
29 p257, E3
An outlet of the largest *nasi kandar* (Penang-style rice and curries) restaurant chain in Malaysia. Ask for the special *kuah campur* (mixed gravy), an assortment of a dozen kinds of curries doused on your white rice or *nasi briyani* (rice cooked with spices and ghee). Very popular with locals, as the food here is both good and cheap.

Spice of India
Lot 417A, Level 4, Suria KLCC. www.spiceofindia.com.my Tel: 03-2164 9221. Open: daily 11.30am–10.30pm. **$$$** 30 p257, D3
Red and yellow lamps cast a dreamy glow in this fine-dining northern Indian restaurant with some southern specialities. Chefs from India and Sri Lanka serve up a fabulous tandoori platter – with chicken, prawns and fish – as well as masala boneless fish and prawn curry. Wednesday is fish-head curry day. Carb-loving diners will go wild over the 13 types of Indian breads.

International

The Apartment Downtown
Lot 139, Ground Level, Suria KLCC. www.attheapartment.com Tel: 03-2166 2257. Open: daily 11am–10pm. **$$$**
31 p257, D3
The trendy ambience and occasional live music performances, rather than the food, are the main reasons to be here. That said, the green chicken curry, king prawn pasta and crunchy crêpes aren't bad at all. After your meal, linger around to enjoy views of the buzzing KLCC park.

Chinoz on the Park
Lot G47, Ground Level, Suria KLCC. Tel: 03-2166 8277. Open: daily 8am–midnight. **$$$** 32 p257, D3
Café and fine dining rolled into one. Young chef Hafiz studied with *enfant terrible* Marco Pierre White and it shows. The food here is excellent; the *dégustation* menu is recommended if you are swamped, as you will be. Restaurateur Teng Wee Jeh has made his mark – this is undoubtedly one of KL's top restaurants.

High Tide
Ground Level, Menara Taipan, Jalan Punchak, off Jalan P. Ramlee. Tel: 03-2072 4452. Open: Tue–Sun L & D. **$$$$**
33 p256, C4
Opened in 2009, this *haute cuisine* restaurant serves practically nothing but fish and seafood, which is flown in fresh every day and served impeccably. Whether you go for king fish, marron (Australian freshwater crayfish), Dover sole or roughy, High Tide will sweep you away.

Italian

Santini
Lot G458, Ground Level, Suria KLCC. Tel: 03-2382 0329. Open: daily 11am–midnight. **$$** 34 p257, D3
Highly recommended bistro with a view of the buzzing KLCC Park. Start with a beef carpaccio or breaded mussels, and move on to the gnocchi with gorgonzola cheese or seafood paella served in a cast-iron pan. End with the delightful panna cotta.

Italian/Japanese

Mezza Notte Italian Restaurant and Sushi Bar
28–40 Jalan Doraisamy, Asian Heritage Row. Tel: 03-2691 5668. Open: Mon–Sat L, daily D. **$$** (buffet lunch), **$$$** (à la carte)
35 p256, B3
A little schizophrenic in its offerings – both Italian and Japanese dishes under one roof – but it seems to work. The rainbow *futomaki* (sushi roll) is delightful, as is the signature Mezza Notte pizza with tomato, bresaola and arugula. Warm, gooey chocolate cake for dessert is recommended. Jazz band in attendance.

Japanese

Kampachi
Hotel Equatorial, Jalan Sultan Ismail. Tel: 03-2162 7777. Open: daily L & D. **$$** (set lunch, dinner), **$$$** (à la carte) 36 p257, D4
Still the finest Japanese restaurant in the city after several decades, with a wine cellar and a sushi counter. The sashimi is flown in fresh from Tokyo. Excellent soft-shell crab *maki* (rolled sushi), beef rolls with *enoki* mushrooms and grilled *unagi* (eel). Popular Sunday

LEFT: drinks at the Apartment Downtown.

brunch and Saturday semi-buffet.

Still Waters
Hotel Maya, 138 Jalan Ampang. Tel: 03-2711 8866. Open: daily L & D. **$$** (set lunch), **$$$** (à la carte) 37 p257, C/D3
Exquisite *sosaku* (creative) cuisine, combining Japanese and Western ingredients. Expect delicate dishes such as *den miso*-gratinated lamb, beef *wasabi* and pan-fried foie gras with daikon. For dessert, try the *pandan chawan mushi* (fragrant steamed egg custard).

Korean

Koryo Won
Lot 19, Arcade West, Main Lobby Hotel Mutiara, Level 2 Kompleks Antarabangsa, Jalan Sultan Ismail. Tel: 03-2142 7655. Open: daily L & D. **$$$** Off map
The first Korean restaurant in Malaysia is still going strong after three decades. Have the barbecue with beef and spare-ribs, accompanied by *kimchi* (pickled vegetables), tofu and spicy cockles. Its *samk yeh tang* (double-boiled chicken soup filled with ginseng and glutinous rice) and *dolsot bab* (boiled red rice in stone pot) are the ultimate comfort food - simply delectable.

Price per person for a three-course meal without drinks:
$ = under RM30
$$ = RM30–60
$$$ = RM60–90
$$$$ = over RM90

Malay

Madam Kwan's
Lot 421, Level 4, Suria KLCC. Tel: 03-2026 2297. Open: daily 10am–10pm. **$$** 38 p257, D3
The humble *nasi lemak* (rice cooked in coconut milk) served with chicken curry, anchovy chilli paste and other side dishes, goes upmarket here. Also delicious is the *nasi bojari*, colourful fried rice paired with crispy fried chicken, tamarind prawns and chicken curry or beef *rendang* (dry beef curry). The Cantonese noodles are recommended. Service is attentive and quick, though there might be a long wait for a table.

Middle Eastern

Bukhara
Lot 137, Level 1, Suria KLCC. Tel: 03-2168 8221. Open: daily 11am–11pm. **$$$** 39 p257, D3
Named after the old city that lies on the Silk Road in Uzbekistan, the restaurant features food from the Far East to the Middle East: baked chicken in filo pastry, Hyderabadi *briyani*, and seafood *la mian* (with hand-pulled noodles). The dining room is adorned with maps and sand features that recall the great trading thoroughfare of yore.

Modern European

Cilantro Restaurant and Wine Bar
MiCasa All Suite Hotel, 368B Jalan 1/68F, off Jalan Tun Razak. www.cilantrokl.com Tel: 03-2179 8048. Open: Mon–Sat D, Fri L only. **$$$$** Off map
Acclaimed chef Takashi Kimura turns out award-winning, exquisite dishes combining French and Japanese cooking styles and ingredients. His *wasabi*-crusted *wagyu* cheek is wonderful, while the *anago* risotto features saltwater eel fried as well as braised in a port reduction with *sake*. Friday set lunches, matched with wines, are popular. This is KL's top restaurant, hands down.

Bars

Bar Italia
29 Jalan Berangan. www.baritaliakl.com Tel: 03-2144 4499. Off map.
This snazzy Italian restaurant/bar offers decent food as well as a great selection of wines and cocktails. You can hang out with the locals on the rooftop or at the bar, where you can admire the gold-plated, hand-crafted espresso machine.

Bar SaVanh
62–64 Jalan Doraisamy, Asian Heritage Row. Tel: 03-2697 1180. 1 p256, B3
With long opium-den style sofas, Buddhist sculptures, a fish pond, candles and incense, this place is beautiful and trendy.

Luna Bar
Pacific Regency Hotel Apartments, Jalan Punchak. Tel: 03-2332 7777. 2 p256, C4
A rooftop outdoor bar with a pool in the middle and views to die for are this exclusive chill-out venue's main draws.

The Pub
Shangri-La Hotel, Jalan Sultan Ismail. Tel: 03-2074 3905. 3 p257, C4
A traditional English pub tucked away in a corner, with pub grub, darts, pool and sports action on TV. A great place to drink, chat and relax. Happy hour should not be missed.

Skybar
Top floor, Traders Hotel. www.skybar.com.my Tel: 03-2332 9888. 4 p257, D4
With spectacular views of the Petronas Twin Towers and the city, this is a comfortable, loungy, cushiony bar, with a pool in the middle. Perfect for tired toes.

Vietnamese/Laotian

CoChine Café and Restaurant
62–64 Jalan Doraisamy, Asian Heritage Row. Tel: 03-2697 1180. Open: Mon-Fri noon–10pm, Sat 5–10pm. **$$$** 40 p256, B3
This beautiful restaurant oozes tranquillity, with soothing water features and elegant statues. The *cha-gio* or Vietnamese spring rolls are succulent and fresh and the Laotian *larb kai* is a delicious chicken dish marinated in lemon juice and chilli, served with roasted pine nuts and mint. On the same site as Bar SaVanh.

KAMPUNG BARU

Stubbornly opposed to modernisation and clinging to its old ways, this "new village", smack in the city centre, retains much of its old communal atmosphere. Its Malay Muslim character is strongly evident in the clothing, food, lifestyle and architecture found here

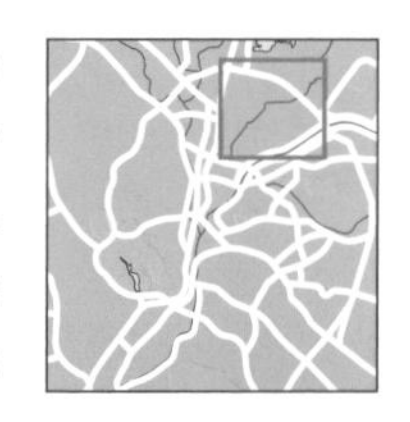

Main Attractions

JALAN RAJA ALANG
KAMPUNG BARU MOSQUE
RAMADAN BAZAAR
NATIONAL THEATRE
TITIWANGSA LAKE GARDENS

Maps and Listings

MAP OF KAMPUNG BARU, PAGE 130
RESTAURANTS, PAGE 149

When the 90-hectare (220-acre) Malay Agricultural Settlement of Kampung Baru (or Bahru) was first established in the late 1890s, it was organised as a Malay *kampung* – a village laid out in a communal setting with houses of wood and *attap* thatching clustered around a common community hall and mosque or *surau* (prayer hall), with a cemetery and school nearby. There were also paddy fields, which provided the main source of food and income. Communal ties were very strong, with families in each house sharing the same space for everything, from sleeping and eating to hosting visitors.

Today, the area remains almost exclusively Malay. Many members of the community are in fact Indonesian, particularly from Java, who rent space from the original local settlers, who have moved out. Many of the traditional wooden houses are slowly being replaced by brick structures and even high-rises. The roads are narrow and some areas have come to resemble shantytowns.

Property and identity

There have been numerous efforts to modernise and develop Kampung Baru, but these have largely been unsuccessful. One reason is that when a title holder of the land here passes away, the property is divided equally among all the children according to Syariah law; getting a consensus on decisions is therefore nigh impossible. There are also concerns within the community itself about restricting ownership to Malays, as residents are divided over whether to develop the area or not. Many purists feel that development could enroach on Kampung Baru's

LEFT: Friday worshippers at the Masjid Kampung Baru. **BELOW:** Malay-style *kampung* houses against the KL skyline.

Malay identity and the rights of the current landowners. In addition, there is distrust of Kuala Lumpur city hall, which has been overruling the administrative board that represents the community. Nonetheless, when the famous Pasar Minggu (weekend market), located just off Jalan Raja Muda Musa, burned down in 2004, it provided a catalyst (and excuse) for the government to launch a RM80 million redevelopment project to turn the area into a cultural attraction. Still, the neighbourhood has a definite charm of its own and prides itself on being the last Malay bastion a multiculutural city riddled with steel and glass.

Jalan Raja Alang ⓮

Religious expression in Kampung Baru is particularly lively, especially on the busy **Jalan Raja Alang**. Many households, besides hanging above their doorways the "*assalamu 'alaikum*" greeting in Arabic script, also decorate their homes with prayer mats and calligraphic works of Koranic verse. Boys who study at the local *madarasah* (religious schools) sport a *songkok* on their heads and an elasticised *sampin* (a wrap worn over trousers) while girls are clad in the *tudung* (headscarf) and traditional *baju kurung* (sarong with long-sleeved tunic).

ABOVE: Kampung Baru Mosque. **BELOW:** white-turbanned Islamic schoolboys at Kampung Baru.

Kampung Baru Mosque ⓯

Address: Junction of Jalan Raja Alang and Jalan Raja Abdullah
Opening Hrs: daily 9am–5pm, except prayer times
Entrance fee: free
Transport: LRT Kampung Baru

A prominent religious landmark in this neighbourhood is the white-domed **Kampung Baru Mosque** or Masjid Kampung Baru at the junction of two busy streets, Jalan Raja Alang and Jalan Raja Abdullah. When it was built, in 1924, it was one of the first concrete structures to be erected in the area.

Almost half a century later, the mosque became the rallying point of the May 13 Incident *(see page 37)*, and has become synonymous with racial tension and protest. During the *Reformasi* period of the late 1990s, the mosque witnessed some of

Ramadan Feasting

Throughout the fasting month of Ramadan, the folks at Kampung Baru get together daily to do community service in the form of a massive cookout of *bubur lambuk* (a peppery rice porridge cooked with minced beef). A portion of it is distributed free to needy people while the rest is sold.This tradition began in the 1950s, and today, during the Ramadan month, giant pots can be seen lining Jalan Raja Abdullah and outside the Kampung Baru Mosque, which reputedly has the best in the city. A phenomenal amount of *bubur lambuk* is consumed during this month; in 2006, a record-setting 30,000 packets were snapped up within two hours by hungry diners.

the riot police's more violent crowd-dispersal methods: tear gas was fired into the mosque to drive out protestors taking refuge inside. Then, in 2006, non-violent protests against US support of Israeli attacks on Lebanon and Palestine, as well as against the Danish newspaper that published caricatures of the Prophet Muhammad, were staged at Masjid Kampung Baru. Fortunately, most of the time, peace reigns.

Ramadan bazaar

Kampung Baru is the best place to experience traditional, home-cooked Malay food. Recipes have been handed down from one generation to the next, and no Malay restaurant in Kuala Lumpur can come close to the cooking standard achieved here. All the regional favourites can be savoured, from the rice-and-curry *nasi padang* (originally from Sumatra) to the famous Kajang *satay*, as well as variations of the spicy noodle dish *laksa* from the northern states of Penang and Kedah. For a more earthy culinary experience, head to Jalan Raja Alang for a Sunday breakfast of *nasi lemak*. All along the road, makeshift stalls dish out plates of fragrant coconut rice from large steaming vats, together with side dishes like hot and sweet *sambal* paste, sliced cucumber, omelette and fried anchovies.

The best time to visit Kampung Baru is in the evening during the annual Ramadan fasting month. At the Pasar Ramadan 3 (Ramadan market), which springs to life from 4pm during this month, the streets are filled with more than 200 itinerant food stalls huddled beneath colourful canopies. A good place to begin wandering around is just outside Masjid Kampung Baru. There is an air of festivity as Muslims on their way home from the office stop here to buy dinner for the *buka puasa* (breaking of fast), which coincides with the *maghrib* evening time of prayer at around 7.30pm. Restaurants here overflow with customers sitting at tables, eagerly waiting

ABOVE: the exterior of the Guru Nanak Darbaar Gurdwara Sahib.

During Ramadan, the ninth month of the Islamic calendar, Muslims refrain from eating and drinking between sunrise and sunset. It is also a time to spend with families and friends, who will often come together for the evening meal. The date of Ramadan varies – moving back about 10 days each year – as it is determined by the lunar calendar; check with the Tourism Malaysia website (www.tourism.gov.my) for the exact dates.

for the announcement of *buka puasa* on the radio or TV before digging into their food.

Guru Nanak Darbaar Gurdwara Sahib ⓰

Even in this overwhelmingly Malay Muslim enclave there is a surprise that reflects the multiculturalism of Kuala Lumpur. At the corner of Jalan Alang and Jalan Raja Bot is a large building that might be mistaken for a mosque but is actually a Sikh temple or *gurdwara* – the **Guru Nanak Darbaar Gurdwara Sahib** (open only to worshippers). After the 1950s, many local Sikh temples started incorporating Indo-Persian architectural elements such as domes, which is why this temple blends so easily into the largely Muslim neighbourhood.

This temple's five pumpkin-shaped domes are adorned at the base with lotus petals made of concrete, with the central dome covered in yellow mosaic. Within is a prayer hall that is the largest in Southeast Asia. This is where the Sikh holy book, the *Guru Granth Sahib*, is kept.

ABOVE: the state-of-the-art National Theatre. **BELOW:** paintings on display at the National Art Gallery.

National Theatre ⓱

Address: Jalan Tun Razak, near Jalan Pahang roundabout, www.istanabudaya.gov.my
Tel: 03-4026 5555
Opening Hrs: check performance schedule
Entrance Fee: charge for performances
Transport: LRT Kampung Baru or Monorail Titiwangsa then taxi/bus: Intrakota 10, 49 or 49A

Just north of Kampung Baru along Jalan Tun Razak is a trio of government buildings constructed during the 1990s – the National Theatre, Gallery and Library. The first you come to, near the roundabout, is the **National Theatre** (Istana Budaya), where major local and international theatre and dance productions are staged; check its website for current listings of programmes. Looking like a rather overblown grand Malay house, its Malaysian architect, Muhammad Kamar Ya'akub, fashioned this theatre after the *wau*, the traditonal giant Kelantan kite, poised in mid-flight. The building's roof is inspired by the *sirih junjung*, which are betel leaves arrayed in a particular manner for use in traditional Malay ceremonies.

National Art Gallery ⓲

Address: 2 Jalan Temerloh, off Jalan Tun Razak, www.artgallery.gov.my
Tel: 03-4025 4990
Opening Hrs: daily 10am–6pm, closed on public holidays
Entrance Fee: free
Transport: LRT Kampung Baru or Monorail Titiwangsa, then taxi/bus rapidKL B114 or Len Seng 169, 165 or 195, or Intrakota 14D

In contrast, the building beside the theatre is a true architectural gem – the **National Art Gallery** (Balai Senilukis Negara). Here, elements of traditional Malay architecture are beautifully incorporated into a completely modern structure. Spread over

13,000 sq metres (140,000 sq ft), the multistorey venue houses five art galleries, with the main gallery on the ground floor showcasing works from the 2,500-piece permanent collection. There is also an outdoor exhibition area, a creative centre for workshops, and a trendy café and resource centre. The permanent collection is showing signs of neglect, but it's worth the trip out here if there is a good exhibition on.

National Library ⓳

Address: 232 Jalan Tun Razak
Tel: 03-2687 1700, www.pnm.my
Opening Hrs: Tue–Sat 10am–7pm, Sun 10am–6pm, closed on public holidays
Entrance Fee: free
Transport: LRT Kampung Baru or Monorail Titiwangsa, then taxi/bus RapidKL B114

East of the National Art Gallery, also along Jalan Tun Razak, is the city's **National Library** (Perpustakaan Negara), which is shaped like a *tengkolok*, the traditional headgear of a Malay man, and inlaid with blue tiles that are intended to resemble the rich texture of *songket*, the gold-threaded material from which the headgear is usually made.

Titiwangsa Lake Gardens ⓴

To the north of this clutch of buildings is a large expanse of greenery known as **Titiwangsa Lake Gardens** or Taman Tasik Titiwangsa (daily 24 hours; free). Covering some 46 hectares (114 acres) of parkland, this popular recreational space, accessed via either Jalan Termeloh or Jalan Kuantan, has jogging trails, a children's playground, a lovely lake with paddleboats and canoes for hire, a sports complex and even horseriding (on weekends only) within an enclosed paddock. Weekends see the most crowds here, with people either picnicking on its lawns or exercising furiously. ❑

ABOVE: one of the five distinctive pumpkin-shaped domes of the Guru Nanak Darbaar Gurdwara Sahib. caption.

RESTAURANTS

Indian

An-Nur Briyani Gam Johor Kampung Baru
15 Jalan Raja Muda Musa, Kampung Baru. Mobile tel: 012-234 3310. Open: Tue–Sun 11am–11pm. **$** ㊶ p257, C2
Nasi briyani gam, originally from the southern state of Johor, is the house speciality here – basmati rice cooked with spices, then steamed together with curried beef, mutton or chicken for the final few minutes for full flavour. Available on Wednesday and Sunday; the usual *nasi briyani* is served on other days. Try also its excellent *sup bandung muar* (yellow noodles in a tomato-based gravy).

Indonesian

Natrabu
3 Lorong Raja Uda 1, off Jalan Raja Muda Abdul Aziz, Kampung Baru. Tel: 03-2691 2701. Open: daily 11am–11.30pm. **$$** ㊷ p257, D2
This is supposedly the best place for *nasi padang* in town, and also the most expensive. Try the *rendang minang* (beef minang style), *ikan teri goring, begedel* (potato and meat balls), *ayam pop* (fried chicken with chilli dip) and the interesting *dendeng alpokat* (avocado juice and chocolate sauce).

Malay

CT Garden Nasi Lemak
Jalan Dewan Sultan Sulaiman, Kampung Baru. Mobile tel: 012-244 4911. Open: daily 6.30pm–5.30am. **$** ㊸ p256, C3
When the craving strikes, people head in droves for the biggest *nasi lemak* (coconut rice) stall in the city, complete with a stunning view of the Twin Towers. The *nasi lemak* is served in a small banana leaf with *sambal* (chilli paste) and a variety of sides, such as deep-fried anchovies, quail eggs or fried chicken. The sambal packs a punch but you'll see people scoffing more than one packet.

Nasi Lemak Antarabangsa
7C Jalan Raja Muda Musa. Tel: No telephone. Open: daily 6pm–5am. **$** ㊹ p257, C2
One of the most revered spots in town, this *nasi lemak* joint has been enjoyed by prime ministers, clubbers and simple folk for ten years. You can't miss it, as it is always, always packed to the gills.

Price per person for a three-course meal without drinks.
***$** = under RM30, **$$** = RM30–60,*
***$$$** = RM60–90,*
***$$$$** = over RM90.*

WELCOME to CLUB
DiGi

BUKIT BINTANG

You can shop til you drop in Bukit Bintang, at which point there is a host of eateries where you can recharge. Alternatively, head to Jalan Conlay, where a heritage museum and a craft centre provide welcome diversions

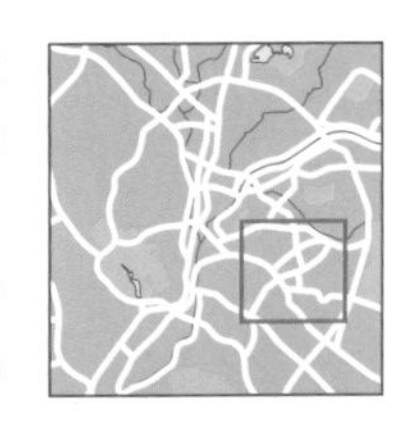

Main Attractions

BINTANG WALK
PAVILION KUALA LUMPUR
STARHILL GALLERY
HUTONG FOOD COURT, LOT 10
BERJAYA TIMES SQUARE
JALAN ALOR
BUKIT CEYLON
BADAN WARISAN MALAYSIA
KUALA LUMPUR CRAFT COMPLEX

Maps and Listings

MAP OF BUKIT BINTANG, PAGE 152
SHOPPING, PAGE 158
RESTAURANTS AND BARS, PAGE 160–3

Back in the 1950s and 1960s you could sing along with Julie Andrews in *The Sound of Music* or root for Charleston Heston's Ben Hur under a starlit sky at one of the open-air cinemas at **Bukit Bintang**. Watching a movie with the cool evening breeze blowing against your face was one of the things for which the Bukit Bintang of yesteryear was noted. Besides the open-air theatres, there were the regular cinemas – Pavilion and Cathay – as well as cabarets and *joget* (Malay dance) clubs, all providing entertainment for city folk.

Much of that is gone, as is the carefree optimism that marked the pre-independence years. Nonetheless, it is Bukit Bintang's tradition of seeking pleasure that prompted development giant YTL Corp to inject huge amounts of money, and both life and style, into a massive redevelopment of the area in 1999. Even back then, Bukit Bintang had the largest concentration of shops, hotels, eateries and nightlife venues. But it was fast being overwhelmed by grime, congestion and vice, not to mention competition from large malls like Suria KLCC and Mid Valley Megamall.

LEFT: the bright lights of Bintang Walk.
RIGHT: taking a stroll down Jalan Bukit Bintang.

Bintang Walk ❶

YTL Corp had a gameplan to rejuvenate Bukit Bintang. After building prime shopping malls like Lot 10 and Starhill Gallery as well as the JW Marriott Hotel, YTL put into place its masterstroke, **Bintang Walk**, a broad landscaped pedestrian boulevard lined with sidewalk cafés, fine dining restaurants, boutiques and live music establishments. Within six months, the hip, trendy and moneyed returned – and have never left.

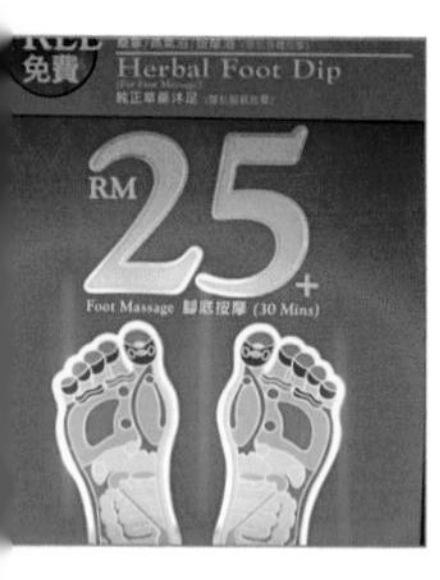

ABOVE: foot reflexology services available along Bukit Bintang.

The 1km (1/2-mile) Bintang Walk begins at the **Pavilion Kuala Lumpur**, a modern, swanky mall on the intersection of Jalan Bukit Bintang and Jalan Raja Chulan, and stretches all the way to the **Lot 10** mall on Jalan Sultan Ismail. The upgrading has also spilled over into the wider Bukit Bintang area, incorporating the T-junction formed by Jalan Sultan Ismail and Jalan Imbi. In fact, with the slew of new speciality shops and serviced apartments, the whole area has gone upmarket.

With its central business location, pen-pushers and number-crunchers make up the bulk of the area's weekday traffic, but come evenings, weekends and school holidays, Bukit Bintang is taken over by young people and families. The weekend nightlife is buzzing, with a wide variety of restaurants, bars and clubs drawing large crowds. New Year's Eve is especially festive here, with roads blocked off, and a street concert and fireworks display taking centre stage.

SHOPPING CENTRES

Shopping is, of course, the major draw of the area, and the malls here

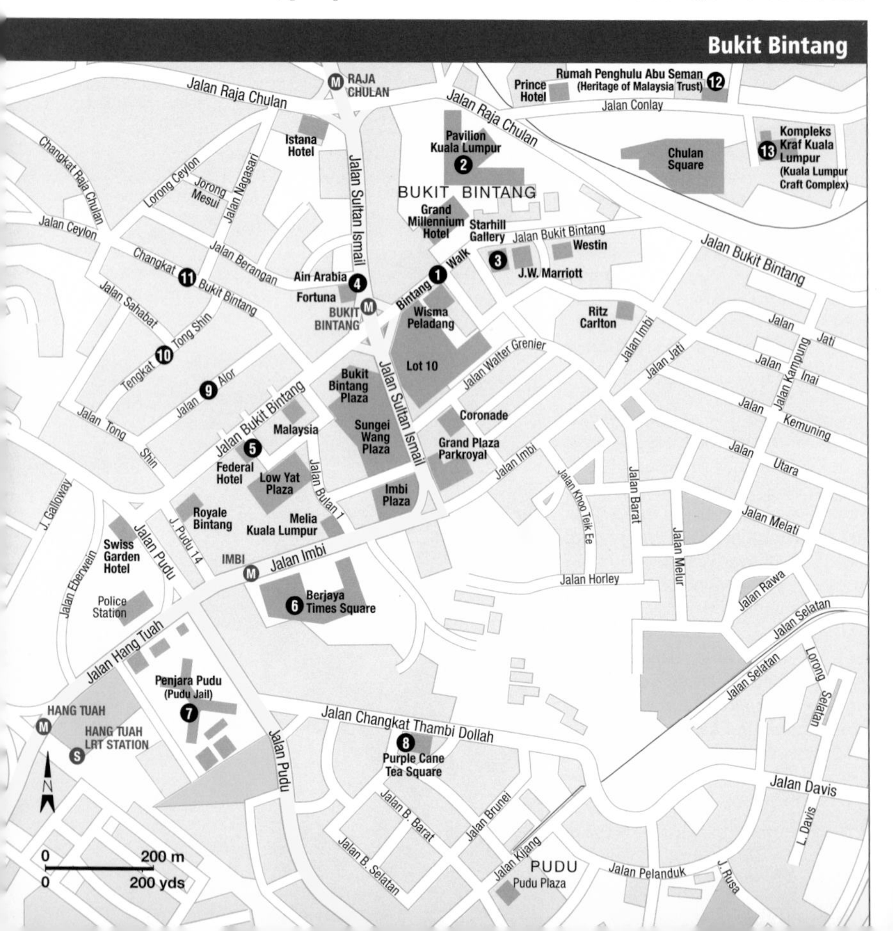

are either luxury (**Pavilion, Starhill Gallery**), mid-range (**Lot 10** and **Berjaya Times Square**) or downmarket (**Bukit Bintang Plaza** and **Sungei Wang Plaza**). For bargain computers and peripherals head to **Imbi Plaza** and **Low Yat Plaza.** In addition, there are also streetside designer boutiques and stores. Note: see Shopping listings *(page 158)* and Shopping chapter *(pages 68–71)* for more details on what and where to buy.

Pavilion Kuala Lumpur ❷

Address: 168 Jalan Bukit Bintang, www.pavilion-kl.com
Tel: 03-2118 8833,
Opening Hrs: 10am–10pm
Entrance Fee: free
Transport: Monorail Bukit Bintang

Pavilion Kuala Lumpur is the most recent addition on this strip. This glamorous, gargantuan mall was not built without controvery, as the venerable Bukit Bintang Girls School, Kuala Lumpur's oldest school, was demolished to make way for it. Protests and petitions from ex-students and heritage buffs failed to stop the developers from going ahead. Check out the food court in the basement. Food Republic serves up very satisfying international and local fare.

Starhill Gallery ❸

Address: 181 Jalan Bukit Bintang, www.starhillgallery.com
Tel: 03-2782 3855,
Opening Hrs: 10am–10pm
Entrance Fee: free
Transport: Monorail Bukit Bintang

The trend among mall developers has been to dedicate whole floors or zones to specialised retail segments. Nowhere is this more evident than in the sharp and luxurious mall called the **Starhill Gallery**. Here, entire floors are dedicated to food and drink – spanning a range of international eateries and fancy bars – and health and beauty shops, including spas. In addition there is an arts floor comprising several art galleries – well worth a visit – as well as stores selling antiques and furniture.

Among the designers who have had a hand in Starhill are New York's famous mall designer David Rockwell and the Tokyo-based Design Spirits Company led by Yuhkichi

TIP

When entering a Starhill Gallery lift, note that it does not use numbers for its different floors. Instead, the floors are labelled as Feast and Relish (restaurants and bars); Indulge, Adorn and Explore (clothing, accessories and other items); Pamper (health and beauty); and Muse (the arts floor).

BELOW: buskers pull in the crowds at Bintang Walk.

ABOVE: busy cross junction at Bukit Bintang with Berjaya Times Square on the left.
BELOW: Cosmo's World indoor theme park at Berjaya Times Square.

Kawai. Inside the mall, "customer service ambassadors" and the concierge desk make sure customers are assured of five-star service. Starhill is also linked to the luxury **JW Marriott** and **Ritz Carlton** hotels by covered walkways.

Hutong Food Court

The renovated **Hutong Food Court** in the basement of Lot 10 is the local foodies' favourite for pork dishes. Enticingly dubbed "lard land", this is a one-stop for the best KL has to offer, with reputable, established stalls hawking old-time favourites like Hokkien *mee* (thick noodles in dark sauce with pork crackling), *bak kut teh* (herbal pork soup), *siu bao* (roasted pork dumplings), pork porridge and much more. Prices are very reasonable, but only venture in if you are really hungry.

Arab quarter

A little Arab quarter has been set up along **Jalan Berangan**, off Jalan Sultan Ismail, to provide a home-away-from-home experience to tourists from the Gulf region. Malaysia has been seriously wooing high-spending Middle Eastern tourists since 2003, when it suddenly saw a massive 40 percent jump in visitors from that region. This is largely because Arabs face difficulties with immigration officers in security-obsessed Western countries and see Malaysia as a Muslim-friendly travel destination – you will see women in top-to-toe flowing black *hijabs* all over the city.

Ain Arabia ❹ – or what should more accurately be called al-Ain al-Arabia, which means Eye of Arabia – encompasses an enclave of Middle Eastern restaurants, barbers and beauty salons, a mini-market selling Arabic provisions such as tobacco, perfumed oils and incense wood chips, as well as souvenir shops and travel agents. The **Sahara Tent** restaurant (*see page 162*) on the ground floor of Hotel Fortuna even has a wide-canopied traditional tent used by Arab nomads, under which *shisha* pipes may be smoked before or after your kebabs and *tabouleh*. The peak period for Middle Eastern tourists – mostly honeymooners and families – is from June to September. Middle Eastern restaurants catering to this market have sprung up throughout the city.

Of the numerous hotels in Bukit Bintang, one that remains an enduring symbol of the city is the **Federal Hotel** ❺ (www.fhihotels.com) at No 35 Jalan Bukit Bintang. Completed just three days before Malaya's independence from the British was declared, it was built at the request of the country's first prime minister, Tunku Abdul Rahman, to house guests for the Merdeka celebrations. It was the grandest hotel around then and its revolving restaurant and nightclub were packed every night. Today, the Federal Hotel, although extensively renovated, lacks the spit and polish of the city's other luxury hotels.

Berjaya Times Square ❻

Address: 1 Jalan Imbi, www.times squarekl.com
Tel: 1-300 888 988
Opening Hrs: daily 10am–10pm
Entrance Fee: free
Transport: Monorail Imbi

At Jalan Imbi, just parallel to Jalan Bukit Bintang, looms the mammoth **Berjaya Times Square**. Currently the largest shopping mall in downtown Kuala Lumpur, with more than 1,000 shops, it also provides ample non-retail diversions like a 48-lane bowling alley and the 12,000 sq metre (130,000 sq ft) indoor **Cosmo's World** theme park (tel: 03-2117 3118; Mon–Fri noon–10pm, Sat–Sun, public holidays and school holidays 10am–10pm; charge), the largest indoor theme park in Asia.

Jalan Imbi

A stone's throw from Berjaya Times Square along **Jalan Imbi** are clusters of hawker stalls and restaurants serving excellent local and Chinese fare. Apart from the makeshift stalls lined up along the street, try the Cantonese fried noodles with freshwater prawns or fried beef *hor fun* noodles at the **Soo Kee Restaurant** on Medan Imbi, off Jalan Imbi; and the pork meat ball noodles at **Kedai Kopi Weng Hing**. The pricey but consistently good Cantonese **Restoran Oversea** is another good bet *(for all these, see pages 160–3)*.

Pudu Jail

Pudu, which is located south of Bukit Bintang, was once tin mine land and covered by thick rainforest, hence its Cantonese name which still lingers today, *Poon San Pa*, which means "half-jungle". The main road, Jalan Pudu, terminates at one end near Petaling Street in the anarchic **Puduraya**, the city's major bus station, where you can get buses and taxis to anywhere in the city and most places farther out of town too.

Occupying prime real estate on the corner of Jalan Pudu and

Prostitution was once rampant in the Bukit Bintang and Pudu areas – a trade that now hovers on the fringes of the area. The old Bukit Bintang still exists, but in small, scattered pockets. The residents of the older flats have moved out and have been replaced by migrant labourers, who hang out at Jalan Alor and its vicinity.

BELOW: Pudu Jail's prison walls.

Jalan Hang Tuah is **Pudu Jail** ❼ (Penjara Pudu), one of the oldest colonial prisons in Southeast Asia, which housed some of the country's most notorious criminals from the time it was built in the 1893 until the prisoners were transferred out in 1996. After that, the building briefly served as a prison museum. Fascinated crowds used to gape at exhibits of items once used for punishment – like a wooden frame and harness to which prisoners would be strapped with their buttocks exposed before being whipped with a *rotan* (rattan cane). Malaysian law allows caning as a means of punishment, something which civil- rights movements in the country are fighting hard to abolish.

In the meantime commercial interests have won out – as with everything else in Bukit Bintang – and today, the prison has been earmarked for demolition, sparking an outcry among artists, conservationists and architects. Developers plan to build another shopping mall, to capitalize on the site's prime location next to Berjaya Times Square, as well as an apartment block. What's left of the prison is being torn down in phases.

ABOVE: silverwork engraving of a *wau* (kite), showing aspects of Malaysian heritage. **BELOW:** the Kuala Lumpur Craft Complex has a vast assortment of handcrafted souvenirs to buy.

Purple Cane Tea Square

From Jalan Pudu turn left into Jalan Changkat Thambi Dollah to reach the rather weary-looking shopping centre called **Shaw Parade**. As with the rest of Pudu, this is happy hunting ground for photographers – everything from equipment and accessories to cleaning and repair services is available. On the second level at L1-01 is **Purple Cane Tea Square** (www.purplecane.com.my; tel: 03-2145 4131; daily 11am–9.30pm) ❽ the largest retail outlet of a chain that sells a range of Chinese teas, teapots and accessories.

Purple Cane also has a Tea Art Learning Centre for training keen tea aficionados in various topics – from tea identification to teapot history and the art of brewing tea. Tourists can do a quick 45-minute course (book one day beforehand, charges apply); the really keen can opt for a 10-lesson elementary course for which a certificate is presented. There are also intermediate and advanced level courses, where you master intricacies from the art of distinguishing between fine teas to the collecting of precious teapots.

Jalan Alor and Tengkat Tong Shin

Just on the other side of Jalan Bukit Bintang and parallel to it is **Jalan Alor** ❾, which was once a paradise for pleasures of the flesh, but is now more famous for its pleasures of the palate. On offer is mainly Chinese fare such as noodles and rice, but there is the odd south Indian stall selling *roti canai* (flaky bread served with curry) and Malay stalls where aromatic *satay* is barbecued. Making a choice can be overwhelming, but you cannot really go wrong with the food here. At night, an additional row of makeshift hawker stalls appears in front of the shops, so that you would sometimes be dining while pressed up close to the cars inching their way along the road.

There is more good food along **Tengkat Tong Shin** ⑩, which is parallel to Jalan Alor. Tengkat Tong Shin has joined the 21st century in recent years, with the arrival of a string of hip backpacker hotels, cafés and pubs that spill over onto the adjoining Changkat Bukit Bintang.

Bukit Ceylon

Changkat Bukit Bintang ⑪ is part of the area known as **Bukit Ceylon** (Ceylon Hill), long a trendy nightlife venue, particularly at weekends, with slick eateries and bars – like the **Frangipani** and **Bijan** restaurants *(see pages 161 and 162)*. Many of these occupy charming old-style bungalows which have been artfully renovated to attract the city's chi chi crowd. The rest of Bukit Ceylon is taken up by luxury condos.

Bukit Ceylon derived its name from the Ceylonese Tamils who set up home in this area during the colonial period. Recruited by the British to fill administrative positions in the colonial government, Ceylonese Tamils were an insular group who socialised little with the wider Indian community until after independence.

Northeast of the Bukit Bintang area, away from the frenzy, are some attractions on **Jalan Conlay**, a quiet section of the city dotted with old bungalows built on sprawling grounds. While similar to those that characterise Jalan Ampang, these buildings are less ostentatious.

Heritage of Malaysia Trust ⑫

Address: 2 Jalan Stonor, www.badanwarisan.org.my
Tel: 03-2144 9273
Opening Hrs: Mon–Sat 10am–5.30pm
Entrance Fee: free
Transport: Monorail Raja Chulan

At the corner of Jalan Conlay and Jalan Stonor is a bungalow that dates back to 1925 and today houses the **Heritage of Malaysia Trust** or Badan Warisan Malaysia. This is a non-governmental organisation that works mainly through advocacy and education for the preservation and conservation of the country's built heritage.

In its grounds is a stunning traditional Malay timber house *(see page 97)* from the northern state of Kedah, the **Rumah Penghulu Abu Seman** (tours Mon–Sat 11am and 3pm; charge). This finely crafted structure was dismantled and relocated piecemeal to Kuala Lumpur, where it was restored by the organisation as a showpiece to raise awareness of Malaysia's fast disappearing heritage. Originally constructed by Penghulu Abu Seman bin Nayan, the chief of a local village, the house's three main sections were built at different periods between the mid 1920s and early 1930s.

Badan Warisan also has a well-stocked **resource centre** (Tue–Sat

EAT

There is excellent street food to be found along Jalan Alor, which is lined with traditional Chinese coffee shops like Dragon View and Wong Ah Wah. There is more good food along parellel street Tengkat Tong Shin, particularly at the roadside Ngau Kee Beef Noodles (daily 6pm–2am), which serves a famous beef noodle soup topped with minced meat.

BELOW: the Frangipani restaurant in Changat Bukit Bintang (Bukit Ceylon) also hosts a hip bar.

SHOPPING

You can buy almost anything in Bukit Bintang, from fashion to electronics to Malayian treasures.

Electronics

Low Yat Plaza
7 Jalan Bintang, off Jalan Bukit Bintang. Tel: 03-2148 3651. www.plazalowyat.com p260, A2
The KL mecca for anything IT. Five floors of everything imaginable for computers, cameras, phones and their accessories. Duty-free too.

Fashion

Malaysian Designers
Yellow Zone, Lot F82-88, Level 1, Sungei Wang Plaza, Jalan Sultan Ismail. Tel: 03-2144 1557. p260, A2
This row of funky shops features emerging and established Malaysian fashion brands and designers. Clothes are quirky and affordable, with a varied selection for both women and men.

Malls

Berjaya Times Square
1 Jalan Imbi. www.timessquarekl.com Tel: 03-2144 9820. p260, A2
A massive 900-outlet mall selling mainly medium-priced and lower-end goods. There's also a cineplex and a large indoor theme park, Cosmo's World.

Bukit Bintang Plaza
111 Jalan Bukit Bintang. Tel: 03-2148 7411. p260, A2
Adjacent to Sungei Wang Plaza, the shops here offer an astounding variety of audiovisual equipment, cameras, bridal outfits, watches, clothes, footwear, batik, leather goods, electrical appliances, books and anything you can imagine.

Lot 10
50 Jalan Sultan Ismail. Tel: 03-2141 0500. p260, A/B2
This green giant, linked to Sungei Wang Plaza, has a curvilinear atrium around which walkways go past upmarket shops selling everything from Thai silks to club wear. The mall's anchor tenant is Japanese store Isetan, which offers a good variety of clothes. The Hutong Food Court in the basement specialises in pork.

Pavilion Kuala Lumpur
168 Jalan Bukit Bintang. www.pavilion-kl.com Tel: 03-2143 8088. p260, A1
The gargantuan mall is anchored by department stores Parkson and Tangs, and has specialist outlets like Kiehl's, Thomas Pink, Shanghai Tang and Diane Von Furstenberg.

Starhill Gallery
181 Jalan Bukit Bintang. www.starhillgallery.com Tel: 03-2782 3855. p260, B1
A glitzy, exclusive mall for high-end fashion labels. Check out the Louis Vuitton Global Store. There are seven themed floors, covering food, art, fashion, and health and beauty.

Sungei Wang Plaza
Jalan Sultan Ismail. www.sungeiwang.com Tel: 03-2144 9988. p260, A2
This popular mall, next to Bukit Bintang Plaza, has 500-odd retail shops with moderately priced products and services. A good place for bargains. Check out the Malaysian *haute couture* on the first floor.

Textiles

Jendela Batik
F21, Explore Floor, Starhill Gallery, 181 Jalan Bukit Bintang. www.jendela-kl.com Tel: 03-2144 9189. p260, B1
Malaysia's traditional textile work is taken to cutting-edge levels at this exclusive atelier. Designs combine traditional and contemporary motifs in breathtaking colours. The quality justifies the higher prices here.

Sim Tan Fine Art
Bukit Ceylon area. Tel: 012-273 9008 (call for address and appointment).
This reclusive but attentive collector has some of the best traditional textiles, jewellery and silverware in Southeast Asia. He also has Peranakan and Malay jewellery and tribal pieces from Nagaland in India.

LEFT: all-electronic at Low Yat Plaza.

10am–4pm; charge; by appointment only) filled with publications, slides and photographs, and a **gift shop** (Mon–Sat 9am–5.30pm) which sells a range of cards and collectables. Visit its excellent website for more information on talks and field trips that it organises for members (fee applies). The website also has a section on some of Kuala Lumpur's historic areas; while the information is dated, the historical data is nonetheless interesting.

ABOVE: late-night eating at Changkat Bukit Bintang.

Kuala Lumpur Craft Complex ⓭

Address: Seksyen 63, Jalan Conlay, www.kraftangan.gov.my
Tel: 03-2162 7459
Opening Hrs: 9am–7pm
Entrance Fee: free
Transport: Monorail Raja Chulan

Further along Jalan Conlay is the sprawling **Kuala Lumpur Craft Complex** (Kompleks Kraf Kuala Lumpur). With its modern and ostentatious interpretation of Malay *kampung* (village) architecture, it's not quite in tune with the subdued tone of the rest of Jalan Conlay. The 3.6-hectare (9-acre) one-stop centre is a gallery and shopping centre for quality – albeit expensive – Malaysian arts and crafts; in short, a government-run upmarket version of Central Market.

The complex also houses the vast **Karyaneka**, a government agency that markets handicrafts produced by cottage industries in Malaysia. With the national emphasis on industrialisation, arts and crafts have taken a step back, and many rich legacies of early craftspeople have been lost. Besides providing an outlet for sales, the government is trying to preserve the country's artistic heritage by organising workshops and providing financial assistance and entrepreneurial training.

Karyaneka has a textile and ready-wear section, where you can see craftspeople working on intricate gold-embroidered *songket* fabric and a souvenir shop where other handicrafts are sold. At its small but interesting **Craft Museum** (daily 9am–5.30pm; charge), exhibits change three times a year.

Walk to the back of the market, where the most interesting sections are found. The **Craft Village** cluster houses artisans who demonstrate various styles of batik artwork, claywork and woodcraft. Behind the craft village is the **Artists' Colony** (daily 9am–6pm), a cluster of 22 huts housing new and established artists who work at their art here and also conduct classes for visitors. Like the artisans at the Craft Village, they are happy to chat and exchange stories; most of their artwork is for sale too.

Also on site are a café, shuttle buses to the complex from nearby hotels, a currency exchange outlet and an information desk where you can book a taxi. ❑

TIP

The Kuala Lumpur Craft Complex hosts National Craft Week, and from time to time, craft-making demonstrations, cultural shows, textile exhibitions and fashions shows. Check the Tourism Malaysia calendar for dates (www.tourism.gov.my).

BEST RESTAURANTS AND BARS

Restaurants

Chinese

Chef Rasa Sayang Sharksfin Restaurant
104–106 Jalan Imbi. Tel: 03-2144 1193. Open: daily noon–10.30pm. **$$**
45 p260, B2
Owner-chef Ah Soon Koh is well known for his shark's fin steeped in superior stock with crab-meat and crab roe. The dim sum, baked freshwater prawns with garlic, braised pork tendon, special seafood dishes and sweet, creamy double-boiled egg custard are also sure to please.

Crystal Jade La Mian Xiao Long Bao
R2 Annexe Block, Lot 10 Shopping Centre, Jalan Sultan Ismail. Tel: 03-2148 2338. Open: daily 11am–10.30pm. **$$** 46 p260, A/B2
Brisk service and delicious Shanghainese and northern Chinese dishes distinguish this casual restaurant that is part of a Hong Kong-based chain. Order the *xiao long bao* (dumplings), which burst with juiciness in every bite. Other notables include noodles with pork ribs and spicy minced meat.

Gu Yue Tien (Fine Circle Restaurant)
Lot B5A Chulan Square, 92 Jalan Raja Chulan. Tel: 03-2148 0808. Open: daily L & D. **$$$**
47 p260, B1
Inventive modern Chinese cuisine by the super-creative chef Frankie Woo. Expect dishes such as soft-boiled egg with foie gras, wok-charred rack of lamb and "Buddha Jumps Over the Wall" soup served in a coconut – all superb. Try also the *chaa siu* (barbecued pork) buns, Shanghai dumplings, and prawn dumplings with caviar and flying fish roe.

Ka-Soh Fishhead Noodles and Seafood Restaurant
205 Jalan Bukit Bintang. Tel: 03-2148 2207. Open: daily L & D. **$$**
48 p260, A2
Meaning "daughter-in-law" in Cantonese, Ka-Soh serves home-style food in an air-conditioned restaurant without frills. Although best known for fish-head noodles in a milky soup, there are plenty of other local favourites too. Try the deep-fried bean curd stuffed with fish paste, and *ha cheung kai* (deep-fried chicken marinated with shrimp paste).

Kedai Kopi Weng Hing
183 Jalan Imbi. Open: daily 7am–midnight. **$**
49 p260, B2
This coffee shop offers the best pork ball noodles in town, served in soup or tossed in gravy. Expect also melt-in-the-mouth *siu yok* (roast pork) and *chaa siu* (barbecued pork), and scrumptious bean curd and chicken braised in soy sauce. Chinese stir-fries and noodles are whipped up for dinner and supper.

Kedai Makanan Goreng Kuey Teow Tong Shin
2 Jalan Rembia, Tengkat Tong Shin. Mobile tel: 016-221 8128. Open: Mon–Sat. **$** 50 p260, A2
This shop, still going strong after 20 years, is run by a husband-and-wife team who turn out delicious *char kway teow* (fried rice noodles) with prawns, *laap cheong* (Chinese sausage), cockles and egg. Other treats include prawn noodles, fried rice and spring rolls.

Noble House
19 Jalan Delima, off Jalan Imbi. Tel: 03-2145 8822. Open: daily L & D. **$$$**
51 p260, C2
Western ingredients prepared by traditional Chinese methods result in the fine modern fare here, served in individual portions. The baked prawns with *foie gras* in tomato is a delight, and so are the braised farm chicken stuffed with dry seafood and the stir-fried baby lobster with salted egg yolk. There's a popular, modestly priced lunch buffet on Sundays.

Restoran Oversea
84–88 Jalan Imbi. Tel: 03-2144 9911. Open: daily L & D. **$$** 52 p260, B2
The Oversea has a loyal following for its Chinese cuisine with contemporary twists. Think butter-fried crab claws, black pepper lamb ribs and crispy cod with pork belly. The classic favourites are excellent too: try the steamed marbled goby fish, *chaa siu* (barbecued pork) and roast suckling pig.

Restoran Teochew
270–272 Jalan Changkat Thambi Dollah, off Jalan Pudu. Tel: 03-2141 4704. Open: daily 7.30am–3pm, 6pm–midnight. **$$**
53 p260, A3
An all-day dim sum place, serving 30 to 40 varieties every day from Monday to Saturday, and a whopping 100 types on Sunday. The *yat chan fung*, literally "a gust of wind" – baked sticky buns filled with barbecued pork, so named because a puff of air gushes out as you bite into each one – are wonderful. There are also other Teochew favourites such as braised goose and fish-paste noodles.

Sek Yuen
313 Jalan Pudu. Tel: 9222 9457. Open: daily L & D. **$$**
54 p260, B4
This is undoubtedly one of KL's top old-style Chinese restaurants, with *kopi-tiam* chairs, wood-fired stoves and grumpy waitresses to boot. The menu is confusing, but favourites include stuffed pork knuckle with chest-

nusts and mushrooms, crispy *pei pa* duck, and village vegetables.

Soo Kee Restaurant
14 Medan Imbi. Tel: 03-2148 1324. Open: Tue–Sun L & D till 1am. **$** 55 p260, B2
Known for its noodles for the last 30 years, Soo Kee's *saang ha min* (egg noodles with huge prawns) and the fried beef and spring onion *kway teow* (flat rice noodles) are especially good. From the English menu board you can also choose meat, fish and vegetable dishes, which are cooked in the big woks facing the street.

Sun Hong Muk Koot Teh
35, 37, 39 & 41 Medan Imbi. Tel: 03-2141 4064. Open: daily 5am–midnight. **$** 56 p260, B2
A good stop for *bak kut teh*, a hearty herbal broth with pork ribs, organ meat and bean curd puffs, eaten with *you tiao* (Chinese crullers) and yam rice. Try the sweet-sourish pig's trotters in black vinegar or chicken in rice wine too. Dim sum is available from Tasty Tasty next door, which is under the same management.

French

Le Bouchon
14 and 16 Changkat Bukit Bintang. Tel: 03-2142 7633. Open: Tue–Fri L & D, Sat–Sun D. **$$$** 57 p260, A1
You'll think you've stepped into a little rustic French country house. Enjoy garlicky spinach escargots, goose liver terrine, braised ox tongue with gherkins, mushrooms and Madeira sauce, or grilled triple-candied rack of lamb provencale. Lots of à la carte choices and fine smelly cheeses to finish with.

Frangipani
25 Changkat Bukit Bintang. Tel: 03-2144 3001. Open: Tue–Sun D. **$$$$** 58 p260, A1
This established chic French fine-dining outlet, with tables set artfully around a pool, offers an intimate environment. Chef Chris Bauer hails from Luxembourg and is completely self-taught, but his eclectic menu proves that he is a true artist. The bar upstairs is perfect for the after-dinner drink and boogie.

International

Bon Ton Restaurant
Lot 10 Shopping Center, Jalan Sultan Ismail, R1 & R2, Lower Ground Floor. www.bontonkl.com Tel: 03-2142 2287. Open: daily noon–2am. **$$** 59 p260, A/B2
This popular restaurant has been given a new lease of life in a new venue but still has its old Asian and Western favourites. The set lunch is an excellent deal – less than RM20 – or you can just stop for some cake and coffee in between shopping.

Island Bistro
Lot C3.10.100, Level 3 Pavillion KL. 168 Jalan Bukit Bintang. Tel: 03-2145 1886. Open: daily 10am–10pm. **$$** 60 p260, B1
Part of Tang's department store outfit Island Shop, this bistro is an excellent pit-stop for lunch or a teatime snack. Sit inside or out to enjoy the black pepper crab *tung hoon* (with glass noodles) or the Singapore *laksa lemak* (curried noodles) with crayfish.

Palate Palette
21 Jalan Mesui, off Jalan Nagasari. www.palatepalette.com Tel: 03-2142 2148. Open: Sun–Thur noon–midnight, Fri–Sat noon–2am; closed Mon. **$$** 61 p260, A1
Stylishly decorated with bright murals and mismatched furniture, Palate Palette serves a varied menu of comfort food, from prawn and avocado salad to fish-and-chips. Popular with a young, grungy crowd, it's a great place to sip a mocktail and people-watch.

Italian

Chiaroscuro Trattoria Pizzeria
Ground Floor, 38 Bidara, 30 Jalan Bedara, off Jalan Nagasari. www.chiaroscurokl.com Tel: 03-2144 8006. Open: Mon–Fri noon–3pm, 6.30pm–midnight, Sat 6.30pm–midnight. **$$$$** 62 p260, A1
Serving fare that is finer than you would normally associate with trattorias, this impresses with its mushroom gnocchi, bresaola (air-cured beef) with grilled mushrooms

Price per person for a three-course meal without drinks:
$ = under RM30
$$ = RM30–60
$$$ = RM60–90
$$$$ = over RM90

RIGHT: Palate Palette.

and proscuitto and rucola pizza. The woodfired pizzas are only available in the evening. Do ask chef Andrea Zanella for recommendations.

Neroteca
Ground Floor, The Somerset, 8 Lorong Ceylon. www.neroteca.com Tel: 03-2070 0530. Open: Wed–Mon 10am–midnight, Tue 6pm–midnight. **$$$$**
63 p260, A1
The menu, which includes cold platters, meats and fish, changes regularly, so its best to ask chef Riccardo Ferrarotti or try the daily specials. The Nerodeli next door is the perfect stop for that special cheese and wine. This place fills up fast, so it's best to make a reservation, or sit at the bar.

Japanese

Dontaku Japanese Restaurant
148 Jalan Bukit Bintang. Tel: 03-2143 4226. Open: Mon–Fri L & D, Sat–Sun noon–10.30pm. **$$**
64 p260 A1/2
A Japanese country-style restaurant with red lanterns brightening up a bamboo facade. Pork dishes stand out here: *katsu don* (deep-fried pork cutlet on rice served with an egg-and-onion sauce), *don kakuni ramen* (noodles in soup with spiced pork cubes) and *gyoza* – fried dumplings with paper-thin skins. Take your pick from the wide variety of set meals.

Gonbei
Relish Floor, Starhill Gallery, 181 Jalan Bukit Bintang. Tel: 03-2782 3801. Open: daily noon–1am. **$$** (set lunch), **$$$$** (à la carte dinner) 65 p260, B1
Dine in a unique decor adorned with Japanese farmhouse paraphernalia. You can choose to sit at the counter for your favourite style of Japanese cooking – sushi, sashimi, *teppanyaki* or *robatayaki*, and watch chefs deftly prepare your dishes. At the *robatayaki* (grill) counter, select the fresh seafood to be grilled. Excellent set meals with *wagyu* beef or mackerel in miso paste.

Tykoh Inagiku
2/F, Podium Block, Menara Keck Sang, 203 Jalan Bukit Bintang. Tel: 03-2148 2133. Open: daily L & D. **$$$$**
66 p260, B1
This understated restaurant is one of KL's top Japanese eateries. The owner is a fishmonger at Tokyo's Tsujiki market, so only the choicest, freshest cuts are flown in every week. Patrons are almost all Japanese and local gourmands. Try the grilled tuna cheek and the seasonal cod milt – if you have a taste for fish sperm.

Malay

Bijan Restaurant
3 Jalan Ceylon. Tel: 03-2031 3575. Open: daily L & D. **$** (set lunch), **$$** (à la carte). Off map
Set in a bungalow with a long patio surrounded by banana trees, Bijan's contemporary interior welcomes with lots of wood, bamboo and colourful batik art. Try the *masak lemak udang tempoyak* (prawns in fermented durian curry), chargrilled short beef ribs with *sambal* (chilli paste) or *kerabu pucuk paku* (jungle fern salad).

Enak
LG2, Feast Floor, Starhill Gallery, 181 Jalan Bukit Bintang. Tel: 03-2141 8973. Open: daily noon–midnight. **$$$** 67 p260, B1
Outfitted in contemporary style, with brass antiques and a wrought-iron fish sculpture. Time-honoured family recipes are on the menu: Acehnese grilled prawns with a piquant fruit salad, slow-cooked beef with spices and herbs, steamed squid stuffed with mushrooms, and more. The young coconut custard meringue is not to be missed.

Kedai Ayam Panggang Wong Ah Wah
1, 3, 5, 7 & 9 Jalan Alor, off Jalan Bukit Bintang. Tel: 03-2144 2462. Open: daily 5pm–3.45am, closed alternate Mon. **$** 68 p260, A2
You'll get local street food at its best here, down a bustling lane. Grilled chicken wings are the main draw, but equally lip-smacking are the grilled fish (such as stingray and mackerel), oyster omelette, crabs in a salted egg sauce, and chilli-fried cockles. There's also satay from the stall in front.

Middle Eastern

Al-Amar
Level 6 Pavillion KL, Jalan Bukit Bintang. Tel: 03-2166 1011. Open: daily noon–midnight. **$$$** 69 p260, B1
The top Lebanese chefs and friendly staff are the secret of this high-end restaurant's success. Tuck into delicate grilled lamb or chicken *briyani* while you listen to the (loud) live music and watch the gyrations of the belly dancer – all in all, a dining experience to remember.

Restoran Tarbush
138 Jalan Bukit Bintang. Tel: 03-2142 8558. Open: daily 10am–1am. **$$$**
70 p260, A2
Fine Middle Eastern cuisine in a casual restaurant that is warmly lit by filigree lamps. Begin with excellent starters like the hummous and *baba ghanoush* (eggplant dip) before enjoying the Tarbush mixed grill of chicken, shish kebab, lamb cubes and chops. Or go for the *shish tawook* – grilled boneless chicken marinated with yoghurt and spices. Another outlet at Starhill Gallery (tel: 03-2144 6393).

Sahara Tent
Ground Floor, Hotel Fortuna, 87 Jalan Berangan, off Jalan Bukit Bintang. www.saharatent.com Tel: 03-2144 8310. Open daily noon–midnight. **$$$** 71 p260, A2
This smart restaurant owned and run by an Iraqi serves excellent Arabic food. However, this is one of the best restaurants to come to

during Ramadan as you get a bit of everything for the buffet price. The meats are mostly grilled and are good on their own or with rice and bread. There is also a shop that sells trinkets and foodstuffs from the Middle East. And, of course, you can round off your meal with a puff on the shisha.

Seafood

Fisherman's Cove
LG10, Feast Floor, Starhill Gallery, 181 Jalan Bukit Bintang. Tel: 03-2782 3848. Open: daily L & D. **$$$$** 72 p260, B1
Savour the freshest seafood in a "boathouse", with sails for walls and bamboo structures up on an upper deck. The dishes, cooked in various styles, range from a seafood soup to sea urchin *ravioli* and ocean trout caviar, to spicy steamed barramundi with eggplant and pumpkin *jus*. The black sesame mousse with aged balsamic ice cream, for dessert, may just take you by surprise.

Jogoya
Relish Floor, Starhill Gallery, 181 Jalan Bukit Bintang. Tel: 03-2142 1268. Open: daily 11am–2am. **$$$** 73 p260, B1
Offers a seafood buffet for lunch and dinner with a slant towards Japanese-inspired dishes such as sushi, sashimi and *tempura* (deep-fried battered seafood and vegetables), in addition to fresh oysters, lobsters, scallops, cod and more. Chinese, Western and Malaysian dishes are on the buffet too – from Shanghainese *xiao long bao* (dumplings) to chicken vindaloo. Pay less after 2pm and after 9.30pm.

Lobsterman
18 Jalan Delima, off Jalan Inai/Imbi. Tel: 03-2141 6772. Open: daily L & D. **$$$** 74 p260, C2
Lobsters from Canada take pride of place in this fine-dining restaurant set in an old bungalow. Have them done any way imaginable – simmered, wrapped in lotus leaf with rice, fried with noodles Cantonese style, in an Indian curry or a Thai *tom yam*. Escargots, oysters, lamb and pasta feature on the menu too.

Price per person for a three-course meal without drinks:
$ = under RM30
$$ = RM30–60
$$$ = RM60–90
$$$$ = over RM90

Spanish

La Bodega
Lot C3.06.00, Level 3, Pavilion KL. www.bodega.com.my Tel: 03-2148 8018. Open: daily 11am–1am. **$$$** 75 p260, B1
The latest addition to this much-loved chain of tapas cafés sits on a cheerful corner of the Pavilion walk. The lamb cutlets and chorizo sausage are recommended, or the heftier seafood paella. The best sangria in town.

El Cerdo
43 and 45 Changkat Bukit Bintang. www.elcerdokl.com Tel: 03-2145 0511. Open: Sun–Fri noon–2.30pm, 6.30–10.30pm, Sat 6.30–10.30pm. **$$$** 76 p260, A2
With its "nose to tail" eating tagline, this is literally a hog fest. The dishes are generous enough for sharing, so they are best enjoyed with company. You can order all manner of Spanish hams and hogs, whole piglets and lambs, and wash it all down with some very good wines.

Vietnamese

Sao Nam Restaurant
25 Tengkat Tong Shin. Tel: 03-2144 1225. Open: Tue–Sun L & D. **$$$** 77 p260, A2
Sao Nam's mangosteen and prawn salad, tangy and creamy, is a must-order, together with the roasted boneless duck in a tart and sweet tamarind sauce and the pepper leaf-wrapped grilled beef *la lot*. Enjoy a glass from the good wine list or the Vietnamese coffee while you take in the American and Vietnamese pop art on the walls.

BELOW: fried fish and beanshoots.

Bars

Borneo Baruk Club
1, Jalan Kia Peng. www.bbc.net.my Tel: 03-2148 0015. 5 p257, E4
This is the only Borneo-themed club in town, built with traditional timber accents It's the only place to indulge in *tuak*, or the traditional rice wine of the head-hunters of Borneo.

Hakka Republic
Level 2, Menara Hap Sang, Jalan P. Ramlee. www.hakkarepublic.com Tel: 03-2078 9908. 6 p257, D4
This Chinese-themed but very swishy bar has one of the best wine lists in town.

Little Havana
2 & 4 Lorong Sahabat (along Changkat Bukit Bintang). Tel: 03-2144 7170. 7 p260, A1
See Cuban culture in action here with Latin music, great wines, fine cigars, good food and hot salsa dancing.

Reggae Bar Changkat
31, Changkat Bukit Bintang. www.reggaebarkl.com Tel: 03-2026 7690. 8 p260, A2
This reggae-themed bar even serves reggae pizza. The perfect venue for hot and humid nights, but gets very full on weekends.

Yoko's
36 Changkat Bukit Bintang. www.yokos-kl.com Tel: 03-2144 3378. 9 p260, A2
Stylish, relaxing Balinese-inspired Japanese bar with great cuisine and live jazz on Friday and Saturday evenings.

LAKE GARDENS, BRICKFIELDS AND BANGSAR

Lush Lake Gardens is a sanctuary of flowers, insects, birds and animals near the heart of downtown Kuala Lumpur. Nearby Brickfields is a fast-disappearing old-world enclave, while to its west, the booming suburb of Bangsar is a veritable all-night party

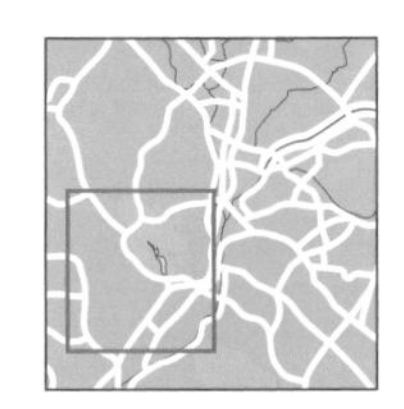

Main Attractions

BUTTERFLY PARK
HIBISCUS GARDEN
KUALA LUMPUR BIRD PARK
ISLAMIC ARTS MUSEUMA
NATIONAL PLANETARIUM
ARULMEGU SREE VEERA HANUMAN TEMPLE
SRI KANDASAMY KOVIL
BANGSAR

Maps and Listings

MAP OF LAKE GARDENS, BRICKFIELDS AND BANGSAR, PAGE 166
SHOPPING, PAGE 170
RESTAURANTS AND BARS, PAGES 172–3

Given the boom in real estate prices in Kuala Lumpur, it's not surprising that the construction of new buildings on prime land continues at breakneck speed. Yet, southwest of the city centre, large swathes of greenery flourish at Lake Gardens, a century-old parkland surrounding a lake. Close to it is Brickfields – Indian in flavour and full of colour – another enclave that has thus far withstood the onslaught of spiralling property prices. In contrast, Bangsar, its neighbouring suburb, has been taken over by upmarket condos and an entertainment strip that parties on till the small hours.

LAKE GARDENS

Spread over 104 hectares (257 acres) in the middle of the city is a verdant expanse of trees and turf surrounding a lake. This is the legacy of Alfred Venning, former chairman of British Malaya's Sanitary Board, who, over a period of 10 years from the late 1880s onwards, created a garden "for health and recreation" by damming a river and taming the jungle to make it appropriately garden-like. Today, portions of Taman Tasik Perdana, or **Lake Gardens** (daily 24 hours; free), as it's more popularly known, have remained unchanged; some of the original plants here date back well over a century. While Venning himself may be all but forgotten, the lush sanctuary he created for recreation is appreciated by all KL-ites.

At dawn and dusk the paths and open spaces are the domain of fitness buffs, while weekends see families hogging the playgrounds and picnicking on the lawns. At night, the park benches are taken over by lovers. Walking is the best way to explore the paths that thread through the gardens, climb up hills and circle the lake. Given the

LEFT: produce at Bangsar night market.
RIGHT: the Butterfly Park.

ABOVE: water lilies at the Lake Gardens.

heat, however, the best time to visit is early morning or evening. From 10am to 5.30pm daily (except during lunchtime), a free shuttle bus, which starts at the **boathouse**, does a 10-minute circuit of the gardens past key attractions, stopping whenever passengers wish to alight. The shuttle runs only when there are enough passengers: it does not follow a timetable. If you are walking around and the bus happens to pass by, just flag it down.

Garden monuments

Start exploring the gardens along the paths north of Jalan Parlimen. First is the **ASEAN Sculpture Garden** ❶, which features modern works by artists from the member states of the Association of Southeast Asian Nations. Just behind is the **National Monument** (Tugu Negara) ❷, a bronze tribute to the soldiers who overcame the Communist threat of the post-war decades. The five soldiers represent the different armed forces of the country, while the slain figures represent the Communists. If the monument looks similar to the Iwo Jima monument in Washington, DC, that's because it was designed by the same sculptor, Felix de Weldon. The crescent-shaped gallery behind

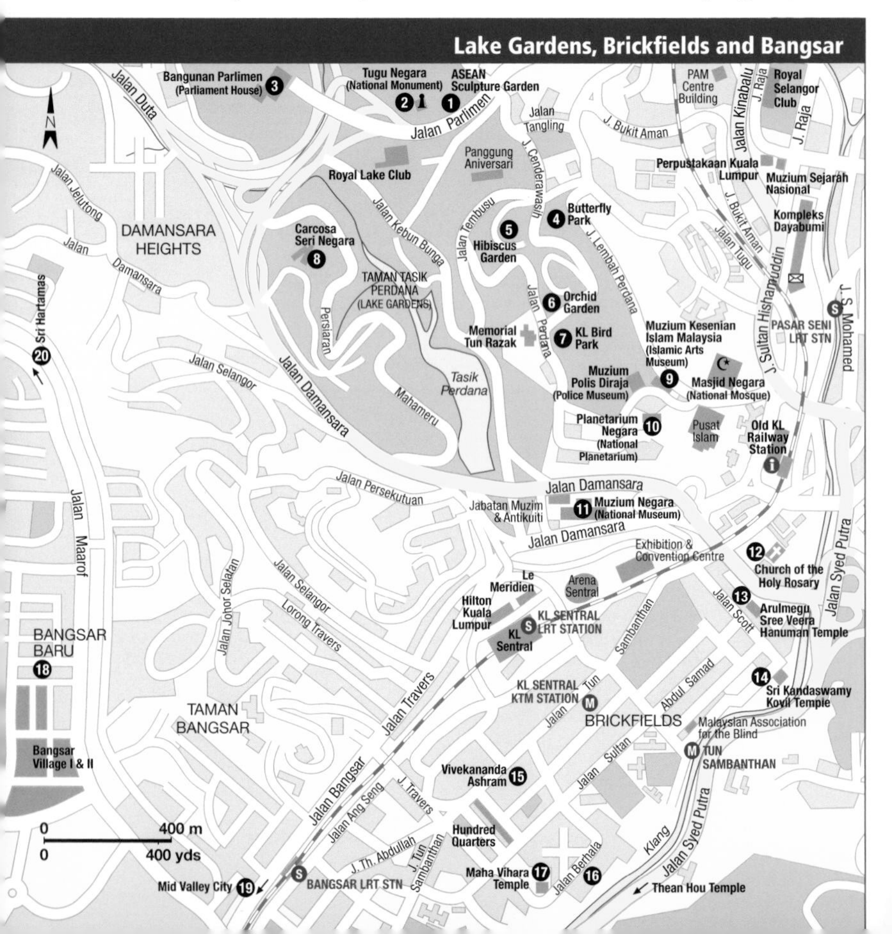

the statue records the names of fighter units, including Malay, British, Australian, Fijian and Maori troops. At the back of the pavilion is the **Cenotaph**, erected to commemorate the soldiers who died in the two World Wars.

Back on Jalan Parlimen, heading west yields a glimpse of **Parliament House** (Bangunan Parliamen) ❸ in the distance. Built after independence, its tower block is clad with concrete "scales" that resemble the skin of a pineapple but which also serve a functional purpose as sunshades. The podium of the complex sports a series of triangular structures fashioned after the traditional Melakan roof form.

ABOVE: the National Monument is a tribute to soldiers who fought against Communists.

Butterfly Park ❹

Address: Jalan Cenderawasih
Tel: 03-2693 4799
Opening Hrs: daily 9am–6pm
Entrance Fee: charge
Transport: LRT Pasar Seni

Cross Jalan Parlimen and continue south along Jalan Cenderawasih into the main section of the gardens, where the **Butterfly Park** is located. This is a sanctuary for more than 6,000 butterflies and moths. The small but lush gardens have been planted with thousands of shrubs and plants to recreate the insects' natural habitat, while ponds filled with koi and turtles punctuate the greenery. Tables set up with honey-laced hibiscus blooms help draw out the butterflies to eye level; look out for the large and distinctive black and electric-green Rajah Brooke's Birdwing, a protected species. A building within the park showcases some of Malaysia's other weird and wonderful insects, reptiles and amphibians, some of which are masters of camouflage.

Hibiscus Garden and Orchid Garden

Return to Jalan Cenderawasih and continue along it to the **Hibiscus Garden** ❺ (daily 9am–6pm; admission charge on weekends and public holidays). This place is a riot of colour, with 2,500 plants of different varieties from all over the world. The hibiscus, called *bunga raya* in Malay, is Malaysia's national flower, although it originates from Hawaii. Also along Jalan Cenderawasih is the **Orchid Garden** ❻ (daily 9am–6pm; admission charge on weekends and public holidays). Here, some 800 species of wild and commercial varieties of orchid can be admired beneath pergolas and from walkways. (In the wild, there are about 2,000 species native to Malaysia.)

Kuala Lumpur Bird Park ❼

Address: Jalan Perdana, www.klbird park.com
Tel: 03-2272 1010
Opening Hrs: daily 9am–6pm
Entrance Fee: charge
Transport: LRT Pasar Seni

Opposite the Orchid Garden, a large net suspended over the trees marks the **Kuala Lumpur Bird Park**. Said to be the largest covered aviary in Southeast Asia, it is spread over 8.5 hectares (21 acres) and contains more than 3,000

The Parliament House is featured on the back of the country's first series of coins, issued by the Central Bank in 1967. It is still in circulation today.

TIP

The National Planetarium has a garden at the bottom of the hill with a scattering of replicas of ancient observatories. See if you can figure out how they work.

birds from almost every major family. Most are caged although some are free flying. The landscaping here is not as pretty as that of the other gardens, but you do get to see spectacular native species, like hornbills, with their prominent beaks and magnificent plumes. Ask at the information counter about feeding times.

Carcosa Seri Negara ❽

At the eastern edge of the Lake Gardens, bounded by Jalan Damansara and Pesiaran Mahameru, is the delightful **Carcosa Seri Negara**. The Lake Gardens was originally set aside as the English quarter of colonial Malaya, with bungalows for the administrators built in the surrounding hills. The grandest of these was British Resident Frank Swettenham's official residence, Carcosa, whose name was derived from the Italian *cara cosa* or "dear place". He also built, on an adjoining hill, a guesthouse called Seri Negara (King's House) for his most important visitors.

Both buildings have been exquisitely renovated and turned into an all-suite luxury hotel. If staying here is out of the question, at least enjoy a traditional English tea (daily 3–6pm) on rattan chairs facing the manicured lawns at **The Drawing Room**, and a stroll through the lobby and public spaces, with their old world Victorian charm still intact, and imagine the grand balls that took place here during colonial times.

BELOW: feeding time for a peacock at the Kuala Lumpur Bird Park.

Islamic Arts Museum ❾

Address: Jalan Lembah Perdana, www.iamm.org.my
Tel: 03-2274 2020
Opening Hrs: daily 10am–6pm
Entrance Fee: charge
Transport: LRT Pasar Seni

At the eastern edge of Lake Gardens, along Jalan Lembah Perdana, is the **Islamic Arts Museum Malaysia** or Muzium Kesenian Islam Malaysia. This spacious museum is a privately owned repository of artefacts and objets d'art from the Islamic world.

The Italian-designed building hosts temporary exhibitions on the lower floors, while the permanent collections occupy the two upper floors. Of note are the detailed architectural models of famous monuments and structures of the Islamic era, such as India's Taj Mahal and the mosques of the holy city of Medina. Painstaking work also went into reconstructing the Ottoman Room, which harks back to the era that is considered the "Renaissance" of Islamic art (1453–1923). Other displays include manuscripts, ceramics, metalwork and arms.

National Planetarium ❿

Address: 53, Jalan Perdana, www.angkasa.gov.my
Tel: 03-2273 4301/5484
Opening Hrs: Tue–Sun 9.30–4.30pm (closed on Hari Raya Puasa and Hari Raya Haji)
Entrance Fee: charge
Transport: KL Hop-on Hop-off, LRT Pasar Seni

Southeast of Lake Gardens along Jalan Perdana is the **National Planetarium** or Planetarium Negara. Besides displays on astronomy, its highlights include an observatory with a 36cm (14in) telescope, a theatre and exhibits like the Arianne IV space engine that launched Malaysia's first satellite, Measat I, in 1996. The dome-screened cinema shows some worthy films.

National Museum ⓫

Address: Jalan Damansara, www.muziumnegara.gov.my
Tel: 03-2267 1000
Opening Hrs: daily 9am–6pm
Entrance Fee: charge
Transport: LRT KL Sentral

South of the planetarium along Jalan Damansara is the **National Museum**, or Muzium Negara. The museum's displays are fairly mundane, but architecturally the building is outstanding. Built between 1959 and 1963 as a statement of national identity by a newly independent country, the museum's monumental roof is Malay in character. It was inspired by the Balai Besar of Kedah, a Thai-influenced 19th-century audience hall for sultans. Resembling a Malay palace, the front facade has a row of pillars, with the entrance positioned in the centre of the building. The 26 concrete pillars – 13 on either side of the main entrance – are meant to represent Malaysia's 26 states. Two batik-inspired murals run the length of the wings, the left panel depicting the country's history and culture, and the right panel its economics and politics. The museum's team of expat volunteers do a good job of giving free tours in five languages (Malay, English, Japanese, French and Mandarin). Do check out the website for special exhibitions, which are often worth the visit.

BRICKFIELDS

South of the Lake Gardens area is **Brickfields**, a lovely old neighbourhood that represents a rapidly vanishing face of Kuala Lumpur. Originally the place where bricks were manufactured to build the city, it is known locally as Batu Limabelas (15th Mile) as it was once a long way from town, and travelling there involved traversing many hills. Today, getting to Brickfields is much easier – both the KL Sentral LRT and Monorail stations are nearby, from where you can easily walk.

At the edge of Brickfields, at No 10 Jalan Tun Sambanthan, spires announce the presence of Gereja Holy Rosary or **Church of the Holy Rosary** ⓬ (tel: 03-2274 2747; daily 10am–4pm; free), a Catholic church established by a French missionary to serve the Chinese community. Built in 1903, it sports the characteristic pointed arches, stained-glass and rose windows of the Gothic style.

Jalan Scott

Brickfields proper begins with **Jalan Scott**, which in the early days comprised Chinese-run shops as well as Indian *dhoby* (laundry) shops, Chettiar moneylenders, and spice and provision shops which served the largely Indian population of Tamils from South India and Sri Lanka. The Tamil immigrants largely worked in the Malayan Railways and the Public Works Depart-

ABOVE: detail of a batik-inspired mural at the National Museum. **BELOW:** an old steam locomotive's final resting place at the National Museum.

ABOVE: the Hainanese Tien Hou Temple.

ment, and were housed in government quarters here. Many also worked in the brick kilns. As a result, Brickfields always had a strong Indian character to it, though that is now changing.

Arulmegu Sree Veera Hanuman Temple ⓭

Address: Lot P.T., 22 Jalan Scott
Tel: 03-2274 0639
Opening Hrs: daily 7am–10pm
Entrance Fee: free
Transport: Monorail Tun Sambanthan

Today, Jalan Scott is blessed with the presence of two Hindu temples. At the junction of Jalan Padang Belia is the **Arulmegu Sree Veera Hanuman Temple.** It honours a deity less commonly seen in Hindu temples – Hanuman, or the monkey god. Depicted in the epic *Ramayana*, Hanuman is worshipped with offerings of butter – applied to the mouth and tail – and garlands of *vadai* (a savoury fritter).

Sri Kandaswamy Kovil Temple ⓮

Address: 3 Lorong Scott, www.srikandaswamykovil.org
Tel: 03-2274 2987
Opening Hrs: daily 5am–1pm, 5–9pm
Entrance Fee: free
Transport: Monorail Tun Sambanthan

At the end of Jalan Scott is the Hindu **Sri Kandaswamy Kovil Temple** with its tall *gopuram* (gateway) of intricately carved deities. Founded by the local Ceylonese (or Jaffna) Tamil community in 1909, this stunning temple was completely reconstructed in 1997. The main deity worshipped here is Subramaniam (Murugan), the same deity worshipped at the Sri Maha Mariamman temple in Petaling Street *(see pages 114)*, which explains why the two temples look similar. At festivals and special occasions, the statue of Subramaniam is paraded around the inner and outer courtyards of the temple.

SHOPPING

Art

Richard Koh Fine Art
Lot No 2F-3, Level 2, Bangsar Village II, Jalan Telawi, Bangsar. www.rkfineart.com Tel: 03-2283 3677.
Specializing in contemporary, young Southeast Asian artists (Thai, Malaysian, Filipino and Indonesian), works here are as stunning as they are pricey. Well-curated and worth the dent in your wallet.

Malls

Bangsar Shopping Centre
285 Jalan Maarof. www.bsc.com.my Tel: 03-2094 7700.
A favourite with expatriates. Trendy shops, expensive restaurants and bars, designer boutiques and a well-stocked Cold Storage, as well as gourmet goodies at KL's first food hall, O Gourmet.

Bangsar Village 1& 2
1 Jalan Telawi Satu. www.bangsarvillage.com Tel: 03-2288 1800.
Another upmarket shopping centre, with anchors like the Village Grocer, which carries international food items. The five-storey sister wing next door specialises in lifestyle and fashion goods.

The Gardens
Mid Valley City, Lingkaran Syed Putra. Tel: 03-2297 0288.
The design of this elegant mall is inspired by the region's flora and fauna. You can easily spend half a day here, browsing its fantastic boutiques offering everything from designer knockdowns to street fashions. There are excellent restaurants, too.

Mid Valley Megamall
Lingkaran Syed Putra. www.midvalley.com.my Tel: 03-2938 3333.
One of Asia's largest malls, with spacious walkways linking over 430 stores, including eateries, an 18-screen cineplex, Pets Wonderland and an entertainment centre for children. Anchor tenants are Metrojaya, Carrefour and Jusco. A bus shuttle operates to the Bangsar LRT station and a walkway connects the mall to the KTM station.

Women's Clothing

Ashes
Level 1, 22A Jalan Telawi, Bangsar Baru. Tel: 03-2287 7911.
This New York loft-style boutique is fuss-free and stocks garments handselected by the owner, Ashley Kwong, herself. New stocks come in from all over every month.

Jovian Mandagie
124 Jalan Maarof, Bangsar. www.jovianmandagie.com Tel: 03-2093 5124.
Young designer Mandagie is the hottest thing in Malaysian fashion. His creations are stunning, sought after by brides, film starlets and women who want something for that special occasion.

Jalan Tun Sambanthan

Brickfield's Indian flavour is most evident in the shops and restaurants lining **Jalan Tun Sambanthan** and the parallel **Jalan Sultan Abdul Samad**. Here, you can get everything from Bollywood DVDs and statues of Hindu deities to plump Indian mangoes, fiery curries on banana leaves and some of the best vegetarian food in town.

At No 220 Jalan Tun Sambanthan is **Vivekananda Ashram ⓯**, established by the followers of the influential spiritual leader of the Vedanta branch of Hindu philosophy, Swami Vivekananda. In front of the ashram, a lovely colonial building, stands a statue of the founder.

Jalan Berhala ⓰

Take a stroll along **Jalan Berhala** (formerly Temple Road) and explore its nooks and crannies to soak up the atmosphere. As its old name suggests, places of worship are clustered here, mostly built before World War II. The area also has schools, bungalows and apartment blocks. Every Thursday, Jalan Berhala and the adjoining stretch of Jalan Sultan Abdul Samad host a *pasar malam* (night market), selling fresh produce as well as hawker food.

Also along this street is the Buddhist **Maha Vihara Temple ⓱** (tel: 03-2274 1141; daily 5.30am–10.30pm) which is very active in community and charity work. Modest in appearance, it assumes an especially festive air come Wesak Day in May as it is the start and end point for a grand night-time float procession. Founded by Singhalese Buddhists from Sri Lanka, this is the focal point of community worship in KL. Opposite, is the **Temple of Fine Arts**, a 25-year-old institution devoted to the theory and practice of Hindustani and Karnatic music. Classes in classical dance forms like Bharatya Natyam and Odissi are also held here.

ABOVE: the night market is a popular spot in affluent Bangsar.

BANGSAR AND SURROUNDINGS

From Brickfields, heading up Jalan Travers and turning left into Jalan Bangsar and right into Jalan Maarof leads to **Bangsar ⓲**, one of the most expensive addresses in town. Property developers in the city frequently tout their latest project as The Next Bangsar, but thankfully there is still only *one* Bangsar, which reigns in terms of exclusivity. Its two main entertainment strips, **Bangsar Baru** and the **Bangsar Shopping Centre** (in Taman Bandaraya) are dense with chic bars, clubs and eateries that are thronged by the city's fashionable set.

Close by are two other areas of note. About 2km (1¼ miles) south of Bangsar is **Mid Valley City ⓳**, comprising offices, condos and hotels that are almost overshadowed by the upsized **Mid Valley Megamall** and its new sister shopping centre called **The Gardens**. About 5km (3 miles) northwest of Bangsar is the bustling suburb of **Sri Hartamas ⓴.** Like Bangsar, this upscale area of expensive houses and luxury condos is chock-a-block with restaurants and bars. ❑

TIP

Along Jalan Rozario is another Brickfields landmark, the Hundred Quarters. A relic of an altogether different era, two rows of identical prewar terraced houses with wooden shuttered windows are separated by a broad back lane whose width is unimaginable in the space-conscious Kuala Lumpur of today.

BEST RESTAURANTS AND BARS

Restaurants

Bangsar

Alexis Bistro
Level 1, Bangsar Shopping Centre, 285 Jalan Maarof. Tel: 03-2287 1388. Open: daily 9am–midnight. **$$** Off map
Alexis serves fine examples from various cuisines: Italian (napoletana and margherita pizzas), English (fish and chips) and Malaysian (Sarawak *laksa*). Order the flavoursome herb rice *nasi ulam*, with a spread of Malay-style dishes such as prawns on lemongrass skewers and jungle ferns in chilli paste.

Basil Thai Nudle Bar
G10, Ground Level, Bangsar Village, 1 Jalan Telawi 1. Tel: 03-2287 8708. Open: daily noon–10pm. **$** Off map
Casual café-style eatery with a menu of traditional Thai dishes. The Special Mix Combo platter, with spring rolls, *wan tan* and fish cakes, is an appetite-whetting good starter. For mains, order the prawn *tom yam* (hot and sour soup), green curry and stir-fried beef with basil.

La Bodega Deli
18 Jalan Telawi 2. www.bodega.com.my Tel: 03-2287 9468. Open: daily 10am–10pm. **$$** Off map
A great selection of cooked breakfasts served in a comfortable, laid-back atmosphere. The selection of Spanish wines and cheeses is excellent, as are the truffles and chocolates.

Cava Restaurant
71 Jalan Bangkung, Bukit Bandaraya. www.cava.my Tel: 03-2093 6637. Open: daily L & D. **$$** Off map
A Spanish restaurant, that also serves Italian, Greek and Moroccan dishes. Tapas like lamb *boulette*, stewed quail in olive and orange sauce, and prawn *pil pil* are great washed down with sangria. For something heartier, order the superb seafood paella or octopus fettucine. Get in by 6pm and pay less for a three-course meal.

Chatterbox
F9, Level 1, Bangsar Village, Jalan Telawi 1. Tel: 03-2287 8833. Open: daily 10am–10pm. **$** Off map
Order the thick toast spread with peanut butter, dipped in egg and deep-fried: it's sinfully good. Then there's the usual *cha chaan teng* (Hong Kong-style bistro) suspects, such as pork chop fried rice in a sweet barbecue sauce and baked with cheese.

Dellcious Café
GF1, Ground Level, Bangsar Village 2, Jalan Telawi 1. www.delicious.com.my Tel: 03-2287 1554. Open: Sun–Thur 9am–midnight, Fri–Sat 9am–1am. **$$** Off map
A much-loved café with a wonderful selection of Western and Asian fare as varied as Vietnamese chicken salad, duck confit pasta, home-made pesto and masala lamb shank. Their desserts are heavenly. Portions here are very generous, so you can definiltely share.

House & Co
Lot S15, Level 2, Bangsar Shopping Centre, 285 Jalan Maarof. Tel: 03-2094 4393. Open: Tue–Sun 10am–6pm. **$$** Off map
A café within a home-decor store. Try the *nasi lemak* (coconut rice) with beef *rendang* (dry beef curry), *acar* (pickled vegetables) and deep-fried *ikan bilis* (anchovies), all beautifully arrayed on banana leaves. Its Nyonya-style *laksa*, with chicken and bean curd puffs swimming in a creamy curry, is enough for two. Superb curry puffs and cakes are served for tea.

Restoran Rebung Chef Ismail
4–2 Lorong Maarof, Bangsar Park. Tel: 03-2283 2119. Open: daily 11am–11pm. **$$** Off map
Authentic dishes from the state of Negri Sembilan, such as aromatic *tempoyak daun kayu* (tapioca leaves in fermented durian curry) and spicy *rendang tok* (beef curry) with young coconut slices, are served at the buffet-style lunch and dinner.

Brickfields

Annalakshmi
116 Jalan Berhala. Tel: 03-2274 3799. Open: L & D Tue–Sun 11.30am–3pm, 6.30–10pm. **$** Off map
For top-rate Indian vegetarian fare, this is one of KL's best. The food is lovingly prepared by chefs and volunteers of the Temple of Fine Arts, and is labelled, which makes choosing very easy. There are breads, rice, lentil and vegetable dishes of many varieties, straddling North and South Indian cuisines.

Gandhi's Vegetarian Restaurant
Scott Sentral Service Suite. Lot G1-G2, Jalan Padang Belia, off Jalan Scott. Open: daily 8am–2am. **$**
78 p258, C4
Gandhi's has moved six times since it opened in Brickfields in 1972. The current location is a bit brightly lit, but the menu more than makes up for it. Buffet-style lunch and à la carte for dinner. No onion or garlic is used.

Jassal Tandoori Restaurant
84 Jalan Tun Sambanthan. www.jesalsweethouse.com Tel: 03-2274 6801. Open: daily 11am–11pm. **$$**
79 p258, B4
At this North Indian restaurant, the mutton vindaloo melts in the mouth and the many varieties of naan are crispy and not too doughy. Foodies have claimed that the *briyani* (fragrant rice with meats) is among the best in KL.

Restoran Chat Masala
259G Jalan Tun Sambanthan. Tel: 2260 3244. Open: daily 8am–midnight. **$** Off map
The dining area is split into two sections, with the smaller smoking room cosier and adorned with beautiful murals. The banana leaf meals and *murtabak* (flaky bread stuffed with meat) are excellent but the afternoon snacks are extra-special. The *puri* (deep-fried dough filled with cheese and chickpeas topped with a chilli tamarind sauce) is perfect with a cup of hot *chai.*

Lake Gardens

Museum Restaurant and Café
Islamic Arts Museum, Jalan Lembah Perdana. www.iamm.org.my Tel: 03-2274 2020. Open: Tue–Sun 10am–6pm. **$$** 80 p258, C2/3
Dine in sumptuous surroundings overlooking a fountain garden. The intricate carvings on the walls and the mirrorwork on pillars are the work of Moroccan craftsmen. Chef Ayman delivers a marvellous lentil soup, tagine lamb, and grilled chicken with tahini.

Mid Valley

Little Penang Kafe
Lot F001 & F100, Level 1, Mid Valley Megamall, Lingkaran Syed Putra. Tel: 03-2282 0215. Open: daily L & D. **$** Off map
Well regarded for its Penang-style noodles, from *char kway teow* (fried flat rice noodles) to the hot and sour *asam laksa* with a spicy tamarind fish gravy, to Hokkien prawn noodles. Order the ice *kacang*, a sweet shaved-ice treat. Another branch at Suria KLCC.

Little Vietnam
Lot T-027, Level 3, Mid Valley Megamall, Lingkaran Syed Putra. Tel: 03-2938 8899. Open: daily 11.30am–9.30pm. **$** Off map
Tastefully appointed restaurant with pretty lampshades and folk art. Order the delicate steamed rice rolls with minced chicken, *pho* (noodles) with juicy beef tendon balls, and the nicely textured five-colour rice flecked with chicken, vegetables and nuts.

Sage Restaurant and Wine Bar
Level 6, The Gardens Residences, Mid Valley City, Lingkaran Syed Putra. www.sagekl.com
Tel: 03-2268 1328. Open: Mon–Fri noon–2pm, 6–10.30pm, Sat 6–10.30pm. **$$$$** Off map
This is one of KL's top dining experiences. Chef Takashi Kimura serves gourmet cuisine in sophisticated surroundings. If the prices give you the shakes, go for the *dégustation* menu, but this should be ordered in advance. Reserve days ahead.

The Yogitree
F-237B, Level 1, The Gardens, Mid Valley City, Lingkaran Syed Putra. www.yogitree.com Tel: 03-2282 6213. Open: daily 10am–10pm. **$$** Off map
As the name suggests, this is a holistic shop that sells everything from meditation CDs and incense to yoga tops and mala beads. And the food here is organic Western and Asian. An all-in-one stop if you're so inclined.

Sri Hartamas

Daorae
9, Level 1, Plaza Crystal Ville Centre, Jalan 23/70A Desa Sri Hartamas. Tel: 03-6203 2616. Open: daily L & D. **$$** Off map
Bulgogi is the reason to head to Daorae. Cook beef marinated in a sweet soy sauce at your own grill, and eat it wrapped in lettuce with bean sauce and *kimchi* (pickled vegetables). A good line-up of other Korean dishes too; try the *dolsot bibimbap*, vegetables and beef on rice in a hot stone bowl, topped with a raw egg.

Jarrod & Rawlins
36, Ground Level, Jalan 27/70A, Desa Sri Hartamas. www.jarrod-rawlins.com Tel: 03-2300 0708. Open: daily 11am–midnight. **$$** Off map
Lots of traditional meat dishes to choose from, including steaks, home-made sausages and lamb cuts, priced by weight. On weekends, there's brunch (their poached eggs are great), Sunday roast or even a hangover special - a bacon and egg "butty" (sandwich) with Alka-Seltzer, Bloody Mary and free aspirin.

BELOW: many restaurants serve Western-style food.

Bars

Backyard Pub
28 Sri Hartamas 8, Taman Sri Hartamas. www.backyardpub.com Tel: 03-6201 0318. Off map.
This neighbourhood pub has pool tables, great Malaysian pub grub and live music every day.

Finnegan's
6 Jalan Telawi 5, Bangsar Baru. www.finneganspubs.com Tel: 03-2284 9024. Off map.
This noisy Irish pub has the largest number of taps in the city and is the only pub with cider. Good retro music on weekends.

Sino The Bar Upstairs
29A Jalan Telawi 3, Bangsar Baru. www.alexis.com.my Tel: 03-2284 2880. Off map.
Award-winning interior, acid jazz playing in the background and fantastic cocktails (try the lychee martini).

Price per person for a three-course meal without drinks:
$ = under RM30
$$ = RM30–60
$$$ = RM60–90
$$$$ = over RM90

STAFF

EXCURSIONS

Kuala Lumpur is a great jumping-off point to a variety of destinations in its surrounds, many of them manageable in a day, others involving overnight stays, but all easily accessible by road

Malaysian roads are generally in good condition. The highways are some of the best in Southeast Asia, a legacy of the colonial powers. On your drive out from the capital city, you'll experience charming and laid-back rural Malaysia with its small towns, rice paddies and villages – although zinc and bricks may have replaced timber and thatch, and rooftop satellite TV dishes are as ubiquitous as fruit trees in neat compounds.

About half an hour's drive north from Kuala Lumpur is the Forest Research Institute of Malaysia (FRIM) in Kepong, its regenerated rainforests containing a wealth of flora and fauna. Equally worth exploring are the labyrinthine Batu Caves, to the east of FRIM and home to fantastical Hindu mythology and the annual Thaipusam spectacle. North of the caves is rural Gombak, where the Ulu Gombak Forest Reserve and the Orang Asli Museum – which showcases the history and diversity of Malaysia's indigenous people – are found.

Further afield from the city, to its north and northeast, are the lofty Titiwangsa mountains, blanketed with millennia-old rainforests. The highlands offer unique vegetation, panoramic views and soothing cool weather. Two contrasting hill resorts here cater to vastly different tastes: frenzied 24-hour Las Vegas-type action in Genting Highlands, and Devonshire cream tea and long walks in the forests of peaceful Fraser's Hill. East of the hill resorts, the Kuala Gandah Elephant Conservation Centre provides unforgettable encounters with gentle Asian elephants.

Thrill-seekers should not miss Kuala Kubu Bahru at the foot of Fraser's Hill, where the swift Sungai Selangor and its tributaries are perfect for whitewater rafting and adventure sports. The undulating currents are dotted with mossy rocks and mirror pools, and there are many waterfalls.

Klang Valley, to the south and southwest of Kuala Lumpur, has many other charms, especially if you like shopping or eating out. Putrajaya, to the south, is a world unto itself, with its over-the-top architecture. ❑

PRECEDING PAGES: incense burning at Chin Swee Temple, Genting Highlands. **LEFT:** Asian elephants at the Kuala Gandah Elephant Conservation Centre. **ABOVE RIGHT:** Kampung Kuala Gandah. **ABOVE LEFT:** Sungai Chiling.

FRIM, BATU CAVES AND GOMBAK

A sprawling tropical rainforest; awe-inspiring limestone caves that come alive during Thaipusam; and a beautiful forest reserve where you can learn about the Temuan tribe – these are the surprises that lie just on the northern fringes of KL

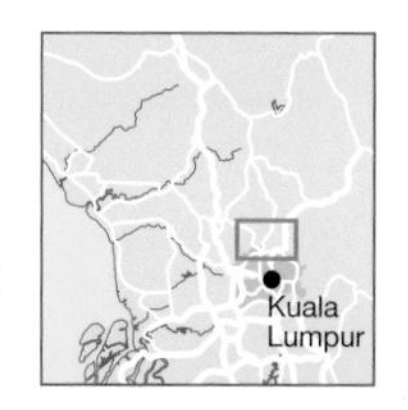

Main Attractions

Maps and Listings

About an hour's drive north and northeast of Kuala Lumpur are several attractions that can each be easily covered in a half or full day. Batu Caves and the Forest Research Institute of Malaysia (FRIM) are surrounded by urban sprawl but they are engaging and disparate worlds unto their own; Gombak is more rural and can also be covered en route to other destination on the Karak Highway *(see page 197)*. Travel agents in Kuala Lumpur sell day tours to Batu Caves and the Ulu Gombak Forest Reserve, but for those who want more control over their time it's worthwhile hiring a taxi.

FRIM

It's not often that earth-bound mortals get to see over the tops of trees, but thanks to the **Canopy Walkway**, a secure network of ladders and ropes stretched over the rainforest canopy, this is now possible. The walkway is the main attraction at the **Forest Research Institute of Malaysia (FRIM)** ❶ (www.frim.gov.my; tel: 03-6279 7575; daily 7am–7pm; admission charge). This is a rainforest research and recreational area in Kepong, 16km (10 miles) north from the city centre (half an hour's drive).

Canopy walkways were first built by scientists to study flora and fauna at treetop level, but now the lay person too has the opportunity to see shoots reaching out to the sun, insects pollinating flowers, and the forest from a top-down perspective. Interest in canopy science is a relatively recent study, but for many first-timers on the Canopy Walkway, the thrill of negotiating the 30-metre (100ft) height is good enough. The walkway stretches over 200 metres (660ft) and is anchored to five large rainforest trees. At these

LEFT: Hindu temple carvings at Batu Caves.
RIGHT: Canopy Walkway at FRIM.

North of Kuala Lumpur
Gading Forest Reserve
Bukit Pokok Pine 1456
Fraser's Hill
Raub
Kg Baharu S. Cetang
Kg S. Chendarawi
Kg S. Delam
Gap
Hulu Bernam Malay Reserve
Kalumpang
Teras
Gading Forest Reserve
Gerachi
Route 55
Semangkok Forest Reserve
Lurah Bilut
Kalumpang (Kg Sejantung)
Kg Gumut
Ulu Selangor Forest Reserve
Sg Gumut
Kerling Hot Spring
Sg Pertak Recreational Forest
Peretak
Kg Baharu Penjuring
Rumah Murah Kg Air Panas
Sungai Selangor Dam
Ulu Selangor Forest Reserve
Kerling
Ampang Pecah
Chiling Waterfall
Kerling
Kuala Kubu Bharu
Kg Gerachi Jaya
Kg Pertak
Kuan Yin Gu See Temple
Buloh Telor
Kg Ampang Pecah
Bukit Kutu
Gunung Rajah 1683
Bukit Kutu Forest Reserve
Bukit Tarek Forest Reserve
Selangor
Bentong
Bentong
Lancang
SELANGOR
Rasa
Kg Perting
Kg Cemeti
Bentong
Ulu Selangor
Sungai
PAHANG
Batang Kali
Batang Kali
Ulu Tamu Hot Springs
Ulu Yam
Ulu Tamu Orchard
Kuala Gandah Elephant Conservation Centre
Ulu Yam Baharu
Genting Highlands
Bandar Bt Beruntung
Kg Temiang
Ulu Yam
Ulu Yam Perdana
Sg Sendat Waterfalls
Bukit Tinggi
Japanese Tea House
Berjaya Hills Colmar Tropicale
Serendah
Kg Lentang
Bukit Tinggi Forest Reserve
Hutan Lipur Lentang (Lentang Forest Recreational Park)
Serendah
Serendah Forest Reserve
Kg Kastam
Ulu Gombak Forest Reserve
Karak Highway
Rawang
Rawang
Batu
Kanching Forest Reserve
Sg Tua Waterfalls
Jungle Lodge Alang Sedayu
Kg Lalang
Kg Batu Dua Belas Gombak
Orang Asli Museum
Gombak
Templer's Park
Empangan Sg Batu
Setapak
Forest Research Institute of Malaysia (FRIM)
International Islamic University
Batu Caves
Empangan Klang Gates
KEPONG
Jinjang Utara
Batu Caves
Taman Melawati
Sungai Buloh
SELAYANG
National Zoo
Wilayah Persekutuan
SETAPAK
KEPONG
WANGSA MAJU
0 5 km
0 5 miles
Petaling
Kuala Lumpur
Titiwangsa Lake
Canopy Walkway
Sungai Kroh Waterfall
Sungai Kroh Picnic Area
Rover Track
Jalan Foxworthy
Salleh Trail
Keruing Trail
Dipterocarp Arboretum
Engkabang Trail
Museum
J. Symington
J. Jelutong
Cafeteria
Coniferatum
Cryto-gamic Garden
Jalan FRIM
Non-Dipterocarp Arboretum
J. Bkt Watson
Kroh
Monocot Arboretum
Ethno-Botanic Garden
J. Kapur
Fruit Tree Arboretum II
FRIM
Entrance
Fruit Tree Arboretum I

vantage points are platforms that give commanding views of the forest and parts of the city through occasional gaps in the foliage. The Canopy Walkway is accessible from the Rover Track *(see below)* and part of it involves a stiff climb. Note: you cannot access the Canopy Walkway (Tue–Thur and Sat–Sun 9.30am–2.30pm; admission charge) without registering first at the **Information Centre** (tel: 03-6279 7575/ 7677; daily 8am–5pm). Be sure to book ahead during school holidays and note that registration closes at 1pm every day.

Trails and arboreta

The rainforest at FRIM, contrary to what people think, does not comprise virgin forest, but is a testament to what can happen if degraded land is left to its own devices for over 60 years. The institute, a leader in tropical forestry research, has also excelled in rainforest conservation and education by putting in place excellent facilities and providing information for the public in their 600-hectare (1,480-acre) site. These include a museum, library, clear signposts, maps, well-marked trails and labels on trees. Check in first at the info centre and they will help you sort out your itinerary, but book ahead for guided tours. The FRIM website is a storehouse of information and maps, and should be the starting point of your research.

For trekkers, there are three short trails, **Keruing Trail**, **Salleh's Trail** and **Engkabang Trail**, which are fairly flat and make for easy walking. Meandering through mature forest and regenerated plantations, and ranging from 1 to 1.5km (½–1¼ miles) long, they each take at most 30 minutes to complete. The toughest trail is the longest, the 3km (1¾-mile) **Rover Track**. This trail cuts through a thick forest, with its huge, straight trees, woody liana creepers and a thick shrub layer. About 10 minutes into this trail, you will come to a fork. The right path leads to a heart-pumping climb up Bukit Nolang (490 metres/1,600ft above sea level) – where the Canopy Walkway is. The left path continues on flatter land and leads to a small waterfall.

An alternative to the walking trails is a network of paved roads that wind

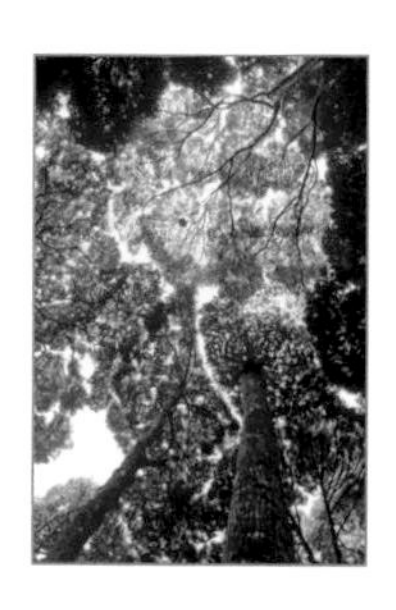

ABOVE: looking up to the canopy layer from the Rover Track at FRIM. **BELOW:** a view of the northern KL city skyline from the Canopy Walkway.

through several lovely **arboreta** (an arboretum is a wide-open space planted with specific tree species). The arboreta at FRIM are a great introduction to the Malaysian rainforest. Some of FRIM's arboreta were started as far back as 1929, when the institution first came into being, and its mature 150-species **dipterocarp arboretum** is world-renowned and widely referenced by scientists. The dipterocarps are the giants of the rainforest.

The forest also has a number of streams and waterfalls; especially popular is the one at **Sungai Kroh**, which during the rainy season (March–May and September–December) is wonderful for splashing around in.

BATU CAVES ❷

About 7km (4 miles) east of FRIM, or 13km (8 miles) from downtown Kuala Lumpur, are the **Batu Caves**, set in a limestone hill and synonymous with the spiritually charged Hindu festival of Thaipusam *(see pages 186–7)*. The hill is riddled with caves and passages, but it is one particular cave midway up its rockface – called the Temple Cave – that has brought it much fame.

ABOVE: waterfall at Sungai Kroh flowing through the rainforest. **BELOW:** Sri Subramaniar Swamy Temple at Batu Caves.

Batu Caves had long been known to, but not inhabited by, the indigenous Orang Asli who once lived in the area. In 1878, the caves were "discovered" by American naturalist William Hornaday; the site soon became known to the public and was turned into a popular picnic spot for British colonials. Shortly after, word spread among the local Hindu population that Batu Caves was a holy site for the deity Murugan (also known as Subramaniam). Given the Hindus' predilection for sacred caves, they started making pilgrimages here. In 1891, the **Sri Subramaniar Swamy Temple**, more commonly known as the Batu Caves Temple, was officially established here by K. Thambusamy Pillai, the founder of the Sri Maha Mariamman temple on Jalan Tun H.S. Lee.

Temple Cave

Today, standing at the base of Batu Caves and visible from afar is a gigantic 43-metre (140ft) tall gilded **statue of Lord Murugan**, to whom the temple is dedicated. From the base, 272 steps lead up to the main **Temple** (or Cathedral) **Cave** (daily 8am–9pm; free). This is a large chamber measuring some 80 by 100 metres (260 by 330ft); the cave opens at one end to a skylight from which shafts of light pour in dramatically at certain times of the day. The main shrine here pays homage to Lord Murugan. If there are worshippers praying at the shrine, keep a respectful distance from them.

Other shrines and caves

Down at the base of the steps leading to Temple Cave are shrines devoted to Ganesha, the Elephant God, and other deities like Meenatchi Amma, Sivan and Saneeswarar (all daily 6.30am–9pm; free). Located in separate structures about 200 metres (220 yards) to the left are shrines to Perumal and Anchaneyar (Hanuman). The

ABOVE: a devotee being blessed by a priest at the Sri Subramaniar Swamy Temple.

latter, the monkey god, is depicted by a 15-metre (50ft) tall statue. Hanuman is a key character in the Indian *Ramayana* epic story.

To the left of the steps, at the base of Temple Cave, are two smaller caves, worth visiting for their artwork (both daily 6am–9pm; single admission charge). One houses the **Gallery of Indian Art** and features brightly coloured, almost garish, wall paintings of Indian myths. The other cave houses **Velluvar Kottam**, which contains colourful clay figurines.

In the gardens near these caves, look out for the **statue of a five-legged bull**. The image honours a real creature that once roamed the area and is now buried at the site.

Dark Caves

Batu Caves are part of an impressive limestone outcrop and were created when rainwater and carbon dioxide dissolved and carved hollows into the porous limestone. In the process, over millions of years, beautiful formations were also created, including stalagmites, stalactites, curtains and dripstones. Batu Caves' limestone ecosystem is extremely fragile; it is also home to a large number of endemic plants and creatures only found in this unique habitat.

To explore the fascinating cave ecosystem, book a guided tour with the **Malaysian Nature Society (MNS)** every third Sunday of the month (tel: 03-2287 9422). The tours will allow you special access to the 2km (1¼-mile) long **Dark Caves**; its entrance is found midway up the steps to the Temple Cave. A range of tours – from a quick 20-minute orientation to a three-hour expedition – are offered by the MNS and the cave operators, and are suitable for children as young as three.

Ulu Gombak Forest Reserve

Heading towards the Titiwangsa Mountain Range is a beautiful forest reserve that has become popular with outdoor training centres. The **Ulu Gombak Forest Reserve** protects virgin lowland and hilly dipterocarp forests, the original homes of the

TIP

Keep a lookout for monkeys on your way up to Temple Cave. These bold creatures have been known to snatch items like cameras, sunglasses and especially food and drink from hapless visitors. so keep these things out of sight. Whatever you do, don't feed the monkeys as this encourages them to be reliant on humans for food.

TIP

If you book a tour of the Dark Caves, rent the overalls and long-sleeved clothes the cave operators will offer; otherwise crawling through tunnels may result in skin scrapes and ruined outfits.

Temuan, the biggest Orang Asli tribe in Selangor (pop. 16,000). Today, the 1,000 or so Temuan in Gombak are mostly urbanised, although some still hunt in the forests. They speak mainly Malay, but also use their own Temuan language, which is similar to Malay.

Orang Asli Museum ❸

A must-visit while in Gombak is the **Orang Asli Museum** (KM 24 Jalan Pahang; tel 03-6189 2113; Sun–Thur 9.30am–5pm; free). Here you can learn about the Temuan and other indigenous peoples of peninsular Malaysia. As the museum is run by the Jabatan Hal-Ehwal Orang Asli (Department of Orang Asli Affairs) and is staffed mostly by non-Orang Asli, some of the wording in the displays can be a little condescending. However, the museum is the only one of its kind in the country, and has excellent historical photographs as well as a large and varied collection of artefacts representing the 100 or so groups of Orang Asli in the country.

Besides displays of Orang Asli implements – from powerful blowpipes and porcupine-quill nose rings to fine weaving – there is a tribute to the Senoi Praaq, a special military elite force almost entirely composed of Senoi people, which was formed to fight the Communist guerrillas. Established in 1956 as British Special Air Service (SAS) protégés, they fought in deep jungles. For those interested in animism, there is a section upstairs on exorcism, with displays of exorcised items such as glass and blades.

The museum also has a souvenir shop with fine examples of masks and carvings. These are crafted by the Mah Meri, an Orang Asli tribe who live in the coastal parts of Selangor. The Orang Asli in Malaysia have had a challenging time with the Malaysian government in the past few years as they continue to fight over the rights to ancestral lands. Much Temuan land has been "seized" by various parties and incorporated into massive building projects like the Sungai Selangor dam in Kuala Kubu Baru and Kuala Lumpur International Airport (KLIA) in Sepang without adequate consultation or compensation. However, the Temuan have been mobilised enough to get legal representation and landmark cases have recently been brought.

BELOW: works by the Mah Meri tribe, among others, are displayed at the Orang Asli Museum.

Jungle Lodge Alang Sedayu ❹

About 10 minutes' drive further up Jalan Pahang, a left turn takes you to one of the access points to the Ulu Gombak Forest Reserve. The narrow road follows the Sungai Gombak, upstream of the historic confluence where Kuala Lumpur began. Here, the river flows swiftly, its clear waters tumbling over rocks and descending over a series of natural steps, looking completely different from its muddy persona in the city.

On the right of the river and road is the forest reserve; on the left, private land. From the junction, drive for another 10 minutes to the **Jun-**

gle Lodge Alang Sedayu (www.junglelodgemalaysia.com; tel: 03-4251 4301; daily 9am–6pm; admission charge for use of all day facilities). The lodge is located on the left, across a bridge over the river. Here, you can spend the day by a 25-metre (82ft) swimming pool in a forest setting, swim in the river or take a tour of the forest.

The 1.4-hectare (3½-acre) timber facility is styled after American summer camps for children, so school holidays and long weekends are usually booked out. Call ahead to check availability. The lodge is a pleasant escape from the city, with fresh air and the sound of gushing water and the rainforest. You may bring your own food, but there is also a canteen that serves local fare and sandwiches. In addition, there are basic accommodation and tents for hire if you've made arrangements to spend the night.

The lodge offers a five-hour tour (10am–3pm) called "A Day in the Rainforest", which includes a pick-up from KL city centre, jungle trekking, lunch and time to relax at the lodge. The trek can be tailored to requirements, so those who want to take it easy may settle for a one-hour rainforest interpretation tour while the more adventurous could enjoy a two-hour trek with river crossings to get to a waterfall. Among all the wildlife here, monkeys are the most likely to be spotted. A special feature of the area is a series of 60-year-old tunnels dug by Communist insurgents (probably with the help of the Temuan). One short tunnel is 10 minutes' walk from the lodge. If you are booked on a tour, ask your guide to point the tunnel out; otherwise, ask the lodge staff for directions to get to it. ❑

ABOVE: local boys play in the Gombak river.

RESTAURANTS

Batu Caves

Pan Heong Restaurant
2 Jalan Medan Batu Caves 2. Tel: 03-6187 7430. Open: daily 8.30am–3pm. **$**
Foodies rave about the humble but spectacular fare at Pan Heong. Notable are the *sang har meen* (tiger prawns and flat rice noodles in an egg sauce) and porridge dishes (with frogs' legs, century egg or pork ribs).

Restoran Ulu Yam
7113 Jalan Len Omnibus, Taman Selayang Bahru. Mobile tel: 012-388 2991. Open: daily 8am–9.30pm. **$**
Tuck into the *loh mee* (noodles in a dark gravy, topped with prawns and pork) that the town of Ulu Yam is famous for. Other must-tries are the chicken curry and deep-fried pork ribs.

Seafood Sin Kee
8 Jalan SG1/10, Pusat Penjaja, Taman Industri Bolton. Tel: 03-6189 7972. Open: daily L & D. **$**
Order the crabs with a spicy-sweet sauce, best mopped up with deep-fried bread rolls. Try also mussels in superior stock and wine, prawns tossed in cheese sauce, and belly pork cooked in soy sauce.

Kepong

Fitou Brasserie
Lot GF2, The Waterfront@ Park City, 5 Persiaran Residen, Desa Parkcity. www.fitougourmet.com Tel: 03-6280 8978. Open: Mon–Sat noon–midnight, Sun 8.30am–midnight. **$$**
Desa Parkcity is a new township built around an artificial lake five minutes from Kepong. Fitou serves Mediterranean-style fare; the Iberico pork ribs and Canadian cod are flown in and the wines are extensive. The champagne brunch is perfect for a lazy Sunday overlooking the lake.

Nice Soup Gang
8 Jalan Daya 11, Taman Daya. Tel: 03-6272 5988. Open: daily L & D. **$$**
Double-boiled soups and other dishes are subtly flavoured with Chinese herbs. Try the shark cartilage soup with dried scallops, bamboo pith and ginseng, steamed fish with ginger and spring onions, or prawns and scallops in sweet corn sauce.

Red Door
Lot F27, Level 1, Jusco Metro Prima Shopping Centre, 1 Jalan Metro Prima, off Jalan Kepong. Tel: 03-6252 6168. Open: daily 10am–10.30pm. **$**
A pretty restaurant adorned with ethnic accents. The coconut rice, coloured blue with the blue pea flower, with thick chicken curry, is an interesting and unusual option. Leave room for desserts such as *pulut inti*, a glutinous rice pudding topped with sweet grated coconut.

Price per person for a three-course meal without drinks.
***$** = under RM30,*
***$$** = RM30–60,*
***$$$** = RM60–90,*
***$$$$** = over RM90.*

Thaipusam – A Festival of Faith

A remarkable sensory experience, the annual Hindu festival of Thaipusam celebrated at Batu Caves is unforgettable

When the star of well-being (*pusam*) rises over the east in the 10th Tamil month of Thai (January/February), Hindus participate in the festival of repentance called Thaipusam. In a riot of colours, sounds and emotions that is unique in the world, over a million devotees in Kuala Lumpur fulfill their vows at the holiest site related to the festival: the Batu Caves temple (*see pages 182–3*) some 272 steps above the ground. Since 1891, it has been associated with the festival's key deity, Murugan, son of Siva and Mariamman. He manifests virtue, valour, youth and vitality and is known as a destroyer of evil forces and dispenser of favours.

At dawn, devotees in a procession begin a 15km (9-mile) journey from Sri Maha Mariamman Temple in Kuala Lumpur (*see pages 114–5*) to Batu Caves. Those who have had a request granted by him carry milk up to the temple to bathe his statue. Milk is sometimes transported in large wooden and metal structures called *kavadi*, some of which weigh over 20kg (44lbs). During their fulfillment of vows, many devotees fall into a trance and several pierce their backs, chests, cheeks or tongues to atone for misdeeds or as a purification ritual. That the piercing is bloodless and painless is, most believe, due to months of strict abstinence in diet and lifestyle.

Above: Thaipusam begins with a dawn procession led by a statue of Murugan in an ox-drawn silver chariot. Devotees wait along the procession route to receive blessings from priests in the chariot.

Above: after making offerings in a consecrated fire ritual, devotees are blessed on the forehead with holy ash. Accompanying family and friends also undergo prayer and blessing rituals.

Right: children and women usually carry a pot of milk (*paal kudam*) wrapped in a saffron-coloured cloth, as their "burden" of devotion. The milk must not be spilled on the journey. The pouring of milk over Murugan's statue symbolises the outpouring of love from the heart.

SYMBOLS OF DEVOTION

As well as being a festival of penance, Thaipusam also commemorates the day Murugan received a *vel*, or trident, from his goddess mother, with which he destroyed evil. The *vel* is synonymous with the deity; the very word is believed to have the power to invoke the grace of Murugan, and is therefore chanted by devotees and their supporters during the fulfilment of vows. Thaipusam is a highly symbolic festival. Besides the *vel*, there are many other tokens derived from various legends associated with Murugan. The carrying of the *kavadi* comes from a myth involving the lifting of a mountain with Murugan at its apex, symbolising the willingness to bear a burden as a test of devotion. A silver chariot with an important and much adorned statue of Murugan is the centrepiece of the procession from the Sri Maha Mariamman Temple in Kuala Lumpur to Batu Caves every year.
Legend has it that after conquering evil spirits, Murugan appeared before his devotees ornamented and in a silver chariot.

LEFT: heads are shaved as a symbol of humility. Cooling saffron-coloured sandalwood paste is applied thereafter, as the colour is associated with sanctity and purity.

BELOW: devotees take a ritual cleansing bath before undertaking their journey of penance. Devotees observe rituals for a month or more before Thaipusam, including fasting, praying and various abstinences.

ABOVE: acts of penance, like the skewering of tongue and body, take centre stage but Thaipusam is actually a communal event. Family and friends support devotees in many ways, from preparing hooks and offerings to keeping their spirits up with the hypnotic drumming of the *urumi mellam* band.

RIGHT: at the foot of the steps leading up to the cave temple at Batu Caves is the world's largest statue of Murugan. It is 43 metres (140ft) tall and covered with 300 litres (66 gallons) of gold paint.

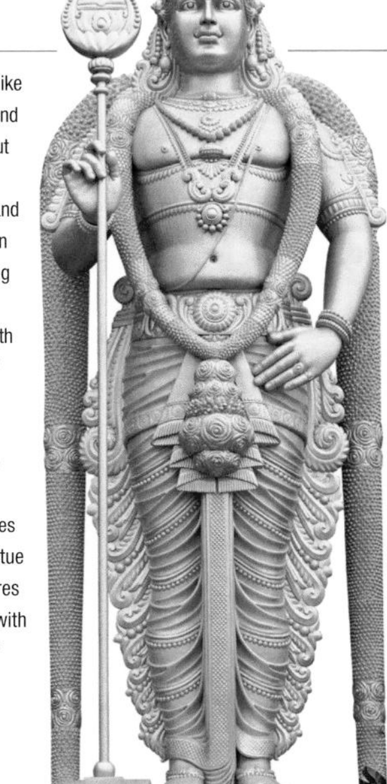

HILL RESORTS AND SURROUNDINGS

Head for the hills to escape the capital's heat and crowds. The Titiwangsa Range's hill stations offer cool weather, lush rainforests and recreational activities. There is also a chance to visit rustic Orang Asli villages, raft on frothing whitewater and visit an elephant sanctuary

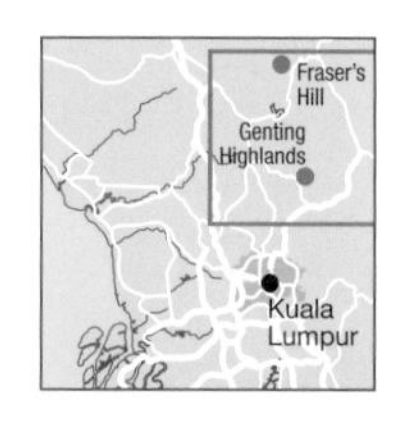

Main Attractions

- KUALA KUBU BHARU
- SUNGAI SELANGOR
- ORANG ASLI SETTLEMENTS
- CHILING WATERFALL
- FRASER'S HILL
- GENTING HIGHLANDS
- LENTANG FOREST RECREATIONAL PARK
- KUALA GANDAH ELEPHANT CONSERVATION CENTRE

Maps and Listings

MAP OF HILL RESORTS AND SURROUNDINGS, PAGES 180 AND 193
RESTAURANTS, PAGE 199

Thrust up during the Jurassic Age about 200 million years ago, the lofty Titiwangsa Mountain Range forms the backbone of Peninsular Malaysia, dividing the east coast from the west. Known also as the Main Range, this mountain chain, whose height is rarely below 1,000 metres (3,300ft), is an attractive destination for its cool air, beautiful scenery and rainforest; its foothills also offer recreational opportunities.

This chapter covers two main areas: Kuala Kubu Bharu and Fraser's Hill, north of Kuala Lumpur; and Genting Highlands and Kuala Gandah Elephant Sanctuary, which are northeast of the capital.

ALONG SUNGAI SELANGOR

Kuala Kubu Bharu

The Titiwangsa is the source of many of the peninsula's rivers, including the 110km (68-mile) **Sungai Selangor**, which discharges into the Strait of Melaka near the town of Kuala Selangor. Like many rivers, Sungai Selangor has charted the course of settlements, including a sleepy town called **Kuala Kubu Bharu** ❺, about an hour's drive or 72km (45 miles) from the capital.

To get to Kuala Kubu Bharu from Kuala Lumpur, drive towards Rawang to get onto Route 1. After about 40 minutes, look out for a signboard indicating a right turn into Kuala Kubu Bharu and Fraser's Hill. Take this turning and, after 15 minutes, you will arrive at Kuala Kubu Bharu, or KKB as the locals call it.

KKB used to be a blink-and-it's-gone type of place on the road to Fraser's Hill. The town itself is small and placid, with small eateries and grocery shops, but in the last decade,

LEFT: the thrills and spills of whitewater kayaking along Sungai Selangor.
RIGHT: visiting the Kuala Gandah Elephant Sanctuary.

its surrounds have become a popular playground for nature and adventure-sports lovers, making it a worthwhile day trip. If Fraser's Hill is your destination, plan to spend at least half a day in KKB before heading up to Fraser's Hill for another day or two.

Sungai Selangor

Adrenalin-seeking **whitewater sports** enthusiasts started paddling in the **Sungai Selangor** stretch near KKB. As word spread, adventure-tour companies began bringing tourists in. Today, the river is a top choice for kayaking, canoeing and rafting, and caters to different proficiency levels *(see Travel Tips page 241)*. For a kayaking course, you need a minimum of three days to gain basic certification. Some operators also offer tubing, which is floating lazily down the river in a rubber tube.

The starting points for whitewater action are along the road leading to Fraser's Hill, part of which skirts the **Sungai Selangor Dam ❻**. This section of the road offers sweeping views of part of the 600-hectare (1,480-acre) forested water catchment area. During the wet season, water overflows into a 30-metre-wide (100ft) spillway, which can be seen from the dam's information centre (Tue–Sun 9am–4pm), located about 5km (3 miles) from KKB.

The dam was completed in 2003 to supply water to parts of Selangor and Kuala Lumpur, but its construction was controversial because of its environmental impact, safety issues and the displacement of two Orang Asli settlements and their land. The Orang Asli here are from the Temuan tribe, Selangor's largest indigenous group.

Safety concerns were raised because the river had been dammed twice before in 1883 and 1926, and had broken its banks both times, drowning the original town of Kuala Kubu that used to sit in the area now called Ampang Pechah ("burst dam"). After the second flood, the town was rebuilt upstream on its present site and renamed *bharu*, which means "new". The new dam sits upstream from the current town. The new town of Kuala Kubu was designed by New Zealand town planner Charles Reade and completed in 1928 in line with

ABOVE: the Orang Asli people rely on the forest for their income.
BELOW: Sungai Selangor Dam.

The Temuan

Like their ancestors, the Temuan people here, who speak little English and are very shy, still live forest-bound lives. About half of them depend on the forest, earning an income through the collection and sale of jungle produce like bamboo and fruit to the townsfolk. Others are forced to find odd jobs around town and in rubber and oil palm estates. A few have also developed new skills and earn an income as nature guides.

If you visit a Temuan village, ask permission from the village head (*tok batin*) before walking around, and bring gifts such as rice, biscuits, tea or coffee. You may see traditional activities like blowpipe-making or basket-weaving; some handicrafts may be for sale.

ABOVE: Orang Asli kids have a splash.

the Garden City movement, which was all the rage after World War I.

According to legend, the first dam broke because the then British district officer, Sit Cecil Ranking, had shot a white crocodile: this was considered a bad omen, and the dam burst that very night, drowning the administrator.

All that was left of him after the waters receded was his hand. The Temuan believed that the shooting had angered several spirit guardians of the river: the crocodile spirit as well as a "red dragon" – in reference to the foaming, red earth-coloured floodwaters that caused the dam to burst.

Orang Asli settlements

Millions of ringgit were paid to compensate the two Temuan communities affected by the building of the dam. Kampung Gerachi and Kampung Pertak were rebuilt, albeit in a contemporary style – reflecting perhaps the political attitude towards Malaysia's indigenous people.

Kampung Gerachi, now called **Kampung Gerachi Jaya** ❼, has a population of 280 and is located before the dam's catchment area (look out for a signboard). The village is perched on a hill and has commanding views of the dam and its surrounds. **Kampung Pertak** ❽, with a population of 300, is 3km (2 miles) further up after the dam's information centre. The village is spread out above the icy-cold Sungai Luit, a beautiful stream which tumbles over boulders. Drive to the end of the village and walk down to the stream for a picnic and swim.

Sungai Chiling area

A popular starting point for whitewater sports is five minutes' drive from Kampung Pertak, at an old steel bridge known locally as the **Rainbow Bridge** because of its arched shape. This bridge is sometimes used by adventure-sports operators for abseiling activities. On the right side of the road is a trail that leads to the lovely

Just around the first corner as you leave Kuala Kubu Bharu for Fraser's Hill is a Hindu temple honouring the Mother Goddess Kali. One year, on the first day of the festival dedicated to the goddess, a white viper wound itself around the head of the deity and stayed there for the entire duration of the holy period before disappearing.

three-tiered **Chiling Waterfall** ❾, which gushes 20 metres (66ft) into a deep pool. The 1½-hour trek follows the swift **Sungai Chiling**, a tributary of Sungai Selangor, and involves six river crossings. Reward yourself at the end with a picnic on the rocks at the bottom-most tier of the waterfall and a swim in its clear waters. Be warned, though, that this canyon is prone to flash floods when it rains.

The forest here is lowland dipterocarp, characterised by tall trees and herbaceous species such as ferns and gingers. Look out for the astonishing variety of seeds and flowers on the ground. The vegetation fringing the river comprises creepers, ferns and semi-aquatic plants that grow well in open areas with strong sunlight. These riverine areas are also important corridors for birds and animals, so keep an eye out for these creatures.

FRASER'S HILL ❿

From Rainbow Bridge, the road winds uphill for about 30km (19 miles) to the turn-off to **Fraser's Hill**, a peaceful hill retreat in the Titiwangsa Mountain Range. The resort actually belongs to the neighbouring state of Pahang. This road, **Route 55**, was built in the late 19th century as the country's first throughway across the mountains, connecting the old towns of Kuala Kubu and Kuala Lipis in Pahang. As you climb, note how the vegetation changes. Hill dipterocarp species start appearing from altitudes of over 300 metres (980ft), and trees get shorter the higher you go. At 1,200 metres (3,940ft), conifers start dominating and moss grows thickly.

The thickly forested winding road made for many excellent ambush points, or so the Communists found during the Emergency of 1948–1960. The then British High Commissioner Henry Gurney was killed in one of these ambushes en route to the hill station in 1951. The spot where Gurney was killed, about 3km (2 miles) from the turn-off to Fraser's Hill, used to be marked, but the sign has disappeared. A small Hindu shrine stands at that same spot, not in honour of Gurney, but because the site happens to be sacred.

Route 55 was constructed to service the Malaysian El Dorado at that time, **Raub**, which lies east of the

BELOW: the long-tailed sibia can be spotted at Fraser's Hill.

mountain range. Back then an 80km (50-mile) bridle path, it was used to transport gold from Raub to Port Klang on the west coast, and to bring supplies to Raub – all by mule.

One of the people who cashed in on the business opportunities on this road was accountant-turned-entrepreneur Louis James Fraser. His diverse businesses also included a gambling den for miners and illicit tin mining in the hills. He mysteriously disappeared one day, leaving behind only the name Bukit Fraser (Fraser's Hill) for the place where he operated. The place vanished from the radar until World War I, when a couple of bishops from Singapore went on a holiday exploration of Bukit Fraser. Though they had to be rescued because they wandered in the forest and became lost, they were enthralled enough to recommend it as eminently suitable for a retreat.

Fraser's Hill became British Malaya's first hill station retreat. When it was completed in 1925, the Chief Secretary Sir George Maxwell prophesied that it would be "the most exquisite and the most dainty hill station in Malaya". Today, it seems the prophecy has been realised, with minimal new development, pleasant average daytime temperatures of 20°C (68°F), and peace and quiet when night falls.

The road up to Fraser's town centre starts at the **Gap**, which, in pre-resort days, was the mid-point rest stop for mule and bullock cart transporters. It was named the Gap as it was literally a gap between the boundaries of the Selangor and Pahang states. Travellers used to take respite at a resthouse here, which still stands today but is poorly maintained.

From the Gap, it is another 20 to 30 minutes' drive uphill on a new one-way road. The passage downhill is the original century-old road. From various points on the new road, you can see the mighty forest below,

ABOVE: creepers and moss cling to a mammoth tree trunk on Fraser's Hill.

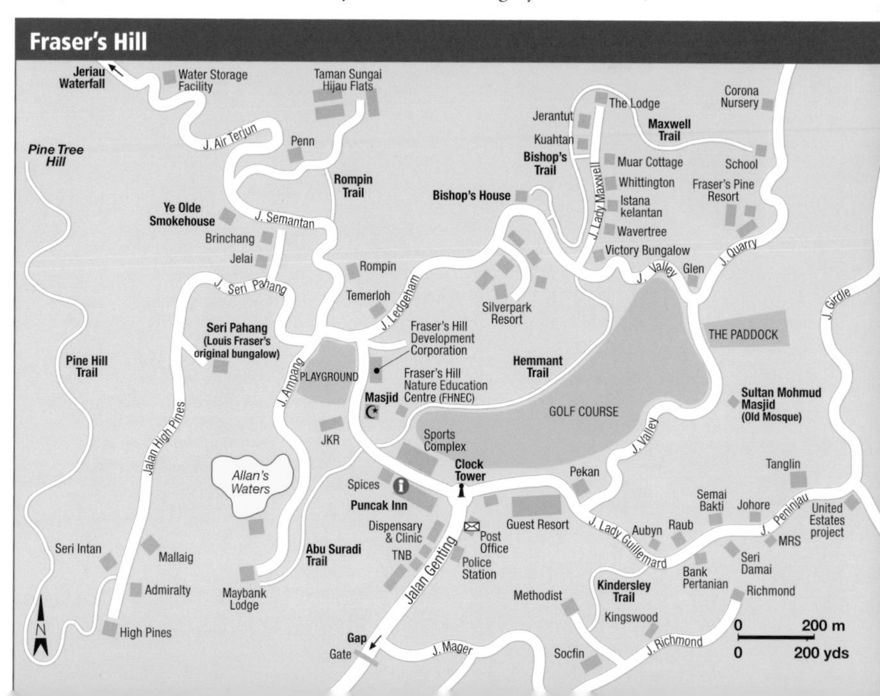

The Mighty Rainforest

Half of Malaysia is covered by ancient tropical rainforests, which flourish thanks to high temperatures, abundant sunlight and heavy rainfall all year round

Malaysia is part of the 2.5-million-sq-km (960,000-sq-mile) Indo-Malayan rainforest block, the second-largest of the world's three major rainforest blocks. Its rainforests have the most diverse and structurally complex land ecosystems on earth, with 40,000 recorded species of higher plants (four times the number found in the entire EU) and an unknown number of lower plant species like fungi and algae. Animal diversity is as high as well; for instance, Malaysia has over 600 species of birds, 280 of mammals and 10,000 of moths. Overall, more than 2,000 higher species are found only in Malaysia and nowhere else on earth. Unfortunately about a fifth are threatened and nearly 4 percent endangered.

In order to understand rainforests, take the opportunity to go on guided tours of the different types of forest habitats. The most common forest types around Kuala Lumpur are the **lowland** and **highland dipterocarp forests**. These are the most luxuriant of all plant communities and a key source of tropical hardwood. Dipterocarps are very large trees – 45 metres (148ft) or taller – that dominate the canopy. Below them is a middle layer of medium-sized trees. There is usually little vegetation on the ground because sunlight cannot filter through.

Swamp forests are found in areas that are under water for long periods or periodically. Freshwater swamp forests thrive in the lower reaches of rivers and fringes of stillwater wetlands. Shaded coastal areas are home to mangrove swamp forests. Swamp forests do not have great species diversity, and host species that have adapted to wet conditions by developing characteristics like stilt or air-breathing roots.

Limestone hills are harsh environments that force highly specialised plants to evolve. This results in a staggering variety of species compared to other habitats. The species are also highly localised, and include herbaceous plants like begonias and orchids.

Up in the mountains, trees are gnarled and more stunted and are covered with moss and epiphytes – these are features of **montane forests**. Where natural forests have been cleared, **secondary forests** evolve, with new grasses and shrubs giving rise to pioneer tree species. After 75 to 100 years a secondary forest will mature, usually with a different composition to the forest it replaced.

Large mammals are frustratingly difficult to spot in rainforests, but smaller creatures are plentiful, varied and fascinating. All are part of an intricate and delicately balanced web of rainforest life that humankind is just beginning to understand. ❑

ABOVE: creepers and moss cling to a mammoth tree trunk on Fraser's Hill.

spreading out like a luxurious green carpet. If you stop to take photographs, make sure the road shoulder is wide enough for safe parking.

Misty montane forests

When you reach the town centre, you will be in the midst of a **montane forest**, which is found only at heights of over 1,500 metres (4,900ft). In the forest, sunbeams dramatically puncture rising and descending mists. Trees are generally shorter here than in the lowlands, growing up to only 30 metres (100ft) tall, and are usually coated with lichens, filmy ferns and orchids. Dominant species are oaks, laurels, tree ferns and conifers. Scientists have found over 30 species of plants that live only in these hills.

Fraser's Hill is also a birdwatcher's paradise, home to 275 recorded species. A major international race is held here each June to sight, identify and record as many species of birds as possible (www.mns.org.my). Besides birds, also look out for monkeys and squirrels in the trees, as well as skinks, trapdoor spiders, beetles and other bugs on the thickly leaf-littered forest floor. If lucky, you may spot a deer or a wild boar. At night, any light will attract all sorts of flying insects.

Colonial architecture

The British had the idea of creating a Little England on Fraser's Hill, and Tudor was the architectural style they favoured. The original granite bungalows were built by colonial government officials and the first four were named after famous World War I gun shelters because limited government funds allowed only small, "knobbly and formidable" (in Maxwell's words) buildings to be erected.

Subsequent buildings were named after British Residents of Pahang or their wives. These have since been renamed according to towns and places in Pahang and can be rented *(see Travel Tips page 233)*.

Later, plantation and large commercial companies built their own bungalows as holiday housing for their staff, while Malaysian royalty erected *istana* (palaces). Some post-independence buildings have attempted to keep to the Tudor theme but with limited success.

Fraser's town centre

The resort's built-up area spreads over seven hills, with all sections accessible by road. The **town centre** has several colonial icons: a clock tower, post office, police station

ABOVE: ferns are common in Fraser's montane forest. **ABOVE LEFT:** old bungalows stand amid rolling hills. **BELOW:** the clock tower on Fraser's Hill.

ABOVE: Bishop's Trail is an easy hiking route.
BELOW: Jeriau Waterfall at Fraser's Hill, an excellent bird-watching location.

and a golf course that was once the ravine mined by Louis Fraser. It is now one of Malaysia's few public golf courses (tel: 09-362 2122; daily 8am–7pm).

To the left of the clock tower is a row of buildings whose upper floors are occupied by the Puncak Inn. The **Information Centre** (tel: 09-362 2201; Sun–Fri 8am–9pm, Sat 9am–10pm), where you can get a free map, is below the inn. You can also book accommodation here. Guided walks and birding tours are available too but you will have to book these a few days ahead. With the exception of the Pine Hill Trail, all the trails are well marked and experienced trekkers will not need a guide, but do check beforehand at the Information Centre on the state of trails and on safety precautions.

Town walks

From the clock tower, several roads loop around the **town centre** and encircle the golf course. The loop makes for a nice, leisurely two-hour walk. In a clockwise direction, walk along Jalan Genting from the clock tower, past the mosque to a junction where some colonial bungalows stand. Take the right fork into Jalan Ledgeham, which is edged by forest. Go past the popular Bishop's Trail jungle walk *(see below)* and connect to Jalan Valley, around part of the golf course. At the Pekan Bungalow, Jalan Lady Guillemard will take you back to the clock tower in the town centre.

The area west of the town centre loop also offers nice walks. At the end of Jalan Genting, the left fork – Jalan Pokok Pine – goes to a popular children's playground. At its end, Jalan Pokok Pine branches out three ways. The left turning, Jalan Ampang, leads to **Allan's Waters**, a small artificial lake where paddleboats are available for hire. The middle turning, Jalan Seri Pahang, leads to more colonial bungalows; of note on this road is Louis Fraser's original bungalow, which he called the Pahang Bungalow. It is now known as **Seri Pahang**, and its current owner is the Sultan of Pahang.

Fraser's Jungle Walks

The most popular jungle trail from Fraser's Hill is the scenic half-hour **Bishop's Trail**, which begins at the Bishop's Bungalow. The equally interesting **Hemmant Trail** begins at the Jalan Valley loop and skirts the golf course to end conveniently at the Information Centre. For a 20-minute walk, take the **Rompin Trail**, which starts opposite the Smokehouse, or the **Abu Suradi Trail**, which goes from the Information Centre to Allan's Waters. Fit trekkers will relish the guided-only 6km (4-mile) **Pine Hill Trail**, which involves a four-hour climb up 1,450 metres (4,750ft) to breathtaking views. For more trail details, see www.wwfmalaysia.org/fhnec/trails.htm.

The right turning off Jalan Pokok Pine goes past another Fraser's Hill institution, **Ye Olde Smokehouse**, and zig-zags for 4km (2 miles) to the **Jeriau Waterfall**. The 10-metre (30ft) high waterfall and its concrete-lined pool sit in a valley accessible by a flight of steps. The fall is not spectacular but its waters offer a refreshing dip, and it is an excellent place for birdwatching.

Tea at the Smokehouse

The road to the waterfall is an easy one-hour walk downhill (you will have to trudge uphill on your return). Time it right and you can reward yourself with a Devonshire tea – warm scones and strawberry jam – in the pretty garden of **The Smokehouse Hotel and Restaurant** (www.thesmokehouse.com.my/fh; tel: 09-362 2226; daily tea 3–5.30pm; *see pages 199, 233*). Erected in 1924, this English cottage-style lodging is one of several bungalows on Fraser's Hill originally funded by the British Red Cross Society and the Order of St John of Jerusalem in England and built "for the benefit especially of ex-members of the imperial forces of 1914–1918 and their dependents".

At sunset, walk down to the lookout at the base of a hillock, and watch the setting sun paint the cotton-wool-like mist and rolling hills a brilliant orange that deepens into purple.

You can explore more of the area if you have a car, particularly the **Jalan Peninjau loop**, east of the town centre, which branches off from the Pekan bungalow. Be warned, though, that this is a very winding road.

GENTING HIGHLANDS ⑪

The **Karak Highway**, which snakes its way northeast up the Titiwangsa Range for over 60km (37 miles), leads to **Genting Highlands** (www.rwgenting.com), a hill resort that is vastly different from the quiet Fraser's Hill. Genting is about 48km (30 miles) from Kuala Lumpur; from the city, drive northeast to reach the Karak Highway. Continue driving for another half an hour before you see a massive multistoreyed rest stop on your right, marking the turn-off to Genting Highlands. From here, a 15-minute drive up a winding road takes you to the resort.

Genting Highlands, the Las Vegas of Malaysia, is immensely popular.

ABOVE LEFT: enjoy tea and scones in the gardens at Fraser's Smokehouse Hotel. **ABOVE:** shady forest ground at Fraser's Hill. **BELOW:** abseiling down Sungai Chiling Bridge.

Visitors might enjoy its mountaintop location – some 2,000 metres (6,500ft) above sea level – but most are really drawn by its man-made rather than natural attractions: in particular, the country's only legal casino. With a slew of other attractions, cheap accommodation and its close proximity to Kuala Lumpur, it's little wonder that Genting gets very crowded on weekends and school holidays.

There are two levels to the retreat. At the peak, the **Genting Highlands Resort** sees non-stop action. The casino, which sits in the Highlands Hotel, one of the seven hotels here, has five themed gaming areas. The casino has a dress code (no T-shirts, shorts or slippers) and Muslims are strictly forbidden from entering it.

Non-gamblers can occupy themselves at the **Genting Theme Park**, which has over 60 thrilling rides, including its signature Flying Coaster and a skydiving wind tunnel; an 80-outlet shopping centre; and over 90 food outlets. International live acts are also staged year round at the hotel's theatre restaurant.

ABOVE: all aboard the carousel at the Genting Theme Park. **BELOW:** Genting's skyway cable car ride.

Awana and Skyway

Midway up the peak and far more laid-back in comparison is the **Awana Genting Highlands Golf and Country Resort** (www.awana.com.my). Its amenities include an 18-hole golf course, heated pools and outdoor adventure sports facilities.

Awana and Genting Highlands resorts are linked by a 24-hour **skyway**, a cable car system that is the world's fastest, covering the 3.4km (2-mile) journey in 11 minutes flat. The cable cars operate every 3 minutes except at night (Sun–Fri 11pm–7.30am, Sat midnight–7.30am) when they operate at 15-minute intervals. If it's not misty, the scenery on this short ride is quite spectacular, with montane vegetation spread out beneath. Free shuttle bus services transport passengers from the hotels to the skyway stations.

FURTHER EAST

Lentang Forest Recreational Park ⓬

From Genting Highlands, continue eastward on the Karak Highway for another 13km (8 miles) to an exit marked "Hutan Lipur Lentang", or **Lentang Forest Recreational Park**, at KM 48. This is a lovely spot for a picnic under shady trees, by brooks that tumble over small rocks.

Kuala Gandah Elephant Conservation Centre ⓭

The not-to-be-missed **Kuala Gandah Elephant Conservation Centre** (tel: 09 279 0391; daily 7.30am-5.30pm, closed for lunch; charge), about 1½ hours drive from Kuala Lumpur, or 120km (75 miles) away, offers a wonderful opportunity to get close to Asian elephants.

From Hutan Lipur Lentang, get onto the Karak Highway and continue east for an hour until you hit the turn-off to Lanchang. Exit the highway and you will come to a T-junction. Turn right onto Route 8 towards Raub, and follow the signs for about 15 minutes.

The centre is home to elephants aged between 7 and 17 years, trained to interact with people *(see picture on page 176)*. An afternoon programme (2.15–3.45pm) allows visitors to ride, bathe and feed them under wildlife officers' supervision. Rides are limited to 100 visitors per day. Do allocate time for browsing through the interpretation centre and to watch the video show.

Threats and conservation

Sadly, Asian elephants are critically endangered in Southeast Asia; in Peninsular Malaysia, less than 1,200 remain in the wild. The activities at the centre help to raise awareness of its original purpose – as a temporary base for elephants that are being relocated from one area to another. When the elephants' natural forest habitats are taken over by creeping urbanisation and conversion to agricultural land, these creatures have no choice but to feed on crops in plantations bordering the remaining forests, and end up being chased away by planters. Elephants who cannot keep up with the herd, including babies and juveniles, are abandoned.

Older elephants are relocated to protected areas such as state and national parks; but babies who find it difficult to adapt back in the wild are doomed to a captive existence in zoos. The centre has an enclosure where elephant babies are cared for, but visitors are allowed to see them only with permission from the wildlife officers. The friendly officers will explain to you how the translocation exercise is carried out using a pair of 60-year-old trained elephants from Thailand. ❑

ABOVE: join in the elephant's daily bathing at the Kuala Gandah Elephant Conservation Centre.

RESTAURANTS

Fraser's Hill

Restoran Hill View
Puncak Inn. Tel: 09-362 2231. Open: daily 10am–9pm. **$**
Operated by a family who have lived here for two generations, this serves Chinese meals and decent pub grub, such as chicken and lamb chops.

The Smokehouse Hotel and Restaurant
Jalan Jeriau. www.thesmokehouse.com.my Tel: 09-362 2226. Open: daily tea 3–6pm, dinner 6.30–9.30pm. **$$$**
You need to dress up to dine here. Superbly prepared English pot roast with Yorkshire pudding, beef Wellington and homemade pies. Or scones with strawberry jam and Devonshire cream for tea.

Genting Highlands

Imperial Rama
Level 2, Highlands Hotel. www.rwgenting.com Tel: 03-6101 1118. Open: daily noon–2.30pm, 6–10pm. **$$**
This self-service Thai-Chinese restaurant offers home-cooked dishes and dim sum favourites. Sit and dine in old-world Chinese charm.

The Olive
Lobby Floor, Genting Hotel. www.rwgenting.com Tel: 03-6105 9668. Open: daily noon–2.30pm, 6–10pm. **$$$**
This award-winning restaurant serves European-style cuisine with contemporary twists. Succulent *wagyu* beef is the speciality, complemented by a good wine and a serenade from the band.

Kuala Kubu Bharu

Gerai-gerai Pejabat Pos
Jalan Abdul Hamid (opposite the Post Office). Open: daily 6am–2pm. **$**
This row of hawker stalls is popular with tourists and adventure-sports operators, who stop by before or after their river and jungle adventures. Try the wild boar curry (stall 7) and the Chinese steamed buns (stall 8).

Kedai Makanan

Govindamah
9 Jalan Abdul Hamid. Tel: 03-6064 5723. Open: daily 7am–1am. **$**
No-frills family-run outlet serving good banana-leaf meals with chicken and mutton curries.

Restoran Ninety Eight
33/34 Jalan Dato' Balai. Tel: 03-6064 1189. Open: Tue–Sun 4pm–midnight. **$**
Offers Cantonese-style dishes such as black pepper venison, crispy-fried pork belly, and chicken and cashew nuts served in a yam (*taro*) basket. If you like your vegetables spicy, try the Four Treasures – long beans, *petai* (stinky bean), aubergine and ladies fingers in garlic and chilli.

Price per person for a three-course meal without drinks.
***$** = under RM30,*
***$$** = RM30–60,*
***$$$** = RM60–90,*
***$$$$** = over RM90.*

KUALA SELANGOR

Taking pride of place in Kuala Selangor is lush Kuala Selangor Nature Park, with its mangrove forests and plentiful wildlife. Combine it with Bukit Melawati's historical sights, visits to traditional industries and a firefly tour for a highly rewarding excursion

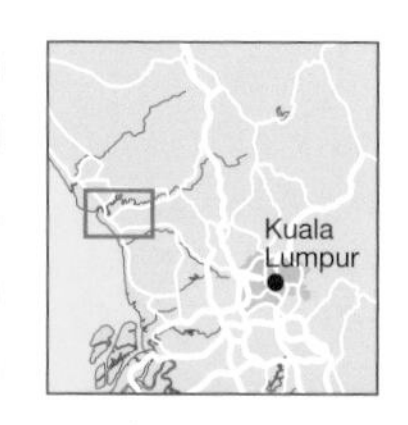

Main Attractions

Maps and Listings

MAP OF KUALA SELANGOR, PAGE 202
RESTAURANTS, PAGE 207

Located 67km (42 miles) from Kuala Lumpur on the estuary of Sungai Selangor is an old Selangor capital, **Kuala Selangor** (www.kualaselangor.info), with beautiful mangroves, fireflies, historical attractions and traditional industries. The quiet town is experiencing a development boom, but still manages to retain its rustic air.

To get to Kuala Selangor from the city, use the North–South Highway heading north, and exit at the Sungai Buloh tollgate. Follow the road through oil palm estates for 45 minutes till you reach the Assam Jawa junction. Turn right here and drive for about 10 minutes to get to Bukit Melawati. At its foot sits the old Kuala Selangor town centre.

Kuala Selangor Nature Park ❶

Start your exploration at the **Kuala Selangor Nature Park**, or Taman Alam Kuala Selangor (tel: 03-3289 2294; charge) on Jalan Klinik behind a housing estate. A 10-minute walk from the old town, the park is operated by the Malaysian Nature Society (MNS) and the Selangor state government. The MNS (www.mns.org.my) was one of the parties that lobbied aggresively to create the 324-hectare (800-acre) area in 1987.

A popular destination for nature lovers, the park protects a complex and important river ecosystem, including a vital crop of mangroves. It also plays an important role in conservation and education.

The park is home to a wide variety of insects, mammals and plants, as well as 157 species of local and migratory birds. The migratory birds

LEFT: lush forests fringe Sungai Selangor, on whose estuary lies Kuala Selangor town.
RIGHT: Kuala Selangor Nature Park is a birder's paradise.

ABOVE: exposed stilt roots of the Rhizophora mangrove plant.

that fly each winter from Siberia to Australia rest and feed here en route (the best time to see them is from September to April).

All visitors have to register at the **Visitors' Centre** (daily 9am–6pm), which has comprehensive information on the park. You can also purchase nature-themed souvenirs, such as books, postcards and T-shirts.

You may wish to explore the park on your own, with the help of a walking guidebook purchased from the visitors' centre. There are 20 stations where you can stop to examine the flora. However, first-time visitors to a mangrove would do well to take a guided tour (book ahead; charges apply). The hour-long nature walk usually starts around 8am and 4pm. The park also offers a 45-minute night walk starting at 9pm, the best time to see fireflies, frogs, crabs, and, of course, sleeping birds.

If you stay overnight at the park's basic chalets and dorms *(see page 234)*, you will have the unforgettable experience of falling asleep to the sounds of droning cicadas and croaking frogs, and waking up to see birds feeding and, maybe, shy resident otters at play.

Park trails

Five **trails** of different lengths wind through different habitats: mangrove forest, mudflats, secondary forest and a lake system. For a half-day walk, begin with the **Egret Trail** from the park headquarters, which goes through the secondary forest to the tallest watchtower; continue anticlockwise on the **Coastal Bund Trail** around the lake; take the **Mangrove Walkway** into the mangrove forest; rejoin the Coastal Bund Trail; and, finally, cross the hanging bridge (five people at a time only) into the **Pangolin Trail** in the secondary forest again, before ending back at the park headquarters.

The Egret Trail meets the Coastal

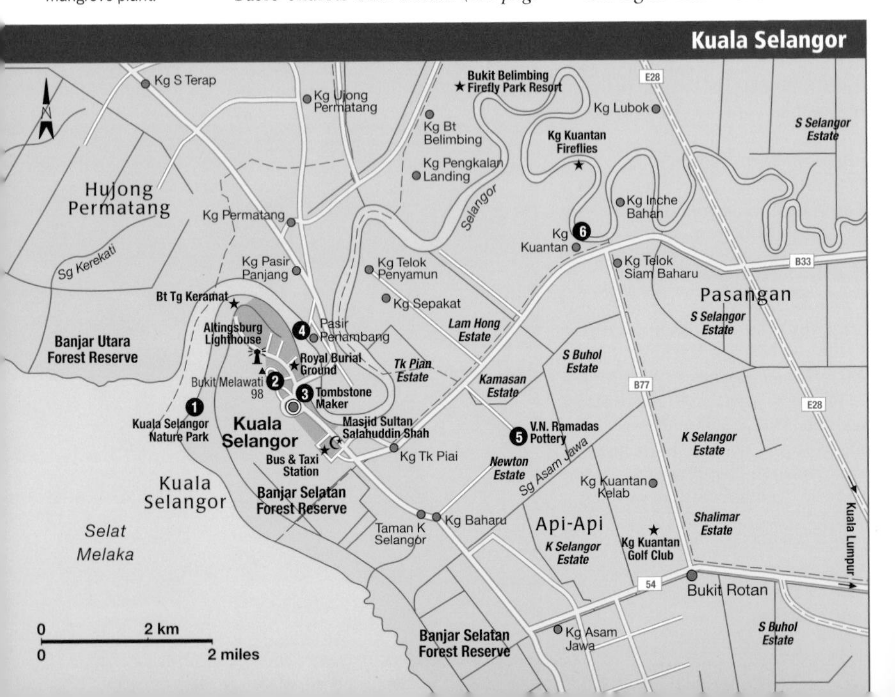

Bund Trail at a canal, where the lucky may spot smooth otters, or at the least, their paw prints in the muddy banks. Bunds were built and a canal dug in the 1940s to drain the area and protect the town against the encroaching sea. As a result, the secondary forest in the first part of the Egret Trail has started taking over the mangrove forest, which could not survive in such dry conditions.

At the end of the Egret Trail, climb the 10-metre (30ft) watchtower. In front is the 10-hectare (25-acre) **lake system** with brackish water – a mix of freshwater and saltwater. The lakes were created to attract birds; a regulated flow of water in and out of the lakes brings in food for the birds.

An experiment that increases the frequency of lake flushing has led to a congregation of hundreds of **grey herons**. You can get a clear view of these birds from the watchtower. A great time to see them is the breeding season at the beginning of the year, when they become very noisy and display elaborate neck movements. The colour of their bills and legs also changes from yellow to deep orange. Once the young are hatched, they maintain a ceaseless loud clicking call. A few purple herons, shy creatures with their snake-like heads, have also started to breed here.

As you walk along the Coastal Bund Trail, keep your eyes peeled for little fluttering birds in the bushes and soaring Brahminy kites overhead. You may also see groups of spiky-haired silver leaf monkeys (possibly with their orange-coloured young) and common long-tailed macaques, as well as smooth-bodied mangrove skinks (lizards) in the underbrush.

The bund will lead to a T-junction where thick **mangroves** front the sea. Here, you will encounter three of the four mangrove species found in the park: Bruguiera with its buttress roots, and Avicennia and Sonneratia with their knee roots. These special roots help the mangroves survive in harsh conditions. Likewise, long and thin fruit shapes enable the fruits to take hold in mud for sprouting; others are round and buoyant so they can easily be carried by tides to new areas.

Get onto the mangrove walkway to see Rhizophora mangroves, which are supported by stilt roots. The walkway

ABOVE: a Bruguiera mangrove seedling sprouting in the mud.
BELOW: birdwatchers at the Kuala Selangor Nature Park.

TIP

If you are exploring Kuala Selangor National Park with a guide, inform them that you want to see the estuary. Getting there involves an adventurous journey through boot-sucking mud and over knotty tree roots till you reach the huge river mouth. Here you get the best view of the convoluted network of roots that exemplifies nature's way of dealing with coastal erosion.

sits above **mudflats** that teem with creatures both weird and wonderful. These include mudskippers, shellfish and fiddler crabs, whose males sport a giant claw for defence. When startled, the creatures will sink back into the mud. Be patient and you will soon be rewarded with the sight of a busy community.

The **secondary forest**, through which the Pangolin Trail winds, is dominated by figs and other coastal trees as well as a few mangroves. Here, some figs, with numerous roots and buttressed trunks, form "pillars" through which the trail passes.

Bukit Melawati ❷

Head back to town to the historic hill of **Bukit Melawati**, where the second Sultan of Selangor built a fort to repel attacks from the Dutch during his reign (1778–1826). The Dutch captured the fort briefly; thereafter, many bloody battles were fought over it. The hill has a lovely landscaped circuit trail shaded by gnarled 200-year-old angsana trees. To complete the circuit, keep left each time you come to a fork.

ABOVE RIGHT: the mangrove ecosystem. **BELOW:** the Kuala Selangor mudflats are home to a variety of wildlife, including mudskippers.

Altingsburg Lighthouse

As you walk up the hill, you will see a **poison well** first. This is a chilly reminder of the fate that awaited traitors: a dip in a poisonous mixture of latex and juice from bamboo shoots. Keep climbing till you see a lighthouse on your right. Named after the Dutch Governor-General, the **Altingsburg Lighthouse** was built in 1907 and is still a working facility; it is off-limits to visitors.

Across the lighthouse is a **lookout**, from where you see a panorama of the Kuala Selangor Nature Park. Peering over the lookout are six cannons from various periods of the Selangor–Dutch war, some of which are replicas; look for the Dutch East India Company (VOC) insignia on the cannon furthest left.

Next to the Dutch cannon is a **watchtower**, where Muslim religious authorities gather to sight the new moon for significant Muslim days such as the beginning and end of the Ramadan fasting month. The new moon is usually seen up to 30 degrees to the right or left of where the sun sets. If the time is right, you may want to pack dinner and camp out on this tower for some moon-spotting.

Watch out for the monkeys here. As they are already regularly fed,

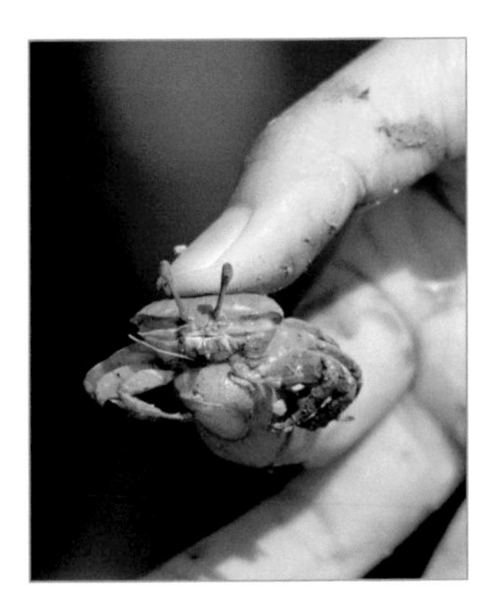

avoid giving them food as this tends to make them more aggressive.

More historic ruins

Keep walking along the trail and it will take you to the **Melawati Gate**, once the gateway to the fort. At its entrance is **Batu Hampar** (Execution Rock), where criminals were beheaded during and after the Selangor Civil Wars of 1863. Legend has it that a palace maiden was also executed here for committing adultery. Her blood was poured over the execution rock and the vicinity as a grim warning against the act.

There are steps leading down from the Melawati Gate to the foot of the hill. Dubbed the **Hundred Steps**, they were once the only pathway to the town of Kuala Selangor from the docks below. The dock area is now part of the Kuala Selangor Nature Park. Continuing on the trail, you will see a mound where the Sultan used to sit and watch his favourite sport of cock-fighting. Further on are ruins of the old **Selangor fort**, the most intact of which is an outer wall complete with three original cannons that point out to sea.

Royal Burial Ground

The hill's final attraction is the **Royal Burial Ground** of the first three sultans of Selangor and their family members. You have to be properly dressed to enter. If not, peep through the wrought-iron gates to see the Penggawa, the sacred cannon ceremonially draped in yellow cloth. A *penggawa* is the sultan's most trusted protector. Discovered in Sungai Buloh, 19km (12 miles) from Kuala Selangor, in 1966, the cannon was first brought to Jugra, Selangor's second capital, to be displayed there, but local lore has it that it "refused" to stay put and was finally brought to its current place to guard the old sultans.

Muslim tombmaker ❸

When you leave Kuala Selangor, drop by the **Muslim tombstone maker**'s little shack on a hillock to the right of the main junction out of Kuala Selangor. Follow the sounds of chipping to Casey, a fifth-generation granite craftsman specialising in hand-hewn Muslim tombstones, and one of probably only two remaining ones in the country. The fact that he is Chinese and a Taoist makes his vocation all the more intriguing – in fact, he has a Taoist altar (made of granite of

ABOVE LEFT: a male fiddler crab shows its large left claw. **ABOVE:** the Altingsburg Lighthouse on Bukit Melwati. **BELOW:** a Dutch cannon at the Bukit Melawati lookout, a remnant of the Selangor–Dutch war.

ABOVE: a V.N. Ramadas pottery maker crafting a pot at the wheel.
BELOW: Casey, the tombstone carver at his workshop just outside Kuala Selangor.

course) by a tree where he prays every day. He taught himself Jawi, including verses from the Al-Fatiha chapter of the Qu'ran. His clients, including Malaysian royalty, come from all over the country.

Casey's raw material is all around him – the hillock and the rocks in the area are all granite. He takes three days to fashion a pair of headstones, which he claims is faster than by machine. He also makes pestles and mortars, as well as grinding stones that are a must for traditional Hindu weddings.

Pasir Penambang ❹

Turn left from the main road towards Tanjung Karang to get to **Pasir Penambang**, a Chinese fishing village and famous seafood haven. You will come to a bridge; look out for a left turn-off after the bridge and follow the road. The riverside wooden buildings are homes as well as seafood processing warehouses. The villagers are used to tourists dropping by to see how they process the seafood.

The village's main street is lined with eateries and shops selling all manner of seafood, from fresh springy fishballs to crunchy prawn snacks and anchovy-based condiments. Some restaurants have lovely river views, and you can dine while enjoying the sea breeze. Look out for boats with pyramids of cockles, which are farmed here. The thriving fishery industry comes courtesy of the mangrove ecosystem, which helps to maintain the nutrient-rich waters.

Traditional Indian pottery

On your way back to Kuala Lumpur, turn left into Jalan Rawang and then right into Jalan Keretapi Lama. Follow this road for around five minutes, keeping your eye out for a house on the right with a large number of pots stacked outside. This is **V.N. Ramadas Pottery** ❺ (tel: 03-3289 1054; appointments necessary), traditional Indian pottery makers. You will probably have passed a number of similar places en route to Kuala Selangor; there are seven such pottery makers in the area. Ramadas, however, is the first and the largest producer.

Its speciality is the round-bottom pot called *mann panai*, used for the Tamil festival of Ponggal (Tamil Thanksgiving). Ponggal is celebrated in the Indian month of Thai (January–February), during which a traditional rice and milk concoction, also called *ponggal*, is cooked in these pots at sunrise and sunset.

The pot-making technique originates in India. At Ramadas it is now practised by a third generation of craftsmen. Other than a modified wheel machine, which goes by the quirky name of *pugmillm jolly jongels*, all the techniques used are traditional, including firing in a brick kiln and sun-drying. The potters also fashion small prayer oil lamps, cooking pots for curry – claypots are believed to

enhance the taste of food – and figurines of Hindu deities as well as those of Guan Yin, the Buddhist Goddess of Mercy.

Kampung Kuantan ❻

When night falls, lights "come on" along the riverside at **Kampung Kuantan**, north of the Ramadas Pottery. This is one of the few places in the world with such a large colony of synchronously flashing fireflies, or *kelip-kelip* (literally, to twinkle) as they are called locally. The tourist jetty (daily 8–10.30pm; ticket office opens 7pm) for this memorable sight is on Jalan Rawang, 7.5km (4½ miles) from the turn-off to the pottery.

Local boatmen will take you out on the river, four to a boat, past the parade of what are actually beetles and not flies, on the drooping branches of the *berembang* (*Sonneratia caseolaris*), a mangrove species. Males flash at a rate of three flashes a second, the females less frequently. The males time their flashing together to enable the females to detect the rhythm, while warning predators off at the same time.

The colony has shrunk in recent years, perhaps due to the influx of tourists, the loss of habitat and the building of the Sungai Selangor dam upstream in Kuala Kubu Bharu, which has affected the water levels. The journey itself is, however, magical. Your local boatman will regale you with firefly facts, and then you drift along silently in the cool night, watching nature's mesmerising display. The phenomenon is best experienced on a moonless and rainless night. ❑

TIP

Most KL tour operators have firefly tours of Kampung Kuantan. Alternatively, tours are also offered by an operator in Kampung Belimbing, north of Kuala Selangor, but they use large boats, which make the tours less personal and whose wake erodes the riverbanks.

ABOVE LEFT: stop over at Pasir Penambang for delicious Chinese-style seafood.

RESTAURANTS

Kuala Selangor

Restoran Waterfall Café
88 Jalan Stesen. Tel: 03-3289 2388. Open: daily 10am–10pm. **$**
This family-owned café does offer standard Western dishes like sandwiches and spaghetti bolognese. But like every eatery in town, its specialities are Chinese seafood dishes.

Pasir Penambang

Restoran Kuala Selangor
1A Jalan Bagan Sungai Yu. Tel: 03-3289 6719. Open: daily 10am–10pm. **$$**
Located a little away from the crowd and right next to a seafood processing warehouse. Must-tries are the stir-fried bamboo shellfish with dried chillies, and sour-spicy "three-sauce" whole fish (you can ask for the fish to be deboned for you). Get a riverside table for good views.

Restoran Makanan Laut Jeti
T26, Jalan Pasir Penampang. Tel: 03-3289 2917. Open: daily 10am–10pm. **$$**
Located right on the main strip of two rows of shophouses, most of them seafood restaurants. Competition is stiff here, but throngs of customers still come back to this one just for the oyster omelette and curried butter crabs. Ask for the special catch of the day or, if you just want a snack, crunchy prawn crackers fresh from the oven.

River View Seafood Restaurant
1 Jalan Besar. Tel: 03-3289 6719. Open: daily 11am–10pm. **$$**
Very popular with tourists, this family-run eatery serves quality seafood dishes. It is pleasantly breezy, and offers commanding views of the bridge, Bukit Melawati and the village. You won't go wrong with dishes such as buttered prawns, and fresh fish in black pepper sauce.

Price per person for a three-course meal without drinks.
***$** = under RM30,*
***$$** = RM30–60,*
***$$$** = RM60–90,*
***$$$$** = over RM90.*

KLANG VALLEY

Among Klang Valley's sprawl are many cultural, natural and recreational attractions – among them, a brilliant art museum and a rich collection of rare plants. There's also the federal administrative capital of Putrajaya with its numerous architectural jewels

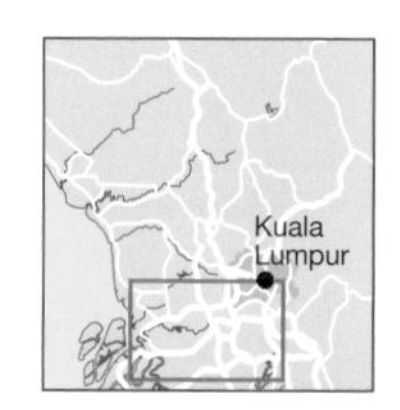

The inevitable spread of urbanisation from Kuala Lumpur outwards into the surrounding state of Selangor has seen more people packed into the area called Klang Valley than anywhere else in the country – about 5 million populate the two main conduits west and south of the capital city. It has the country's largest suburb, its main port and two other capital cities. Among the mass housing and light industrial areas are some recreational and cultural gems that are worth visiting.

The entire area is named after **Sungai Klang**, but it is only the western conduit that really follows the 120km (75-mile) long river. Parallel to the waterway is the six-lane **Federal Highway** (Route 2) that links Kuala Lumpur to the country's main port, Port Klang.

PETALING JAYA ❶

The first city along the Federal Highway from Kuala Lumpur, 20km (13 miles) away, is **Petaling Jaya**, established in the 1950s to encourage industrial development and to overcome housing problems caused by massive rural–urban migration. Based on post-war British town development plans, Petaling Jaya, or PJ as it is popularly called, became a model for new town development in the recently independent Malaysia.

Although PJ was originally intended for the resettlement of squatters from a crowded Kuala Lumpur, demand for housing from middle-class KL-ites has led to better quality homes. Its original population of 70,000 has swelled to almost seven times that number today. In 2006, PJ was granted city status, and now faces the same urban issues as Kuala Lumpur did in the 1950s. This

LEFT: Putra Mosque.
RIGHT: the Kota Darul Ehsan arch marks the border between KL and PJ.

TIP

A great way to get a sense of the Klang Valley is to travel by Light Rail Transit (LRT), which circumvents Federal Highway traffic and, because it is elevated, gives you a good view of the suburban sprawl.

has prompted the middle class to seek a less chaotic lifestyle yet again, even farther out.

Kota Darul Ehsan

If you are coming from Kuala Lumpur on the LRT's E line, right after the Universiti stop look out on your right for an arch across the road. Opened in 1982, the **Kota Darul Ehsan** marks the border between Kuala Lumpur and Selangor, and commemorates the ceding of part of the Selangor Sultan's land to form a Federal Territory. Made of marble, the Moorish-style arch is guarded by ancient cannons.

Gurdwara Sahib Petaling Jaya ❷

Address: 4 Lorong Utama B, off Jalan Utara
Tel: 03-7955 8645
Opening Hrs: Fri–Wed 9am–5pm
Entrance Fee: free
Transport: LRT Asia Jaya

For a first-hand experience of Sikh culture, visit the **Gurdwara Sahib Petaling,** one of the most active Sikh *gurdwara* (temples) in the Klang Valley, with a large congregation of around 400. It is located close to the Tun Hussein Onn Eye Hospital and within walking distance of the Asia Jaya LRT station. In the main hall upstairs, the *Guru Granth Sahib*, the Sikh holy book, is placed on a richly decorated platform under a beautiful domed canopy.

There is always something happening at the temple, particularly between 7 and 9pm from Monday to Thursday and on weekends from 10am to noon. Sunday morning prayers are from 9am to noon. At the temple's community kitchen, the *langar,* visitors can help themselves to some of the best home-cooked Punjabi vegetarian food found in Kuala Lumpur, in return for a small donation.

School holidays are particularly popular periods for Sikh weddings,

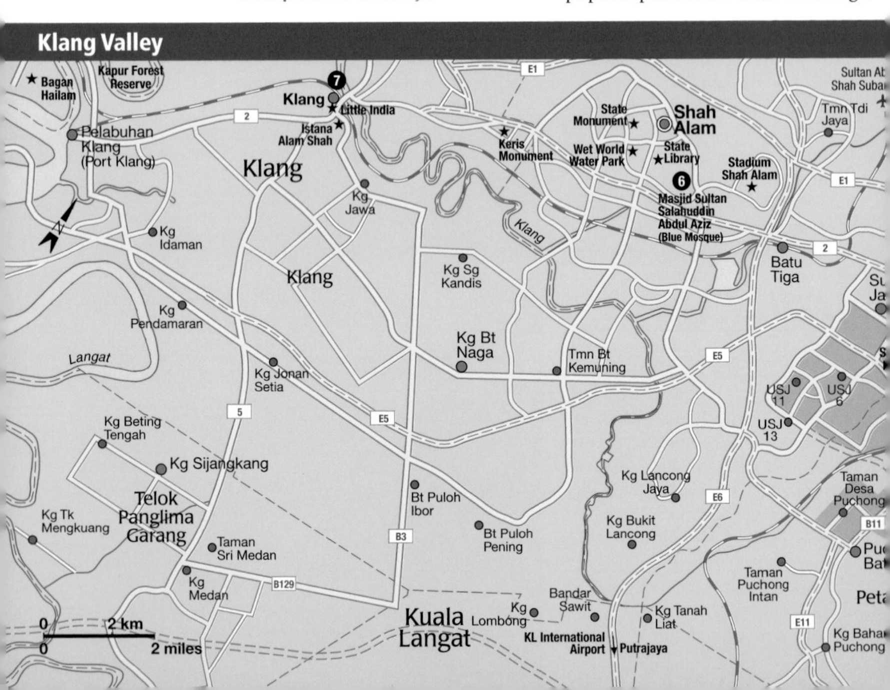

colourful events with singing, *bhangra* dancing and eating. Another big event, to which visitors are welcome, is the Vaisakhi celebration or *mela*, the harvest festival in India. Held for several days leading up to and on 14 April, it is a deeply religious day for Sikhs.

Wat Chetawan ❸

Address: 24 Jalan Pantai 9/7
Tel: 03-7957 2255
Opening Hrs: daily 7am–9.30pm
Entrance Fee: free
Transport: LRT Taman Jaya

Get off at the Taman Jaya LRT stop and walk past Amcorp Mall across Jalan Timur towards the lake, and then turn right into Jalan Pantai 9/7. You will pass some large houses and a church before you see the glinting roofs of the beautiful Thai temple complex, **Wat Chetawan**. One of the few temples outside Thailand sponsored by the Thai monarch, this stunning edifice is both religious and community centre for Thai Malaysians. Many non-Thai Buddhists pray at this temple too.

The ends of its steep, multi-tiered, orange-tiled roofs are decorated with *chofah* (sky tassels). Intricate carvings and miniature glass tiles adorn the rest of the buildings. Gold is used liberally everywhere. The grandest building is the main prayer hall, marked by eight pillars, indicating that it is consecrated ground. It houses a large Buddha statue flanked by smaller ones, and just outside it there is a belfry equipped with a bell and drum to sound the time for prayers and ceremonies.

There are several outdoor *sala* or traditional open-sided pavilions in the grounds. One houses a four-faced statue of Buddha, watching over the four corners of the world. Some people say this statue represents Brahma, the creator in the Hindu pantheon of gods. Another pavilion is dedicated to Guan Yin, the Goddess of Mercy. Facing the main prayer hall is a hall with

ABOVE: a four-faced Buddha seated in an open-aired pavilion at Wat Chetawan. **BELOW:** PJ's Sikh community cooks and dines together at the Gurdwara Sahib.

TIP

A visit to the Herbal Sauna Treatment Centre (tel: 01-6324 9834/01-3336 3273; Tue–Fri 2–8pm, Sat–Sun and public holidays 10am–8pm; charge) on the premises of Wat Chetawan, can help with a myriad of ailments and improve blood circulation.

four lifelike statues that pay tribute to Buddhist religious leaders in the country. Interestingly, these abbots have Malay titles, pointing to their northern Peninsular Malaysian and southern Thai origins.

The grounds also house accommodation for monks, a meeting hall and a columbarium. At the end furthest from the main hall is a *bodhi* tree with beautiful spreading branches. The temple is most colourful during Thai festivals like Songkran and Loy Krathong, as well as Wesak, the celebration of the Buddha's birthday and the most important festival in the Buddhust calendar.

Amcorp Mall Antiques Flea Market

Address: Amcorp Mall, 18, Persiaran Barat, off Jalan Timur
Tel: 03-7958 5318
Opening Hrs: daily 10am–10pm
Entrance Fee: free
Transport: LRT Taman Jaya

Right across from the Taman Jaya LRT station and within walking distance of the temple is Amcorp Mall, noted for its Sunday antiques flea market, with the city's top antiques dealers selling everything from toys, watches and glassware to gramophones and cutlery. If you like antiques-hunting, this is the best place to get some precious finds.

ABOVE RIGHT: treasure hunting at Amcorp Mall Antiques Market. **BELOW:** the Museum of Asian Art has an excellent textile collection, including this rare *patola* cloth.

Museum of Asian Art ❹

Address: Universiti Malaya, Jalan Universiti
Tel: 03-7967 3805
Opening Hrs: Mon–Thur 9am–noon, 2–4pm, Fri 9am–noon, 2.45–4pm, Sat 9am–12.45pm
Entrance Fee: free
Transport: LRT Universiti

From Wat Chetawan, take a taxi to **Universiti Malaya** (www.um.edu.my). This is the country's first and premier university. and has two attractions worth visiting.

To get to the university's **Museum of Asian Art**, or Muzium Seni Asia, go through the Jalan Universiti entrance and follow the road till you reach a four-way junction, then turn left. When you come to a fork, turn left again and follow the signs.

On display in this handsome three-storey museum are some 6,000 pieces of art spanning 4,000 years of history in Asia. The museum's permanent collection has a strong Southeast Asian focus, and ceramics comprises about 60 percent of its collection.

The museum has the world's largest public collection of *kendi* (a handle-less water container with a spout), which spans 1,000 years and represents different countries in East and Southeast Asia. The shapes and designs of the *kendi* are fascinating indicators of the cultural and social practices in the region as well as trade patterns during different periods of history. An interesting fact about the *kendi* is that while it was used locally, it was never manufactured in Malaysia, but in neighbouring countries and even in Japan.

The museum also has the largest collection of early Vietnamese pottery outside Vietnam, as well as Malaysia's most important collection of Thai ceramics from the Ban Chiang period (from as early as 4000 BC) and from the key ceramic-producing areas of Sukhothai and Sawankhalok. Of note is the extremely rare ceramic Sawankhalok elephant, which has a mahout and a rider on its back, and a warrior at each of the beast's legs.

Also noteworthy is the textile collection, which includes the ancient *patola* (double-*ikat*) cloth, a precious trading commodity at the height of the Melakan empire in the 15th and 16th centuries.

The main exhibits change every two months, and eight temporary exhibitions are held annually. Guided tours are available if you book a week in advance.

Rimba Ilmu

Address: Universiti Malaya, Jalan Universiti, www.rimba.um.edu.my
Tel: 03-7967 4686
Opening Hrs: Mon–Thur 9am–noon, 2–4pm, Fri 9am–noon, 2.45–4pm
Entrance Fee: charge
Transport: LRT Universiti

To get an idea of what a Malaysian rainforest is like, visit the Universiti Malaya's informative 80-hectare (198-acre) tropical botanical garden called **Rimba Ilmu**. One of the most important biological conservatories in Malaysia, it was set up in 1974 and coordinated by one of the country's top botanists, Dr. K.M. Wong. Rimba Ilmu (literally "Forest of Knowledge") has over 1,500 species of plants found mainly in Malaysia and Indonesia.

Start off by visiting the centre's **interpretive exhibition** on rainforests and the environment. It is probably the most comprehensive of such exhibitions in the country. The section on biodiversity displays winged dipterocarp seeds and features interesting plants like the pitcher plant and the Rafflesia, the world's largest flower.

The **rainforest garden** is not formally landscaped – making for a more authentic experience – and has a wetland area in the middle. Its 750-metre loop trail winds through five core collections: medicinal plants, palms, citrus and citroids (lime family), ferns and bamboo. A corner of the garden is being turned into a younger version of the regenerated forest found in the Forest Research Institute of Malaysia *(see pages 179–82)*. As you walk in the garden, take a deep breath from time to

ABOVE: winged dipterocarp seeds on display at the Rimba Ilmu interpretive exhibition. **BELOW:** rainforest trail at Rimba Ilmu.

ABOVE: a hair-raising ride in the amusement park at Sunway Lagoon. **BELOW:** splashing around in the family-friendly pool at Sunway Lagoon.

time, and all sorts of fragrances will hit you.

You can do the 45-minute walk around the garden on your own as the trail is well marked and labels are ample. You can also buy the three guidebooks on the garden from the information counter to better understand what you are seeing.

Rare plant conservatory

A guided tour will give you access to a real gem – the **Conservatory of Rare Plants and Orchids**, housed in a 40 by 30-metre (130 by 98ft) plant house. It is not accessible without a guide. Beautifully laid out on the grounds and hanging from the ceiling are 1,500 plants that are rare or are becoming rare because of habitat destruction or over-collection. Among these are the delicate slipper orchids, one of the 300 species of orchids housed here; the pretty begonia Rajah; and the four unusual *Johannesteijsmannia magnifica* or "umbrella leaf" palm species. Book a week ahead for the guided tour (charge applies). A free 3-hour guided tour is conducted for Malaysian Nature Society (MNS) members on the first Saturday of each month at 9am (just sign up for MNS membership; tel: 03-2287 9422).

Sunway Lagoon ❺

Address: 3, Jalan PJS 11/11, Bandar Sunway, www.sunway.com.my/lagoon
Tel: 03-5639 0000
Opening Hrs: Mon, Wed–Fri 11am–6pm, Sat–Sun 10am–6pm, public holidays and school holidays 10am–6pm
Entrance Fee: charge
Transport: Komuter Subang or LRT Kelana Jaya, then taxi

Further down the Federal Highway towards Klang is **Sunway City**. This award-winning development was built on rehabilitated tin-mining land, a resort-in-the-city complex that hosts the popular **Sunway Lagoon**. The family-friendly venue, fashioned after South Africa's Sun City, is spread over 32 hectares (80 acres) and offers three different theme parks, the world's largest man-made surf beach, complete with artificial waves, and the world's longest pedestrian suspension bridge.

The adjoining **Sunway Pyramid** (daily 10am–10pm; tel: 03-7494 3000) is a rather kitschy Egyptian-themed shopping mall anchored by a giant lion in a sphinx-like pose. Besides shops and food outlets, the shopping centre has the largest indoor ice-skating rink in the country, a 10-screen cineplex and a 48-lane bowling alley. The front of the mall is lined with outdoor cafés, serving everything from American coffee to sushi and hawker fare from Penang.

Next to the shopping centre is the five-star **Sunway Resort Hotel and Spa**, which also takes a leaf from Sun City but has sculptures and decor inspired by Malaysian rather than African beasts, as well

as a coconut- tree-lined free-form swimming pool with waterfalls.

SHAH ALAM

From Sunway City, the Federal Highway goes past Subang Jaya and USJ, two development schemes that are collectively among the largest housing estates in the country.

The Federal Highway then takes you to **Shah Alam**, the capital of Selangor, about 25km (16 miles) from Kuala Lumpur. Named after the fifth Sultan of Selangor, the city was built to host the state's administration, which moved out of Kuala Lumpur in 1978. After the PJ experience, careful thought was put into its development, resulting in one of the best planned cities in the country.

Sultan Salahuddin Abdul Aziz Mosque ❻

Address: Persiaran Masjid, Shah Alam
Tel: 03-5519 9988
Opening Hrs: Mon–Fri 9am–5pm, except prayer times
Transport: Komuter Shah Alam, then taxi

There is not much here for tourists but the most imposing sight and worth a stop is the **Masjid Sultan Salahuddin Abdul Aziz**, also known as the **Blue Mosque**. Commissioned to commemorate Shah Alam's status as capital, this Arabic-influenced mosque is one of the country's largest, able to accommodate more than 16,000 worshippers. Its popular moniker refers to its massive blue-and-white dome – larger than London's St Paul's Cathedral – that reaches a height of 107 metres (350ft) and has a diameter of 52 metres (170ft). At night, the dome lights up, creating the illusion of a desert scene on a starry night. The mosque's four minarets also reach record heights of 140 metres (460ft).

KLANG ❼

The Federal Highway ends in the Selangor royal city and former capital, **Klang**, 32km (20 miles) from Kuala Lumpur. A 2,000-year-old settlement, it has a few highlights, which can be covered easily in a few hours. The wooden **Gedung Raja Abdullah** (tel: 03-5519 7604; daily 9am–4pm) on Jalan Tepi Sungai, a historic warehouse for tin, is now

The Muzium Sultan Alam Shah on Persiaran Perdagangan in Shah Alam (tel: 03-5519 0050; Tue–Sun 9.30am–5.30pm) is a repository of the state's historical, cultural and communal artefacts. Of note are the Selangor sultanate's collection and the innovative temporary exhibitions.

LEFT: the Egyptian-inspired Sunway Pyramid shopping mall. **BELOW:** the Blue Mosque, with its striking blue-and-white dome.

EAT

The Old Stall in Klang (Lorong Stesen Saru, next to a car park; daily 5–11am) is where the Chinese dish of *bak kut teh* is said to have originated. Klang is famous for this herbal pork soup concoction, believed to have been brought here by an émigré from Fujian. The stall serves it with strong Chinese tea, for breakfast only.

fittingly a tin museum – though not a very good one.

The golden-domed **Masjid Sultan Sulaiman** on Jalan Timur, sporting a mix of Art Deco, neoclassical and local architectural styles, is the royal mosque. **Istana Alam Shah** (closed to the public), the Sultan's official residence on Jalan Istana, stands on top a hill.

One of Klang's best walks awaits at **Little India**, which has the Klang Valley's largest conglomeration of Indian shops. The area centres on Jalan Tengku Kelana and its vicinity, and starts from the historic **Masjid India Klang**, stretching southwards. From spices to saris and music to *muruku* (deep-fried snacks), the colours, cacophony and aromas assault from all corners. The Deepavali festival in November is a great time to visit as the area is at its most vibrant.

Klang, or rather, Port Klang (Pelabuhan Klang), is well known for its seafood. Two good places to go are **Muara Ikan Bakar** at the Tanjung Harapan esplanade for Malay fare, and **Bagan**, a fishing village with restaurants on stilts, where Chinese dishes are served. Getting to these places is not easy, so hire a taxi.

PUTRAJAYA

The conduit heading south from Kuala Lumpur that is part of the Klang Valley has several expressways leading to the Kuala Lumpur International Airport, 70km (43 miles) away. This corridor, which is anchored in the capital at the Kuala Lumpur City Centre, is also known as the Multimedia Supercorridor (MSC), the Malaysian government-led version of Silicon Valley. Information and communications technology (ICT) has been identified as the means to enable the country to leapfrog to developed-nation status in this information-driven era.

Key to the MSC is **Putrajaya** (www.ppj.gov.my), the country's federal administrative capital. For

BELOW: Indian sweet stall in Klang's Little India.

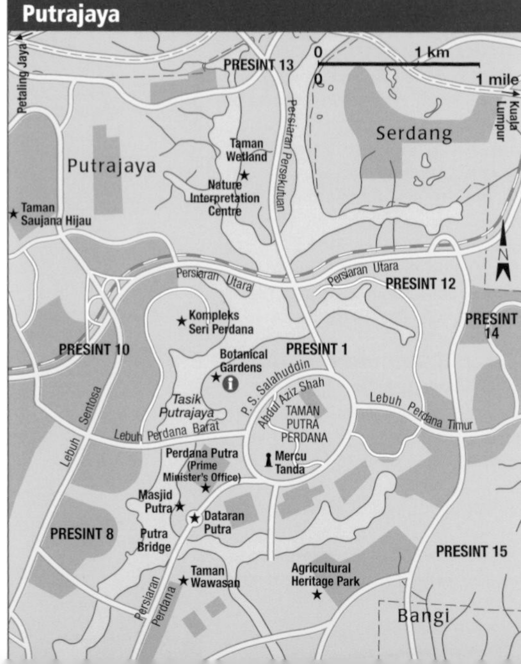

almost a decade now, the machinery of the Malaysian government has operated out of this ultra-modern township. Located 25km (16 miles) south of Kuala Lumpur, Putrajaya was the country's largest-ever real estate development project. One of former prime minister Mahathir Mohamad's pet mega-projects of the 1990s, this "intelligent city", which doubles as a garden city, covers 4,900 hectares (12,200 acres). It is impressive for the sheer scale of all its components, which range from imposing government administrative buildings and national monuments to expansive public spaces and highly elaborate bridges, right down to its impossible-to-miss lampposts. Many of the country's top architects have had their hand in key buildings here, and the result is a hotchpotch of futuristic buildings with no particular theme. The wide, paved boulevards lined with monoliths of steel, glass and chrome are very popular with film crews.

In short, Putrajaya embodies the gargantuan aspirations of a nation drunk on a decade of giddy economic growth rates (which fell dramatically after the 1997 Asian financial crisis). Devoid of the teeming humanity and character of Kuala Lumpur, most people find Putrajaya rather impersonal and unwelcoming. The sheer scale of its architecture, however, is something to behold.

Presint 1

Putrajaya is named after the country's first prime minister, Tunku Abdul Rahman Putra al-Haj. Its government and commercial developments sit in

ABOVE: futuristic lamppost design along Putrajaya Boulevard.

SHOPPING

As well as the usual shopping malls with their big-name department stores, the Klang Valley still has a few speciality things to offer.

Crafts

Gerai OA
Tel: 019-751 8686 (Reita Rahim)
Gerai OA, or Gerai Orang Asli, is a mobile, volunteer-run stall that stocks handmade, hand-crafted pieces from many indigenous tribes from east and west Malaysia. These beautiful things are sold mostly at local flea markets and fairs. Call to find out where they will be next or check out their Facebook page for updates.

Electronics

Digital Mall
2 Jalan 14/20, Section 14, 46100 Petaling Jaya.
www.digitalmall.com.my
Tel: 03-7968 3311
This is a smaller version of Bukit Bintang's Low Yat Plaza in the heart of suburbia. Lots of gadgets and toys for those who cannot get enough of technology.

Gaming

Wolf's Game Shop
16A-3, Jalan 14/20, Section 14, 46100 Petaling Jaya.
www.wolfgameshop.com Tel: 012-259 9952.
Vintage gaming shops are more or less extinct in KL but this one still remains. Owner Wolf stocks vintage games, miniatures and a whole lot more for the real enthusiast.

Malls

1 Utama
1 Lebuh Bandar Utama, Bandar Utama, Petaling Jaya. www.1utama.com.my
Tel: 03-7710 8118.
This sprawling mall has two sections, an old wing and a new, offering shoppers a choice of 600 shops – including anchor tenants Parkson and Jusco – eateries and two cinema complexes. If you need a break, take a stroll in the tropical rainforest zone and feed the fish.

The Curve
100 Jalan PJU 7/2, Mutiara Damansara, Petaling Jaya.
www.thecurve.com.my
Tel: 03-7710 6868.
Anchored by Ikea Home Furnishings, Ikano Power Centre, Tesco Hypermarket and Metrojaya, this pedestrianised shopping centre has all-weather walkways connecting its alfresco dining courtyards and shops.

Sunway Pyramid
Bandar Sunway, Petaling Jaya. www.sunway.com.my/pyramid Tel: 03-7494 3000.
Behind a 25-metre-tall (82ft) statue of a sphinx-like lion is an Egyptian-themed shopping centre, complete with an ice-skating rink, cineplex, bowling alley and a variety of shops, anchored by Jusco and Parkson, plus 10 speciality stores. It has a good IT section in the basement. Some restaurants overlook Sunway Lagoon theme park.

The Multimedia Supercorridor comprises "intelligent" communities linked to one another and the world by a high-bandwidth fibre-optic backbone, where new applications are developed, new lifestyles lived and new learning done – all based on ICT. The concept is tantalising, but its realisation will probably take decades.

a core area called **Presint 1**. Around this core, bordered by a lake, are residential and recreational areas. Be warned that Putrajaya is not easy to navigate; the signposting is poor and the names of places sound similar.

Take a drive on the circular road in Presint 1 – called **Persiaran Sultan Salahuddin Abdul Aziz Shah** – for a look at the government buildings. Stop at the **Information Centre** (tel: 03-8888 7272; daily 8.30am–6pm;) in Kompleks B to get a map. The road goes around a hill that is the highest point in Putrajaya. On it sits the luxury **Putrajaya Shangri-La Hotel** and a park, **Taman Putra Perdana**, from where there are panoramic views of the city. Standing among the gazebos and fountains is the **Putrajaya Landmark** (Mercu Tanda), which symbolises the city's beginning and contains a time capsule. From here extends the 4.2km (2.6-mile) **Persiaran Perdana**. It links four squares and two bridges, and is the site of a colourful parade whenever Putrajaya hosts the National Day (31 August) celebrations.

Back at the bottom of the hill, turn into the first of the squares, **Putra Square** (Dataran Putra), a circular space that has a star-shaped centrepiece representing the country's states. The square is bordered by several buildings. To the north is the impressive **Perdana Putra**, the Prime Minister's Office Complex, with its lofty onion-shaped and glazed-mosaic main dome.

BELOW: the pink-domed Putra Mosque.

Putra Mosque

Address: Dataran Putra, www.masjidputra.gov.my
Tel: 03-8888 5678
Opening Hrs: daily 9am–5pm, except during prayer times
Entrance Fee: free
Transport: KLIA Express Putrajaya

West of Putra Square is the stunning **Putra Mosque** (Masjid Putra), which reflects a 16th- to 18th-century Persian Islamic architectural style. The building is embellished with rose-tinted granite mosaic, and the main entrance is fashioned after the gates of public buildings in Persia. Three-quarters of the mosque extends onto the lake, so from certain angles the mosque looks like it's floating on the waters of Tasik Putrajaya.

Putrajaya Lake

There are altogether seven bridges in Putrajaya that span the man-made **Putrajaya Lake** (Tasik Putrajaya). The one closest to Putra Square is the 435-metre (1,430ft) **Putra Bridge**. Modelled after the 17th-century Khaju Bridge in the Iranian town of Isfahan, it sports decorated arches and pavilions and has three levels – for vehicles, pedestrians and future monorail tracks – with its main pillars housing fine-dining restaurants. At the foot of the Putra Bridge is the jetty for **Cruise Tasik Putrajaya**, which offers 1½- to 2-hour cruises on the lake (www.cruisetasikputrajaya.com; tel: 03-8888 5539; daily 9am–7pm). This is an enjoyable way to see the rest of Putrajaya and you can also combine it with a land tour.

If you want something more adventurous, getting wet is an option too. You can wakeboard, waterski, barefoot ski or kneeboard at the lake too *(see page 242)*. ❑

BEST RESTAURANTS AND BARS

Restaurants

Klang

Sri Baratha Matha Vilas Restaurant
34 Jalan Tengku Kelana. Tel: 03-3372 9657. Open: daily 7am–10.30pm. **$**
While many places serve it, this is *the* place to have *mee goreng* (spicy fried noodles). Owner S. Govindasamy selects the spices himself, sautéing them over a slow fire, and then frying the noodles. Served on a banana leaf, with slices of crispy battered prawn cake.

Teluk Pulai Bah Kut Teh
32 Jalan Batai Laut 5, Kawasan 16, Taman Intan. Tel: 03-3344 5196. Open: daily 7am–3pm. **$**
Located off the Federal Highway before Klang town, this is the most popular of several claypot *bak kut teh* outlets here, dishing up various cuts of chunky meat in a hearty herbal soup. Try the yam or "oily" rice as accompaniment to the soup.

Petaling Jaya

Borneo Rainforest Café
0B-K5, Sunway Pyramid, Bandar Sunway, 3 Jalan PJS 11/15. Tel: 03-5635 0888. Open Tue–Sun 5pm–1am. **$$**
Owned by local actress and celebrity Tiara Jacquelina, this restaurant's speciality is rice noodles in a spicy, prawn-based soup, drenched in coriander, chilli paste and lime. The outdoor area is lush and plays host to local musicians as well.

Greenview Restaurant
6 and 8 Jalan 19/3. Tel: 03-7958 1076. Open: daily 11am–11pm. **$$**
The best dish here is the *sang haar meen* (eggy noodles with freshwater prawns). The crispy noodles are drenched in an eggy sauce, and flanked by large prawns. The bamboo clams in chilli and garlic are very good too.

Kayu Nasi Kandar
64 Jalan SS2/10. Tel: 03-7876 4767. Open: daily 24 hrs. **$$$**
Order the spicy fried squid with your *nasi kandar* (Penang-style rice and curries). Worth trying as well are the *roti tisu* (a long, crispy, tissue-thin bread with sugar coating) and *roti telur* (thin pancake with egg and curry).

King Crab Restaurant
103–107 SS25/2, Taman Mewah Jaya. Tel: 03-7808 2388. Open: daily 10.30am–2.30pm, 5.30–10.30pm **$$$**
This is the place to come for crab dishes. Crabs are prepared in every possible way, be it steamed, curried, with salted egg or black peppered, for example. Choose your crab(s) of choice from the restaurant's water tanks.

Paya Serai
Hilton Petaling Jaya, 2 Jalan Barat. Tel: 03-7955 9122. Open: Mon–Thur 6am–3am, Fri–Sun 24 hours. **$$**
There is nothing Malaysians love more than a good buffet. And the popularity of the one at this casual, open-concept coffeehouse is testament to its quality. The spread comprises a large variety of tasty Malay dishes, including favourites like beef *rendang* (dry beef curry) and *sambal* (chilli paste) grilled fish. Breakfast and high tea spreads are equally generous.

Sri Pandi's
25 Jalan Chantek 5/13. Tel: 03-7958 7004. Open: daily 6am–10pm. **$**
Opposite Wat Chetawan is a road to this no-frills outlet, which serves some of the best southern Indian curries in PJ. Breakfast sees a range of delicious chutneys to go with freshly made breads, while for lunch and dinner there's an array of curries as well as vegetables.

Tanjung Bungah
117 Jalan SS2/6. Tel: 03-7877 4531. Open: Fri–Wed 10am–3pm, 5–10pm. **$$**
Penang Nyonya food with an infusion of Thai flavours. Dishes include *jiu hu char* (dried cuttlefish and shredded vegetables eaten with fresh lettuce), *otak-otak* (steamed curry fish paste in banana leaf), spicy mango *kerabu* (salad) and the restaurant's speciality, Nyonya chicken (fried chicken served in a tangy sweet and sour sauce). Among the divine deserts are *sago gula melaka* (sago with palm sugar) and *cendol* (a dessert with green pea jelly strips).

Price per person for a three-course meal without drinks:
$ = under RM30
$$ = RM30–60
$$$ = RM60–90
$$$$ = over RM90

Bars

Raw Bar and Murmur Lounge
J-0G-09, Soho KL, Solaris Mont Kiara. Tel: 03-6203 6869.
This Melbourne-inspired cocktail bar serves up favourites like blood orange and passionfruit martini and the Mebournian sling.

Sid's Pub
34 Lorong Rahim Kajai 14, Taman Tun Dr Ismail. www.sidspubs.com Tel: 03-7726 6832.
Sid's serves up authentic English pub grub and draught beers and cider in a cosy setting.

Souled Out
20 Jalan 30/70A, Desa Sri Hartamas. www.souledout.com.my Tel: 03-2300 1955.
Chill out in a large airy area outside - the dance floor is upstairs. A favourite with soccer fans, the crowd streams in on weekends.

INSIGHT GUIDES TRAVEL TIPS
KUALA LUMPUR

Transport

Accommodation

Activities

A – Z

Language

Further Reading

Transport

Getting There and Getting Around

Getting There

By Air

Kuala Lumpur is a key gateway between Asia and the West and a transportation hub for Southeast Asia. **Kuala Lumpur International Airport**, or KLIA (tel: 03-8776 0888 KLIA 1Touch; www.klia.com.my), is located 70km (43 miles) south of the city in Sepang. It is one of Asia's largest and most modern airports. Facilities are top-notch and it's not a bad airport to while away a few hours in if you're in transit. Planes arrive and depart from four satellite arms, which are linked to the main terminal building via a convenient aerotrain (with departures at 3- to 5-minute intervals).

The national carrier is **Malaysia Airlines** (24-hour call centre tel: 03-7843 3000; 1300-883 000 toll-free within Malaysia; www.malaysiaairlines.com), which flies to more than 100 international and domestic destinations. Local budget airline **AirAsia** (24-hour call centre tel: 03-6008 5999, 1300 889 933 toll-free within Malaysia; www.airasia.com) offers cheap fares online for both domestic and overseas destinations. Budget airline **Firefly** (tel: 03-7845 4543; www.fireflyz.com.my) also has competitive fares.

Malaysia Airlines' flights depart from KLIA while AirAsia flights depart from the **Low Cost Carrier Terminal** (LCCT; tel: 03-8776 0888 KLIA 1Touch; www.lcct.klia.com.my), about 20km (12 miles) from KLIA. Feeder buses running at 20-minute intervals link the two terminals.

Flying from UK or US

Airlines that fly to KL from the UK and US include Aer Lingus, Air France, Alitalia, Austrian Airlines, EVA Air, Finnair, Iberia, Japan Airlines, KLM, Lufthansa, Malaysia Airlines and Singapore Airlines.

Passengers from the UK and EU can fly direct to KLIA in about 13 hours, though stopover flights are cheaper. Airlines that fly non-stop include EVA Air, Malaysia Airlines and Thai Airways.

Travel time from the US is longer. Flying from the west coast takes about 16 hours and involves a connection in Tokyo, Taipei or Hong Kong; the east coast route via Europe takes about 19 hours. Malaysia Airlines operates flights from New York (Newark) to KLIA via Stockholm. US carriers fly via Singapore, where you connect with Singapore Airlines to KL.

By Rail

National Railways, or **KTMB** (tel: 03-2267 1200; www.ktmb.com.my), operates services that are clean, cheap and reliable. The rail links KL with Thailand in the north; Singapore in the south; and the east coast of the peninsula. In KL, the rail terminus is **KL Sentral**.

If travelling from Bangkok, you need to change trains in Hatyai (south Thailand) or Butterworth (near Penang). The express journey takes about 20 hours. A less travelled route is via the east coast through the Thai town of Sungai Kolok and the Malaysian town of Rantau Panjang, from where you take a bus to Kota Bharu and then the train to KL. From Singapore, the express journey takes 8 hours.

Express trains are air-conditioned and offer simple meals on board. There are sleeping berths on the night services, with dormitories as well as compartments for two. You can book seats up to 60 days ahead. Regular trains stop at numerous stations and can take twice as long to reach your destination. Ask about the **Visit Malaysia Rail Pass**, which is valid for travel on all KTMB services in Peninsular Malaysia (including Singapore). Passes are valid for either 5, 10 or 15 days.

To travel in style, opt for the elegant and charming luxury **Eastern and Oriental Express** (Singapore tel: 65-6395 0678; www.orient-express.com/e&o). Travelling several times a month between Singapore and Bangkok, it makes a stop at the Old KL Railway Station on certain days.

By Road

KL is connected by the North–South Expressway to Thailand along the west coast via Bukit Kayu Hitam, and to Singapore via two causeways. These are serviced by long-distance express buses and share taxis.

From Thailand, buses travel to KL along the west coast from Hatyai, a journey of about 9 hours. Many buses from Hatyai, Bangkok and Phuket terminate in Butterworth, from where you can take a local express bus. The east coast route from Thailand is via Sungai Kolok and Kota Bharu, where there are various overland options to KL. The main bus terminus in KL is at **Puduraya**.

From Singapore, the bus journey takes about 5–6 hours. While the crowded and chaotic Puduraya is the main bus terminus for the cheaper bus services, several of the pricier operators terminate at various places in the city. These include **Aeroline** (tel: 03-6258 8800; Singapore tel: 65-6723 7222; www.aeroline.com.my), which terminates at Jalan Ampang, at Corus Hotel near KLCC, and Petaling Jaya; **Nationwide Interstate Coach Executive Express (NICE)** (tel: 03-2274 0499; Singapore tel: 65-6256 5755; www.plusliner.com) which terminates at the Old KL Railway Station; and **Transnasional** (tel: 03-4047 7878; Singapore tel: 65-6294 7034; www.nadi.com.my/transportation_home.asp), which terminates at the Malaysia Tourism Centre along Jalan Ampang.

These companies operate the more expensive and more comfortable VIP or Executive (24-seater) express coaches which have comfortable reclining seats, a host or hostess on board to serve drinks and meals and, on some services, individual TV screens. Cheaper non-express coaches make several stops on the way, including a 30-minute-long meal stop.

Long-distance shared taxis provide flexibility since they operate 24 hours. However, they cost at least twice as much as buses and will usually wait until there are four passengers before departing unless you book the whole car. The KL terminus is Puduraya but you could ask to be taken to your accommodation for a small additional fee.

Bus Tours

Always buy your bus ticket from a ticket counter and not from a tout, and check the date and departure time. Illegal operators, especially at Puduraya, wait until a bus is full before departing, make numerous stops along the way, have daredevil drivers, and operate without licence or insurance. You have been warned!

By Sea

Travellers can visit from Sumatra, Indonesia via Port Klang, boarding a ferry from Dumai (in Riau) or Tanjung Balai Asahan (in North Sumatra). To or from Dumai, **Doyan Shipping** runs the Indomal/Malaysia Express (tel: 03-3167 1058). To or from Tanjung Balai Asahan, try **Aero Speed** (tel: 03-3165 2545/3073).

Getting Around

To and from KLIA

The journey from KLIA to the city centre takes 30–75 minutes, depending on the mode of transport and traffic conditions. Many city hotels offer complimentary airport transfers or can arrange one for a small fee.

By Train

The fastest mode of travel from KLIA is the high-speed **KLIA Ekspres** (tel: 03-2267 8000; www.kliaekspres.com), which takes you to the **Kuala Lumpur City Air Terminal** (KL CAT) at **KL Sentral** directly in 28 minutes. Trains run every 20 minutes from 5am to midnight, and every 15 minutes between 5 and 9am and 4 and 10pm. Taxis at KL Sentral can take you to other points in the city, but it will add to your travel time.

The half-hourly **KLIA Transit** service stops at three intermediate stations – Salak Tinggi, Putrajaya/Cyberjaya, Bandar Tasik Selatan and LCCT. The journey takes 36 minutes and the service hours are 5.52am–1am.

Tickets can be purchased from vending machines or counters at KLIA and KL CAT, at hotels and through appointed travel agencies.

Passengers departing on Malaysia Airlines, Cathay Pacific and Royal Brunei may check in at KL CAT with a valid KLIA Ekspres ticket at least two hours before departure. You will be issued a boarding pass and a claim tag for checked-in baggage.

By Taxi

Airport Limo taxis (tel: 03-8787 3378) operate a meet-and-greet service 24 hours from KLIA and are air-conditioned. A range of taxis is available. Buy coupons from the Airport Limo counter just before you exit the international arrivals gate, or just outside the domestic arrivals gate. The journey to the city centre takes anywhere from 40 to 60 minutes and, depending on the type of car used (Budget, Premier, Luxury or 8-seater van service), will cost between RM70 and RM180.

When leaving the country, you can call the Airport Limo (tel: 03-9223 8080 8am–midnight); tel: 03-8787 3030 midnight–8am) or take any city taxi to the airport. The latter's fare comprises the meter rate plus toll fares, a surcharge of RM12 and an extra charge for luggage placed in the boot. The total will add up to RM60–80. **Public Cab** (tel: 03-6259 2020) also offers a limo service to the airport that seats six. You can also book a taxi the night before for an early morning flight. Note that there is a surcharge for services from midnight to 6am.

By Bus

The **Airport Coach** (tel: 03-6203 3067) makes a 75-minute journey to Hentian Duta (RM20) and Jalan Chan Sow Lin LRT station (RM10), and runs every 45 mins. From Duta the only available public transport is taxis, which usually charge a hefty flat fee, whereas from Chan Sow Lin you can take a train to town.

To and from LCCT

Take the feeder bus to KLIA (daily 5.55am–12.35am) and use the transport options listed above. KLIA Ekspres now has a stop at LCCT, and this is probably the most efficient way to get to KL Sentral. Alternatively, the **Skybus** (www.skybus.com.my) to KL Sentral runs every 15–30 minutes from 7.15am to 12.30am. The journey takes 90 minutes (RM9) and tickets can be purchased from counters at the terminal or on board AirAsia flights. The **Airport Coach** (tel: 03-6203 3067) runs every 45 minutes between 5am and 12.30am to Hentian Duta (RM20) and to Jalan Chan Sow Lin LRT Station (RM10). The journey takes about 75 minutes. Depending on the type of car used (Budget, Premier or or 8-seater van service), a taxi to the city centre will cost RM60–150.

PIRATE TAXIS

Unlicensed taxi operators called *teksi sapu* or *kereta sapu* often hang around airport, train, bus and ferry terminals, and charge a flat rate, usually higher than official rates. They are also not insured and sometimes go round gathering a few passengers before departing. Always opt for a licensed cab.

Orientation

Located on the west coast of the peninsula, KL is bordered on the east by the Titiwangsa Mountains and anchors the Klang River basin. The most densely populated and developed part of the country, it covers 234 sq km (90 sq miles) and comprises an old city centre around Independence Square (Dataran Merdeka) and a new one around the KL City Centre (KLCC).

Getting around KL is easy, and most of the city's attractions are accessible using a combination of walking and the train system. Avoid road transport during the peak hours of 7–10am and 5–8pm, and particularly if it is raining. Taxi drivers are increasingly reluctant to drive during these periods. While the public transport system has improved, it is still clumsily integrated and there are pockets of the city which are not linked, particularly further away from the city centre.

Though the city is far from pedestrian-friendly, walking is still a quick way to get around.

Public Transport

Trains

KL's rail system consists of three types of services – the LRT which covers most of the city and inner suburbs; the semi-circular KL Monorail which loops through the Golden Triangle; and the KTM Komuter for trips to the outer suburbs. The main rail terminus is **KL Sentral**, where you can get on any of these systems. **RapidKL** now combines all bus and rail services in the Klang Valley.

The **Light Rail Transit (LRT)** (tel: 03-7885 2585; www.rapidkl.com.my/network/rail) has two lines that intersect at Masjid Jamek station: the **Ampang** and **Sri Petaling** line which runs from northern KL (Sentul Timur station) to Ampang in the east and Sri Petaling in the south; and the **Kelana Jaya** line that runs from Terminal Putra station in Gombak in northeastern KL to Petaling Jaya, ending at Kelana Jaya station in the southwest.

Trains run every 7–8 minutes (every 3 minutes during peak hours) from 6am to 11.50pm (11.30pm on Sundays and holidays). Senior citizens pay half price but need to get a concession card from the station. Tickets for single and return journeys can be purchased at vending machines and customer service counters. Monthly travel cards can also be purchased.

The elevated **Kuala Lumpur Monorail** (tel: 03-7885 2585; www.rapidkl.com.my/network/rail) has a single line that covers central KL, from KL Sentral to Titiwangsa station from 6am to midnight, with trains running every 7–10 minutes (4–5 minutes during peak hours). Note that the Monorail's KL Sentral station is poorly signposted and getting there requires walking 250 metres/yds from the main station across a busy street (Jalan Tun Sambanthan). However, you can also hop on the free shuttle bus from 7am to 7pm. Single tickets can be purchased at station counters; RM20 and RM50 stored-value tickets are also available.

The **KTM Komuter** (tel: 03-2267 1200; www.ktmb.com.my) is an intra-city commuter train service covering greater KL. It runs two lines, namely **Sentul–Port Klang** and **Rawang–Seremban**. The interchange is at KL Sentral. Tickets can be purchased from vending machines and counters at stations.

Buses

RapidKL's City Shuttle buses (tel: 03-7885 2585; www.rapidkl.com.my/network/bus/busroutes) cover most major areas in the city and provide feeder services to train (mainly LRT) stations. City Shuttle buses have a red disk on their windscreens and side windows near the front door, and they ply routes 101 to 115. The fare is RM2 for the whole day; buy a ticket on the bus on your first ride and flash it at the driver for all subsequent rides. Have exact change ready, especially during peak hours. You can also buy a Rapidpass for unlimited rides for RM40 and an integrated LRT/ Rapid KL ticket for RM100.

Services run by other bus operators are more chaotic and information is lacking, but you can get buses to outlying areas in Petaling Jaya, Shah Alam and Klang from major stops in the city, such as the Klang Bus Station, and at the Bangkok Bank near Petaling Street.

Taxis

Taxis are abundant (they operate 24 hours), safe and air-conditioned. Taxis are required by law to use meters, with fares starting at RM3 for the first kilometre, with a 10-sen increase every 200 metres/yds. From midnight to 6am, there is a surcharge of 50 percent on the metered fare, and extra passengers (more than two) are charged 20 sen each. Surcharges also apply for bookings (RM1) and baggage placed in the boot (RM1 per piece). Many taxis refuse to use the meter with tourists, so be sure to check before you get in. If you're already in the taxi and think you're being taken for a ride, ask to be let out as soon as possible. Take down the taxi's registration number and report it to the cab company.

Taxis are operated by several different companies, but all will have a sign at the top, which, when lit, means the taxi is available. Note that there are premium taxis that have a RM4 starting charge and charge a bit more for each kilometre travelled. There are taxi stands but you can usually wave taxis down anywhere.

Often, during peak hours, taxis will not go to places where traffic is horrendous and passengers are hard to come by on the return leg. In such cases, drivers either decline passengers or will charge a flat rate. If you have to bargain, keep in mind that fares around town start at RM5 and it should cost you no more than RM10 to go across the central city area.

KL Sentral and tourist places like the KL Tower have taxi counters that require you to buy a prepaid coupon. Such fares are higher than the meter system but are lower than flat rates. Reliable radio taxi services can be booked with **Comfort Taxi** (tel: 03-2692 2525), **Public Cab** (tel: 03-6259 2020; www.publiccab.com.my), **Supercab** (tel: 03-2095 3399), **Sunlight Radio Taxi** (tel: 03-9057 1111) and **Selangor Radio Taxi** (tel: 03-2693 6211).

Driving

Avoid driving in the city unless you are used to challenging driving conditions and ill-mannered drivers. KL drivers are notorious for cutting into lanes, not signalling and just being plain rude. However, driving out of the city on excursions is a pleasure, and, in fact, should not be missed. Petrol stations are plentiful, even along highways. Note that signs are in Bahasa Malaysia and can be inadequate. Buy a good (recent) KL roadmap (like the *Kuala Lumpur and Klang Valley Street Directory* by NAVI Map) and plan your route. Another good map source for Malaysia is found at www.jkr.gov.my/RoadMap.

Drive on the left. An international driver's licence is required except for tourists from the US, EU, Australia, New Zealand, Japan and Singapore. Major car rental companies have 24-hour counters at the KLIA, as well as branches in other major cities where you can drop off your car. Rental starts from RM150 for the compact Malaysian-made Proton car, and includes insurance and unlimited mileage. Chauffeur-driven cars are also available. Reputable companies include:

Avis Malaysia, tel: 03-7628 2300, 1800 88 1054; www.avis.com.my

Hertz Malaysia, tel: 03-7718 1266, 1800 883 086; www5.hertz.com

Hawk Rent A Car, tel: 03-5631 6488; www.hawkrentacar.com.my

Pacific Rent-A-Car, tel: 03-2287 4118/4119; www.iprac.com

Trips Out of KL

By Road

Malaysia has a good dual-carriageway highway system covering 66,000km (41,260 miles). To head south and southwest (to Shah Alam, Klang, Putrajaya and KLIA), you can choose to take the Lebuhraya Damansara–Puchong (LDP), New Klang Valley Expressway (NKVE) or Federal Highway. Using the North–South Expressway, you can go north all the way to Thailand, and south to Singapore. To get to the east coast, take the Karak Highway, which links KL to the East Coast Expressway.

On expressways, the speed limit is 110km/h (68mph), although it is lower on trunk roads, in large urban areas, in rural settlements and on hilly roads. Every expressway has a toll system; tolls can be paid using cash or the Touch 'n Go card *(see below)*.

Driving on narrow trunk roads can be a little more hazardous, with maniacal lorry drivers, potholes and non-existent road signs. Slow down near villages in case of animals on the road.

For driving directions out of the city to various excursion destinations, see the respective Excursions chapters.

By Bus

Three types of interstate buses operate in Malaysia: non-air-conditioned buses plying between the states, air-conditioned

TOUCH 'N GO CARD

This easy-to-use card can be used on all major public transport systems in the Klang Valley, highways in Malaysia, and some parking spaces and theme parks. Buy one for RM10 and top up at toll booths, train stations and selected banks and petrol kiosks (tel: 03-7628 5115; www.touchngo.com.my).

express buses connecting major towns, and non-air-conditioned buses that provide services within each state. Buses generally run from 6am to midnight daily. Apart from express buses, these seldom adhere to schedules, although they are frequent enough between 7am to 10pm.

The main bus terminus for interstate travel is **Puduraya** on Jalan Pudu (tel: 03-2070 0145). However, many buses heading for the east coast states of Terengganu, Kelantan and Pahang leave from either **Hentian Putra** on Jalan Putra (tel: 03-4041 4642) or the **Pekeliling Bus Station** on Jalan Pekeliling (tel: 03-4042 7988). Some northbound buses leave from **Hentian Duta** on Jalan Duta (tel: 03-6203 3150).

A good nationwide company for bus travel is **Transnasional** (tel: 03-2070 3300; www.transnational.com.my).

By Taxi

Taxis allow you the greatest flexibility. Share taxis from **Kuala Lumpur Outstation Taxi** (tel: 03-2078 3525; www.infotaxi.org) in **Puduraya** can take you to smaller towns, where you can change to local taxis to get to specific attractions. Note that licensed taxis are rare in these towns and *kereta sapu* (unlicensed taxis) may be your only option.

Alternatively, hire a KL taxi for the day *(see page 223)*. The fare usually comprises a rate for driving you to/from your destination, which includes a waiting time of 1–2 hours. Beyond this, a per-hour waiting fee is charged, starting from RM10 per hour. Toll charges are additional. Once you reach your destination, sort out the charges to get around locally before you explore an area.

Many hotels also offer car-and-driver services. Check if an operator is licensed and has insurance. Be clear about where you want to go, how long you expect to engage a driver's services, and whether charges cover petrol, tolls, parking and meals. Be sure to take down the driver's name, car registration and company contact number.

Interstate Bus Hints

Some outlying bus stations are not accessible by public transport and taxis can be hard to hail or will charge a flat rate, especially after midnight. Also, keep a wary eye out for snatch thieves and pickpockets, especially when waiting for night coaches.

Buses will stop at the main bus stations in the respective towns, and you can hop on local buses from there. Be sure to ask about the frequency of these buses and what time the last bus runs. Keep small or exact change for these journeys.

By Rail

The LRT and KTM Komuter take you to parts of the Klang Valley and Selangor. The KLIA Ekspres travels to Putrajaya/Cyberjaya and the south en route to the airport. To go further afield north, south or east, hop on the KTMB interstate trains.

FRIM, Batu Caves, Gombak

FRIM

By Taxi: Buses do not service FRIM, so hire a taxi for the day (RM25–30 per hour) to guarantee transport back to your hotel. You can also take the KTM Komuter train to Kepong station and hop into a taxi from there (RM10). Be sure to arrange with the taxi driver to take you back to the station when you are done.

Batu Caves

By Taxi: As with FRIM, the most efficient way to get to Batu Caves is by taxi. A ride from the city centre will cost about RM20 one way. You can easily get a taxi from Batu Caves back to town. Alternatively, take the LRT to Putra and then take the RapidKL Bus No 203 to Batu Caves. Note that Batu Caves feature in day tours offered by many KL tour operators.

Above: the KL monorail

Gombak

By Taxi: The best way to get here is to hire a taxi for the day (RM25–30 per hour). Alternatively, take the day tour offered by **Jungle Lodge Alang Sedayu** (tel: 03-4251 4301; www.junglelodgemalaysia.com). They will pick you up from the city centre.

Hill Resorts and Surroundings

Kuala Kubu Bharu

By Bus: From **Puduraya**, take the half-hourly Mega Kota bus No 66 to Tanjung Malim, which stops at Kuala Kubu Bharu (KKB). Buses run from 5.30am to 8pm and the journey takes about 90 minutes. Alternatively, take the KTM Komuter to **Rawang** and catch the local bus from there to KKB (about 1 hour).

By Taxi: A share taxi from **Puduraya** costs RM200 one way (negotiable). The journey takes 75 minutes. From **Rawang**, the cost is RM30 one way and the ride takes 30 minutes.

Fraser's Hill

By Bus: Bus travel is inconvenient unless you time your trip perfectly. You have to get to Kuala Kubu Bharu (as above) in time to catch the 10.30am shuttle bus (Pahang Lin Siong Bus Co) to Fraser's Hill, which takes 90 minutes.

By Taxi: A share taxi from **Puduraya** costs RM160 one way, and takes 2 hours. From **Rawang**, the fare is RM80 and travel time is 1½ hours.

Genting Highlands

By Bus: The Genting Express Bus (tel: 03-2279 8989; www.rwgenting.com) leaves **KL Sentra**l every hour from 8am to 7pm. Buses are only allowed to go up to the Skyway cable car station, except for selected weekend services. The fare includes the Skyway cable car fare. Buses to Genting also leave from **Puduraya** (tel: 03-2072 6863) half-hourly from 7am to 7pm, and the fare is RM9.60, including the Skyway fare; and from Gombak LRT Terminal, 1 Utama mall and Kajang.

By Taxi: Genting-bound taxis are based in **Puduraya** (tel: 03-2078 5353) and can pick you up from hotels in the city centre. They are only allowed as far as the Skyway cable car station. Fares are RM60–70 and the journey takes 1 hour.

Lentang

By Bus: Board the Temerloh express bus at the **Pekeliling Bus Station**. Tell the ticket seller you want to be dropped off at Lanchang town and remind the bus driver as well. Buses run from 8am to 8pm and the journey to Lanchang is 75 minutes. From Lanchang, take a taxi to Lentang and make sure you arrange to be picked up from there.

By Taxi: The KL Outstation Taxi (tel: 03-2078 3525) in **Puduraya** charges RM240 for a round trip to Lentang (35 minutes one way).

Kuala Gandah

By Bus: Take the same route as to Lentang and then hire a taxi (20 minutes) to the Kuala Gandah Elephant Conservation Centre. Be sure to get on the early bus if you want to get to the elephant centre in time for the 2pm feed.

By Taxi: *See Lentang.*

Kuala Selangor

By Bus: From **Puduraya**'s platform 23, take bus No 141, which departs every 30 minutes from 5am to 7.30pm. The last bus leaves Kuala Selangor for KL at 7.30pm. The ride takes about 2 hours. From the **Kuala Selangor Bus Station**, you can take a local taxi to Kampung Kuantan and Pasir Penambang. Make sure you arrange for return journeys and negotiate the price before you board.

By Taxi: Shared taxis from **Puduraya** cost RM50–60 one way and the journey takes just over 1 hour.

Klang Valley

Petaling Jaya

By Bus: RapidKL buses (tel: 03-7885 2585; www.rapidkl.com.my/bus/busroutes) service many parts of PJ. No 33D goes from the Bangkok Bank near Petaling Street, along the Federal Highway to Kelana Jaya, and stops near Jalan Universiti. No 906A does a pick-up at the Universiti LRT Station and winds through the Universiti Malaya campus.

By Taxi: Almost all taxis will go to PJ. From KL Sentral, the cost is about RM10 to get to the fringe of PJ; travel time can range from about 30 to 45 minutes, depending on traffic.

By Rail: The Kelana Jaya LRT line serves most of the PJ routes and travelling time is 15–25 minutes from the heart of the city. You can also take the KTM Komuter which stops at the Petaling station; from here you can take a taxi to various attractions.

Sunway City

By Taxi: From KL Sentral, the cost is about RM20 and travel time is about 40 minutes.

By Rail: Take the Kelana Jaya line to the Kelana Jaya LRT Station, from where shuttle buses to Sunway (50 sen) run every 30 minutes.

Shah Alam

By Bus: RapidKL bus No 63 and No 338 from KL Sentral go to the centre of Shah Alam. There are bus services within Shah Alam. Alternately, hop on any Shah Alam bus from Klang Bus Station near Central Market. These buses will drop you off in front of the PKNS Plaza mall, from where you can easily flag down taxis.

By Taxi: Not all taxis will go to Shah Alam. For those that will, be sure to ask the drivers to use their meters or negotiate a rate before you board. The fare is usually RM30–40 and the journey is about 50 minutes.

By Rail: The KTM Komuter line to Port Klang stops at the Shah Alam station, from where you can take a taxi to get to local attractions.

Klang

By Bus: There are several buses from the Klang Bus Station near the Central Market to Klang. They stop right across from the Mydin departmental store in Klang town.

By Taxi: Not all taxis will go to Klang. For those that will, be sure to ask the drivers to use their meters or negotiate a rate before you board. It costs about RM40 one way and the journey takes about 1 hour.

By Rail: The KTM Komuter line to Port Klang stops at the Klang station in town, which is just a 10-minute walk across the bridge to Little India.

Putrajaya

By Bus: Take the CityLiner Bus No 868 from the Mydin building on Jalan Tun Perak, or RapidKL bus No 868 from the Sinar Kota Shopping Centre near Petaling Street. Travel time is 1 hour. In Putrajaya, take Nadi Putra bus No 100, No 200 or No 300 to get around the city.

By Taxi: Book a radio taxi to get there. The fare is usually RM40–50 for the 1-hour journey.

By Rail: From KL Sentral, take the KLIA Ekspres, which runs every 30 minutes, and alight at Bandar Tasik Putrajaya. From there, take Nadi Putra bus No 100, No 200 or No 300 to get to your destination.

Accommodation

Some Things to Consider Before You Book The Room

Choosing a Hotel

Kuala Lumpur has some of the region's best hotels in every price range. There is a good choice of international brands, home-grown chains, resort-themed accommodation and boutique establishments, not to mention serviced apartments, as well as simple guesthouses and backpacker hostels. Hotels are star-rated from 1 to 5 according to international criteria such as size, facilities, food and beverage outlets and staff-to-guest ratio. See the **Malaysian Association of Hotels** website (www.hotels.org.my) for more information.

Outside of luxury hotels, however, the service can often be wanting; this is mainly due to poor training, so exercise patience when dealing with hotel staff. Note that, like hotel eateries, non-smoking rooms or floors are not always smoke-free. If you are not sure, always ask to inspect a room first. An increasing number of hotel eateries serve only halal food, so expect "beef bacon" and "turkey ham" on the menu.

Hotel Areas

Most 5-star hotels are clustered in the Golden Triangle, with views of the Petronas Twin Towers and/or KL Tower as selling points. Many are also close to the Jalan Sultan Ismail entertainment area.

Bukit Bintang offers accommodation from 3-star boutique hotels to 5-star luxury hotels, which are surrounded by great nightlife, restaurants and shops. Behind Bukit Bintang, in Tengkat Tong Shin and its surrounds, are the new-breed "flashpacking" budget places, occupying classy, refurbished prewar shophouses that are a hop away from the nightlife of Jalan Sultan Ismail and the Asian Heritage Row.

The more established backpacker hostels are in Petaling Street, and the adjacent Puduraya and Masjid India areas, in the midst of local bustle as well as historical and cultural attractions.

The moderately priced hotels along Jalan Tuanku Abdul Rahman are popular with Asian business travellers. Newer hotels like The Royale Chulan and Anggun KL in the Bukit Bintang area offer a Malaysian ambience, whilst the Grand Millennium has the perks of a glitzy 5-star Vegas hotel. More modest accommodation is available nearby in the older enclave of Brickfields.

Outside of KL, Petaling Jaya hotels cater mainly to medium budgets, with the exception of the 5-star, family-oriented Sunway Resort Hotel. Putrajaya has several luxury hotels but there is little reason to stay here unless you are attending a convention or are on government business.

Prices and Bookings

Hotels are required to quote net prices (including 10 percent service and 5 percent government tax), and most include buffet breakfast with the room. Actual rates are usually lower than published rates, and discounts can be negotiated for longer stays. Ask about packages as tours or admission fees to attractions are sometimes thrown in.

Book in advance for stays over long weekends, Malaysian and Singaporean school holidays, public holidays – particularly Chinese New Year and Hari Raya Puasa – the Formula 1 Grand Prix period, and the super peak months of July and August, when Arab tourists flock to the country. There is usually a surcharge during these periods too.

As in most big cities, internet rates are lower than walk-in or call-in rates, so check individual hotel websites or the Malaysian Association of Hotels website (www.hotels.org.my).

Accommodation Listings

Historic Heart

Budget

Heritage Station Hotel Kuala Lumpur
Bangunan Stesen Keretapi, Jalan Sultan Hishamuddin
Tel: 03-2273 5588
www.heritagehotelmalaysia.com
1 p259, C3
Located in the beautiful Old KL Railway Station, this hotel harks back to when it was *the* place to stay in colonial times. Designed by A.B. Hubbock, the hotel hosted many eminent literary figures in the 1920s and 30s, including Herman Hesse and Anthony Burgess. The fixtures have been retained, including the clanking old lift, a bistro area adorned with historical wall hangings, and lovely arched Moorish windows. Room sizes have been halved and the fittings modernised. The rooms are comfortable though slightly worn. The dorms can sleep six people, and there are laundry facilities. NICE buses serving Singapore and Penang stop here. The old city centre and Lake Gardens are an easy walk away.

Petaling Street and Surroundings

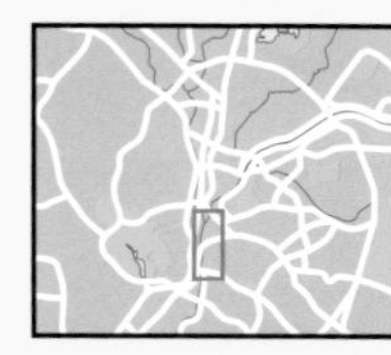

Moderate

Ancasa Hotel
Jalan Tun Tan Cheng Lock
Tel: 03-2026 6060
www.ancasa-hotel.com
2 p261, F2/3
Great location between Petaling Street and the Puduraya bus station, with markets and historical areas close by, as well as cheap Chinese food available. Don't expect too much of the service, but the clean rooms are good value for money.

Citin Hotel Pudu
38 Jalan Pudu
Tel: 03-2031 7777
www.citinpudu.com
3 p261, F2
Opposite the Puduraya bus station. Recently renovated, this offers pleasant and clean accommodation. Rooms are generally small, except for the family rooms. Baby cots are available on request. Historical and cultural attractions are a short walk away.

Hotel Malaya
Jalan Hang Lekir
Tel: 03-2072 7722
www.hotelmalaya.com.my
4 p261, E3
In business since 1966, this 3-star hotel has been renovated several times, and the rooms are warm and pleasant. A great location to experience the day and night rhythms of Petaling Street, which is right on its doorstep. Its Kafetien 1966 restaurant serves delicious Nyonya fare.

Swiss-Inn Kuala Lumpur
62 Jalan Sultan
Tel: 03-2072 3333
www.swissinkualalumpur.com
5 p261, F3
Converted from an early 20th-century Chinese shophouse, this popular hotel fronts a street with wonderful Chinese eateries, teashops and souvenir outlets, while its back opens out directly to the Petaling Street bazaar. Cast in pastel shades, rooms are basic with small bathrooms, but clean and offer value for money. A non-smoking floor is available. Internet rates are much lower than published rates.

Budget

Hotel China Town 2
70 and 72 Jalan Petaling
Tel: 03-2072 9933
www.kl.hotels.com/chinatown2
6 p261, F3
A cross between a hotel and a hostel. Quiet and air-conditioned rooms have attached bathrooms with hot showers; only some rooms have windows. Wi-fi access, lockers, laundry and phone services.

Hotel China Town Inn
52–54 Jalan Petaling
Tel: 03-2070 4008
www.chinatowninn.com
7 p261, F3
In the heart of Petaling Street, this friendly and very popular hotel has rooms with fans or air conditioning. Early check-in from 7am.

StayOrange
16 Jalan Petaling
Tel: 03-2070 2208
www.stayorange.com
8 p261, E3
This budget hotel is inspired by Japanese cube hotels, with simple, basic rooms dipped in orange paint. If you time your booking right, you can get a bed in a two-bunk room with Wi-fi and air conditioning for RM2.

Le Village
99A Jalan Tun H.S. Lee
Mobile tel: 013-355 0235
9 p261, E2
Housed in a century-old shophouse, this simple outfit with basic fan-cooled rooms is a stone's throw away from Central Market as well as trains and buses. Homely and laid-back with artwork on its walls and a rooftop garden for chilling out.

Price Categories

Price categories are for a double room with breakfast and taxes:
Luxury = above RM400; **Expensive** = RM300–399; **Moderate** = RM100–299; **Budget** = under RM100

Jalan TAR and Surroundings

Moderate

Hotel Grand Centrepoint
316 Jalan Tuanku Abdul Rahman
Tel: 03-2693 3988
⑩ p256, B3
A cheerful medium-priced hotel at the northern end of the Jalan TAR silk stretch and opposite the Maju Junction Mall, with an LRT station on its doorstep and Kampung Baru within walking distance. Rooms have ample soundproofing from the busy traffic. Offers tour bookings, laundry services and transfers to the Jalan Duta bus terminus for airport-bound guests.

Palace Hotel
40–46 Jalan Masjid India
Tel: 03-2698 6122
www.palacehotel.com
⑪ p256, B4
Frills-free accommodation in Little India, the ethnic enclave filled with curry smells, Hindi music and *azan*, the call to Muslim prayer. The single, double and quad rooms are air conditioned and have hot showers. The Masjid India LRT interchange is a 5-minute walk away.

Quality Hotel City Centre
Jalan Raja Laut
Tel: 03-2693 9233
www.quality.com.my
⑫ p256, A3
At the lower end of the mid-budget category, this family-friendly place has large beds. Its coffee house serves a good buffet breakfast. Close to malls – particularly Pertama Complex for cheap and good leather products, and the Japanese department store Sogo.

Budget

Coliseum Café and Hotel
98–100 Jalan Tuanku Abdul Rahman
Tel: 03-2692 6270
⑬ p256, B4
Soak up the lovely old-world charm of this hotel, which dates back to the 1920s. It once housed less salubrious colonial characters who would drown their sorrows in the bar and dine in the adjacent restaurant on sizzling steaks prepared by thecity's best Hainanese chefs. Today, a mostly backpacker crowd fills the rooms. Doubles are air-conditioned; singles are fan-cooled. Both the bar and the eatery –

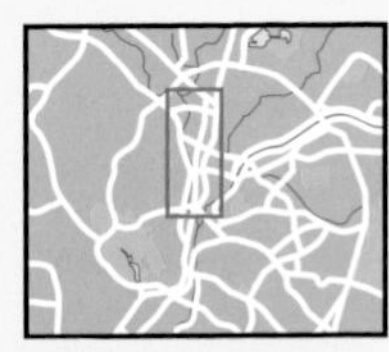

slightly frayed but still dishing out the same solid fare – are good places to mingle with and watch the locals.

Tune
316 Jalan Tuanku Abdul Rahman
Tel: 03-2692 3300
www.tunehotels.com
⑭ p256, B3
Budget home-grown airline AirAsia has applied its no-frills philosophy to the hospitality scene, but with a little more pizzazz. You get branded mattresses, but you have to buy soap, air conditioning and everything else.

Kuala Lumpur City Centre

Luxury

The Ascott
9 Jalan Pinang
Tel: 03-2142 6868
www.the-ascott.com
⑮ p257, D4
Located across from the KLCC, the Ascott is a serviced apartment with splendid views of the city from its rooftop pool. Offerings range from studio to three-bedroom apartments, all with fully equipped kitchens and facilities that cater to both families and business folk. Within walking distance of a wide array of eateries.

Mandarin Oriental
Kuala Lumpur City Centre
Tel: 03-2380 8888
www.mandarinoriental.com
⑯ p257, D4
If you don't mind splurging for ultimate comfort, pick this hotel, often touted as a "6-star" facility. It has large guest rooms that combine traditional and contemporary furnishings with cutting-edge modern technology. The windows stretch from floor to ceiling and offer fabulous views of the Petronas Twin Towers. Art aficionados can marvel at the 300-odd original artworks displayed throughout the hotel. The restaurant and bars are innovative and its breakfast has often been described as "the best buffet experience". The Thalgo Marine Spa provides a relaxing if expensive diversion from the hustle of city life.

Shangri-La Hotel
11 Jalan Sultan Ismail
Tel: 03-2032 2388
www.shangri-la.com/kualalumpur
⑰ p257, C4
This hotel has lovely gardens, a pool area nestled among skyscrapers, a large, fully equipped gym and capacious rooms. Its foyer is always busy and its lounge often crowded. The hotel restaurants are popular on weekends, so book a table if you are dining there. This is a large hotel, so while service is good it is not always quick. Party-goers will rel-

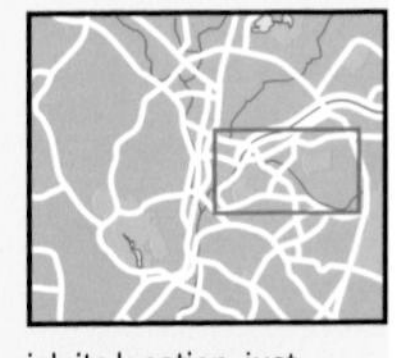

ish its location, just across from the pulsating clubs of Jalan Sultan Ismail. The KL Tower and lush Bukit Nanas Forest Recreational Park are right behind the hotel.

Sheraton Imperial
Jalan Sultan Ismail
Tel: 03-2717 9900
www.starwoodhotels.com
⑱ p256, B3
Part of Starwood's "luxury collection", this plush modern hotel is located close to the Jalan Sultan

Ismail entertainment stretch, and right next to the swish Asian Heritage Row. The Monorail is a 5-minute walk away. Polished timber, Italian marble and original art pieces feature throughout the hotel, but the rooms may be a little below international standard. Despite being positioned as a business hotel, both rooms and suites are extremely child-friendly.

Expensive

Crowne Plaza Mutiara
Jalan Sultan Ismail
Tel: 03-2148 2322
www.crowneplaza.com
19 p257, D4
This 36-storey hotel sits on a beautifully landscaped 5-hectare (12-acre) property. Recently refurbished, it now sports a fresh, contemporary look, with spacious rooms equipped with large bathrooms and heavenly rain showers. Guests in executive club rooms and suites enjoy complimentary breakfast, cocktails, drinks and pre-dinner snacks. The hotel has also been scoring marks for its quality service.

Hotel Equatorial
Jalan Sultan Ismail
Tel: 03-2161 7777
www.equatorial.com/kul
20 p257, D4
This pioneer hotel has pleasant, functional and comfortable rooms, with amenities geared towards business travellers. Its food and beverage outlets are among the city's most favoured, and are particularly renowned for high tea and Japanese fare. A shuttle goes daily to its sister resort in Putrajaya, useful if you are attending a convention there.

Hotel Maya
138 Jalan Ampang
Tel: 03-2711 8866
www.hotelmaya.com.my
21 p257, C/D3
Innovative use of space and an award-winning interior design combined with personalised service. This stylish boutique hotel has rustic timber flooring and floor-to-ceiling glass panels overlooking the Twin Towers or KL Tower. Its guests-only Sky Lounge provides views of both. The food outlets are excellent, especially the Still Waters restaurant, where *sosaku* (Japanese–Asian fusion cuisine) is served.

Hotel Nikko
165 Jalan Ampang
Tel: 03-2161 1111 or 1800-883 292 (toll-free)
www.hotelnikko.com.my
22 p257, E3
A contemporary Japanese-style hotel in the business district. Nikko offers great service, tastefully furnished rooms and excellent amenities. Has a complimentary shuttle service to and from the KLCC, Bintang Walk and Lot 10. Food options include a Japanese restaurant with fresh and seasonal offerings and an excellent Chinese restaurant.

Pacific Regency Hotel Apartments
Menara PanGlobal, Jalan Punchak, off Jalan P. Ramlee
Tel: 03-2332 7777
www.pacific-regency.com
23 p256, C4
Longer-staying tourists will appreciate this serviced apartment located opposite the KL Tower. Choose from studios and two-bedroom family-style units, all with fully equipped kitchenettes and free wireless broadband access. Besides a range of fine-dining and casual eateries, it has an in-house mini-mart and delicatessen. The establishment's chic rooftop Luna Bar is one of the city's top chill-out places.

Traders Hotel
Kuala Lumpur City Centre
Tel: 03-2332 9888
www.tradershotels.com
24 p257, D4
Connected to the KL Convention Centre and occupying levels 5 to 34, this sleek hotel – part of the Shangri-La chain – is a popular business and incentive destination, with five exclusive Traders Club floors. The contemporary styled rooms have large picture windows with views of either the city or to-die-for panoramas of KLCC Park and the Petronas Twin Towers. It's connected via the convention centre to KLCC Suria mall, which is really useful during inclement weather when you are carting back loads of shopping bags.

Moderate

Concorde Hotel
2 Jalan Sultan Ismail
Tel: 03-2144 2200
www.concorde.net/kl
25 p257, C4
One of the older hotels in the city, Concorde has held its own with large and airy rooms. Its Premier Executive wing (which falls into the expensive price category) is particularly nice, offering free limousine transfers from the airport, complimentary refreshments at its lounge, and a separate reception area. Filipino bands in the lounge remain as popular as ever, while right next door is the Hard Rock Café.

Impiana KLCC Hotel and Spa
13 Jalan Pinang
Tel: 03-2147 1111
www.impiana.com/klcc.html
26 p257, D4
A spa retreat for business travellers, this elegant addition to the KLCC hotel cluster offers busy executives a health bar and a wide choice of massages and therapies at the Swasana Spa. It has an infinity pool with an edge that appears to extend to the horizon. Other features are a wine lounge and cigar bar, while a walkway connects to the KLCC Convention Centre.

Renaissance KL Hotel
Corner of Jalan Sultan Ismail and Jalan Ampang
Tel: 03-2162 2233
www.marriott.com/property/propertypage/kulrn
27 p257, C3
Comprising two sections, the fancier West Wing and the more modest East Wing, this large European-themed hotel is popular with business travellers. The rooms are large but a little worn, but the beds are comfortable, the facilities are great and the buffet breakfast a real treat. The LRT and Monorail are within walking distance.

Price Categories

Price categories are for a double room with breakfast and taxes:
Luxury = above RM400; **Expensive** = RM300–399; **Moderate** = RM100–299; **Budget** = under RM100

Bukit Bintang

Luxury

Grand Millennium Kuala Lumpur
160 Jalan Bukit Bintang
Tel: 03-2117 4888
www.millenniumhotels.com
28 p260, A/B1
Located smack in the middle of Bintang Walk, this luxurious hotel boasts top-notch service, vibrant bars and restaurants. The city is literally at your doorstep.

The Ritz-Carlton
168 Jalan Imbi
Tel: 03-2141 0828
www.ritzcarlton.com
29 p260, B2
A business hotel, but family-friendly too. It has one of the city's best personalised butler services, along with charming touches like chilled aromatherapy towels and butler-drawn baths. Indulge in outdoor spa baths and therapies at its Spa Village.

The Westin
Jalan Bukit Bintang
Tel: 03-2731 8333
www.westin.com
30 p260, B1
Located next to the Starhill Gallery, this stylish and contemporary hotel boasts large rooms with luxurious beds and bathrooms. Parents will appreciate its Kids Club and babysitting services, while party-goers should not miss Qba, a fancy Latin venue with a wine/cigar bar.

Expensive

JW Marriott
183 Jalan Bukit Bintang
Tel: 03-2715 9000
www.marriott.com
31 p260, B1
This luxury hotel has all the required mod-cons for business travellers, including separate work areas in the rooms. It's part of the Starhill Gallery complex, so hotel guests can use the Starhill's spa and health facilities, as well as charge their dining expenses at the mall's Feast Village to their rooms.

The Royale Chulan
5 Jalan Conlay
Tel: 2688 9688
www.theroyalechulan.com.my
32 p260, C1
Built with local architecture in mind, this hotel boasts hand-crafted timber details and finishings. Rooms are opulent and spacious. Also has long-term serviced apartments.

Moderate

Anggun Kuala Lumpur
7 and 9, Jalan Tengkat Tong Shin
Tel: 03-2145 8003
www.anggunkl.com
33 p260, A2
One of the few boutique hotels in KL, this elegant hotel has tastefully furnished rooms and furnishings. Located on a busy street surrounded by food and nightlife outlets, it is a pleasant oasis from the hustle and bustle of the city.

Bintang Warisan
68 Jalan Bukit Bintang
Tel: 03-2148 8111
www.bintangwarisan.com
34 p260, A2
This 10-storey heritage boutique hotel is just behind the Jalan Alor hawker stalls. Has clean, adequately sized rooms, room service until 10.30pm, laundry service and airport transfers.

Dorsett Regency Hotel
172 Jalan Imbi
Tel: 03-2715 1000
www.dorsettregency.com.my
35 p260, B1/2
This 4-star facility has a stylish inside that belies its bland exterior. Most rooms have good views of the Twin Towers. The Esquire Club rooms and packages are great value, with complimentary services such as airport transfers and free internet access.

The Federal
35 Jalan Bukit Bintang
Tel: 03-2148 9166
www.fhihotels.com
36 p260, A2
Built at the request of the first prime minister just in time for the country's 1957 independence celebrations, this city landmark has kept up with the times and the competition. It has an eco-floor boasting plastic-free and organic features. Its revolving restaurant, with live music and a panoramic view of the city, serves fine-dining Western meals.

Budget

The Green Hut Lodge
48 Tengkat Tong Shin
Tel: 03-2141 3339
www.thegreenhut.com
37 p260, A2
This spotless and safe backpacker's place boasts ethnic interiors, bold colours and a well-designed common area. There are dorms, and twin-share and single rooms. All rooms are air conditioned and have hot showers.

Number Eight Guesthouse
8–10 Tengkat Tong Shin
Tel: 03-2144 2050
www.numbereight.com.my
38 p260, A2
This friendly, top-of-the-budget-range accommodation with Straits Chinese decor has dorms, twins, doubles and en-suite rooms. Amenities include air conditioning/fans, hot showers and free 24-hour internet access (including Wi-fi).

Pondok Lodge
20–22C, Jalan Changkat Bukit Bintang
Tel: 03-2142 8449
www.pondoklodge.com
39 p260, A1
Located above the teeming Ceylon Bar, this laid-back, gay-friendly guesthouse offers rooms that are not always top-notch, so ask to view a room before crashing. The rooftop terrace is a hangout for exchanging travel tales.

Pujangga Homestay
21 Jalan Berangan, off Jalan Nagasari
Tel: 03-2141 4243
www.pujangga-homestay.com
40 p260, A1
Simple and understated, this is reminiscent of a middle-class KL dwelling. It is separated from the street by a garden courtyard and rooms can fit up to 11 guests in various configurations. It oozes KL charm.

Lake Gardens, Brickfields and Mid Valley

Expensive

The Gardens Hotel and Residences
Mid Valley City, Lingkaran Syed Putra
Tel: 03-2268 1188
www.gardenshtlres.com
This is the plushest of the hotels in the Mid Valley area – and also the priciest. Like its tropical flora-inspired sister establishment, The Gardens mall, the hotel is an interior designer's dream. The residences offer longer lets.

Hilton Kuala Lumpur
3 Jalan Stesen Sentral
Tel: 03-2264 2264
www.kuala-lumpur.hilton.com
41 p258, B4
KL Hilton's bright and airy rooms have floor-to-ceiling windows with views of the city, luxurious beds, rain showers and 107cm (42in) plasma TVs (plus TVs in the bathrooms). Other features include a freeform pool, a multi-restaurant enclave, and the Zeta Bar, where you can rub shoulders with KL's glitterati.

Le Meridien
2 Jalan Stesen Sentral
Tel: 03-2263 7888
www.lemeridien.com
42 p258, B4
A swanky establishment with contemporary decor, Jim Thompson upholstery, luxurious marble bathrooms, and a lovely landscaped pool area. Like the rooms, the restaurants have great views of the city. Located in the rail transport hub of KL Sentral, so access to and from the airport or any other part of town is easy.

Moderate

Boulevard Hotel
Mid Valley City, Lingkaran Syed Putra
Tel: 03-2295 8000
www.blvhotel.com
This modern business hotel is located in the Mid Valley area, which boasts two enormous malls, so it is great for shopaholics. The rooms are large, have classy furniture, flat-screen TVs and beautiful artworks. It's a short drive to KL Sentral and Bangsar, and the KTM Komuter train station is within walking distance. Provides a complimentary shuttle to the Bangsar LRT station.

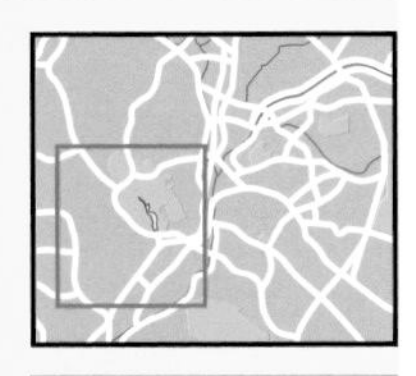

Budget

YMCA Hostel
95 Jalan Padang Belia
Tel: 03-2274 1439
www.ymcakl.com/hostel.htm
43 p258, B4
A simple hostel in Brickfields, a stone's throw from KL Sentral and public transport to the airport and city. Rooms are clean, most with bathrooms, air-con, TV and IDD phone. Just outside is great Indian food and a charming old neighbourhood to explore.

Fraser's Hill and Genting Highlands

Moderate

Colmar Tropicale
KM 48, Persimpangan Bertingkat Lebuhraya Karak, Berjaya Hills, Pahang
Tel: 09-288 8888
www.berjayahills.com
This Alsace-themed resort lies on the border of Selangor and Pahang. Rooms are in French country-style and the restaurants have French names. The Japanese village within the compound has an authentic teahouse and eight tatami-style suites.

Genting Highlands Resort
Tel: 03-2718 1118
www.rw.genting.com
Choose from six hotels with over 10,000 rooms, ranging from the 3-star First World Hotel (said to be the world's largest hotel) to the 5-star Highlands Hotel (where the casino is). Rooms range from the simple to the sublime. Expect a wide range of facilities and food and beverage outlets in these hotels.

Highland Resthouse Holdings
Suite 3-2, Level 3, Capsquare Signature Office B, 9 Persiaran CapSquare, Capital Square
Tel: 03-2693 6996
www.hrhbungalows.com
These renovated colonial bungalows provide contemporary comfort with old-world charm. Complete with dining and living rooms as well as English-style gardens, its three 3-bedroom and two 4-bedroom bungalows are only available for rent as a whole, whereas the six Temerloh chalets and eight Pekan bungalow rooms can be rented individually. Rates vary from under RM300 to RM1,500 a day, and are halved on weekdays. Housekeepers, who can cook your meals, can be arranged. Not to be confused with the government-run FHDC bungalows.

The Smokehouse Hotel
Jalan Jeriau
Tel: 09-362 2226
www.thesmokehouse.com.my
Built in 1924, this Tudor-style gem of a hotel has beautiful stone masonry and manicured gardens. Rooms are cosy, and each one is different, offering a choice of hill or garden views. The public spaces are filled with chintz and memorabilia. Be sure to try its delicious Devonshire cream tea. Guests are required to dress up for dinner.

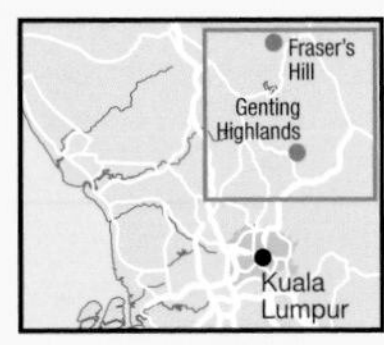

Price Categories

Price categories are for a double room with breakfast and taxes:
Luxury = above RM400;
Expensive = RM300–399; **Moderate** = RM100–299; **Budget** = under RM100

Transport
Accommodation
Activities
A – Z
Language

Kuala Selangor

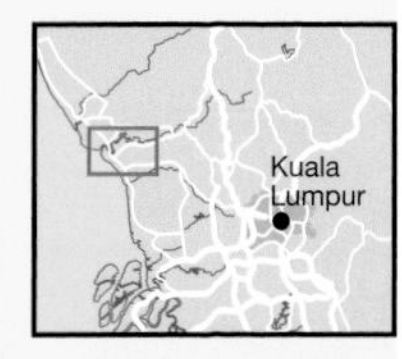

Budget

Kuala Selangor Nature Park
Jalan Klinik
Tel: 03-3289 2294
Email: ksnaturepark@yahoo.com
Stay at the Kuala Selangor Nature Park if you want to catch dawn bird choruses and otter sightings. Accommodations are basic: four A-frame huts (twin-share), 12 chalets (triple-share), two dorms (20 beds) and a hostel (14 rooms, maximum 7 guests per room). You need to bring your own towels and toiletries, but there is running water and 24-hour electricity, as well as a communal kitchen. You can also rent a pitch at the campsite but need to bring your own gear and effective mosquito repellent. For meals, the old town centre is only a 10-minute walk away.

Klang Valley

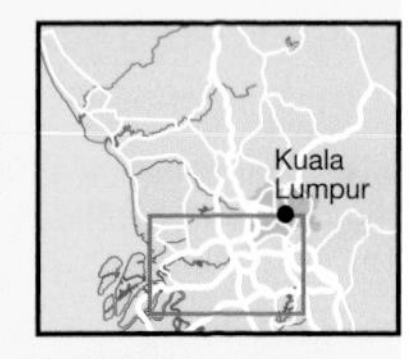

Luxury

Cyberview Lodge Resort and Spa
Persiaran Multimedia, Cyberjaya
Tel: 03-8312 7000
www.cyberview-lodge.com
Plush lodgings with the finest of amenities in beautifully landscaped gardens. The wooden chalets and rooms are private, spacious and airy. Food outlets are varied, and recreational opportunities, from fishing and mountain biking to horse riding, abound.

Hotel Equatorial Bangi-Putrajaya
Off Persiaran Bandar, Bandar Baru Bangi, Bangi-Putrajaya
Tel: 03-8210 2222
www.equatorial.com/bng
Built like a Spanish villa, this eight-storey hotel is perched majestically atop a hill amid lush tropical gardens, and has an expansive 27-hole championship golf course. Offers a host of services including traditional massages and a fitness centre. A shuttle bus goes several times a day to its sister hotel in the heart of KL.

Putrajaya Shangri-La
Taman Lrt Perdana, Presint 1, Putrajaya
Tel: 03-8887 8888
www.shangri-la.com
This luxurious oasis away from the bustle of KL is modelled on the concept of a "hotel in a park and a park in a hotel". Beautifully designed and landscaped, this hotel has a 5-star spa and "techno-gym" along with a host of water-based activities. Rooms are stunning. Enjoy a romantic dinner on the Azur Terrace from where the sunset view is breathtaking.

Sunway Resort Hotel and Spa
Persiaran Lagoon, Petaling Jaya
Tel: 03-7492 8000
www.sunway.com.my/hotel
A family-friendly hotel with easy access to Sunway Lagoon and the Sunway Pyramid Shopping Mall with its myriad food and entertainment outlets. The decor is a kitschy Malaysian version of South Africa's Palace of the Lost City (at Sun City). It's built into the ground, so try to avoid rooms just beneath the lobby as it can be noisy overhead.

Expensive

Pan-Pacific KL International Airport
Jalan cta 4B, KLIA, Sepang
Tel: 03-8787 3333
www.panpacific.com/KLairport
Those who want to get up in more leisurely fashion for a flight or are on overnight transit will appreciate this hotel, which is linked to the airport. A buggy service ferries passengers to the airport. Rooms are spacious, modern and spotless, with in-room broadband internet access.

Moderate

Eastin Hotel
13 Jalan 16/11, Pusat Dagang Seksyen 16, Petaling Jaya
Tel: 03-7665 1111
www.eastin.com
A good business hotel, linked by a network of highways to suburbs like Bangsar, Mont Kiara and Damansara. Rooms are spacious and comfortable. The Chinese restaurant is good, particularly for dim sum. Try also the strip of eateries behind the hotel.

Hilton Petaling Jaya
2 Jalan Barat, Petaling Jaya
Tel: 03-7955 9122
www.hilton.com
Located just off the Federal Highway, with airy rooms, delicious local cuisine, a popular pub that serves excellent steaks, and a Davidoff cigar store. The gym is good for fitness buffs and the spa next to it does wonders for muscle soreness afterwards.

Shah's Village Hotel
3 and 5 Lorong Sultan, Seksyen 52, Petaling Jaya
Tel: 03-7956 9322
www.shahsresorts.com
This family-run hotel has quaint rooms with endearing details such as batik sarongs for guests' use. Boasts a tropical resort feel with swaying palm trees surrounding the swimming pool. A great local bar, Waikiki, is next door, and the LRT is a short walk away.

ACTIVITIES

THE ARTS, NIGHTLIFE, SIGHTSEEING TOURS, SPORTS, SPAS AND CHILDREN'S ACTIVITIES

THE ARTS

Two of the best sources of information on the arts are *TimeOut KL* (www.timeoutkl.com) and **KLue** (www.klue.com.my). Both magazines and websites have the most up-to-date listings of events and venues in KL. See also **The Arts Scene** chapter *(pages 59–63)*.

Performing Arts Venues

The Actors Studio
Rooftop, Lot 10 Shopping Centre, Jalan Bukit Bintang
Tel: 03-2142 2009
www.theactorsstudio.com.my
Modern contemporary performing arts space run by the country's top theatre company, featuring mainly local productions; scheduled performances are held almost every week. Shows start at 8.30pm or 3pm on Sunday matinees.

Dewan Filharmonik Petronas
Ground Level, Tower 2, Petronas Twin Towers
Tel: 03-2051 7007
www.mpo.com.my
This purpose-built classical concert hall has a full programme of classical music all year round performed by the resident Malaysian Philharmonic Orchestra as well as guest orchestras and soloists from all over the world, including renowned jazz and world music exponents. A dress code is imposed for evening performances. Sunday matinees are good value for money. Mon–Fri 10am–6pm, opening nights 10am–9pm, Sun noon.

Kuala Lumpur Performing Arts Centre (KLPAC)
Sentul Park, Jalan Strachan
Tel: 03-4047 9000
www.klpac.com
A beautiful, award-winning space managed by The Actors Studio – with a 500-seat main theatre, as well as other performance spaces. About 60 percent of its productions are local. Getting to this venue by public transport is a little tricky. Daily 10.30am–6.30pm. Shows open at 8.30pm.

National Theatre (Istana Budaya)
Jalan Tun Razak
Tel: 03-4026 5555
www.istanabudaya.gov.my
Modelled after the Kelantan kite, the country's largest theatre stages big local and international acts including Broadway musicals and symphonic orchestra performances. Mon–Fri 9am–6pm, Sat 9am–1pm.

PJ Live Arts
2A-3, Block K, Jaya One, 72 Jalan Universiti, Petaling Jaya
Tel: 03-7960 0439
www.pjla.com.my
Intimate new theatre in the heart of a multi-level commercial complex. Only open for performances. Check website for show times.

Malaysia Tourism Centre Auditorium
109 Jalan Ampang
Tel: 03-9235 4848
www.matic.gov.my
This tourism centre has a lovely auditorium and outdoor arena, which hosts sporadic productions from drama to dance.

Other Venues

Central Market (Pasar Seni)
Jalan Hang Kasturi
Tel: 03-2272 9966
www.centralmarket-kl.com.my
Cultural performances regularly take place in the main foyer area and outdoor stage, while alternative arts performances are staged at The Annexe Gallery.

Sutra House
12 Persiaran Titiwangsa 3
Tel: 03-4021 1092
www.sutradancetheatre.com
Owned by the respected Indian classical dance guru Ramli Ibrahim, Sutra House has a landscaped outdoor stage where Indian dance and music recitals are held under the stars; there is also an indoor art gallery.

Other venues with occasional performances are **Panggung Bandaraya** (Jalan Raja; tel:

03-2617 6307; www.dbkl.gov.my); the **Experimental Theatre**, home of the National Arts, Culture and Heritage Academy (Jalan Tun Ismail; tel: 03-2697 1777; www.aswara.edu.my); and the **Temple of Fine Arts**, which hosts classical Indian art forms (Jalan Berhala; tel: 03-2274 3709; www.tfa.org.my).

Art Galleries

Most contemporary art on view in the capital is created by home-grown artists, some of whom have gained significant international exposure; many more are emerging artists. Exhibitions by overseas artists, including regional talent, can also be found at the many art galleries in and around the city. Check newspapers and lifestyle publications for listings.

The Annexe Gallery
Level 1 and 2, Central Market, Jalan Hang Kasturi
Tel: 03-2070 1137
www.annexegallery.com
Showcases the most experimental, edgy work in KL in the form of film screenings, art fairs, dance, music, performance art and more. Mon–Thur 11am–8pm, Fri–Sat 11am–9.30pm.

Galeri Chandan
15, Jalan Gellenggang, Damansara Heights
Tel: 03-2095 5360
www.galerichandan.com
Founded by a collective of artists and designers, this slick gallery space showcases more experimental work from younger, less established artists. Mon–Fri 10am–6pm.

Galerie Taksu
17Jalan Pawang, Bukit Keramat
Tel: 03-4251 4396
www.taksu.com
Housed in a gorgeous bungalow, this contemporary art space, with a leaning towards the new and the original, has a busy exhibition schedule. Also conducts an artist-in-residence programme. Mon–Sat 10am–6pm, Sun by appointment.

House of Matahati
6A, Jalan Cempaka 16, Taman Cempaka, Ampang
Tel: 03-9285 6004
www.houseofmatahati.blogspot.com
Owned and run by five Malay painters, this space showcases their own work and work from emerging artists. Very diverse styles; work is fantastic. Mon–Fri 11am–6pm, Sat 1–6pm.

MAP
Solaris Dutamas, 1 Jalan Dutamas 1
Tel: 036207 9732
www.mapkl.org
This ambitious space in a retail complex in the middle of a wealthy suburban area is trying to bring art to the masses. The White Box and Black Box are the two spaces used for art and live performance. Mon–Sat 10am–6pm.

National Art Gallery (Balai Senilukis Negara)
2 Jalan Temerloh, off Jalan Tun Razak
Tel: 03-4025 4990
www.artgallery.gov.my
With a permanent collection of over 2,500 artworks, including ceramics, textiles and sculptures, this modern facility has five galleries as well as a café and an outdoor exhibition area. Daily 10am–6pm.

NN Gallery
53A and 56, Jalan Sulaiman 1, Taman Ampang Hilir
Tel: 03-4270 6588
www.nngallery.com.my
Specialising in abstract and expressionist art, this gallery has an eclectic and interesting collection of works in different media by established and young artists. Mon–Sat 9am–6pm.

Petronas Gallery (Galeri Petronas)
341–343, Level 3, Suria KLCC, Kuala Lumpur City Centre
Tel: 03-2051 7770
www.galeripetronas.com
This compact space, a marriage of art and architecture, provides a beautiful setting for traditional and modern artistic – including multimedia – expression. Tue–Sun 10am–8pm.

RA Fine Arts Gallery
6 Jalan Aman, off Jalan Tun Razak
Tel: 03-2161 7341
Email:rafinearts@gmail.com
Owned and run by poet and art patron Raja Ahmad Aminullah, this gallery throws focus on a range of genres, particularly on the work of young and established Malay painters. Mon–Sat 11am–6pm.

Sutra Gallery
12 Persiaran Titiwangsa 3, Taman Tasik Titiwangsa
Tel: 4021 1092
www.sutradancetheatre.com
Work focuses on Indian dance and culture, mainly art and photography. Housed in a leafy, green bungalow which doubles as a dance school and an outdoor amphitheatre. Mon–Sat 9am–5pm.

Valentine Willie Fine Art
Level 1, 17 Jalan Telawi 3, Bangsar Baru
Tel: 03-2284 2348
www.vwfa.net
With a busy calendar of exhibitions, this contemporary art gallery and consultancy has an extensive selection of Malaysian and Southeast Asian paintings, sculptures and drawings. Mon–Fri noon–8pm, Sat noon–6pm.

Wei-Ling Gallery
8 Jalan Scott, Brickfields
Tel: 03-2260 1106
www.weiling-gallery.com
A three-storey gallery in a refurbished shophouse that showcases the works of Malaysian artists, ranging from the forefathers of Modernism in Malaysia to up-and-coming contemporary talents. Mon–Fri noon–7pm; Sat 10am–5pm.

Cinema

KL's cinemas are air-conditioned, comfortable and cheap, with some offering THX sound and luxury halls. Cinemas screen mainly mainstream offerings by Hollywood, Bollywood and Hong Kong as well as a scattering of local Malay-language films, Southeast Asian fare and arthouse releases. Blockbusters often get released the same day – in order to foil video pirates – as in the US, UK and Hong Kong, and queues can be long. Non-Malay language movies have subtitles in Bahasa Malaysia and Chinese.

For listings, click on www.cinema.com.my. There are three main cinema operators, whose halls are located in malls. **Golden Screen Cinema** (GSC; tel: 03-8312 3456; www.gsc.com.my) theatres are located in the Mid Valley Megamall, Berjaya Times Square and 1 Utama (Petaling Jaya). **Tanjung Golden Village** (TGV; tel: 03-7492 2929; www.tgv.com.my), has theatres at Suria KLCC, 1 Utama and Sunway Pyramid (Petaling Jaya). The smaller **Cathay Holdings** (tel: 03-7727 0724; www.cathayholdings.com) has cinemas at The Curve and City Square. Thanks to digital video, Malaysian film-makers have been carving an international reputation for making noteworthy and award-winning short films, with new talent being unearthed at every turn. Among established names are Amir Muhammad, James Lee, Ho Yuhang, Liew Sang Tat and Tan Chui Mui. Meanwhile, the late Yasmin Ahmad's films still lead in feature-length, groundbreaking productions that deal with love affairs that cut across ethnic boundaries. Check media listings for **short film/indie film festivals**, usually held at the Help Institute in Petaling Jaya and the KLPAC in Sentul.

Nightlife

Kuala Lumpur's nightlife starts rocking by about 11pm, with Friday and Saturday nights seeing the most action throughout the city. The partying ends between 2 and 3am but many clubbers adjourn for the obligatory post-party supper at hawker centres and the 24-hour *mamak* joints. If you are in a large group, it is best to book a table at popular clubs on weekends. KL-ites tend to dress up to go the fancier clubs. Some places enforce a dress code, which, for men, stipulates a collared T-shirt, long trousers and covered shoes, while other places have a no jeans, shorts and sandals rule. Most clubs adhere to the 21-year-old age limit (the legal drinking age in Malaysia) but sometimes this is openly flouted.

Driving and parking can be difficult, and cops are always out to get drink drivers, so take a cab. Clubs charge an entry fee from 10 or 11pm, which is inclusive of one drink. Wednesday is ladies' night in most places, which means free drinks for women. Happy hour is usually 5.30–9pm when drinks are half-price, and should be taken advantage of, since alcohol is very expensive in Malaysia. Beers start at RM16 a glass and RM40 a jug, spirits RM23 a glass, and wine about RM23–25 a glass and RM100 a bottle. Wines have become very popular, and a wide range is available, especially in wine and cigar bars. You can keep a tab going till you leave. Waiters generally expect a tip.

Live music starts at around 10pm at most places. For more information on nightlife, see the **After Dark** chapter *(page 65)*.

Nightlife Listings

Besides newspapers, you can get information from local magazines like *TimeOut KL* (www.timeoutkl.com) or *KLue* (www.klue.com.my) which you can buy at any newsstand. These two magazines have comprehensive listings for artistic events, nightlife and eating out in the Klang Valley. Another good magazine is *Vision KL* (www.visionkl.com). For underground music listings check www.thericecookershop.com or http://ricecooker.kerbau.com.

Nightclubs

Kuala Lumpur City Centre

The Beach Club Café
97 Jalan P. Ramlee
Tel: 03-2166 9919
www.beachclubcafe.com
A popular tropical-themed hotspot which plays chart music. Also serves Asian food. Animal-rights supporters might be upset by the tanks of baby sharks (yes, live) amid the loud music. Join the scantily clad women and ladyboys among the throng of happy clubbers for a wild time.

Dragonfly
1, Jalan Kia Peng
Tel: 03-2143 1999
www.dragonflykl.com
From the same stable as the legendary Dragonfly in Jakarta, this club pretty much guarantees a good time.

Envie Club Lounge
14–16 Changkat Bukit Bintang
www.envieclublounge.com
If you want a good night out, head to Envie. The hardworking DJs keep the music going on and on. Fridays see female DJs spinning and Saturday is R&B night. Interiors are pink and white, like frilly cotton candy.

Hard Rock Café
Level 1, Wisma Concorde, Jalan Sultan Ismail
Tel: 03-2715 5555
This oldie-but-goldie international chain keeps them coming with live local and regional bands playing mainstream music. Attracts a mainly young crowd. Good American-style fare in large portions served in the café.

Quattro
Lot G4,5 and 6, M8A and 9, Ground and Mezzanine Level, Avenue K, 156 Jalan Ampang
Tel: 03-2166 6566
www.clubquattro.com
This ultra-cool club has gone for a seasonal theme, with a summer restaurant, spring lounge, autumn club and winter bar, with each room even enjoying appropriate weather. Located across the road from KLCC.

Rum Jungle Restaurant and Bar
1 Jalan Pinang
Tel: 03-2170 6666
This tropical oasis mimics a rainforest setting with four different

bars, each playing different music. A bit over-the-top with the decor but if you're in the mood for something outrageous, this is worth a stop.

7atenine
Ascott Kuala Lumpur, 9 Jalan Pinang
Tel: 03-2161 7789
www.sevenatenine.com
A facelift in 2010 by design god Ed Poole, the ice bar and the tag "you'll never know who you'll meet at the rendezvous for KL's chic" is enough to tempt restless souls into this upmarket bar/restaurant.

Zouk
113 Jalan Ampang
Tel: 03-2171 1997
www.zoukclub.com.my
This dome-shaped Singapore-owned club strikes all the right chords. Velvet Underground's popular Wednesday Mambo-Jambo nights draw the crowds with its 1980s retro music, while the ever changing line-up of local and international DJs at its three other clubs, Phuture, Aristo and Barsonic, keep the electronic music crowd happy.

Asian Heritage Row

Elysium
44,46,48 Jalan Doraisamy
Tel: 016 678 1384
Its name inspired by the classical penchant for drinking and being merry, Elysium has two whole floors of dance space.

The Loft-Upstairs
28–40 Jalan Doraisamy
Tel: 03-2691 5668
Spread across four shop lots, clubbers dance till late to DJ-spun music at this large open club. Has a steady, loyal clientele, mostly large groups of Chinese. Also houses Cynna, which has an extensive menu of vodka shots.

Maison
8 Jalan Yap Ah Syak
Tel: 03-2381 2088
Inspired by warehouse rave parties. The bare brick walls here are married with chandeliers and wrought iron within a Peranakan heritage mansion. Every day has its own theme from R&B to funky house and hip-hop.

Bukit Bintang

Qba
Westin Kuala Lumpur, Jalan Bukit Bintang
Tel: 03-2731 8333
Samba, cha-cha and salsa to a live Latin band at this Havana-styled club. Cigars and boutique wines are other attractions of this classy two-storey place. Be sure to try its rum-based mojitos and caipirinhas.

Bangsar and KL Sentral

MILK
18 Jalan Liku, Bangsar
Tel: 03-2282 2018
www.mistclub.com.my
The heart and soul of R&B in KL, DJs here put on a show every night. Black leather and a metal ceiling add to the funk of the place.

Zeta Bar
Hilton Kuala Lumpur, 3 Jalan Stesen Sentral, KL Sentral
Tel: 03-2264 2264
www.kl-studio.com/zetabar.html
Styled after the Hilton London's namesake nightclub, this sophisticated place is patronised by the celebrities of KL. DJs who spin rock to 1980s retro alternate with live bands.

Klang Valley

EUPHORIA by Ministry of Sound
Sunway Resort Hotel and Spa, Persiaran Lagoon, Bandar Sunway, Petaling Jaya
Tel: 03-7495 1786/1788
www.euphoria.com.my
Undoubtedly one of the country's best clubs, this branch of London's Ministry of Sound fits 1,000 people, and it's also the only non-smoking club in the city. Expect an awesome sound system and a clientele on a mission to party.

Live Music

Kuala Lumpur City Centre

Alexis Ampang
Lot 10, Ground Level, Great Eastern Mall, 303 Jalan Ampang
Tel: 03-4260 2288
www.alexis.com.my
Hosting local and international singers and groups, including top jazz acts, this sophisticated space also offers terrific food and a choice of 300-plus wines. Shows on Friday and Saturday. A bit pricey, but well worth it if you're a jazz lover.

Bukit Bintang

Delucca
L-G-2, Ground Level Office Tower, One Residency, 1 Jalan Nagasari, off Jalan Raja Chulan
Located directly across from No Black Tie, Delucca is somewhere you come for the music – the food is decidedly lacklustre.

No Black Tie
17 Jalan Mesui, off Jalan Nagasari
Tel: 03-2142 3737
www.noblacktie.com.my
Run by classical pianist Evelyn Hii, this pioneering space for local musician/songwriters features quality acts ranging from jazz to Western classical music and poetry readings. Enjoy the music downstairs or upstairs in its cosy and contemporary all-wood setting and nibble on Japanese food. Showtime is 10pm; you'll have to pay a cover charge.

Various locations

Laundry Bar
Lot G75 & 76, Ground Level, The Curve, 6 Jalan PJU 7/3, Mutiara Damansara, Petaling Jaya
Tel: 03-7728 1715
www.laundrybar.net
Hosts singer-songwriter events or bands of various genres from indie to emo and Indonesian rock-influenced groups. Patrons are a mix of music lovers, social butterflies and football fans. Sit near the bar if you want to hear the music.

Karaoke

The largest chain is **Red Box Karaoke** (www.redbox.com.my/redbox/eng/default.asp) with outlets in Low Yat Plaza (tel: 03-2710 1883), Sungei Wang Plaza (tel: 03-2145

7788), Sogo shopping centre (tel: 03-2694 7788) and Sunway Pyramid (tel: 03-5633 6669). There are also high-end karaoke lounges with plush private rooms, the latest AV equipment and "guest relations officers". These include **Club De Macau** behind the Renaissance Hotel on Jalan Ampang (tel: 03-2163 2632) and **Club De Vegas**, also on Jalan Ampang (tel: 03-2163 2632). This is where serious drinking and lots of business deals are done.

Vanity Mansion
8–26, Jalan Kamunting
Tel: 03-2694 6460
www.heritage-mansion.com
This is high-end karaoke. Rub shoulders with A-list KL glitterati with a glass of Moet in hand.

Gay and Lesbian Venues

Kuala Lumpur City Centre

Blue Boy
50 Jalan Sultan Ismail
Tel: 03-2142 1067
Malaysia's oldest gay club, which is almost 20 years old now, is still the place to be. Packed on weekends, especially after midnight, it's friendly and cruisy but can be smoky. Mainly Malay crowd. Good house dance tracks.

Café Café
175 Jalan Maharajalela
Tel: 03-2145 8141
This is a truly extraordinary place. The decor is fastidiously Parisian and decadent. Food is generally good, desserts better.

Bukit Bintang

Frangipani
25 Changkat Bukit Bintang
Tel: 03-2144 3001
A seductive gay bar that attracts a stylish crowd. Offers a large selection of fine cocktails and shooters as DJs spin house music. Restaurant downstairs serves fine French fare amid equally chi chi surroundings.

Shook!
Starhill Gallery, Jalan Bukit Bintang
Tel: 03-2719 8535
This classy gay-friendly hangout, which is spread over half the basement level, has a circular cocktail bar where you can chill listening to live jazz. Enormous array of food choices here and at the surrounding restaurants.

Sixty Nine Bistro
14 Jalan Kampong Dollah, off Jalan Pudu
Tel: 03-2144 3369
www.69bistro.com.my
A tribute to the 1960s, this hangout is located in a prewar shop house near Berjaya Times Square. Wholesome comfort food and tarot readings are available after 4.30pm.

Sightseeing Tours

Most hotels offer their own shuttle bus or van tours around the city. It's best to check with the hotel concierge or the reception desk. Half-day 3-hour city tours are priced at RM44–65 per person. Full-day tours of 8 hours cost RM200–220 per person. There are also individual tour guides who charge a per-hour fee but be sure to use the services of a licensed guide. Contact the **Kuala Lumpur Tourist Guide Association**: tel: 03-9221 0688 for more details.

To avoid being scammed, choose travel agents that are certified by the **Malaysian Association of Tour and Travel Agents** (tel: 03-9287 6881; www.matta.org.my). The following tour agencies offer half- and full-day tours of KL and its environs as well as longer and more comprehensive tours of various destinations in Malaysia.

Asian Overland Services
tel: 03-4252 9100;
www.asianoverland.com.my

Holiday Tours and Travel
tel: 03-6386 6000;
www.holidaytours.com.my

Mayflower Acme Tours
tel: 03-6252 1888;
www.mayflower.com.my

Diethelm Travel
tel: 03-2161 1922;
www.diethelmtravel.com

Sri America Travel Corporation
tel: 03-2142 9155.

KL Hop-On Hop-Off

Another handy service is the **KL Hop-On Hop-Off Bus**. Launched in 2007, this double-decker bus service offers a convenient way of visiting the city's tourist sights. Plying 22 stops around the city, the buses run from 8.30am to 8pm daily. Waiting time is roughly 30 minutes and you can board and alight from the bus at any of the designated stops along the way. Prerecorded commentaries in eight languages (Malay, English, Mandarin, Hindi, Arabic, Japanese, French and German) are available on headsets attached to the seats. One-day tickets at RM38 for adults and RM17 for children and senior citizens can be purchased on the bus itself, at selected hotels and travel agents or online at its website at www.myhoponhopoff.com. For inquiries call KL Hop-On Hop-Off City Bus Tour at tel: 03-2691 1382.

Sports

Participant Sports

Bowling

Cosmic Bowl
Level 3, Mid Valley Megamall
Tel: 03-2287 8280
This 38-lane bowling alley has state-of-the-art equipment and glow-in-the-dark features. Sun–Thur 11am–1am, Fri–Sat 11am–2am. Fees: before 5pm RM5, 5–9pm RM6, after 9pm RM7.

Pyramid Megalanes
Level 1, Sunway Pyramid, Bandar Sunway, Petaling Jaya
Tel: 03-7492 6307
A 48-lane bowling alley that is also the training ground for the national squad and venue for international

competitions. Daily 11am–10pm. Fees: RM6 per game.

Fitness and Yoga

Most gyms are located within hotels and sell expensive one-day passes to non-guests. However, several fitness centres outside of hotels also sell walk-in passes. Yoga has also become a trend, with instruction offered in hotels and fitness centres.

Celebrity Fitness
www.celebrityfitness.co.id
With branches all over Malaysia, Indonesia, India and more, this gym chain offers a wide selection of classes, including bodycombat, yoga, hip-hop and even pole-dancing. Visitors are allowed to use the facilities for RM50 a day.

Clark Hatch
Level 3, Block A Plaza Mont Kiara
Tel: 03-6201 6177/2698 6080
www.clarkhatch.com.my
Has an indoor heated swimming pool along with state-of-the-art equipment and a Bali-Asian spa. Guest walk-in rate RM52 per visit.

Energy Yoga
Plaza Damas, Sri Hartamas
Tel: 03-6201 7888
www.tsm-energy.com
Has over 180 classes a week for different levels. Walk-in rates are RM25–30 per class.

Fitness First
Ground Level, Menara Manulife RB, 6 Jalan Gelanggang, Damansara Heights
Tel: 03-2093 8050
www.fitnessfirst.com.my
This well-known gym has a myriad of fitness equipment, offers lots of classes and has qualified personal trainers. Walk-in rates are RM65 per person.

Golf

There are more than 50 courses within an easy hour's drive from Kuala Lumpur, some of which offer night golfing under floodlights. Some are designed by golf luminaries like Ronald Fream, Jack Niklaus and Robert Trent Jones. For more information, contact the **Malaysian Golfing Association** (tel: 03-9283 7300; www.mgaonline.com.my).

Bukit Jalil Golf and Country Resort
Jalan 3/155B, Bukit Jalil
Tel: 03-8994 1600
www.berjayaclubs.com/jalil
Spread over 67 hectares (165 acres), this 18-hole Max Wexler-designed course offers scenic views. Green fees cost RM84–180.

Kuala Lumpur Golf and Country Club
10 Jalan 1/70D, off Jalan Bukit Kiara
Tel: 03-253 1111
www.klgcc.com
A 36-hole course with a fully computerised driving range. Visitors must produce their handicap cards upon registration. Fees for non-members are RM120 for 9 holes and RM180 for 18 holes during weekdays; and RM165 for 9 holes and RM250 for 18 holes on weekends.

Royal Selangor Golf Club
Jalan Kelab Golf, off Jalan Tun Razak
Tel: 03-9206 3333
www.rsgc.com.my
One of the city's oldest golf courses, this 45-hole parkland golf course right in the heart of the city is open to non-members on weekdays 8.30–10am only. Green fees are RM400.

Saujana Golf and Country Club
Seksyen U2, Shah Alam
Tel: 03-9206 3333
www.saujana.com.my
Two award-winning Ronald Fream-designed courses are set in a former oil palm and rubber estate, with the Palm Course regarded as the country's best course. Green fees start at RM220 for 18 holes.

Tropicana Golf and Country Resort
Jalan Kelab Tropicana, Petaling Jaya
Tel: 03-7804 8888
www.tropicanagolf.com
This scenic 27-hole championship golf course has two courses catering to both champion and amateur golfers. Green fees start at RM75 for 9 holes.

Art of Bargaining

Other than in departmental stores and boutiques, goods are always priced with the expectation that they will be knocked down by the customer. Bargaining is also a way to interact with locals. Shop around so you know what the price range is. Start by knocking off 50 percent of the price then increase the amount you are prepared to pay as the salesperson reduces the price. Throw in a few local terms like *"Mahal sangat!"* (too expensive!) or *"Boleh kurang?"* (can you reduce the price?). If you are not prepared to pay the "final price" offered, walk away. If your price is within the shop's profit range, the salesperson will call you back. If not, you know you have gone too low. The first and last customers of the day usually get the best prices, and cash always gets you the best deals.

Jogging/Running

There are special sprung jogging trails at the **Lake Gardens** and **KLCC Park**. **Taman Tasik Titiwangsa**, behind the National Art Gallery, also has jogging and walking trails. For other trails, check with the **Kuala Lumpur Hash House Harriers** (www.motherhash.org; tel: 03-7876 0439), a running and beer-drinking group with roots in colonial Malaysia. Family-oriented fun runs are carried out on trails all over the city and its suburbs.

Rock Climbing

Camp 5
Level 5, 1 Utama Shopping Centre, Bandar Utama
Tel: 03-7845 5561
www.camp-5.com
This climbing facility, within a 24-metre (79ft) high, air-conditioned environment, offers roped climbing and bouldering. Open Mon–Fri 2–11pm, Sat–Sun and public holidays 10am–10pm. Also

organises expeditions to various rock-climbing spots in Malaysia.

Sports Centres

Bangsar Sports Complex
3 Jalan Terasek
Tel: 03-2284 6065
Tennis, squash and badminton courts are available for hire here and there is also a swimming pool. Courts are open from 7am till late at night. Pool hours are 9.30am–noon, 2–4.30pm and 6–8.30pm.

Kompleks Sukan Titiwangsa
Taman Tasik Titiwangsa
Tel: 03-4023 9558
Public sports complex with tennis courts, squash courts and a gymnasium available for use daily 8am–11pm. Rates start at RM4 per hour with rates doubling at night. Shower facilities available.

Kompleks Tenis Negara
Jalan Duta
Tel: 03-6201 5482
The National Tennis Complex has open and covered tennis courts for rental starting at RM6 per hour, 7am–10pm (night charges are double). Shower facilities available.

YMCA
95 Jalan Padang Belia
Tel: 03-2274 1768
www.ymcakl.com
Four tennis courts are available for rental at RM6 per hour (daily 7am–5pm). There are also basketball, volleyball and netball courts. Just sign up for membership.

Swimming

Chinwoo Stadium
Jalan Hang Jebat
Tel: 03-2070 5025
www.chinwoo.org.my
Olympic-sized swimming pool open Mon–Fri 2–8pm, Sat–Sun 9am–8pm. Other activities here are *wushu*, *tai chi*, basketball, table-tennis and lion dancing.

Whitewater, Adventure and Extreme Sports

For information on nature-based activities and listings of operators who adhere to sustainable tourism, check www.tourismselangor.gov.my. This state-run website lists comprehensive activities for many outdoor activities in the areas surrounding Kuala Lumpur. Other useful websites are www.wildasia.org, www.nature-escapes-kuala-lumpur.com and www.greenselipar.com.

Asian Overland Services
39C and 40C Jalan Mamanda 9, Ampang Point
Tel: 03-4252 9100
www.asianoverland.com.my
Established outfit offering adventure and nature-based tours throughout the country. Also handles regular inbound tours.

Endemicguides.com
Mobile tel: 016-383 2222
www.endemicguides.com
Small nature-based operator working with local communities; has jungle-trekking, birdwatching and caving tours in destinations around Kuala Lumpur and at various national parks.

Khersonese Expeditions
55, Jalan Rahim Kajai, TTDI, Taman Tun Dr Ismail
Tel: 03-7722 3511
www.thepaddlerz.com
Offers day trips to Sungai Selangor, Sungai Itik (Gombak) and the challenging Sungai Singor in Hulu Perak, as well as well-organised multi-day rafting expeditions.

KL Tower Jump
2 Jalan Punchak, off Jalan P. Ramlee
Tel: 03-2020 5444
www.kltowerjump.com
Since its first BASE jump off KL Tower in 1999, giant leaps have been happening annually.

Nomad Adventure
525 Jalan 17/13, Petaling Jaya
Tel: 03-7958 5152
www.nomadadventure.com
Pioneer whitewater outfit operating mainly in Gopeng but also in other whitewater destinations. Conducts courses and also runs exciting adventures and treks.

Oxbold Sports (Extreme Sports Malaysia)
Suite 663, MBE Bangsar Village LG-K1, 1 Jalan Telawi Satu
Hotline: 019-663 8336
www.oxbold.com
Specialists in all kinds of extreme sports – aerial, land, water; the sky is the limit, literally. You can fly a Cessna, jump off a plane or go car drifting.

Tracks Adventure
Lot 11, Jalan Lengal, off Jalan Tembak, Kuala Kubu Bharu
Tel: 03-6065 1767
www.tracksadventures.com.my
Based in Kuala Kubu Bharu, this outfit offers half-day whitewater trips on Sungai Selangor (11am and 3pm) with hardshell canoes, and American Canoe Association certification (minimum 3 days). Also offers other adventure sports and jungle trekking.

Waterfall Survivors
Mobile tel: 014 630 3999
www.waterfallsurvivors.blogspot.com
This diehard group of waterfall junkies plan elaborate excursions to waterfalls around KL and beyond. They organise waterfall cleanups, camping, star-gazing and quirky, food-related trips.

Spectator Sports

Football

Malaysians love football, which they call *bola*, whether it's the English Premier League or Malaysia Cup matches. Live matches see almost rabid club or state football support at stadiums throughout the city (see the **Football Association of Malaysia** website at www.fam.org.my). Fans also congregate at pubs and 24-hour *mamak* outlets or hawker centres to cheer their teams in live matches on huge TV monitors.

Formula One

Sepang International Circuit
Sepang, Selangor
Tel: 03-8778 2222
www.malaysiangp.com.my
Motorsports' premier event heats up the tracks annually. You can book tickets online or purchase them at the door. During this time, the city goes into party overdrive too.

Horse Racing

Selangor Turf Club
Jalan Kuda Emas, off Jalan Sungei Besi
Tel: 03-9058 3888
Able to accommodate 25,000 people and with over 350 colour monitors and 24 video wall systems, races are beamed live from its three circuits to the rest of the country and internationally.

Watersports

Waterski and Wakeboard @ Putrajaya
Maritime Centre, Presint 5, Waterski and Wakeboard Site, Putrajaya
Tel: 03-8926 1054
www.waterski.com.my
Hosts major international competitions for waterskiing and its sister sport, wakeboarding, or you can have a go yourself. Check website for details.

Spas and Massage

Kuala Lumpur has always been behind the region in terms of spa offerings, but it is now catching up. A slew of beautifully designed spas – many housed in hotels and catering to the mid- and high-end market – have opened up. The hotel spas combine a wide variety of recreational activities with spa treatments. Prices at such day spas are high; an hour-long massage can cost RM150–250. At the lower end are simple massage centres in the Brickfields area which hire blind masseurs who charge as little as RM40 for a full body massage. Along Bukit Bintang are several massage centres dispensing cheap foot reflexology and Chinese-style acupressure massages.

Andana Spa
Level 7, Menara Citibank, Jalan Ampang
Tel: 03-2161 3368
www.andanaspa.com
This enormous, award-winning men-only spa is regarded as one of the top spas in the country. Saunas, Roman-style baths and a diversity of treatments are complemented by an all-day food and drink menu.

Angsana Spa Kuala Lumpur
Level 5, Crowne Plaza Mutiara Kuala Lumpur, Jalan Sultan Ismail
Tel: 03-2141 4321
www.angsanaspa.com/resortspas/kualalumpur
Occupying 1,000 sq metres (11,000 sq ft), this exquisite spa has 22 rooms, including outdoor spa pavilions. Treatments include the signature 90-minute Angsana massage, which works on pressure points. Ask about promotional day packages.

Ayurvedium Medispa @ The Gardens
Lot FF-229, Level 5, The Gardens, Mid Valley City, Lingkaran Syed Putra
Tel: 03-2282 5066
www.ayurvedium.com
Specialises in 5,000-year-old Indian holistic treatments. You'll be assessed by a certified physician and prescribed personalised treatments that will balance your *dosha* (constitution).

Energy Day Spa
Level 4, Great Eastern Mall, Jalan Ampang
Tel: 03-4256 8833
www.energymindbodyspirit.com
This facility offers facial, body and therapeutic massage in 10 beautiful treatment rooms. Also has branches in Mont Kiara and Gleneagles Intan Hospital.

Hammam
Lot 3F-7, 3F-B, Bangsar Village II, Jalan Telawi 1, Bangsar Baru
Tel: 03-2282 2180
www.hammambaths.com
This *hammam* (Turkish bath) replicates a Moroccan bathhouse, complete with hanging lamps, mosaics, carpets and alcoves. Try the "hammam and gommage", which literally takes off a layer of skin.

Kenko Reflexology and Fish Spa
Lot 5.01.09, Pavilion Kuala Lumpur, 168 Jalan Bukit Bintang
Tel: 03-2141 6651
www.kenko.com.sg
The Fish Spa provides an interesting experience, though it's not for everyone. You immerse your feet in a clear tank and let countless *garra rufa* fish nibble away at your toes, heels and calves. It's a bizarre, ticklish sensation.

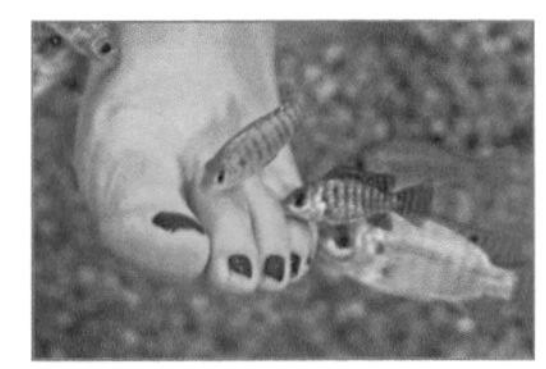

Above: fish spa therapy.

Ozmosis Health and Day Spa
Level 1, 14 and 16 Jalan Telawi Dua, Bangsar Baru
Tel: 03-2287 0380
www.ozmosis.com.my
This lovely Balinese-inspired spa in the Bangsar area has the full range of exfoliating scrubs, wraps, facials and massage treatments for men and women. Check its website for current promotions.

Spa Indrani
S20 and 27 Pamper Floor, Starhill Gallery, Bukit Bintang
Tel: 03-2782 3868
www.spaindrani.com
Only organic and high-quality French-made Phytomer products are used at this well-designed spa. Expect a pampering experience in one of its eight treatment rooms, after which you can relax at the hydrotherapy pool. Has a much larger branch at Jalan Stonor (tel: 03-2142 7808).

Spa Village Kuala Lumpur
Ritz-Carlton, 168 Jalan Imbi
Tel: 03-2142 8000
www.ritzcarlton.com
Tropical-inspired spa with eight spacious treatment suites and an array of treatments inspired by Chinese, Peranakan, Malay and Western healing traditions.

Thalgo Marine Spa
Mandarin Oriental Kuala Lumpur
Tel: 03-2380 1138
www.mandarinoriental.com
Try the rejuvenating blitz shower, warm water-based balneotherapy or detoxifying marine algae wrap. There is also a wide selection of facials and massage therapies.

Combine three or more treatments for a day-long indulgent treat. Daily 10am–9pm.

CHILDREN'S ACTIVITIES

Aquaria KLCC
Concourse Level, Kuala Lumpur Convention Centre
Tel: 03-2333 1888
www.klaquaria.com
More than 5,000 creatures from local and international marine and terrestrial worlds displayed in tanks and exhibits.

Cosmo's World
Level 5, Berjaya Times Square, Jalan Imbi
Tel: 03-2117 3118
www.timessquarekl.com
Located over two floors of a mall, with 14 rides grouped into two sections. Galaxy Station has hair-raising rides and Fantasy Garden's kiddie rides are suitable for younger children.

Genting Theme Park
Genting Highlands Resort
Tel: 03-2718 1118
www.rworldgenting.com
This expansive theme park comprises indoor and outdoor sections, with a total of 60 rides. The outdoor park features such signature rides as the hang-gliding Flying Coaster and Corkscrew roller-coaster. The Sky Venture wind tunnel offers a skydiving experience at 193km/h (120mph). There is also a SnowWorld, X-pedition wall and the Ripley's Believe it or Not Museum.

KLCC Park
Kuala Lumpur City Centre
Tel: 03-2382 3359
Kids love the 0.8-hectare (2-acre) children's playground and wading pool (bring swimmers) as well as the "dancing" fountain display.

Kuala Gandah National Elephant Conservation Centre
Kuala Gandah, Lancang, Pahang,
Tel: 09 279 0391
www.wildlife.gov.my
Get there by 2pm to start the day's activities of feeding, bathing and riding the Asian elephants. These activities help raise awareness of the centre's role as a temporary base for elephants that are being relocated *(see pages 198–9)*.

Kuala Lumpur Craft Complex
Jalan Conlay
Tel: 03-2162 7533
www.kraftangan.gov.my
Make your own batik, pottery and woodcraft at the Craft Village; instruction and all materials supplied.

Lake Gardens
Jalan Perdana
Wildlife experiences can be found at the Kuala Lumpur Bird Park and Butterfly Park, while playgrounds and vast green spaces for picnics make this a lovely place to spend the day.

National Science Centre (Pusat Sains Negara)
Jalan Persiaran Bukit Kiara
Tel: 03-2092 1150
www.psn.gov.my
Encased in an upside-down cupcake-like building, various exhibits show how science relates to the environment, religion and daily life.

National Zoo (Zoo Negara)
Jalan Ulu Kelang, Ampang, Selangor
Tel: 03-4108 3422
www.zoonegara.org.my
While getting rather tired, the zoo is still a good place for children to be introduced to Malaysian wildlife as well as to animals from the rest of Asia and Africa. A shuttle takes visitors around the gardens. More than 5,000 animals are housed here.

Petrosains
Level 4, Suria KLCC
Tel: 03-2331 8787
www.petrosains.com.my
This interactive science discovery centre offers the best children's activities in town, with innovative displays that provide hours of fun and learning.

School of Hard Knocks
Royal Selangor Visitor Centre, 4 Jalan Usahawan 6, Setapak Jaya
Tel: 03-4145 6122
www.royalselangor.com
Create your own pewter masterpiece with a few simple tools in this hour-long pewter-smithing workshop. Bookings required.

Sunway Lagoon
3 Jalan PJS 11/11, Bandar Sunway, Petaling Jaya, Selangor
Tel: 03-5639 0000
www.sunwaylagoon.com
This 32-hectare (80-acre) park has an array of exciting wet and wild rides as well as the world's largest man-made surf beach and longest pedestrian suspension bridge. Explore the Extreme Park, Water Park, Amusement Park, Wildlife Park and Scream Park. Also has a Nite Park.

COOKERY CLASSES

Azrah's Home of Culinary Arts
19 Lorong Terasek Kanan, Bangsar Baru
Tel: 012-307 0420/2284 7385
Malay, Indian, Chinese, Nyonya, Thai and vegetarian cooking classes by cookbook author Azrah Kamala. It's first to the market at 8.30am, then to class (8–10 people) to learn three or four dishes, and then lunch.

LaZat Malaysia Home Cooking Class
584 Jalan 17/17, Section 17, Petaling Jaya
Tel: 03019 238 1198
www.malaysia-klcookingclass.com
Has excellent facilites for preparation and cooking of local Malaysian dishes. Classes (Tue–Sat 10am–2pm) are kept small, with 3 to 10 people.

The French Culinary School in Asia
HTC in Asia, Level 8, Annexed Block, Menara IMC (next to Concorde Hotel), 8 Jalan Sultan Ismail
Tel: 03-2078 7969
www.htcinasia.com
This top-notch culinary school offers the best in French cooking and more: "cooking with tea", "clams and scallops", "all about chocolate" and bread-making classes. Join chef Jean Michel and his team in learning how to make things like roast duck with red tea and honey.

A – Z

AN ALPHABETICAL SUMMARY OF PRACTICAL INFORMATION

Addresses

Finding your way around KL is quite easy with the help of good maps. All road signs and place names are in Bahasa Malaysia but many also appear in English. What is a little confusing is that some places are referred to by their English names while others are commonly identified by their Malay names. In this guidebook we have chosen to use the names which are most commonly used by the locals – sometimes it's English and sometimes Malay.

Tourist attractions, train stations and RapidKL bus stops are well marked, but signposting for drivers could be improved. Note that the lowest two floors of multistorey buildings are usually referred to as the ground floor (G/F) or ground level and first floor (1/F) or level 1. As the Chinese associate the number "4" with death, in some lifts the fourth floor button is marked as "3A" instead. In some high-rises, the 13th floor is 12A or 14.

Admission Charges

There is quite a disparity between charges for government-owned institutions and private ones. Government art galleries and museums are primarily free or have a minumim charge; the privately owned Islamic Arts Museum charges around RM10 for special exhibits. Entertainment venues like Sunway Lagoon and Aquaria charge hefty admissions, beginning at RM30. Tickets to theatre productions start at around RM40 and can go up to RM300, depending on the venue. Matinee shows are much cheaper.

Budgeting for Your Trip

KL is a bargain, particularly in off-peak seasons. Rooms in 5-star hotels cost a fraction of what they do in New York or London. Decent budget accommodation starts at RM60; on average, RM250–300 gets you a room in a good 4-star hotel. Many hotels include breakfast with the room rate.

Street food is very cheap; a meal with a soft drink can be as little as RM5. Generally, budget RM20–30 for a main meal. Alcohol is very expensive, with beers going for RM15–20 a pop, so do take advantage of happy hours. Admission fees for attractions and theatre tickets are generally reasonable, and matinee theatre shows are discounted. Public transport is cheap, but taxis may charge double by insisting on a flat rate during peak hours and levy a 50 percent surcharge between midnight and 6am. Car hire is reasonably priced, but parking in the city centre and at 5-star hotels is very expensive.

If you are frugal, you can get by on RM120 a day; RM150–200 per day is a fair budget.

Business Travellers

There is no lack of hotels and business centres catering to business travellers. Kuala Lumpur International Airport (KLIA) has a business centre (Plaza Premium Lounge), which is open to all travellers, in its Satellite Building, where you can enjoy food and drinks, showers, movies, high-speed internet access, the use of computers and massage chairs and more.

Most hotels in the city centre target business travellers with business centres and meeting rooms equipped with free Wi-fi, as well as secretarial services. In-room facilities often include broadband and/or wireless internet access, increasingly for free. A number of business centres around town offer short-term office space and secretarial services.

The government body dealing with doing business is the **Malaysian Industrial Development Authority** (tel: 03-2267 3633; www.mida.gov.my).

Children

It's safe to travel with children in KL, though the city is not so baby-friendly – facilities for breast-feeding, nappy-changing and strollers are inadequate. However, Malaysians love children, so a helping hand is never far away. In fact, locals don't hesitate to pinch your child's cheeks or even take babies in their arms. Some hotels, 4-star or above, have kids' clubs, with activities and minders for children all day long. Bigger malls and fast-food outlets have play areas, and there are enough attractions in the city to keep the young ones happy.

Children may be more susceptible to heat and food- and water-related ailments. Always carry sunblock, hats, insect repellent and lots of water. While pharmacies, such as Caring and Guardian, are well stocked with children's medications, do bring along any special medications.

Climate

Malaysia's weather is generally hot and sunny all year round, with temperatures ranging from 32°C (89.6°F) during the day to 22°C (71.6°F) at night. It is slightly colder in the highlands like Fraser's Hill and Genting Highlands. Humidity is high, at 80 percent, and there are regular quick showers and thunderstorms. The heaviest rainfall occurs during the inter-monsoon periods of April to May and October to November. The months of January to March are hot and dry. As in many places, though, climate change means the rains have become unpredictable.

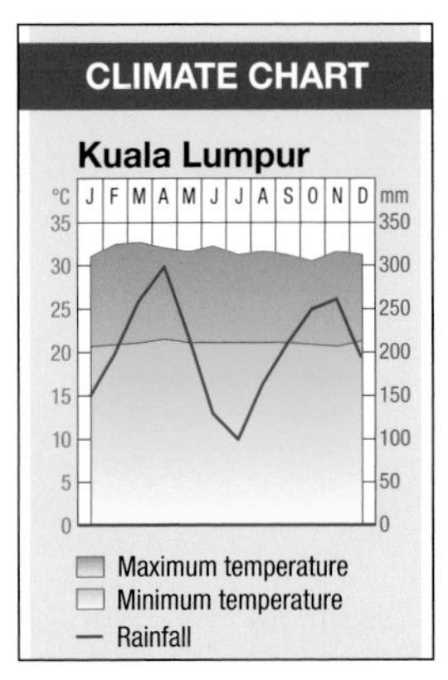

Thick haze has been recurrent in Malaysia's skies for some years, especially in July. Most of the smoke and soot is blown in by the southwest monsoon from parts of Indonesia hit by forest fires, which have been worsened by the dry weather caused by the El Niño phenomenon.

For more details on local weather, visit the **Malaysian Meteorological Department** website at www.met.gov.my.

What to Wear

Light and loose clothes work best in Malaysia's climate, so pack cottons and natural fibres. Sunglasses, sunblock and umbrellas or raincoats are advisable. Shoes should be removed before entering temples and homes, so slip-ons and sandals are handy. Shorts and T-shirts are generally acceptable attire, including in shopping malls. KL-ites do tend to dress up for a night out in town. Women should dress more conservatively when entering places of worship, and outside KL.

Because of the heat and humidity, business dress is often casual. The standard formal office wear for men is dark trousers, a light-coloured long-sleeve shirt and tie without a jacket, but bring one in case you need it for a formal dinner. Some women wear skirt or trouser suits for work, but most wear dresses or long-sleeve blouses and skirts. Many non-Muslim women choose to wear the *baju kurung* (long-sleeved blouse over a long skirt) on Fridays, as a mark of respect for the Muslim day of worship.

Crime and Safety

Kuala Lumpur has become rather notorious for snatch and petty thefts. Snatch thieves tend to be two men on a motorcycle or men leaning out of moving cars to grab your bag. If your bag is snatched, give in, because many thieves carry knives which they will not hesitate to use. On pavements, always walk in the direction of oncoming traffic and make sure your bag is on the side away from traffic. When sightseeing, take only what you need with you. If you do not trust your hotel room safe, leave your valuables and passport with the hotel reception. At night, keep to well-lit areas.

The **Tourist Police** (tel: 03-2149 6590) patrol tourist spots. Their uniforms are distinguished by a checkered hatband, dark-blue shirt and trousers, and a red-and-blue badge with the letter "I" (for information) on the breast pocket. They can help with lost passports and other documents as well as give general advice. Otherwise, do not hesitate to head to any police station or booth when you need help (tel: 999).

Common Scams

Although KL-ites are friendly, they rarely approach foreigners or engage them in conversation. Always be on guard and walk away if they ask you to meet a "relative" who has "always wanted to visit your country", or to partake in a gambling session with "guaranteed winnings".

Be aware of people pretending to be police and demanding to see your ID. The police will not do so unless you have committed an offence or you are in a nightspot that is being raided.

Never buy anything from touts, whether bus or train tickets, or other admission tickets.

Electricity

Electrical outlets are rated at 220 volts, 50 cycles, and serve three-pin, flat-pronged plugs. American products do not work here, but most supermarkets stock adapters. Major hotels can supply an adapter for 110–120 volt, 60Hz appliances.

Customs Regulations

When you arrive in Malaysia, you must declare all prohibited and dutiable goods. The former includes drugs, dangerous chemicals, pornography, firearms and ammunition. Note that possession of drugs carries a mandatory death sentence. Items such as cameras, watches, pens, perfume, cosmetics and lighters are duty-free. Visitors bringing in dutiable goods may have to pay a deposit for temporary importation – usually 50 percent of the value – refundable on departure (remember to keep your receipt of purchase and to get an official receipt for any tax or deposit paid). For details, call the **Customs Department** (tel: 03-8776 8055, www.customs.gov.my).

Disabled Travellers

Basic disabled-friendly facilities, like extra-wide parking bays and toilets, and wheelchair ramps, can be found in major hotels, malls, theatres, fast-food chains and some government buildings. KLIA and the Light Rail Transit (LRT) system are also disabled-friendly. But in general, KL falls short on accommodating the disabled, with uneven pavements, potholes and unsympathetic drivers. Taxis will usually not transport people in wheelchairs.

Embassies/Consulates

Australia, 6 Jalan Yap Kwan Seng; www.australia.org.my; tel: 03-2146 5555. Visas: Mon–Fri 8.30am–noon; tel: 03-2146 5642.
UK, 185 Jalan Ampang; www.britain.org.my; tel: 03-2170 2200. Visas: Suite 19-05, Wisma MCA, 163 Jalan Ampang; Mon–Fri 8am–12.30pm; tel: 03-2164 9323.
Canada, 17/F, Menara Tan and Tan, 207 Jalan Tun Razak; www.canadainternational.gc.ca; tel: 03-2718 3333. Visas: Mon–Thur 8am–4.30pm, Fri 8am–1.30pm; tel: 03-2718 3385.
Indonesia, 233 Jalan Tun Razak;www.kbrikualalumpur.org; tel: 03-2116 4000. Visas: Mon–Fri 9am–1pm; tel: 03-2116 4100.
New Zealand, 21/F, Menara IMC, 8 Jalan Sultan Ismail; www.nzembassy.com/malaysia; tel: 03-2078 2533; Mon–Thur 8am–4.45pm, Fri 8am–12.30pm.
Singapore, 209 Jalan Tun Razak; www.mfa.gov.sg/kl; tel: 03-2161 6277. Visas: Mon–Fri 8.30am–noon.
Thailand, 206 Jalan Ampang; www.thaiembassy.org/kualalumpur; tel: 03-2148 8222. Visas: Mon–Fri 9.30–11.30am.
United States, 376 Jalan Tun Razak; www.malaysia.usembassy.gov/; tel: 03-2168 5000. Visas: Mon–Tue, Thu–Fri 2–4pm.

Etiquette

Malaysians are remarkably tolerant and forgiving of foreigners' gaffes, but there are some things you should keep in mind.

Greetings

Seniority is much respected and it is considered rude to address older people by their names. See **Language** *(pages 252–3)*. Unless you know your business associates well or you know otherwise, always use titles such as Mr (Encik), Madam (Mrs) or Ms (Cik).

If you are a man, you must never offer to shake a Muslim lady's hand unless she offers it first. A simple nod or smile will suffice. Similar rules apply to women wanting to shake a Muslim man's hand. If you get what you think is a limp handshake, it is actually a Malay greeting (*salam*), which involves brushing the palm of the other person and placing the hand on one's heart. This signifies "I am pleased to meet you from the bottom of my heart".

Head and Feet

The Hindu religion regards the head as the wellspring of wisdom and

Emergencies

Police: 999 (112 from mobile phone)
Civil Defence: 991
Fire Brigade: 994
Gas Emergency: 995

the feet as unclean, so it is insulting to touch another adult's head, point one's feet at anything or step over another person. Malays consider it rude to point the index finger at something, so when indicating direction, make a fist with the right hand and the thumb folded on top, and then aim at the subject.

At Home

In Malaysian homes, it is rude, especially for women, to cross your legs in front of your host. If entering a Malaysian home, remove your shoes. It is courteous to come bearing a gift, no matter how small. Never refuse drinks or snacks served to you, even if it is just to take a sip or bite. In a Malay home, when passing in front of someone, bow slightly while walking and point an arm down to indicate the path to be taken.

At Places of Worship

Remove your shoes before entering any place of worship. At the mosque, non-Muslims are prohibited from entering certain areas; signs are clearly displayed. Conservative clothing is advisable – meaning visitors, both men and women, must have their arms and legs covered. Some mosques, like the Putra Mosque in Putrajaya, provide robes to wear and scarves for wrapping your hair.

Certain Hindu temples are not open to non-Hindus to keep the place "purified" from people who consume beef. If you enter a Sikh temple be sure to cover your hair. Be sensitive about photographing worshippers in prayer.

Public Behaviour

While holding hands is common, displaying other forms of affection in public is considered bad form. The government is particular about upholding Islamic and Asian moral values, so such behaviour in public places is unacceptable, especially if you are with a local or look like one. Shouting and talking loudly, even outside a nightspot, is considered rude.

Gay and Lesbian

KL has a sizeable gay and lesbian community, unofficially estimated at 60,000. As in other Asian countries, Malaysian society is generally tolerant – though not of public displays of affection – and appreciative of the pink dollar. Homosexual visitors can travel safely and without fear of persecution in KL, usually facing only minor harassment from police, if it happens at all. However, note that there are provisions in the Penal Code and for Muslims (Islamic Syariah laws) that penalise same-sex sexual acts and cross-dressing.

Nonetheless, KL's nightlife in is interesting and varied. See **After Dark** (*page 65*) and **Gay and Lesbian Venues** (*page 239*). Comprehensive information and newsgroups are available on gay portal **Utopia** at www.utopia-asia.com/ and www.fridae.com.

For more information on the community, contact community rights and AIDS/HIV outreach organisation **PT Foundation** (tel: 03-4044 4611; www.ptfmalaysia.org). For lesbians, www.purplelab.net has listings and a community chat forum. Http://tiltedworld.org is a website that champions the LGBT community and gay issues in Malaysia.

Health and Medical Care

Visitors entering Malaysia are not required to show evidence of vaccination for smallpox or cholera, but it is a good idea to immunise yourself against cholera, hepatitis A and B and tetanus. There are periodic outbreaks of dengue fever, for which there is no immunisation, so take preventive measures like using insect repellent, especially outside of the city areas. If you suffer from a very high fever while (or shortly after) visiting Malaysia, consult a doctor immediately.

Should you be in KL during the haze period (July), be aware that the haze affects those with respiratory illnesses, especially asthmatics. Stay indoors or wear a mask when outdoors. Thankfully, the monsoon season right afterward helps clear the air. The risk of Avian Influenza (bird flu) in Malaysia is believed to be very low. As a precaution, avoid visiting live animal markets and poultry farms, and ensure poultry and egg dishes are thoroughly cooked. For more information, visit the **Institute for Public Health** website, www.iku.gov.my

Many first-time visitors to a tropical country take a while to adjust to the heat and humidity; make sure you drink at least 2 litres (8–10 glasses) of water per day to keep hydrated. Keep out of the sun during the hottest part of the day (11am–1pm). Tap water in KL is potable but, to be on the safe side, drink boiled or bottled water. Avoid ice cubes at street-side stalls and small coffeeshops, as they are usually made using unboiled water. Refrain from eating peeled fruit at street stalls. Otherwise, food served in restaurants and hawker centres is fine.

Dental Clinics

The quality of dental work is generally very good, and costs are reasonable. Most hospitals and medical centres have dental clinics. Clinics are also found in major shopping malls and shopping areas like Bukit Bintang and the KLCC. For a complete list of clinics, check the **Malaysian Dental Association** (www.mda.org.my).

Dentalpro Dental Specialist Centre, 8 Lengkok Abdullah, Bangsar Utama; tel: 03-2287 3333.

Pristine Dental Clinic, F-074 Level 2, Mid Valley Megamall; www.pristinedental.com.my; tel: 03-2287 3782.

Twin Towers Medical Centre KLCC, 401 F&G, Level 4, Suria KLCC; www.ttmcklcc.com.my; tel: 03-2382 3500.

Hospitals

KL offers advanced medical care in both government and private hospitals, which are well equipped and have specialised clinics and good medical staff. Government hospitals charge a fraction of what private ones charge, but there is usually a longer waiting period. See the **Ministry of Health** website at www.moh.gov.my for a hospital list.

Hospital Kuala Lumpur, Jalan Pahang; www.hkl.gov.my; tel: 03-2615 5555. The largest government hospital, it has 23 clinical departments, a large specialist team and good facilities.

Tung Shin Hospital, Jalan Pudu (near Puduraya); www.tungshinhospital.com.my; tel: 03-2072 1655. A good, medium-sized private hospital offering Western and traditional Chinese treatments.

Gleneagles Intan Medical Centre, Jalan Ampang; www.gimc.com.my; tel: 03-4255 2786. A medium-sized private hospital with top-notch medical services. Favoured by expatriates, it offers special services for overseas patients, such as emergency airlift transfers.

Medical Clinics

For minor problems, there are many private clinics around the city, some open 24 hours. All major hotels have an on-premise clinic or a doctor on call. There are also specialist and family clinics, and alternative medicine practitioners, from chiropractors and homeopaths to practitioners of traditional Chinese medicine (TCM), reflexology and Ayurveda.

Pharmacies

Pharmacies are found everywhere, especially in malls, usually operated by chains like **Watsons**, **Guardian** and **Caring**. Usually, a licensed pharmacist will be on duty on weekdays from 10am to 5pm. A doctor's prescription is required for controlled drugs. Do check the expiry dates. Pharmacies also stock nutritional and personal-care products.

You can find homeopathic and natural product remedies in large malls. There are also many Chinese medical halls selling traditional and herbal medications.

Internet

Broadband internet access is readily available in the city, from the airport to hotels of all categories. Wireless broadband (Wi-fi) is becoming quite widespread. In cafés, Wi-fi is usually free with purchase of food or drinks; the cashier will give you a log-in name and password. Internet cafés are found in major shopping areas like Petaling Street and KLCC. However, many internet cafés are used for gaming and therefore filled with noisy youngsters.

Left Luggage

Hotels usually provide free left-luggage services for their guests. **KLIA** (tel: 1Touch KLIA 03-8776 0888; www.klia.com.my) has locker rental services in the Satellite Building and counter storage services in the Main Building. **KL Sentral** (tel: 03-2279 8888; www.klsentral.com.my) has lockers on Level 1 and 2. There are also left luggage services at **Puduraya** (tel: 03-2070 0145; 8am–10pm).

Lost Property

For any lost property or passport, call the **Tourist Police** immediately on 03-2149 6590 or lodge a report at the nearest police station. There is a Lost and Found service at **KLIA** (Main Building, tel: 1Touch KLIA 03-8776 0888) and **KL Sentral** (tel: 03-2279 8888).

Maps

Basic maps are available for free at most hotels. You can also purchase decent maps from any good bookshop or convenience store. The *Insight Fleximap Kuala Lumpur* is a good one to get. Also check out www.kuala-lumpur.ws/maps for a basic online map.

Media

Newspapers/Magazines

Malaysia's English-language dailies include *The Star*, *The New Straits Times*, *The Sun* (free) and *Malay Mail*. The first two offer comprehensive coverage of local and international news. Most major hotels provide free local English-language newspapers every morning, or you can purchase them at any bookshop, newsstand or convenience store. Business coverage is provided weekly by *The Edge*. You can also buy *The Asian Wall Street Journal*, *The International Herald Tribune*, *USA Today* and leading international periodicals and magazines at bookshops and hotel newsstands. Local newspapers also come in Bahasa Malaysia, Chinese and Tamil languages.

TimeOut KL and KLue are the best local lifestyle and entertainment magazines, with news and listings.

Radio

There is a range of English-language broadcasts on FM radio. English-language news is broadcast hourly. The popular stations are the Business Station BFM 89.9, which plays 1980s music; Traxx 90.3 and Hitz 92.9, which play mainly American hits; Mix 94.5, which plays a mixture of new and old hits; and Light n' Easy 105.7, which plays retro and classics. KL-only stations are Radio Music KL 97.2, which has programmes for visitors and travellers, and Fly FM 95.8, which is broadcast out of KLIA.

Television

Cable TV, with channels such as CNN, BBC, Al Jazeera, CNBC and HBO, is available in most hotels. The specialist hotel programme package is called Vision 4. Free-to-air local TV stations are run by RTM (TV1 and TV2) and by private stations TV3, NTV7 and 8TV. Except for TV1, which is a Malay-language station, all have news reports in English, American programmes and religious Islamic programmes. The two paid satellite TV stations (Astro and MiTV) have as many as 100 channels.

Money

The Malaysian Ringgit (RM) is divided into 100 sen. Bank notes are in units of RM1, 2, 5, 10, 20, 50 and 100, and coins are in 1, 5, 10, 20 and 50 sen denominations.

ATMs

Automated teller machines are available at most shopping centres. Local ATMs operate 6am–midnight but some international banks operate 24-hour machines. You can use your credit card to withdraw money from these machines. Banking networks available are MFPS, Cirrus, Maestro and Bankcard.

Changing Money

Changing currency is easy as money-changers are located everywhere in the city, including the main bus and train terminals as well as KLIA. Banks charge a commission but money-changers do not. Rates vary slightly from one money-changer to another, so shop around. Larger amounts of currency get you better rates.

Credit Cards

American Express, Diners Club, Visa and MasterCard are widely accepted at major shopping malls, hotels and petrol stations. Note that some retailers add an extra 2–3 percent surcharge for the privilege of using plastic – so ask first before paying. As with everywhere in the world, be watchful of credit card fraud.

American Express, tel: 03-2050 0000

Diners Card, tel: 03-2161 1055 (office hours), tel: 03-2161 2862 (after office hours)

MasterCard, tel: 1800 804 594

Visa, tel: 1800 802 997

Travellers' Cheques

All major brands of travellers' cheques and cash in major currencies are readily accepted in KL. Some big hotels will exchange travellers' cheques for cash but their rates are not as good as the rates offered by banks.

Opening Hours

Government offices and some businesses operate Mon–Fri 8.30am–5.30pm, with a 1-hour lunch break from 12.30pm. There is a longer lunch break 12.45–2.45pm for Muslim prayers on Fri. Some companies also operate Sat 9am–1pm.

During the Muslim fasting month of Ramadan, government office hours are Mon–Thur 8am–4.30pm, Fri 8am–4pm. Hours for private businesses vary, though most retain the same hours.

Banking hours are Mon–Fri 9.30am–4.30pm, although banks in shopping malls and areas like Masjid India, Golden Triangle, Jalan Ampang and Bangsar open 10am–7pm on weekdays and 10am–1pm on Sat. Money-changing kiosks in the city are open till 7pm daily. Shops and departmental stores open 9–11am and close 9–10pm Mon–Sat, and are open 10am–8pm on Sun. Malls are generally open 10am–10pm daily. You can find 24-hour convenience stores all over the city.

Restaurants usually open 11am–2.30pm and 5–11pm while café hours are 7am–10pm. They close later on weekends. *Mamak* outlets that serve Indian and Malay food are open 24 hours a day; some hawker places only open for dinner and close at 4am.

Tipping

Tipping is not obligatory as bills usually include a 10 percent government tax and 5 percent service charge. However, tips are appreciated. Porters are tipped RM2–5, restaurant and bar staff are usually left loose change or change from bills rounded off to the nearest RM10. But, obviously, you can tip according to how you feel about the quality of service. Otherwise, a simple thank you (*terima kasih*) and a smile will do.

Photography

Camera shops are widely found in malls and tourist areas. Cameras and accessories are good bargains, as they are duty-free here. Most shops offer digital photo transfers to CD, and print services. For camera repairs and second-hand equipment, head to the Pudu area. Likewise, video equipment and digital tapes are affordable.

Be prepared for rain, even on sunny days, and always have a plastic bag handy for your equipment. Note that rainforest excursions are damaging to cameras because of the humidity. Pack a dry non-lint cloth for wiping your camera. Although there are no restrictions on what you can photograph or film, use your discretion in religious places. When in doubt, ask for permission. Some attractions charge a fee for cameras.

Postal Services

The Malaysian postal service, **Pos Malaysia** (www.pos.com.my) is not the most efficient in the world and delays are inevitable. However, it does offer the full range of services, including registered mail, parcels and courier services (Poslaju) as well as the cashing of postal and money orders. Most post offices are open Mon–Fri 8am–5.30pm and Sat 8am–1pm. The **General Post Office** (tel: 03-2274 1122; Mon–Sat 8am–6.30pm, Sun 10am–1pm) is located at Kompleks Dayabumi, beside the Central Market. Post offices with extended hours from Mon to Sat are located in **Bangsar** (until 10pm), **Mid Valley Megamall** (until 9pm), **Suria KLCC** (until 6pm) and **Sungei Wang Plaza** (until 6pm). There is also a post office in the Main Building in **KLIA**. Most big hotels can mail letters for you.

International courier services include the following:
Federal Express (FedEx), Damansara Uptown, Petaling Jaya; tel: 1800 886 363; www.fedex.com.my
United Parcel Services (UPS), 11 Jalan Tandang, Petaling Jaya; tel: 03-7784 2311; www.ups.com
Deutsche Post (DHL), Level 27, Menara TM, off Jalan Pantai Baharu; tel: 1800 888 388

Public Holidays

Some holidays are fixed while others have variable dates as they are governed by the lunar calendar. Check specific dates with **Tourism Malaysia** (tel: 03-1300 885 0505; www.tourism.gov.my).
New Year's Day: 1 Jan
Federal Territory Day: 1 Feb
Chinese New Year: Jan/Feb
Labour Day: 1 May
Wesak Day: May
Agong's Birthday: first Saturday in June
National Day: 31 Aug
Prophet Muhammad's Birthday: date varies
Deepavali: Oct/Nov
Hari Raya Puasa: date varies
Hari Raya Haji: date varies
Christmas: 25 Dec

School Holidays

School holidays start on the Sat closest to these dates: 30 Jan–4 Feb, 29 May–8 June, 6–14 Sept, 23–27 Oct, 8 Nov–4 Jan. When planning your trip, take note that during these times, attractions will be packed with families and school children. For exact dates, check www.moe.gov.my. For Singapore school holiday dates, check www.moe.gov.sg/schools/terms-and-holidays.

Religious Services

As the majority of the population is Muslim, mosques are very common and all public buildings have at least a *surau* (prayer room). There are also ample places of worship for Buddhists, Taoists, Hindus, Sikhs and followers of other faiths. Of the various Christian denominations, below is a list of churches that offer English-language services.

Anglican

St Mary's Cathedral, Jalan Raja; tel: 03-2692 8672; www.stmaryscathedral.org.my. Sun services 7am, 8.30am, 10.30am, 6pm.

Catholic

Cathedral of St John, 5 Jalan Bukit Nanas; tel: 03-2078 1876; www.stjohnkl.net. Sat Mass (and Novena) 6pm, Sun Mass 8am, 10.30am and 6pm.
Church of the Holy Rosary, 10 Jalan Tun Sambanthan, Brickfields; tel: 03-2274 2747; Sat Mass 5pm, Sun Mass 8.30am.
Church of Our Lady of Fatima, Jalan Sultan Abdul Samad, Brickfields; tel: 03-2274 1631; Sun Mass 7am and 10.30am, Tue–Sat Masses 6.30am.

Tailoring and Repairs

KL has good tailors who can handle both Western and ethnic clothing. Tailors abound in Jalan Masjid India and along Jalan Tuanku Abdul Rahman, with textile shops offering quality tailoring. There are also tailors in major shopping malls, as well as at laundry or dry-cleaning shops in malls and big hotels. If you want an inexpensive tailor, scout around Bukit Bintang and Pertama Complex on Jalan Tuanku Abdul Rahman. These also do alterations and mending.

Tax

Most services are subject to a 10 percent service charge and a 5 percent government tax. These are listed on bills; if not, you are welcome to tip more.

Time Zone

Malaysian time is 8 hours ahead of GMT and 16 hours ahead of US Pacific Standard Time.

Telephones

Most hotel rooms have phones with **International Direct Dialling** (IDD) facility, but charges are high. To call overseas, dial 00 followed by the country code, area code and phone number. The **country code** for Malaysia is 60 and the **area code** for KL and Selangor is 03. Each state in Malaysia has a different area code. To call KL from outside Malaysia, dial 603 followed by the number; within KL drop the prefix 03. For local and international **telephone directory** assistance, dial 103 (20 sen per call), and for **operator-assisted** calls, dial 101 (RM1.50 per local call, RM5 per international call).

You can also buy **prepaid cards** that offer cheaper rates for international calls to certain destinations. These use voice-over-internet-protocol (VOIP) and the connection may not be as clear.

Public Phones

The minimum cost of a local call from a public phone is 30 sen per 3 minutes. Booths are either coin-operated or use phone cards. Phone cards in denominations of RM5–50 can be bought at phone shops, newsstands and petrol stations. Around Bukit Bintang, there are also many shops providing IDD services.

Mobile Phones

Malaysian mobile phones – which use the prefixes 010, 012, 013, 014, 016, 017, 018 and 019 – use the **GSM** network. If your mobile phone has a roaming facility with your home service provider, it will automatically hook up to one of the country's digital networks (like Celcom, DiGi and Maxis). Otherwise, prepaid SIM cards, with which you get a local mobile number, are very affordable, starting at RM20 for registration and air-time. These allow you to call locally and overseas, and can be topped up at phone shops, newsagents and petrol stations.

Toilets

Public restrooms can be dirty and wet, and many still have squat toilets, which visitors may not be used to. Toilet paper is not always available, although you can sometimes buy small tissue packs at the entrance. Most malls charge a toilet entrance fee of 20–50 sen. If you are very particular, use hotel toilets.

Tourist Information

For detailed and comprehensive information and updates, visit the **Tourism Malaysia** website at www.tourism.gov.my, or call the infoline, tel: 1300 885 050. Tourist offices have helpful staff and ample brochures and maps.
Visitor Service Centre, KLIA, Level 3, Main Building; daily 24 hours; tel: 1Touch 03-8776 0888. Offers airport and flight information, as well as details on accommodation, transport and attractions.
Malaysia Tourism Centre, 109 Jalan Ampang; www.mtc.gov.my; tel: 03-9235 4848; daily 7am–10pm. This has tourist literature and computers for surfing state tourism homepages, and hosts a tour agency, a restaurant and the Transnasional coach company. Cultural performances are held on Tuesday, Thursday, Saturday and Sunday, while theatre performances are staged occasionally at its auditorium.
Tourism Malaysia Headquarters, 17/F, Menara Dato' Onn, Putra World Trade Centre, Jalan Tun Ismail; tel: 03-2615 8188.

Overseas Offices

Australia, Level 2, 171 Clarence Street, Sydney; tel: 61 2 92994441/4442/4443; email: mtpb.sydney@tourism.gov.my.
Canada, 1590-1111, West Georgia Street, Vancouver; www.tourism malaysia.ca; tel: 60-4-6898899.
UK, 57 Trafalgar Square London, London; tel: 44-20 7930 7932; email: mtpb.london@tourism.gov.my or info@tourism-malaysia.co.uk.
India, 4th Floor, Vijaya Towers, 4 Kodambakkam High Road, Chennai; www.malaysiajao.com; tel: 91 44 4506 8080/8181/8282.
Netherlands, 4th Floor, The Hague Equinox, J.P. Coenstraat 7, Den Haag; tel: 31 (0) 70 799 9173/31 (0) 70 799 9172.
USA, 120 East, 56th Street, Suite 810, New York; www.tourismmalaysiany.com; tel: 1-212-7541113.

Visas and Passports

Passports must be valid for at least six months at the time of entry. Visa requirements change from time to time, so check with a Malaysian embassy/consulate or the **Immigration Department** website (www.imi.gov.my) before travelling. Citizens of the Commonwealth (except Bangladesh, India, Nigeria, Pakistan and Sri Lanka), ASEAN countries, the US, Switzerland, the Netherlands, San Marino and Liechtenstein do not need a visa. Some EU, South American, South African and Arab nationals do not need visas for visits shorter than three months.

Tourist visas can be extended at the **Immigration Office** in KLIA (tel: 03-8776 8001/3681) or at the **Immigration Department** in the Federal Government Administration Centre, Putrajaya (tel: 03-8880 1000), or by making a trip to Thailand or Singapore and back.

Websites

Aliran, www.aliran.com. News and information site run by the country's foremost human-rights group.
All Malaysia, www.allmalaysia.info. General site on all things Malaysian with content from leading English newspaper, *The Star*.
Bibliobibuli, www.thebookaholic.blogspot.com. Insider info on literary events in KL: readings, book launches, spoken-word events, poetry slams and more. Kept alive by Sharon Bakar, writer, teacher and literary activist.
Fried Chillies, www.friedchillies.com. Honest reviews of and guide to food in KL and Malaysia.
Journeymalaysia, www.journeymalaysia.com. Comprehensive information related to travel.
KLue, www.klue.com.my. Listings of entertainment events.
The Malaysian Insider, www.themalaysianinsider.com. Alternative news portal to government-sanctioned newspapers.
myGovernment, www.gov.my. The government's portal, with information and links, including those for ministries and tourism.
Screenshots, http://asiancorrespondent.com/jeff-ooi-blog. Malaysia's most famous blogger has insightful and acerbic commentary on politics and society.
Wildasia, www.wildasia.net. Excellent non-profit site promoting responsible tourism.

Weights and Measures

Malaysia uses the metric system, although orally, traditional measurements, like *kati* (600g) and miles (for distance), are used.

Women Travellers

It is safe for women to travel alone in KL, but Western women may have the image of being "easy", no thanks to Hollywood movies. Wear a wedding band, or just say, "Yes, I'm married" to queries on marriage status. If you are approached, be polite but firm and walk away if you are uncomfortable. Although KL-ites are generally open, clothes that are too revealing will draw stares. You should dress more conservatively in places of worship and outside the city. Topless bathing at swimming pools is prohibited. KTMB (Malaysian Railways) has just launched a "Ladies Only At All Times" carriage on its train routes from Sentul to Port Klang and Rawang to Seremban. Look out for the pink sticker on the carriages. If successful, more routes will follow, so keep your eyes peeled.

Language

Understanding The Language

Bahasa Malaysia

Bahasa Malaysia is Malaysia's official name for the Malay language, an Austronesian language also spoken in Indonesia, Singapore, Brunei, the Philippines and southern Thailand. Although there is a standard Bahasa Malaysia taught in schools and used formally, there are actually many regional Malay dialects that are not mutually intelligible. This is in addition to a simplified form of Bahasa Malaysia known as "bahasa pasar" or "bazaar Malay". Today's urban youth also speak "bahasa rojak" or mixed language, which is formed from creolisation and pidginisation and includes English, Chinese dialects, Tamil and other languages.

Bahasa Malaysia is also known as Bahasa Melayu and popularly abbreviated as BM. Since it is the official language and all signboards and public displays of writing are in Bahasa Malaysia, it is useful to learn some words. It is an easy language to learn, and in Malaysia it is written in the Latin alphabet.

The language is polysyllabic, with variations in syllables to convey changes in meaning. Words are pronounced as they are spelt. However, the spelling can be tricky, for despite standardisation efforts, place and street names, for example, still follow different spellings. For instance, *baru* (new) is standard but appears as *bahru*, *bharu* and *baharu*. Another two examples are *cangkat* (hillock), which is sometimes spelt *changkat*, and *tingkat* (lane) as *tengkat*.

Root words are either nouns or verbs, and prefixes and/or suffixes are added to change the meaning of the word. Therefore, while *makan* is "to eat", *makanan* is "food" and *memakan* is "eating". The adjective always comes after the noun, so "my husband" is *suami saya*. To indicate plural, you often just repeat the noun, so "many rooms" is *bilik-bilik*.

Pronunciation Tips

In general pronunciation is the same as in English, with some exceptions. The "a" is pronounced "ar" as in tar when it appears in the middle of a word, but when it ends a word, it is pronounced with an "er" sound as in observe. Therefore *apa* (what) is pronounced as "arper". The "e" also has an "er" sound as in observe.

The "i" is pronounced with an "ee" sound unless it ends as an "-ik" or "-ih", in which case it is pronounced like the "a" in agent, so *bilik* (room) is pronounced "bee-lake". The "u" has an "oo" sound unless it ends as an "-uk", "-up", "-uh" or "-ur", in which case it has an "oh" sound. Therefore *sepuluh* (ten) is pronounced "sir-poo-loh". "C" is pronounced "ch" as in chair; "sy" is pronounced "sh"; and "ai" is pronounced "i". A tricky one involving "ai" which you are likely to use is *air* (water) which is pronounced "i-yeah".

The "g" is always hard, as in gun; the "h" is always pronounced, and you will come across "ny" and "ng" sounds which might not be common in your native language.

Forms of Address

When addressing someone formally, the form for men is *encik* (sir), which can be used on its own or may precede a person's name, eg *Encik* Razak. The female equivalent for married or older women is *puan* (madam) and *Puan* Miriam (Mrs Miriam), and for single or younger women is *cik* (miss) and *Cik* Ros (Ms Ros). For men and women who are about the same age, you may use "comrade" as in *saudara* (men) and *saudari* (women).

The informal form for older men of your father's age is *pakcik* (literally "uncle"), and *abang* (literally "older brother") for men slightly older than you. For women the equivalent is *makcik* (literally "aunty") and *kakak* (literally "older sister"). Meanwhile the gender-free informal form for younger men and women as well as children is *adik* (younger brother/sister).

Regardless of formal or informal use, the word for "you" (*anda*, etc) is rarely used as it is considered rude. Instead replace it with the form of address or name, for example, "*Encik dari mana?*" or "*Encik Razak dari mana?*" ("Where are you from?") Note that, other than for older people, the English pronoun "you" has become common, for example, "You *dari mana?*"

Vocabulary

You will find Sanskrit, Arabic, Tamil, Portuguese, Dutch and Chinese words in Bahasa Malaysia. English words are also increasingly being incorporated into the language, particularly in relation to business and technology. In spoken Bahasa Malaysia, short forms are usually used, and these are indicated within [ ] below too. Here are some useful words and phrases to get you going.

Numbers

One Satu
Two *Dua*
Three *Tiga*
Four *Empat*
Five *Lima*
Six *Enam*
Seven *Tujuh*
Eight *Lapan*
Nine *Sembilan*
Ten *Sepuluh*
Eleven *Sebelas*
Twelve *Dua belas*
Twenty *Dua puluh*
Twenty-one *Dua puluh satu*
One hundred *Seratus*
One thousand *Seribu*

Days of the Week

Monday *Isnin*
Tuesday *Selasa*
Wednesday *Rabu*
Thursday *Khamis*
Friday *Jumaat*
Saturday *Sabtu*
Sunday *Ahad*

Prounouns

I/Me Saya/Aku
You *Anda/Awak/Kamu [Mu]/Engkau [Kau]*
He/she *Dia*
We (inclusive of person being addressed) *Kita*
We (exclusive of person being addressed) *Kami*
They *Mereka*

Directions

Where Di mana
Right *Kanan*
Left *Kiri*
Turn *Belok*
Go *Pergi*
Stop *Berhenti*
Follow *Ikut*
Near *Dekat*
Far *Jauh*
Inside *Dalam*
Outside *Luar*
Front *Hadapan or Depan*
Behind *Belakang*
Here *Sini*
There *Sana*

Driving

Road Jalan
Lane *Lorong*
Street *Lebuh*
Highway *Lebuhraya*
Bridge *Jambatan*
Junction *Simpang*
Danger *Awas* or *Bahaya*
No overtaking *Dilarang memotong*
Slow down *Kurangkan laju*
Speed limit *Had laju*
Enter *Masuk*
Exit *Keluar*
Keep left/right *Ikut kiri/kanan*
One-way street *Jalan sehala*
North *Utara*
South *Selatan*
East *Timur*
West *Barat*

Useful Words and Phrases

How do you do? *Apa khabar?*
Fine/good *Baik*
Good morning *Selamat pagi*
Good afternoon *Selamat petang*
Good night *Selamat malam*
Goodbye *Selamat tinggal*
Bon voyage *Selamat jalan*
Thank you *Terima kasih*
You're welcome *Sama-sama*
Please *Tolong/sila*
Excuse me *Maafkan saya [Maaf]*
May I ask you a question? *Tumpang tanya?*
I am sorry *Minta maaf [Maaf]*
What is your name? *Siapa nama anda?*
My name is... *Nama saya...*
Please be careful *Berhati-hati*
Yes *Ya*
No *Tidak [Tak]*
How much? *Berapa harganya?*
Can you help me? *Bolehkah cik tolong saya?*
Where is this place? *Di mana tempat ini?*
How far? *Berapa jauh?*
I want to go to... *Saya hendak pergi ke...*
Please stop here *Tolong berhenti di sini*
When? *Bila?*
Expensive *Mahal*
Lower the price *Kurangkan harganya*
Too big *Besar sangat*
Too small *Kecil sangat*
Any other colour? *Ada warna lain?*
Drink *Minum* (verb) *Minimum* (noun)
Eat *Makan* (verb) *Makanan* (noun)
Water *Air*
Hot (spicy) *Pedas*
Hot (heat) *Panas*
Cold *Sejuk*
Sweet *Manis*
Sour *Masam*
Bitter *Pahit*
Delicious *Sedap*
A little *Sedikit [Sikit]*
A lot *Banyak*
This *Ini [Ni]*
That *Itu [Tu]*
Clean *Bersih*
Dirty *Kotor*
Beautiful *Cantik*
Open *Buka*
Close *Tutup*
Sometimes *Kadang-kadang*
Toilet *Tandas*
Male *Lelaki*
Female *Perempuan*

Further Reading

General

The Encyclopedia of Malaysia. An collection of Malaysiana with lovely illustrations, covering such topics as architecture, politics, plants, animals, and early history.

Insider's Kuala Lumpur by Lam Seng Fatt. Interesting expositions on aspects of the city's landmarks.

Paradoxes of Mahathirism: An Intellectual Biography of Mahathir Mohamad by Khoo Boo Teik. Carefully researched study on the former prime minister's ideas on nationalism, capitalism and Islam, among other things.

History and Society

A History of Malaysia by Barbara Watson Andaya and Leonard Y. Andaya. Traces how modern Malaysia was shaped by cultural heritage and trade.

The Kampung Boy by Lat. This classic by the country's most beloved cartoonist is still a best-seller; it provide an insightful, rib-tickling look at Malaysians.

Malaysia – A Pictorial History 1400–2004 by Wendy Khadijah Moore. A painstakingly researched pictorial account of Malaysian history.

The End of Empire by T.N. Harper. A thoughtful analysis of how Malaya was created by a plural society caught in crisis.

A Malaysian Journey by Rehman Rashid. Stylish and sharp, if dogmatic, treatises on contemporary Malaysia.

I am Muslim by Dina Zaman. Essays and reflections on what it means to be a liberal Muslim woman in Malaysia.

What Your Teacher Didn't Tell You by Farish A. Noor. A deeply provoking alternative on the country's history and politics.

Malaysian Politicians Say the Darndest Things compiled by Amir Muhammad. A hilarious selection of actual quotes by Malaysian politicians. Has to be read to be believed.

Malaysian Maverick by Barry Wain. Initially banned in the country, the book takes a cold-hearted look at the nation's most feared, and revered prime minister, Mahathir Mohamad.

Literature

25 Malaysian Short Stories: Silverfish New Writing 2001–2005 edited by Nesa Sivagnanam. Compilation of popular post-colonial written work by Malaysians.

Harmony Silk Factory by Tash Aw. A gripping tale of 1940s Malaya told from three perspectives by a critically acclaimed UK-based Malaysian author.

The Long Day Wanes (The Malayan Trilogy) by Anthony Burgess. Biting satire on the waning days of the British empire – first published in 1964.

Green is the Colour by Lloyd Fernando. A tale of racial and religious tolerance set against the shadow of the 1969 riots in Kuala Lumpur.

Evening is the Whole Day by Preeta Samarasan. Beautifully crafted novel about an Indian family in Malaysia. Revisits controversial events in the nation's history.

Cookery

The New Malaysian Cookbook by Nor Zailina Nordin and Fatihah Seow Boon Hor. Covers all-time Malaysian favourite dishes.

Nonya Flavours: A Complete Guide to Penang Straits Chinese Cuisine edited by Julie Wong. Definitive cookbook of Malaysia's unique Nyonya cuisine.

Art and Culture

Kuala Lumpur – A Sketchbook by Chin Kon Yit and Chen Voon Fee. Annotated collection of beautiful watercolour paintings of old Kuala Lumpur.

Lillian Too's 168 Feng Shui Ways to a Calm and Happy Life by Lillian Too. Malaysia's world-famous feng shui proponent provides tips on enhancing happiness in the home.

Spirit of Wood by Farish A. Noor and Eddin Khoo. Well-written tribute to the Malay art of woodcarving and its symbolisms.

Malay Magic by Walter William Skeat. The definitive guide on theory and practice of Malay magic and shamanism.

Natural History

The Natural and Other Histories of Batu Caves by Shaharin Yussof. Fine research study on the various caves at Batu Caves.

Wild Malaysia: The Wildlife and Scenery of Peninsular Malaysia, Sarawak and Sabah by Junaidi Payne. A well-received study of natural history and peoples by one of the country's top conservationists.

The Malay Archipelago by Alfred Russel Wallace. An extensive sociological and anthropological guide.

Other Insight Guides

The Insight Guides series includes several titles on the region, including *Malaysia*, *Singapore*, *Indonesia* and *Fleximap Kuala Lumpur*.

Kuala Lumpur Street Atlas

The key map shows the area of Kuala Lumpur covered by the atlas section. An index of street names and places of interest shown on the maps can be found on the following pages. For each entry there is a page number and grid reference

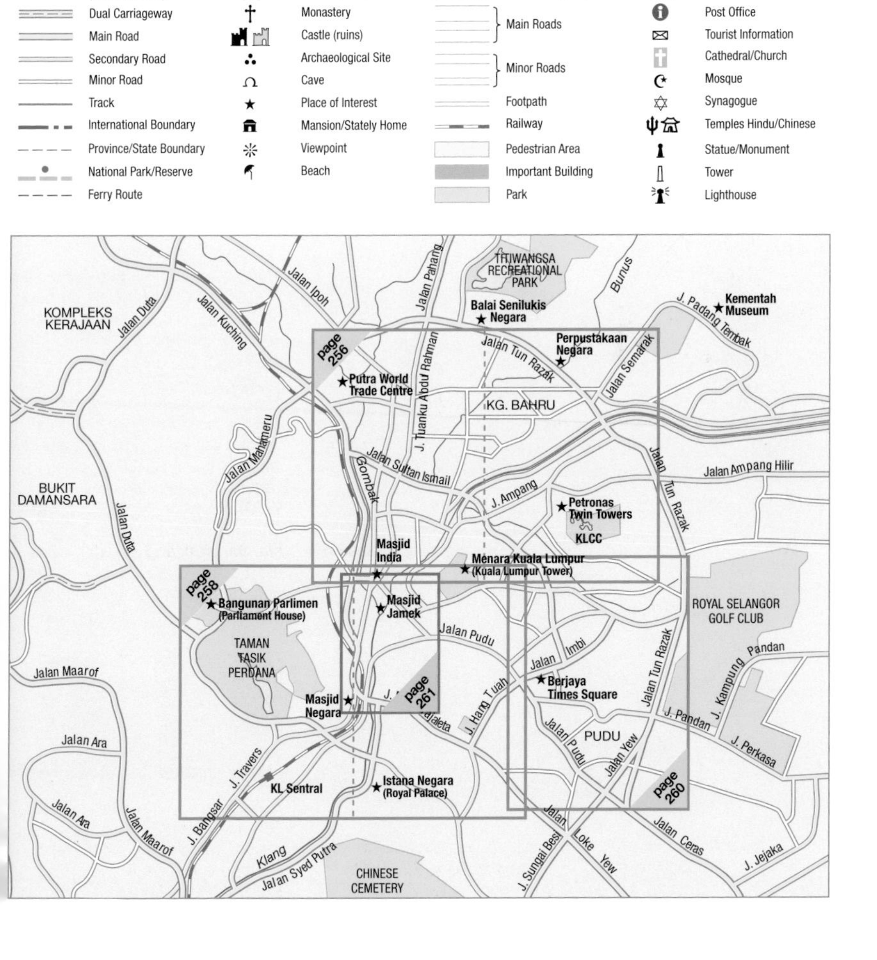

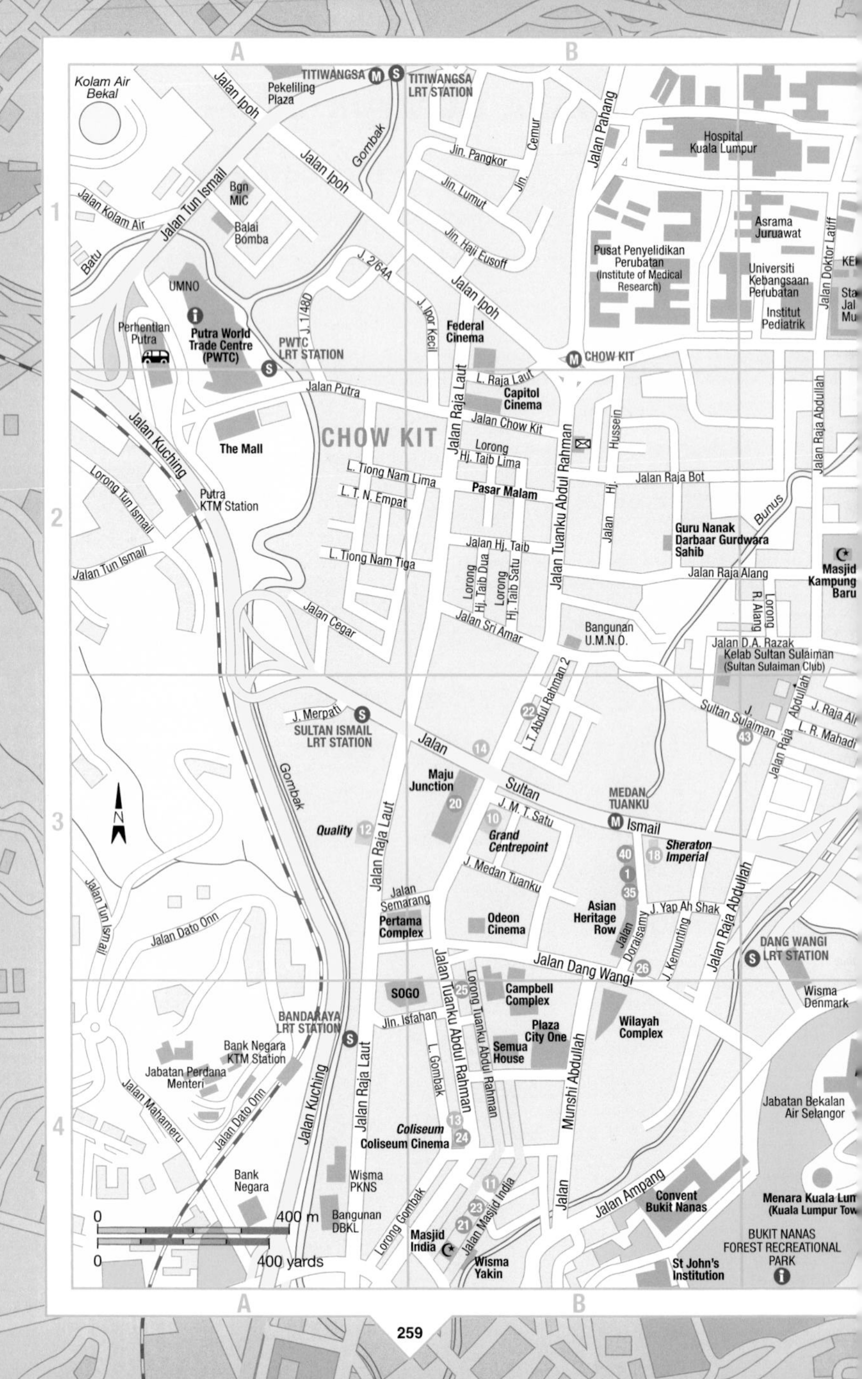
A
B
1
2
3
4
Kolam Air Bekal
Jalan Ipoh
Pekeliling Plaza
TITIWANGSA
TITIWANGSA LRT STATION
Gombak
Jln. Pangkor
Cemur
Jln.
Jalan Pahang
Hospital Kuala Lumpur
Jln. Lumut
Jln. Haji Eusoff
Jalan Kolam Air
Jalan Tun Ismail
Bgn MIC
Balai Bomba
Batu
Asrama Juruawat
Pusat Penyelidikan Perubatan (Institute of Medical Research)
Universiti Kebangsaan Perubatan
Institut Pediatrik
Jalan Doktor Latiff
J. 2/64A
J. 1/48D
J. Ipor Kecil
UMNO
Perhentian Putra
Putra World Trade Centre (PWTC)
PWTC LRT STATION
Federal Cinema
CHOW KIT
L. Raja Laut
Capitol Cinema
Jalan Putra
Jalan Raja Laut
Jalan Chow Kit
Jalan Raja Abdullah
The Mall
CHOW KIT
Lorong Hj. Taib Lima
Hussein
Jalan Tuanku Abdul Rahman
Jalan Kuching
L. Tiong Nam Lima
Jalan Raja Bot
Lorong Tun Ismail
Putra KTM Station
L. T. N. Empat
Pasar Malam
Jalan Hj.
Bunus
Guru Nanak Darbaar Gurdwara Sahib
Jalan Hj. Taib
Jalan Tun Ismail
L. Tiong Nam Tiga
Lorong Hj. Taib Dua
Lorong Hj. Taib Satu
Jalan Raja Alang
Masjid Kampung Baru
Lorong R. Alang
Jalan Cegar
Jalan Sri Amar
Bangunan U.M.N.O.
Jalan D.A. Razak
Kelab Sultan Sulaiman (Sultan Sulaiman Club)
L.T. Abdul Rahman 2
J. Merpati
SULTAN ISMAIL LRT STATION
22
J. Sultan Sulaiman
Abdullah
J. Raja Al
L. R. Mahadi
43
Jalan Raja
14
Jalan Sultan Ismail
Gombak
Maju Junction
20
MEDAN TUANKU
10
J. M. T. Satu
Quality
12
Grand Centrepoint
40
18
Sheraton Imperial
Jalan Raja Laut
J. Medan Tuanku
1
35
Jalan Semarang
Asian Heritage Row
J. Yap Ah Shak
Jalan Raja Abdullah
Jalan Tun Ismail
Pertama Complex
Odeon Cinema
Jalan Doraisamy
J. Kemunting
Jalan Dato Onn
DANG WANGI LRT STATION
Jalan Dang Wangi
26
Wisma Denmark
SOGO
25
Campbell Complex
Lorong Tuanku Abdul Rahman
BANDARAYA LRT STATION
Jln. Isfahan
Plaza City One
Wilayah Complex
Bank Negara KTM Station
Semua House
Munshi Abdullah
Jabatan Perdana Menteri
L. Gombak
Jalan Tuanku Abdul Rahman
Jabatan Bekalan Air Selangor
Jalan Mahameru
Jalan Dato Onn
Jalan Kuching
Jalan Raja Laut
13
Coliseum
24
Coliseum Cinema
Bank Negara
Wisma PKNS
11
Jalan Masjid India
Jalan Ampang
Convent Bukit Nanas
Menara Kuala Lum (Kuala Lumpur Tow
0
400 m
Bangunan DBKL
23
21
Lorong Gombak
Jalan
Masjid India
BUKIT NANAS FOREST RECREATIONAL PARK
400 yards
Wisma Yakin
St John's Institution

259

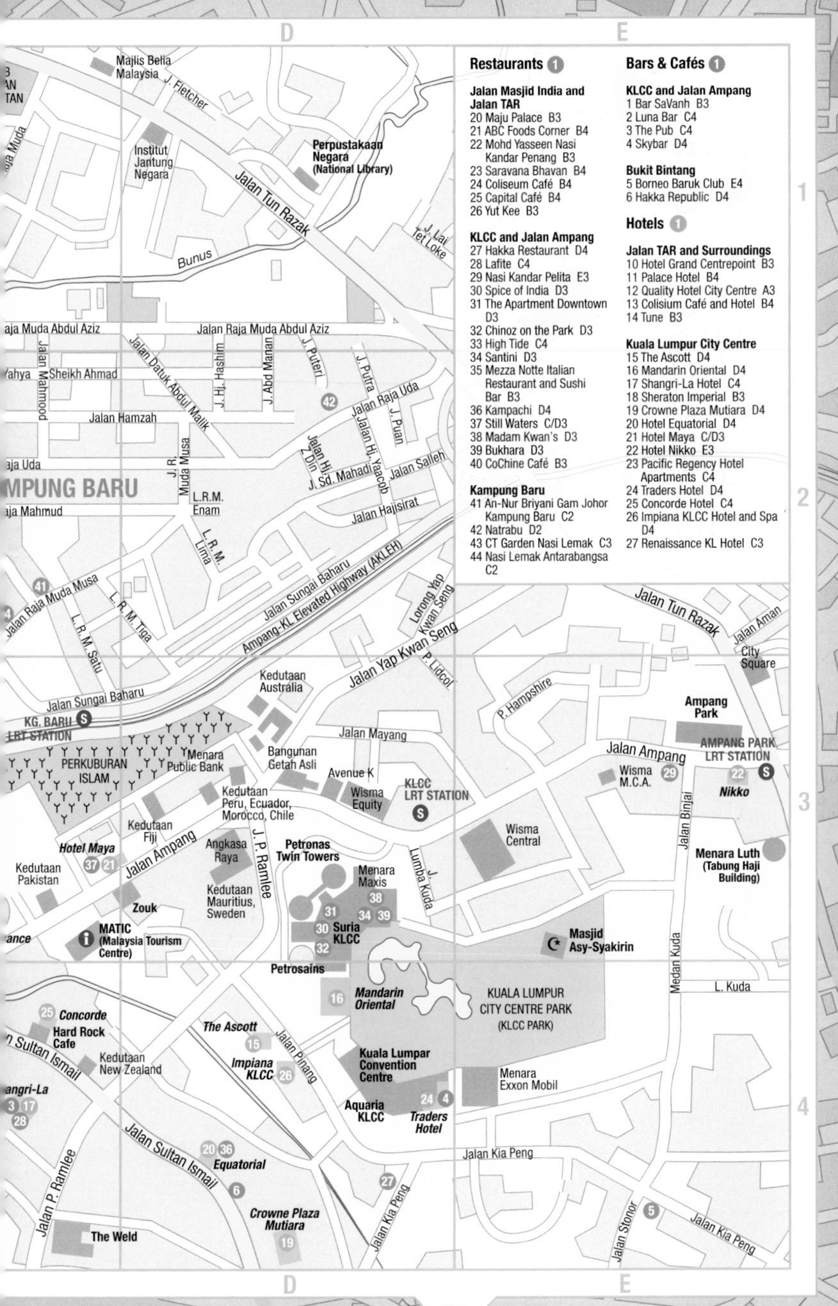
D
E
Restaurants 1
Jalan Masjid India and Jalan TAR
20 Maju Palace B3
21 ABC Foods Corner B4
22 Mohd Yasseen Nasi Kandar Penang B3
23 Saravana Bhavan B4
24 Coliseum Café B4
25 Capital Café B4
26 Yut Kee B3
KLCC and Jalan Ampang
27 Hakka Restaurant D4
28 Lafite C4
29 Nasi Kandar Pelita E3
30 Spice of India D3
31 The Apartment Downtown D3
32 Chinoz on the Park D3
33 High Tide C4
34 Santini D3
35 Mezza Notte Italian Restaurant and Sushi Bar B3
36 Kampachi D4
37 Still Waters C/D3
38 Madam Kwan's D3
39 Bukhara D3
40 CoChine Café B3
Kampung Baru
41 An-Nur Briyani Gam Johor Kampung Baru C2
42 Natrabu D2
43 CT Garden Nasi Lemak C3
44 Nasi Lemak Antarabangsa C2
Bars & Cafés 1
KLCC and Jalan Ampang
1 Bar SaVanh B3
2 Luna Bar C4
3 The Pub C4
4 Skybar D4
Bukit Bintang
5 Borneo Baruk Club E4
6 Hakka Republic D4
Hotels 1
Jalan TAR and Surroundings
10 Hotel Grand Centrepoint B3
11 Palace Hotel B4
12 Quality Hotel City Centre A3
13 Colisium Café and Hotel B4
14 Tune B3
Kuala Lumpur City Centre
15 The Ascott D4
16 Mandarin Oriental D4
17 Shangri-La Hotel C4
18 Sheraton Imperial B3
19 Crowne Plaza Mutiara D4
20 Hotel Equatorial D4
21 Hotel Maya C/D3
22 Hotel Nikko E3
23 Pacific Regency Hotel Apartments C4
24 Traders Hotel D4
25 Concorde Hotel C4
26 Impiana KLCC Hotel and Spa D4
27 Renaissance KL Hotel C3
1
2
3
4
Majlis Belia Malaysia
J. Fletcher
Institut Jantung Negara
Perpustakaan Negara (National Library)
Jalan Tun Razak
Bunus
J. Lai Tet Loke
Jalan Raja Muda Abdul Aziz
Jalan Mahmood
Sheikh Ahmad
Jalan Datuk Abdul Malik
J. Hj. Hashim
J. Abd Manan
J. Puteri
J. Putra
J. Puan
Jalan Raja Uda
Jalan Hamzah
Jalan Hj. Z. Din
Jalan Hj. Yaacob
J. Sd. Mahadi
Jalan Salleh
J. R. Muda Musa
L.R.M. Enam
L.R.M. Lima
Jalan Hajisirat
MPUNG BARU
Jalan Sungai Baharu
Ampang-KL Elevated Highway (AKLEH)
Lorong Yap Kwan Seng
Jalan Yap Kwan Seng
P. Lidcol
Jalan Raja Muda Musa
L.R.M. Tiga
L.R.M. Satu
Kedutaan Australia
KG. BARU LRT STATION
PERKUBURAN ISLAM
Menara Public Bank
Bangunan Getah Asli
Jalan Mayang
Avenue K
Wisma Equity
KLCC LRT STATION
P. Hampshire
Jalan Ampang
Wisma M.C.A.
Ampang Park
AMPANG PARK LRT STATION
Nikko
City Square
Jalan Aman
Kedutaan Peru, Ecuador, Morocco, Chile
Kedutaan Fiji
Hotel Maya
Kedutaan Pakistan
Angkasa Raya
J. P. Ramlee
Petronas Twin Towers
Wisma Central
Jalan Binjai
Menara Luth (Tabung Haji Building)
Kedutaan Mauritius, Sweden
Menara Maxis
J. Lumba Kuda
Zouk
MATIC (Malaysia Tourism Centre)
Suria KLCC
Masjid Asy-Syakirin
Petrosains
Mandarin Oriental
KUALA LUMPUR CITY CENTRE PARK (KLCC PARK)
Medan Kuda
L. Kuda
Concorde
Hard Rock Cafe
Jalan Sultan Ismail
The Ascott
Jalan Pinang
Kedutaan New Zealand
Impiana KLCC
Kuala Lumpar Convention Centre
Menara Exxon Mobil
Aquaria KLCC
Traders Hotel
Shangri-La
Jalan Kia Peng
Equatorial
Crowne Plaza Mutiara
Jalan P. Ramlee
The Weld
Jalan Stonor

260

A
B
1
2
3
4
0
400 m
0
400 yards
N
P. Tun Ismail
Psn Sultan Salahuddin
Jabatan Pelajaran
Jalan Parlimen
Wisma Ekran
PAM Centre Building
Bangunan Parlimen
(Parliament House)
Tugu Negara
(National Monument)
ASEAN Sculpture Garden
Bukit Aman Police HQ
Jalan Tangling
Jalan Bukit Aman
Royal Lake Club
Panggung Aniversari
Perpustakaan Kuala
(KL City
Jabatan Perancang Bandar & Desar
Jalan Tembusu
Butterfly Park
Hibiscus Garden
Jalan Cenderawasih
Hospital Tanglin
Jalan Kebun Bunga
TAMAN TASIK PERDANA
Jalan Perdana
Jalan Lembah Perdana
Jalan Cendera
Orchid Garden
Persiaran
KL Bird Park
Memorial Tun Razak
Muzium Polis Diraja
(Police Museum)
Muzium Kesenian Islam Malaysia
(Islamic Arts Museum)
J. Selangor
Jalan Damansara
Mahameru
Tasik Perdana
80
Jalan Perlis
Planetarium Negara
Pusat Islam
Jalan Negeri Sembilan
Jalan Persekutuan
Jalan Damansara
Istana Hinggap N. Sembilan
Istana Hinggap N. Kedah
Jabatan Muzim & Antikuiti
Muzium Negara
(National Museum)
Jalan Damansara
Police Station
Exhibition & Convention Centre
Arena Sentral
Hilton Kuala Lumpur
41
42
Le Meridien
KL Sentral
KL SENTRAL LRT STATION
Jalan Tun Sambanthan
YMCA
43
Jalan Kandang Kerbau
J. Sultan Abdul Samad
KL SENTRAL KTM STATION
Jalan Tun Sambanthan
J. Thambapillay
BRICKFIELDS
TUN SAMBA
Jalan Anthony
Jalan Sultan Abdul Samad
Vivekananda Ashram
79

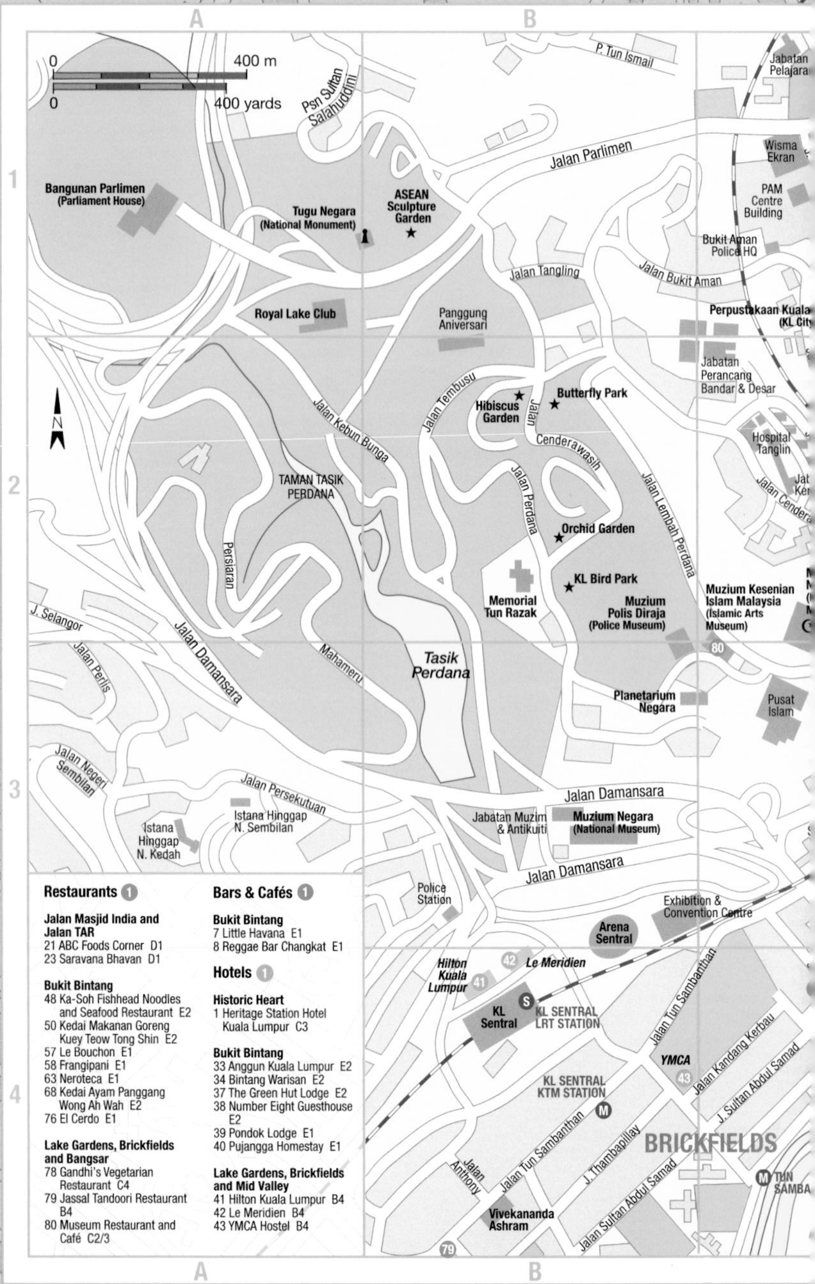

Restaurants 1

Jalan Masjid India and Jalan TAR
21 ABC Foods Corner D1
23 Saravana Bhavan D1

Bukit Bintang
48 Ka-Soh Fishhead Noodles and Seafood Restaurant E2
50 Kedai Makanan Goreng Kuey Teow Tong Shin E2
57 Le Bouchon E1
58 Frangipani E1
63 Neroteca E1
68 Kedai Ayam Panggang Wong Ah Wah E2
76 El Cerdo E1

Lake Gardens, Brickfields and Bangsar
78 Gandhi's Vegetarian Restaurant C4
79 Jassal Tandoori Restaurant B4
80 Museum Restaurant and Café C2/3

Bars & Cafés 1

Bukit Bintang
7 Little Havana E1
8 Reggae Bar Changkat E1

Hotels 1

Historic Heart
1 Heritage Station Hotel Kuala Lumpur C3

Bukit Bintang
33 Anggun Kuala Lumpur E2
34 Bintang Warisan E2
37 The Green Hut Lodge E2
38 Number Eight Guesthouse E2
39 Pondok Lodge E1
40 Pujangga Homestay E1

Lake Gardens, Brickfields and Mid Valley
41 Hilton Kuala Lumpur B4
42 Le Meridien B4
43 YMCA Hostel B4

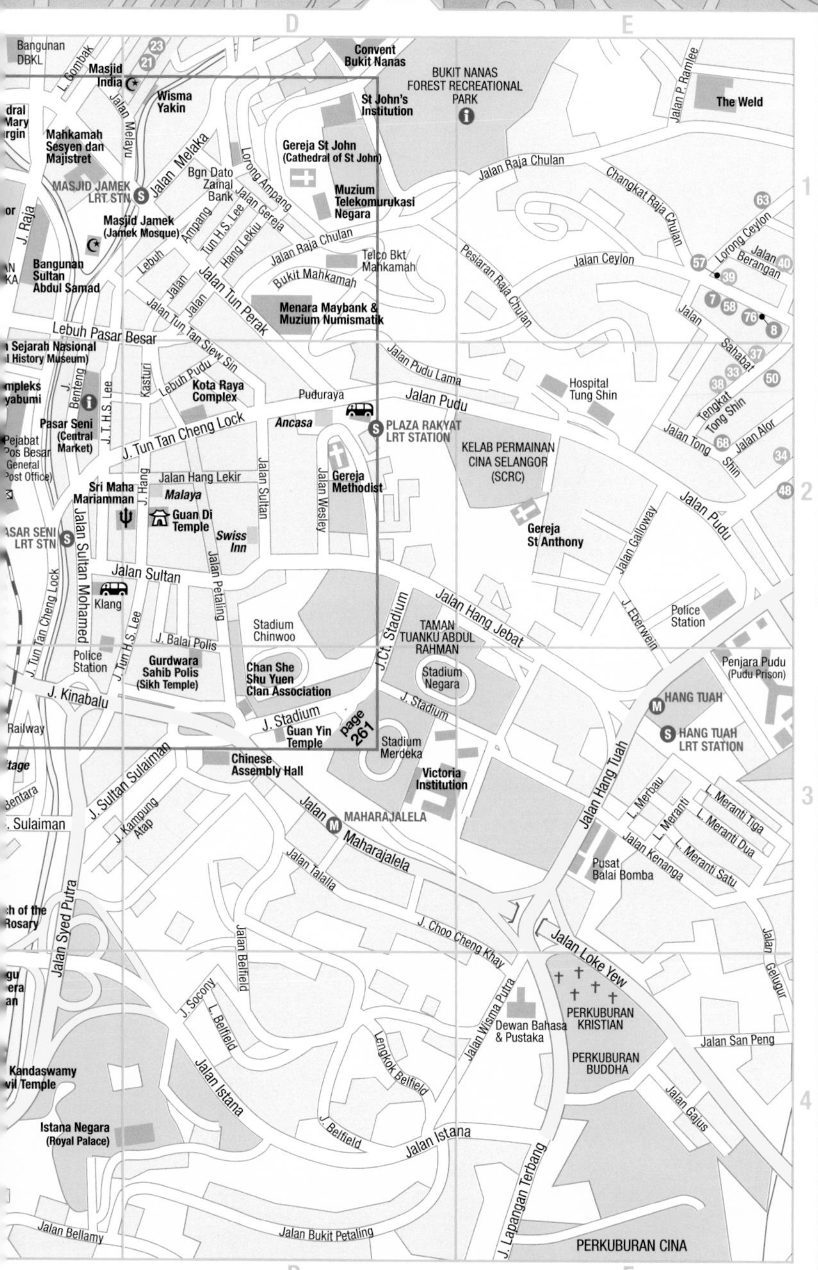

256
260
page 261
Bukit Nanas Forest Recreational Park
The Weld
Convent Bukit Nanas
St John's Institution
Gereja St John (Cathedral of St John)
Muzium Telekomurukasi Negara
Masjid India
Wisma Yakin
Mahkamah Sesyen dan Majistret
Masjid Jamek LRT Stn
Masjid Jamek (Jamek Mosque)
Bangunan Sultan Abdul Samad
Bangunan DBKL
Bgn Dato Zainal Bank
Telco Bkt Mahkamah
Menara Maybank & Muzium Numismatik
Kota Raya Complex
Puduraya
Ancasa
Plaza Rakyat LRT Station
Pasar Seni (Central Market)
Sri Maha Mariamman
Guan Di Temple
Malaya
Swiss Inn
Gereja Methodist
Kelab Permainan Cina Selangor (SCRC)
Gereja St Anthony
Hospital Tung Shin
Police Station
Penjara Pudu (Pudu Prison)
Hang Tuah
Hang Tuah LRT Station
Klang
Stadium Chinwoo
Chan She Shu Yuen Clan Association
Gurdwara Sahib Polis (Sikh Temple)
Taman Tuanku Abdul Rahman
Stadium Negara
Stadium Merdeka
Guan Yin Temple
Chinese Assembly Hall
Victoria Institution
Maharajalela
Pusat Balai Bomba
Dewan Bahasa & Pustaka
Perkuburan Kristian
Perkuburan Buddha
Perkuburan Cina
Kandaswamy Temple
Istana Negara (Royal Palace)
Jalan Raja Chulan
Jalan Ceylon
Jalan Pudu
Jalan Pudu Lama
Jalan Hang Jebat
Jalan Sultan
Jalan Sultan Mohamed
J. Tun Tan Cheng Lock
Jalan Tun Perak
Lebuh Pasar Besar
Jalan Melaka
Jalan Melayu
Lorong Ampang
Jalan Tun Tan Siew Sin
Jalan Hang Lekir
Jalan Petaling
Jalan Wesley
Jalan Galloway
J. Eberwein
Jalan Hang Tuah
Jalan Maharajalela
Jalan Talalla
J. Choo Cheng Khay
Jalan Loke Yew
Jalan Istana
Jalan Syed Putra
J. Sultan Sulaiman
J. Kinabalu
J. Stadium
Jalan Belfield
Lengkok Belfield
Jalan Wisma Putra
J. Lapangan Terbang
Jalan Bukit Petaling
Jalan Bellamy
Jalan San Peng
Jalan Gajus
Jalan Gelugur
Jalan Kenanga
L. Merbau
L. Meranti
L. Meranti Tiga
L. Meranti Dua
L. Meranti Satu
Jalan Alor
Tengkat Tong Shin
Jalan Tong Shin
Jalan Sahabat
Jalan Berangan
Lorong Ceylon
Changkat Raja Chulan
Pesiaran Raja Chulan
Jalan P. Ramlee
Jalan Balai Polis
J. Kampung Atap
J. Socony
L. Belfield
J. Belfield
Railway

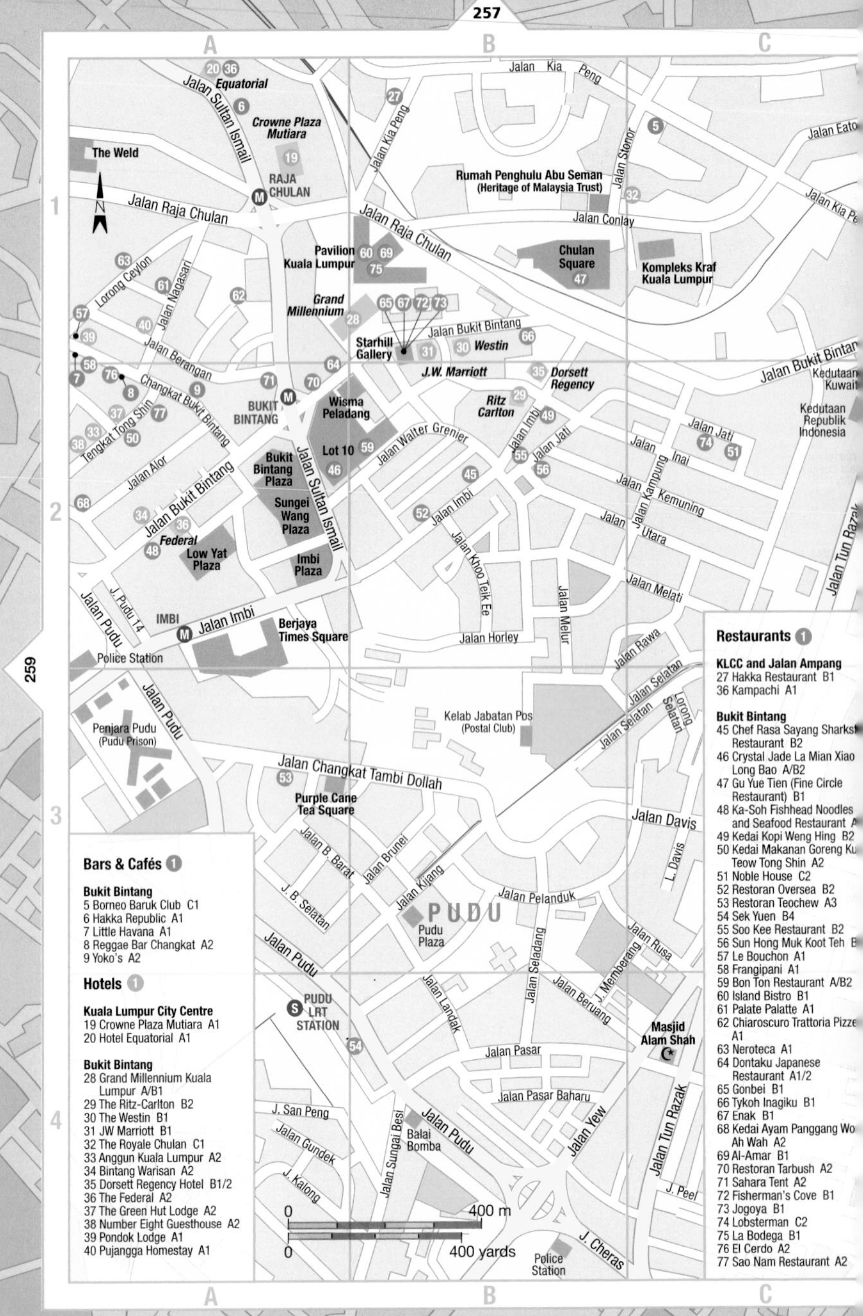

257
259
A
B
C
1
2
3
4
Equatorial
Jalan Sultan Ismail
Crowne Plaza Mutiara
The Weld
RAJA CHULAN
Jalan Raja Chulan
Jalan Kia Peng
Jalan Stonor
Rumah Penghulu Abu Seman
(Heritage of Malaysia Trust)
Jalan Conlay
Jalan Eaton
Pavilion Kuala Lumpur
Chulan Square
Kompleks Kraf Kuala Lumpur
Grand Millennium
Lorong Ceylon
Jalan Nagasari
Jalan Berangan
Starhill Gallery
Jalan Bukit Bintang
Westin
J.W. Marriott
Dorsett Regency
Kedutaan Kuwait
Kedutaan Republik Indonesia
Changkat Bukit Bintang
Tengkat Tong Shin
BUKIT BINTANG
Wisma Peladang
Ritz Carlton
Jalan Imbi
Jalan Jati
Jalan Inai
Lot 10
Jalan Walter Grenier
Jalan Alor
Bukit Bintang Plaza
Sungei Wang Plaza
Jalan Kampung
Jalan Kemuning
Jalan Utara
Jalan Tun Razak
Federal
Low Yat Plaza
Imbi Plaza
Jalan Khoo Teik Ee
Jalan Melati
Jalan Pudu
J. Pudu 14
IMBI
Berjaya Times Square
Jalan Horley
Jalan Melur
Jalan Rawa
Police Station
Jalan Selatan
Lorong Selatan
Penjara Pudu
(Pudu Prison)
Kelab Jabatan Pos
(Postal Club)
Jalan Changkat Tambi Dollah
Purple Cane Tea Square
Jalan Davis
L. Davis
Jalan B. Barat
Jalan Brunei
Jalan Kijang
J. B. Selatan
Jalan Pelanduk
PUDU
Pudu Plaza
Jalan Rusa
J. Memberang
Jalan Seladang
Jalan Beruang
Jalan Landak
PUDU LRT STATION
Masjid Alam Shah
Jalan Pasar
Jalan Pasar Baharu
Jalan Yew
J. San Peng
Jalan Gundek
J. Kalong
Jalan Sungai Besi
Balai Bomba
J. Peel
J. Cheras
Police Station
0
400 m
0
400 yards

Bars & Cafés 1
Bukit Bintang
5 Borneo Baruk Club C1
6 Hakka Republic A1
7 Little Havana A1
8 Reggae Bar Changkat A2
9 Yoko's A2
Hotels 1
Kuala Lumpur City Centre
19 Crowne Plaza Mutiara A1
20 Hotel Equatorial A1
Bukit Bintang
28 Grand Millennium Kuala Lumpur A/B1
29 The Ritz-Carlton B2
30 The Westin B1
31 JW Marriott B1
32 The Royale Chulan C1
33 Anggun Kuala Lumpur A2
34 Bintang Warisan A2
35 Dorsett Regency Hotel B1/2
36 The Federal A2
37 The Green Hut Lodge A2
38 Number Eight Guesthouse A2
39 Pondok Lodge A1
40 Pujangga Homestay A1

Restaurants 1
KLCC and Jalan Ampang
27 Hakka Restaurant B1
36 Kampachi A1
Bukit Bintang
45 Chef Rasa Sayang Sharks
Restaurant B2
46 Crystal Jade La Mian Xiao Long Bao A/B2
47 Gu Yue Tien (Fine Circle Restaurant) B1
48 Ka-Soh Fishhead Noodles and Seafood Restaurant A
49 Kedai Kopi Weng Hing B2
50 Kedai Makanan Goreng Ku Teow Tong Shin A2
51 Noble House C2
52 Restoran Oversea B2
53 Restoran Teochew A3
54 Sek Yuen B4
55 Soo Kee Restaurant B2
56 Sun Hong Muk Koot Teh B
57 Le Bouchon A1
58 Frangipani A1
59 Bon Ton Restaurant A/B2
60 Island Bistro B1
61 Palate Palatte A1
62 Chiaroscuro Trattoria Pizze A1
63 Neroteca A1
64 Dontaku Japanese Restaurant A1/2
65 Gonbei B1
66 Tykoh Inagiku B1
67 Enak B1
68 Kedai Ayam Panggang Wo Ah Wah A2
69 Al-Amar B1
70 Restoran Tarbush A2
71 Sahara Tent A2
72 Fisherman's Cove B1
73 Jogoya B1
74 Lobsterman C2
75 La Bodega B1
76 El Cerdo A2
77 Sao Nam Restaurant A2

256
D
E
F
Masjid India
Wisma Yakin
Jalan Melayu
Klang
Cathedral of St Mary the Virgin
Gombak
Jalan Raja Laut
Panggung Bandaraya (Old Town Hall)
Mahkamah Sesyen dan Majistret (Old FMS Survey Office)
Old High Court
J. Tun Perak
Jalan Melaka
MASJID JAMEK LRT STN
CINB Bank (Oriental Building)
Lorong Ampang
Bangunan Dato Zainal Bank
St John's Institution
Gereja St John (Cathedral of St John)
Muzium Telekomurukasi Negara
Jalan Gereja
Lorong Ampang
Jalan Raja
J. Raja
DATARAN MERDEKA (INDEPENDENCE SQUARE)
Royal Selangor Club
Bangunan Sultan Abdul Samad
Masjid Jamek (Jamek Mosque)
Gian Singh Building
L. Ampang
J. Tun H.S. Lee
J. Hang Lekiu
Jalan Raja Chulan
Telco Bkt Mahkamah
Bukit Mahkamah
Medan Pasar
Lebuh Ampang
Textile Museum
Muzium Sejarah Nasional (National History Museum)
Lebuh Pasar Besar
J. Tun H.S. Lee
J. Hang Lekiu
Jalan Tun Tan Siew Sin
Jalan Tun Perak
Menara Maybank & Muzium Numismatik
Jalan Pudu Lama
Bangunan Persekutuan
Kinabalu
Jalan Raja
Kompleks Dayabumi
Jalan Benteng
Pasar Seni (Central Market)
J. Hang Kasturi
Jalan Tun H.S. Lee
Lebuh Pudu
Kota Raya Complex
(Jalan Silang)
Puduraya
Ancasa
PLAZA RAKYAT LRT STATION
259
Sin Sze Si Ya Temple
Jalan Tun Tan Cheng Lock
Rex Cinema
Gereja Methodist
Bukit Aman
Hishamuddin
Pejabat Pos Besar (General Post Office)
Klang
Jalan Hang Lekir
Lee Rubber Building
Malaya
Jalan Petaling
Jalan Sultan
Jalan Wesley
Guan Di Temple
J. Hang Kasturi
Jalan Tun H.S. Lee
Sri Maha Mariamman Temple
Swiss Inn
PASAR SENI LRT STN
Jalan Sultan Mohamed
Jalan Sultan
Jalan Hang Jebat
Jalan Tun H.S. Lee
Jalan Petaling
Klang
0
200 m
0
200 yards
J. Tun Tan Cheng Lock
Old KL Railway Station
N
1
2
3
4
D
E
F
259
Restaurants
Historic Heart
1 Restoran Ahamedia E2
2 Restoran Yusoof Dan Zakhir E2
3 Restoran Seri Asia E2
4 Secret Recipe E2
5 Ginger Restaurant E2
6 Oh Malaya E2
7 Sin Seng Nam E2
8 Precious Old China Restaurant and Bar E3
Petaling Street and Surroundings
9 Chinatown Seng Kee E3
10 Hong Ngek Restaurant F2
11 Koon Kee E3
12 Nam Heong Restaurant E3/4
13 The Oriental Bowl F2
14 Soong Kee Beef Noodles E2
15 Lotus Family Restaurant E2
16 Peter Hoe Beyond E3
17 Old Town Kopitiam E3
18 Cintamani F3
19 Yin Futt Kuok F3
Hotels
Petaling Street and Surroundings
2 Ancasa Hotel F2/3
3 Citin Hotel Pudu F2
4 Hotel Malaya E3
5 Swiss-Inn Kuala Lumpur F3
6 Hotel China Town 2 F3
7 Hotel China Town Inn F3
8 StayOrange E3
9 Le Village E2

Street Index

Art and Photo Credits

akg images 24B, 25T&B
H. Berbar/HBL 26T, 58, 129, 132L&R
Corbis 1, 6BR, 23L, 27T&B, 34T, 35L, 36B, 37, 38L&R, 39L&R, 49, 60, 139
V. Couarraze/HBL 4T
Mary Evans Picture Library 24T
Getty Images 7TR, 12/13, 36T
iStockphoto.com 77B, 192, 197TR
Robert Lendrum/HBL 19
Muzium Negara, Malaysia 31, 33L
onasia.com 40/41
Private archives 28, 29, 30, 32, 33R, 34B, 35R, 98B
Jon Santa Cruz/APA 5T, 6TR, C&BC, 7BL&BR, 10T&B, 11L, 14/15, 17, 21L&R, 43, 51, 52, 54T&B, 55(all), 56R, 59, 67, 70T, 75, 82/83, 85L&R, 92T&B, 93L, 94T&B, 109T&B, 112B, 113L&R, 115L, 117L&T, 125B, 135L, 137T&B, 141, 142, 146T, 147, 150, 153, 155, 158, 159, 161, 164, 173, 174/175, 177L&R, 189, 190T&B, 194T, 212T, 216, 218, 220, 222, 226, 235, 242, 244, 252
Shangri-La Hotels and Resorts 228
Sipa Press/Rex Features 50B
Stuart Spivack 163
Superstock 96T
Arthur Teng 89, 96B
Topfoto 26B, 98T
Tourism Malaysia 7TL, 8B
Nikt Wong/APA 4BL&BR, 5B, 6L, 7CL, 8T, 9T&B, 11R, 16, 18, 20L&R, 22, 23R, 42, 44, 45L&R, 48, 50T, 53, 56L, 57, 61T&B, 62, 63, 64, 65, 66, 68, 69, 70B, 71, 74, 76, 77T, 78, 79, 80/81, 84, 88, 91T&B, 93R&B, 95T&B, 97T&B, 99T&B, 100L&R, 101, 102, 106, 107, 108T&B, 110(all), 111T&B, 112T, 114L&R, 115T&R, 116T&B, 117BR, 118T&B, 120, 121, 123T&B, 125T, 126, 128, 131, 133T&B, 134T&B, 135R, 136, 140T&B, 144, 145, 146B, 148T&B, 149, 151, 152, 154T&B, 156T&B, 157, 165, 166, 167, 168, 169T&B, 170, 171, 176, 178, 179, 181T&B, 182T&B, 183, 184, 185, 188, 191, 193, 194B, 195(all), 196T&B, 197L&B, 198T&B, 199, 200, 201, 202, 203T&B, 204T&B, 205(all), 206T&B, 207, 208, 209, 211T&B, 212B, 213T&B, 214T&B, 215T&B, 217

Photo Features

46/47: all images **Corbis** except 46CR **Getty Images**

72/73: Corbis 72BL, 73CR; **Jon Santa Cruz/APA** 72BR, 73BL; **Nikt Wong/APA** 72/73, 72CR, 73TR, CL&BR

104/105: all images **Nikt Wong/APA** except 104BL **Jon Santa Cruz/APA**

186/187: Corbis 186/187, 186CR&B, 187BL; **iStockphoto.com** 187BR; **KPA/Zuma/Rex Features** 187TR&CL

Original cartography: Berndtson & Berndtson updated by Stephen Ramsay and APA Cartography Department

Production: Tynan Dean, Linton Donaldson, Rebeka Ellam
Picture Research: Tom Smyth

General Index

N

O

P

R

S

Restaurants

Bars and Cafés

INSIGHT GUIDE
KUALA LUMPUR

Series Editor
Rachel Lawrence
Series Manager
Rachel Fox
Art Director
Steven Lawrence
Picture Manager
Tom Smyth

Distribution

UK & Ireland
Dorling Kindersley Ltd,
a Penguin Group company
80 Strand, London WC2R 0RL
customerservice@dk.com

United States
Ingram Publisher Services
One Ingram Blvd, PO Box 3006
La Vergne TN37086-1986
customer.service@ingram
publisherservices.com

Australia
Universal Publishers
PO Box 307
St Leonards, NSW 1590
sales@universalpublishers.com.au

New Zealand
Brown Knows Publications
11 Artesia Close, Shamrock Park
Auckland, New Zealand 2016
sales@brownknows.co.nz

Worldwide
Apa Publications GmbH & Co.
Verlag KG (Singapore branch)
7030 Ang Mo Kio Avenue 5
08-65 Northstar @ AMK
Singapore 569880
apasin@singnet.com.sg

Printing

CTPS-China

First Edition 2007
Second Edition 2011
Reprinted 2012

www.insightguides.com

About This Book

What makes an Insight Guide different? Since our first book pioneered the use of creative full-colour photography in travel guides in 1970, we have aimed to provide not only reliable information but also the key to a real understanding of a destination and its people.

Now, when the internet can supply inexhaustible (but not always reliable) facts, our books marry text and pictures to provide that more elusive quality: knowledge. To achieve this, they rely on the authority of locally based writers and photographers.

This new edition of *City Guide Kuala Lumpur* was commissioned by Series Editor **Rachel Lawrence** and Commissioning Editor **Carine Tracanelli.** The history and features chapters were thoroughly updated by **Siew Lyn Wong**, a Malaysia-born freelancer who specialises in travel and environmental writing. A foodie and nature-lover, she loves Kuala Lumpur's eclectic blend of chaos, cosmopolitanism and multifariousness. She also wrote the chapters on Kuala Lumpur's people and its nightlife, as well as the photo feature on Thaipusam. She has contributed to numerous Insight Guides, including *Insight Guide Southeast Asia*, *Insight Guide Malaysia*, *Pocket Guide Penang and Langkawi* and *Step-by-Step Kuala Lumpur*.

The Places section and the Travel Tips were updated by **Bernice Chauly**, a KL-based writer and photographer. She has worked as a journalist, radio correspondent, magazine editor and food writer, and has also written for the stage and screen.

The text of writers who contributed to previous editions has been updated for this book. They include **Lam Seng Fatt**, **Kathy Rowland**, **Eu Hooi Khaw**, **Leng Ng**, **Shanon Shah** and **Fong Peng Khuan**.

Most of the images were taken by **Jon Santa Crus** and **Nikt Wong**.

The book was copy-edited by **Stephanie Smith**, proofread by **Janet McCan** and indexed by **Helen Peters**. Thanks also go to **Alison Howard** and **Astrid deRidder**.

Send Us Your Thoughts

We do our best to ensure the information in our books is as accurate and up-to-date as possible. The books are updated on a regular basis using local contacts, who painstakingly add, amend, and correct as required. However, some details (such as telephone numbers and opening times) are liable to change, and we are ultimately reliant on our readers to put us in the picture.

We welcome your feedback, especially your experience of using the book "on the road". Maybe we recommended a hotel that you liked (or another that you didn't), or you came across a great bar or new attraction that we missed.

We will acknowledge all contributions, and we'll offer an Insight Guide to the best letters received.

Please write to us at:
Insight Guides
PO Box 7910, London SE1 1WE
Or email us at:
insight@apaguide.co.uk

Kuala Lumpur Rail Transit

Tanjung Malim
Kuala Kubu Bharu
Rasa
Batang Kali
Serendah
B RAWANG
Kuang
Sungai Buloh
Kepong
Segambut
A SENTUL
Putra
Bank Negara
Kuala Lumpur
F KL SENTRAL
Angkasapuri
Pantai Dalam
Petaling
Jalan Templer
Kampung Dato Harun
Seri Setia
Setia Jaya
Subang Jaya
Batu Tiga
Shah Alam
Padang Jawa
Bukit Badak
Klang
Teluk Pulai
Teluk Gadong
Kampung Raja Uda
Jalan Kastam
A PORT KLANG

D C SENTUL TIMUR
Sentul
F TITIWANGSA
PWTC
Sultan Ismail
Bandaraya
Masjid Jamek
Pasar Seni
Chow Kit
Medan Tuanku
Dang Wangi
Bukit Nanas
Raja Chulan
Bukit Bitang
Imbi
Hang Tuah
Maharajalela
Tun Sambathan
Plaza Rakyat
Pudu
Chan Sow Lin
Cheras
Salak Selatan
Bandar Tun Razak
Bandarb Tasik Selatan
Sungai Besi
Bukit Jalil
D SRI PETALING

E TERMINAL PUTRA (Gombak)
Taman Melati
Wangsa Maju
Sri Rampai
Setiawangsa
Jelatek
Dato Keramat
Damai
Ampang Park
KLCC
Kg. Baru
Bangsar
Abdullah Hokum
Kerinchi
Universiti
Taman Jaya
Asia Jaya
Taman Paramount
Taman Bahagia
KELANA JAYA

C AMPANG
Cahaya
Cempaka
Padnan Indah
Pandan Jaya
Maluri
Miharja

Mid Valley
Seputeh
Salak Selatan
Serdang
Kajang
UKM
Bangi
Batang Benar
Nilai
Labu
Tirol
SEREMBAN B

Putrajaya and Cyberjaya
Salak Tinggi
LCCT
KL INTERNATIONAL AIRPORT

A Sentul - Port Klang
B Rawang - Seremban
C Ampang line
D Sri Petaling line
E Kelana Jaya line
F KL Sentral - Titiwangsa
Aerocity commuter
Aerocity express

Interchange station
Interchange station within walking distance

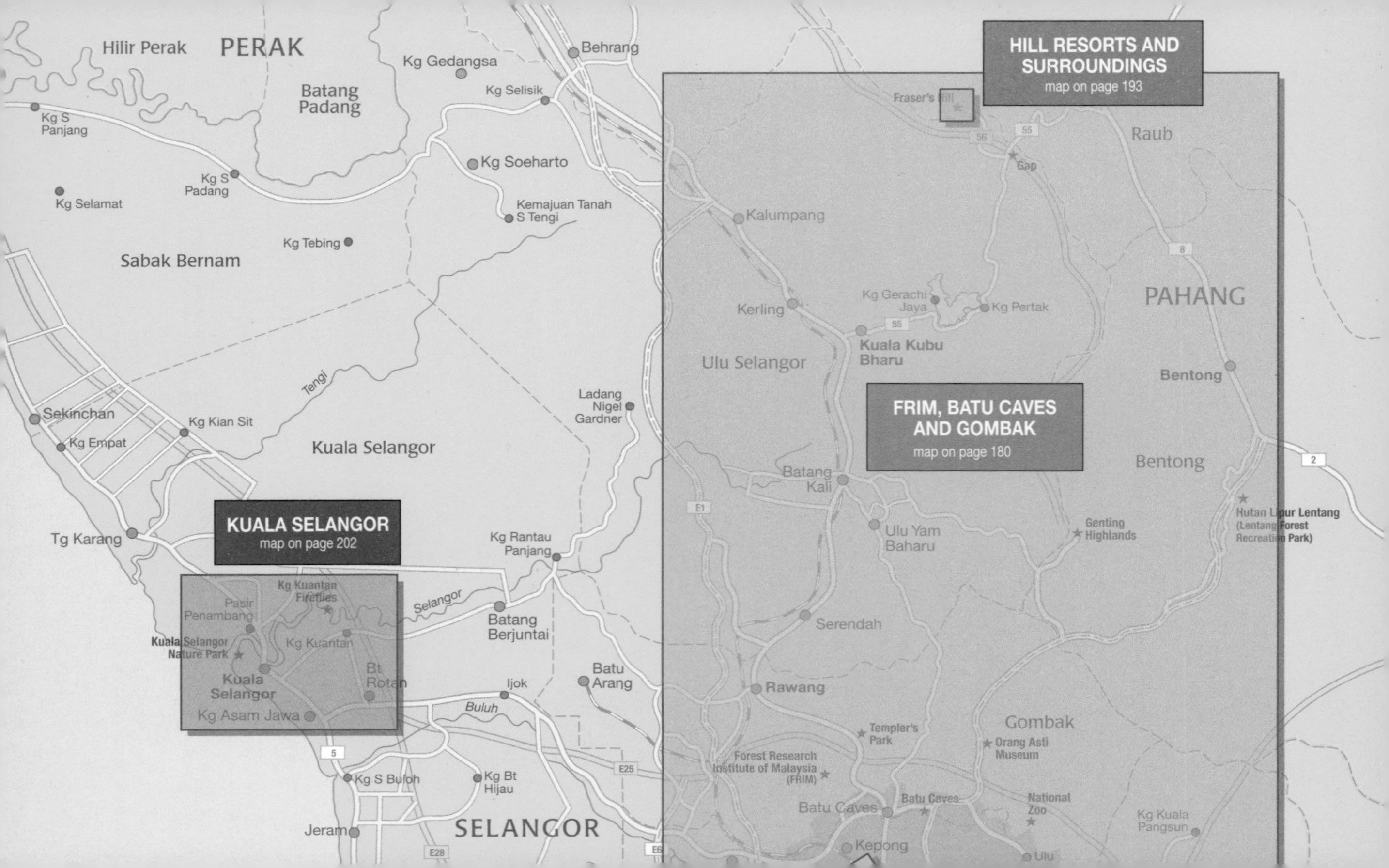

HILL RESORTS AND SURROUNDINGS
map on page 193
FRIM, BATU CAVES AND GOMBAK
map on page 180
KUALA SELANGOR
map on page 202
PERAK
PAHANG
SELANGOR
Hilir Perak
Batang Padang
Sabak Bernam
Kuala Selangor
Ulu Selangor
Raub
Bentong
Gombak
Kg S Panjang
Kg S Padang
Kg Selamat
Kg Gedangsa
Kg Selisik
Behrang
Kg Soeharto
Kemajuan Tanah S Tengi
Kg Tebing
Tengi
Sekinchan
Kg Empat
Kg Kian Sit
Tg Karang
Ladang Nigel Gardner
Kg Rantau Panjang
Selangor
Batang Berjuntai
Batu Arang
Ijok
Buluh
Pasir Penambang
Kg Kuantan Fireflies
Kg Kuantan
Kuala Selangor Nature Park
Kuala Selangor
Bt Rotan
Kg Asam Jawa
Kg S Buloh
Kg Bt Hijau
Jeram
Fraser's Hill
Gap
Kalumpang
Kerling
Kg Gerachi Jaya
Kg Pertak
Kuala Kubu Bharu
Batang Kali
Ulu Yam Baharu
Genting Highlands
Hutan Lipur Lentang (Lentang Forest Recreation Park)
Serendah
Rawang
Templer's Park
Orang Asli Museum
Forest Research Institute of Malaysia (FRIM)
Batu Caves
National Zoo
Kg Kuala Pangsun
Kepong
Ulu
2
5
8
55
56
E1
E25
E28